D0213672

Rainbow at Midnight

RAINBOW AT MIDNIGHT

Labor and Culture in the 1940s

———

George Lipsitz

University of Illinois Press
Urbana and Chicago

© 1994 by the Board of Trustees of the University of Illinois
Manufactured in the United States of America
1 2 3 4 5 C P 5 4 3 2 1

This book is printed on acid-free paper.

Library of Congress Cataloging-in-Publication Data

Lipsitz, George.
   Rainbow at midnight : labor and culture in the 1940s / George Lipsitz.
    p. cm.
   Rev. ed. of: Class and culture. 1981.
   Includes bibliographical references and index.
   ISBN 0-252-02094-4 (cloth). — ISBN 0-252-06394-5 (paper)
   1. Working class—United States—History—20th century. 2. Labor—United
States—History—20th century. 3. Industrial relations—United States—History—
20th century. 4. Industrial mobilization—United States—History—20th century.
5. Reconstruction (1939–1951)—United States. 6. Strikes and lockouts—United
States—History—20th century. 7. United States—Economic policy—1945–1960.
8. United States—Economic policy—1933–1945. 9. United States—Social
conditions—1945– 10. United States—Social conditions—1933–1945.
11. Popular culture—United States—History—20th century. 12. United States—Race
relations—History—20th century. I. Lipsitz, George. Rainbow at midnight.
II. Title.
HD8072.5.L56 1994
305.5′0973—dc20
                                                       93-36425
                                                         CIP

Contents

Acknowledgments

———

Teaching and learning are acts of sharing. They succeed only when we acknowledge the ways in which we have learned from each other. Many people have helped me while writing this book; I would like to thank some of them individually.

My mother and late father, Paulette and Herbert Lipsitz, shared their love of learning and passion for justice with me, and I will always owe a debt to their guidance and example. Ramon Gutierrez, Kathy Corbett, Mary Bufwack, Ed Robbins, and Peter Fuss read early drafts of this work and offered helpful criticisms. Stanley Aronowitz contributed by example and by practical assistance, and Jim Fleming, Richard Wentworth, and Becky Standard provided excellent editorial guidance.

James Neal Primm of the University of Missouri–St. Louis changed my life by showing me that it was possible to do socially responsible intellectual work. I will always be proud to think of myself as his student. George Rawick did more to shape my understanding of politics and history than any other individual. As a colleague and friend, he generously shared his time and his extraordinary talents. Tom McCormick's careful scholarship, fine teaching, courageous politics, and exuberant love of life make my friendship with him one of the most important things in my life.

While revising and expanding this book for its 1994 publication, I have been helped enormously by encouragement from Melvin Oliver, David Roediger, and Barbara Tomlinson. Stan Weir's knowledge about working people and his commitment to them provide an inspiring example. He may not agree with everything I have written in this book, but I hope he will notice how much I have learned from him.

Finally, I also have to thank the best group of teachers I have ever had. In the early 1970s, a group of rank-and-file Teamsters in St. Louis organized an extra-union caucus to deal with the issues that appear in this book. They taught me more in a short time than I was ever able to learn in all my years of formal education. It is to all of them, but particularly to Ron Gushleff, Jan Hill, Elmer Matyi, and Porter Thompson, that this book is dedicated.

Why Write about Workers?

"Of course it is difficult to maintain the faith and keep working toward the new time if you've had no *experience* of it, not *seen* ordinary people actually transform selves and societies."

Toni Cade Bambara

WRITING ABOUT workers is no easy task in the 1990s. For almost twenty years, working people and their interests have been absent from most public discussions about our national political and cultural life. As deindustrialization and economic restructuring have radically transformed U.S. society, the people and communities most immediately affected by these changes have been virtually erased. Business initiatives dominate the economic, political, and social agenda of the nation, while labor's perspectives and needs remain almost invisible within most of the country's mainstream media and educational institutions.

The disappearance of the working class from popular consciousness has left a terrible void in our national life. Left unchallenged, business principles lead to rule by the rich and to the exclusion of the majority of the population from any meaningful participation in the decisions that affect their lives. The ruthless competition and selfishness promoted by an enterprise-oriented society too often leave individuals adrift and unconnected to any broader community or moral purpose.

Even in economic terms, the policies pursued by elite investors and entrepreneurs in the eighties have directed capital away from productive investments and toward grandiose speculative ventures. This reckless pursuit of profit has left the nation deeply in debt, poorly positioned within the world economy, and dangerously close to dismantling the educational, medical, and environmental infrastructures necessary for faith in the future.

For twenty years, business realities have been the only realities represented in politics, the media, and in education. Politicians competing for corporate support ignore the social costs of business failures like the collapse of the savings and loan industry. Television news programs and newspapers regularly provide business "reports," but almost never acknowledge the existence of a labor perspective. Colleges and universities give graduate degrees in management, but have few programs about labor. University and private laboratories carry on research and development projects subsidizing the indirect costs of doing business for corporations while offering no comparable resources to labor.

It is not as if labor's side gets presented fairly and then loses the argument, but rather that the business world appears as the only world. The needs, aspirations, and ideas of working people appear only when they become a problem for business. Deficiencies of productivity and competitiveness are blamed on workers and unions rather than on investment and administrative decisions by management. Occupational health and safety regulations become characterized as "needless regulation" of business. Organized labor gets labeled as a "special interest," while industrialists and bankers benefit from government bailouts and specially designed tax breaks. Workers on strike in Gdansk, Poland, get more exposure on the network news in the United States than do striking workers in Weirton, West Virginia. Politicians, journalists, and business representatives blame union rules for undermining the competitiveness of U.S. corporations, but they raise little outcry when twenty-four workers burn to death in a Hamlet, North Carolina, chicken processing plant because their employer locked the fire doors on them to make sure that no one walked away with a few extra pieces of chicken. Tax expenditures for social welfare programs routinely receive blame for the inability of U.S. companies to compete with foreign corporations, even when those competitors often operate in countries that demand higher taxes to help support universal medical care and day care programs far superior to what exists in the United States.

The erasure of the working class from public consciousness hides the disaster that deindustrialization, economic restructuring, and computer-generated automation have brought to the majority of the population. As one factory shutdown follows another, good jobs are lost forever. Tax cuts and bailouts for failed businesses take money that used to go to state and local school budgets, while higher education increasingly becomes reserved for only the children of the elite. Millions of young people face the future with few prospects for upward mobility, while their parents and grandparents watch the collapse of the industrial and social infrastructure they helped to build. Social networks that once held people together in relations of mutual respect and trust have dissolved in the wake of the abandonment of neighborhoods and cities by investors, while institutions that formerly

provided ordinary people with a sense of sharing power have been eviscer-
ated by the increased influence and power of the rich over politics.

This book is an effort on my part to call attention to what we can learn
from labor during one important historical period—the years immediately
following World War II. In that era, workers staged the largest strike wave
in U. S. history. They voiced radical demands to restructure society along
more democratic lines. They took direct action to advance their interests
through strikes and demonstrations that seemed to signal an important cultural break with the past. Fighting for full employment and high-wage jobs,
they created an active public sphere of action and debate that encouraged
communities to confront the important problems facing them. Their collective and individual actions won important concessions, and provoked enormous repression. But failure to transform local protests into a coordinated
national movement surrendered advantages to leaders of business, government, and labor unions, and their defeat created the preconditions for the
enduring economic and social problems that plague us in the present.

This volume is a greatly revised version of a book that I first published a
decade ago under the title *Class and Culture in Cold War America: A Rainbow at Midnight*. At that time, I did not understand fully how the history
I wrote about the forties illumined many of the key issues of deindustrialization and economic restructuring that would come to dominate the
eighties. I did not comprehend completely how the compromises fashioned
to end the class contestations of the post–World War II era made race and
gender more important than ever as categories constitutive of opportunities and life chances. After three printings in its original version, this new
one gives me the opportunity to address these questions more fully and to
make use of research materials that have recently become available. I have
also benefited from the contributions made by the many excellent social
and labor history studies that have appeared over the past ten years.

I have revised all of the chapters of the original book and added several new ones. The chapters in part 1 explore how mobilization for war
changed the nature of class, gender, and race in U.S. society. In part 2 I
examine postwar reconversion and the extraordinary wave of mass demonstrations and general strikes that it engendered. The chapters in part 3
focus on politics, the Taft-Hartley Act, the Marshall Plan, and the impact
of the cold war on labor relations at home. Part 4 addresses issues of class
and culture, including the emergence of new consumer practices, attitudes
toward authority, and connections between class issues and commercial
film, television, radio, and music products. This introduction and a new
conclusion serve to frame (and reframe) the descriptions, evidence, argument, and analysis in chapters 1–13.

In this book, I hope to draw out in greater detail the implications of labor's struggles in the forties for what has happened since. I believe that today's problems and tomorrow's possibilities can come into clearer focus if we understand the ways in which political battles of the postwar era shaped the contours of this country's economic, cultural, and political life.

What can we learn from labor? The invisibility of labor in the present keeps us from comprehending its accomplishments and its errors in the past. For most of this century, working people have been a powerful force for democratic change in the United States. At the point of production they have struggled over the purpose, pace, nature, and rewards of work. In community life, they have created and sustained institutions designed to provide more democratic access to education, housing, medical care, and recreation. Political mobilization by workers in the thirties forced business and government to establish meaningful unemployment insurance, old-age pensions, and home-loan assistance. The upheavals of the forties that are described in this book won a high-wage, high-employment economy responsible for what we have come to know as the American standard of living, with high levels of broad-based consumer spending and intergenerational upward mobility.

Yet it would be foolish to make a caricature out of complex social relations by portraying workers as always virtuous, noble, or democratic while stereotyping those who work for salaries or dividends as innately immoral, greedy, and elitist. Workers have a long history of self-serving, bigoted, and undemocratic behavior, while people from all levels of society can point with justified pride to their own histories of public-spirited, egalitarian, and moral political action. People in business have made important (if far too infrequent) contributions to movements for social justice over the years, while workers and their organizations have too often been the opponents of social justice. Trade unions have sometimes served as powerful vehicles for working-class solidarity and democratic social change, but they have also often functioned as conservative bureaucracies policing the workplace on behalf of management, as self-centered monopolies allowing organized workers to make gains at the expense of the unorganized.

In addition, it is important to resist the temptation to evoke a past "golden age" for workers and their allies. While there certainly have been better times for workers than the present, the working class has always functioned as a subordinate force in American history, a group often capable of winning important concessions from those in power, but never capable of mobilizing itself and its allies sufficiently to set the direction for the nation's economic and political life.

One thing we need to learn from labor's history is why workers lose most of the battles they fight. We also need to analyze these defeats to learn how victory might have been possible, to see what was salvaged in the process of losing, and to understand how each victory or defeat creates a new context for the future. Why did the trade unions and political parties in the forties fail to provide the necessary organizational and institutional mechanisms for challenging entrenched power? How did divisions among the working class in that era contribute to its defeats? What kind of movement would workers have needed to realize the aspirations that they articulated so powerfully in the forties? How do today's problems stem from the unresolved agenda of the postwar era?

Learning from labor does not mean looking for perfect people or for times without troubles. Rather it means trying to understand the roots of present problems in past policies, to understand how societies act in times of transformation, and to position ourselves for the future by understanding the legacy of labor's struggles for democracy in the past.

I know how difficult it can be to learn about labor. In the early seventies, I worked with a collective of students and ex-students on an underground newspaper in St. Louis. Through that paper, we encountered a group of rank-and-file Teamsters who had organized an extra-union caucus to advance their demands for a more democratic union and a more democratic workplace.[1] They provided us with a wonderful education about social class, the workplace, and the nature of movements for social change. Watching them work together, analyze their problems, and take collective action to solve them gave us a tangible sense of how individuals and societies might change that has stayed with me ever since. Yet their eventual defeat also educated me about the painful costs of social struggle, about what happens to individuals and groups when they cannot find a way to change the institutions that shape their lives.

My reasons for writing this book initially stemmed from my efforts to understand the origins of the problems facing that insurgent caucus in the Teamsters Union. But it was difficult for me initially to find scholarly studies that addressed adequately the complexity of their struggle. Scholarly work on labor seemed segmented into institutional, political, and cultural categories. Many excellent works illumined important aspects of trade-union history, of the role played by workers in political conflict, and of the nature, contradictions, and possibilities within working-class culture. But in the insurgency that I saw close up, these categories could not be separated from one another.

For the rank-and-file Teamsters that I knew, the trade union as an institution could not be separated from the workers' cultural and political identities outside it, while their identities as citizens or creators and receivers of culture could not be detached from their experiences as waged workers and union members. In this book, I have tried to show how working-class institutions, politics, and culture are part of a broader social canvas, and that within the working class and within society at large, politics, culture, and social life are mutually constitutive of one another rather than separate and discrete categories of their own.

In making revisions for this new work, I have been aided immeasurably by the splendid scholarship that has emerged in the past few years on working-class life in the thirties and forties. Spurred on by the social crises of the eighties, young scholars sensitive to the interconnectedness of class, race, and gender have created a rich body of literature about the lives of working people. Refusing to conflate the history of aggrieved populations with the history of the institutions purporting to represent them, these scholars have produced richly nuanced and subtle studies of the multiple identities people take on as they live their lives.

This new scholarship places special emphasis on the nature of social and political protest movements and on the centrality of race and gender in U. S. society. For example, in his extraordinary book *Hammer and Hoe*, Robin D. G. Kelley shows how an African-American culture of opposition enabled black workers in Alabama in the thirties to turn that state's Communist party into a vehicle for their own political and economic aspirations. Lizabeth Cohen's *Making a New Deal* details the ways in which the ascendancy of mass popular culture and the decline of ethnic fraternal organizations during the depression combined to create the preconditions for the New Deal coalition. George Sanchez explains how the labor movement of the thirties played an important role in transforming people of Mexican ancestry in Los Angeles into people who identified themselves as Mexican Americans rather than as Mexicans in his book *Becoming Mexican American*. Vicki Ruiz in *Cannery Women, Cannery Lives* delineates the importance of race and gender in the creation of class consciousness among Chicana workers in the thirties and forties. Earl Lewis's *In Their Own Interests* and Joe Trotter's *Coal, Class, and Color* explore the "racialized class consciousness" of southern black workers. In Wendy Kozol's brilliant study of family images in *Life* magazine, *Life's America*, and in Lynn Spigel's superb *Make Room for TV*, a study of the introduction of television sets into U. S. homes in the forties and fifties, we learn how an emerging corporate consumer culture presented images of the patriarchal family as the center of American life in a way that obscured class and gender identities.[2]

The exciting arguments and analyses presented in these recent studies often destabilize traditional categories of academic inquiry, but they do so in order to give us richer and more carefully multidimensional accounts of the past than we have had before. In their sensitivity to issues of race and gender, in their sophistication about the relationships among politics, economics, and culture, these studies also help explain the enduring relevance of the nation's industrial history to its postindustrial present.

I have tried to follow these leads and examine the meaning of the upheavals of the forties for the deindustrialized and restructured economy of the present. I didn't know when I was working with the insurgent rank-and-file caucus in the Teamsters Union that they had come into being at a crucial moment in U. S. labor history. Spurred on by the oppositional social movements of the sixties and squeezed by the unprecedented combination of rising inflation and rising unemployment, workers all across the country in the early seventies waged militant battles with management and unions. Rank-and-file workers felt the economic crisis of that era first, because companies and unions brought it home to them in the form of production speedups, plant closings, and stagnant wages. From strikes by postal workers and teamsters in 1970 to the insurgencies in the auto, steel, mining, and trucking industries in the years that followed, rank-and-file workers fought back against employers trying to unilaterally void the postwar bargain between management and unions.

The spread of rank-and-file caucuses in industry in the early seventies seemed to many of us at the time as the logical extension of the movements for democratic change that had transformed so much of U. S. society during the sixties. It seemed as if an important new era might be starting with the self-activity of rank-and-file workers responding to and joining similar mobilizations by students, environmentalists, aggrieved racial minorities, and women. But sometimes what seems to be a sunrise can really be a sunset.[3] We were not witnessing the dawn of a new movement for democracy in U. S. industry in the early seventies, but rather the beginnings of a new era of inequality and injustice ushered in by deindustrialization and economic restructuring.

The combination of an energy crisis, capital shortages, increased foreign competition, and the accumulated costs of war overseas and social neglect at home led business to new strategic directions after 1973. They mobilized politically through the American Enterprise Institute, the Heritage Foundation, and the John M. Olin Foundation to campaign for reduced federal and local expenditures on social programs in order to free up more capital for private enterprise. Large corporations used their influence and power to secure subsidies for overseas investment and computer automation at home, while pushing for increased defense spending as an indirect way of recapitalizing business. Most important, in the late seventies, the business community unilaterally broke the bargain that it had made with labor in the forties and aggressively campaigned against unions and their power. They not only resisted the spread of union organizing through their influence with Congress and the National Labor Relations Board but they began to roll back union memberships through aggressive bargaining, supplanting strikers with permanent replacements, and moving production to areas known for nonunion labor. Even more important, they responded to the accumulated consequences of their own failures to modernize U. S. factories with a collective decision to move industrial production overseas. Rather than rebuild the nation's manufacturing capacity, they decided to restructure the United States into a high-tech, low-wage, low-employment economy. By the time that union leaders realized the full dimensions of management's strategy (and some have not realized it yet), it was too late.

Twenty years later, organized labor holds far less power than it did in the seventies. Union membership has fallen below 16 percent of the work force, its lowest level since the twenties.[4] Trade unions have offered no comprehensive political program or shop-floor strategy to oppose the new corporate assault on working people. The intelligent and militant young workers that I knew didn't rise to positions of influence within the trade-union movement; most could not even hold on to the jobs they had when economic restructuring crippled the industrial infrastructure of their cities. The great contributions they might have made to society have not been realized because no political movement emerged that was capable of giving voice to their needs and interests.

For me, watching that caucus and the powerful solidarity that it forged offered important lessons in working-class life. It made it essential for me to learn where these people had come from and why they had lost. What currents did they draw on in fashioning their activism? How had unions become such an obstacle to the wishes and interests of the rank and file? Under what circumstances could the processes I saw emerging within that caucus become generalized throughout society? I didn't know enough then to know what had happened, and I turned to this research as one way for me to find part of the answers to these questions.

Of course, the same kinds of moving personal experiences that help us learn can also hinder our knowledge. It might be tempting for me to rewrite the history of the forties working class to suit my own needs, to have the struggle that ended sadly for me in real life come out "right" on paper. In a country where workers suffer so many defeats, it would be understandable if sympathetic historians found consolation by exaggerating the achievements of past generations of militants as a way of convincing ourselves that change is still possible today. But that would be bad history and bad politics. A school of labor history where workers never suffer defeats does not help us understand the very real problems that actual workers have faced in the past and are facing in the present.

Yet, I also think that it is important to guard against another kind of subjectivity, one that writes pessimism in the present back into the past. Just as it would be detrimental to turn working-class history into an exercise in raising morale for the present, it would be equally harmful to become so demoralized with the history of defeats for labor that it becomes impossible to see how much contestation, struggle, and triumph there has been in the past. As Toni Cade Bambara argues about her own writing, "It's defeatist to dwell always on the consequences of risks. It's proracist to assume we can't take a chance. I am not interested in collaborating with the program of the forces that systematically underdevelop."[5] To pose our work as scholars as a matter of having to choose between realistic pessimism and ungrounded optimism is to oversimplify and distort our challenge. Only the truth will help us, but discerning what the truth is requires an open mind, a predisposition toward either pessimism or optimism depending on what we discover in the evidence.

Because workers and working-class life have been so systematically erased from most accounts of U. S. society, any focus on them understandably evokes associations with what we have come to understand as marxism. It is, I think, a measure of the hegemony of pro-business ideologies that makes people assume that one would only notice the existence and importance of the working class in the United States if one were under the "thrall" of marxist ideology. I refuse to give in to what I consider the anti-intellectualism and anticommunism of this position by distancing myself from the rich analyses of alienated labor, history, and politics that I find in writings by Marx and by those working in his tradition. But I also cannot accept what we have come to identify as the marxist project in respect to labor—identifying the working class as the sole possible agent of change, as the revolutionary grave digger destined to bring an end to capitalism.

While finding much to admire in the marxist tradition, the identification of the working class as the only potential agent of social change does not seem plausible or desirable to me. Marx's own formulations on this subject contain great unresolved contradictions; on the one hand he tells us that workers grow ever more alienated from their own potential under capitalism, and on the other hand that somehow they come to see their circumstances so clearly that they become the ones to critique and overthrow the system. Attempts to resolve that contradiction have often made it worse; one justification for the Leninist party has been that professional revolutionaries must stand in for the alienated proletariat and make the revolution for them. In this book, I try to show the terrible costs exacted on workers' movements in the forties by this vanguardist tradition. The long overdue demise of Stalinist dictatorships in the former Soviet Union and the countries of Eastern Europe is only the most recent manifestation of the failure of this vision.

Yet I think it would be foolish to allow the shortcomings of marxism to give capitalism a free ride, to excuse as inevitable or necessary the very real pain that its inequalities, exploitations, and alienations produce. On the contrary, the disappearance of Leninist states may now take away capitalism's justification for itself as the lesser of two evils, and it may allow us to examine anew the many injustices perpetrated for the sake of profits. In addition, the important historical forces set in motion by shipyard workers in Gdansk, Poland, in the early eighties serves as a reminder of the power of mass politics, of the potential for even seemingly powerless groups of working-class militants to ally with other sectors of society to undermine hierarchy and exploitation. In most countries (including our own), the working class remains the group most capable of meaningfully interrupting or reversing the business agenda, and the labor movement remains the largest potential source of organized collective struggle against greed and exploitation. Leninism and state socialism may have suffered fatal defeats, but popular struggles for democratic power, dignity, and decent lives remain as relevant as ever.

My sympathies and commitments begin with people rather than with theories. I believe that marxism has been important in history because it has been one of the vehicles that workers and others have used to help them struggle against hierarchy and exploitation. When the process is reversed, when workers and their struggles have been vehicles for marxists to gain power, the results have always been disastrous. Labor radicalism in the United States has gained much from marxist formulations and from the activities of individual marxists, but fights over the nature, pace, purpose, and rewards of production, over the distribution of wealth and power in the society, and over the gap between the way people live and the way that they want to live have hardly originated in marxism. As Paul Buhle demonstrates in *Marxism in the United States*, organic working-class radicalism in this country has drawn on indigenous traditions rooted in abolitionist, feminist, spiritualist, and communitarian struggles. The origins of U.S. radicalism lie within the energy and anger of ethnic communities, in resistance to racism led by people of color, and in the diverse critiques and contestations by feminists. All of these movements have had their working-class dimensions, but they have also contained a democratic vision that made cross-class coalitions possible.[6]

Class conflict is not the only source of social change; nor is it inevitable that labor and management will fight over political power. But class tensions represent one of the key places where contradictions exist in our society that might well give rise to fundamental change. It has been among workers that crucial forms of direct-action protest have developed historically, and it has been workers who have voiced the most comprehensive critiques of capitalism as a way of life, not just as a system of production.

For some, marxism outlines immutable laws, predicts the future, and describes the only possible alternative to capitalist production and consumption. But I have always been more intrigued by the more useful tradition outlined by Marx in the *Eighteenth Brumaire of Louis Bonaparte*, where he talks about the complicated and unpredictable nature of political struggle, and in *The Civil War in France*, where he salutes the thoroughly bourgeois reforms of the Paris Commune because they reflected a process of direct democracy allowing ordinary people to determine their own destinies. These examples are useful, not because they tell us about something called "marxism," but rather because they help us understand how people in history struggle for a better life for themselves and for others.

Like other social categories including race and gender, class never appears by itself. No one lives their life completely in class terms; any experience with class is automatically inflected by race, gender, region, sexual preference, and dozens of other identities. When I talk about class consciousness or incipient class formation in this book, I am talking about an awareness of the connections among individuals and institutions, about a political vision of a just society formed in the process of self-aware political activity. I am not saying that workers are better people than others, that they automatically know more than members of other classes, or that they have any innate predispositions because they perform manual labor or get paid by the hour. Following E. P. Thompson and others, I view class consciousness as something that comes out of organizational learning, social contestation, and political mobilization.

The history of the working class is the history of people, their problems and their choices, their potential to change social relations, as well as their powerlessness to bring about change. Learning from them does not mean sanctifying an abstraction called the working class, as if it were a totem encapsulating all that is good in the world. Instead, it means taking seriously the limitations and accomplishments of ordinary people as they try to address the gap between who they want to be and the lives they have to lead.

In the United States, questions of class can seem even more complicated than they do elsewhere. Unlike their European counterparts, American workers have engaged in no prolonged struggle with titled aristocrats. They have enjoyed the benefits of widespread political participation and relatively easy access to land. They have participated in coalition political parties rather than establishing their own. Individual economic mobility has generally overshadowed unified class action in the United States, and ethnic differences have traditionally provided more compelling attachments than class loyalty.

Yet, if titles have not been inherited in the United States, money and power have. The relatively open availability of land, money, and political rights for ordinary people may have limited the power of elite groups, but

it has never seriously challenged the exploitation and oppression perpetrated by concentrated wealth. Individual economic mobility and ethnic
loyalty have been class strategies for survival as well as individual means of
escape, and the nation's overall distribution of wealth has remained markedly stagnant despite well-publicized instances of those who have gone
from rags to riches. The dearth of organized working-class movements may
tell more about the strength of capitalists than about the absence of class
consciousness among workers.

The concept of an American working class can be useful in at least three
respects. First, it provides a useful way of categorizing the empirical fact
that large numbers of people make their living by selling their labor power
to someone else in return for wages. In the post–World War II era, nearly
60 million Americans fit that description, and they shared at least some
common experiences because they did. Second, class offers a coherent explanation for otherwise mysterious activity. Millions of people engaged in
strikes and demonstrations after the war because of their consciousness
of themselves as part of a working class. Even when they had no direct
personal stake in a particular dispute, they often took action out of a conviction that those who performed society's necessary labor had common
concerns. Third, class presents an effective means of comprehending the
ways in which the structure and inner logic of American capitalism influence social behavior. Regardless of their perceptions at any given moment,
workers and employers alike hold a relationship to production that shapes
their consciousness and activities. Positing hostility between the seller and
buyer of labor power because the exchange deprives the seller of control
over the rewards, nature, pace, and purpose of work, a class analysis can
identify working-class strategies of independence as manifestations of long-
repressed needs stemming from the process of production itself.

Thus, class represents both an ideological perception and a historical
experience. From the first days of settlement in North America, tensions
have existed between the producing classes and those whom they viewed
as parasites living off the labor of others. With the advent of industrialism,
those tensions hardened into class antagonisms that manifested themselves
in resistance to capitalist time-work discipline, mass uprisings, strikes, and
attempts to build trade unions. By the late forties, workers had inherited
a long tradition of struggle and self-identification based on the exploitation of their labor and its attendant consequences. Their strategies of independence attempted to fulfill some very old aspirations under very new
circumstances.

One additional aspect of class contains crucial importance for understanding working-class strategies of independence in the postwar years.
Managing, controlling, and profiting from labor plays a central role in

the capitalist system, and consequently, workers' efforts to control the nature and rewards of work play an equally important role in any challenges to that system. Working-class movements often express more than a simple awareness of present inequalities; sometimes they demand fundamental changes that would alter the way all groups in society relate to one another. Yet, that potential has been realized only sporadically in the history of the American working class, and workers have never emerged as a force capable of leading a total reorganization of society. Instead, the working class has all too often been defensive, particularistic, and interest-conscious.

The working class has been defensive by trying to retain past privileges, rather than anticipating and controlling future changes. It has been particularistic by relying on the direct shared experiences of small groups of workers as the basis for resistance, hampering efforts at unity with other groups and exacerbating divisions within the work force. Workers have been interest-conscious, demanding immediate gains within the framework of hierarchical and exploitative production, often at the expense of other groups and carrying within them no alternative vision of social relationships.

For most of its history, the American working class has battled for its interests without an independent affirmative vision of its own and with insurmountable divisions along racial, gender, and caste lines. The consolidation of corporate-liberal power during and after World War II further weakened the working class by destroying some traditional forms of resistance, but in the process it also helped create circumstances in which old barriers could be transcended. One purpose of this book is to understand how that happened and what it means for the present.

The working class has no predetermined mission for the future, no inevitable destiny outside of itself. It is not innately radical; it is not essentially conservative. But it has a history of struggle with an enduring relevance to prospects for democratic change in the United States.

A few years ago, I organized a public forum at a local university on the history of social protest. One of the speakers was a veteran labor activist from the electrical industry. Someone asked him if workers had really gained anything from the struggles of the past and whether there was any point in continuing the fight in the future. He replied, "If it hadn't been for organizing and organizing protest, this country would have gone by the wayside. It's only when people join together and organize and fight the bosses and raise hell that they get anything accomplished. When the working people unite, when the working people get their backs up, when the working people fight, they can whip any damn boss."[7]

Many of the people in the audience thought he was too optimistic, that he had a "romantic" notion of the capacity for change among working people. I know that many who read his remarks here will feel the same way, But, if these comments reveal romanticism, I think it is the romanticism of an organizer, the habit of someone accustomed to looking for an opening, to seeing where change would come from if it were possible.[8] To me, he seemed like a quarterback in a football game before the snap of the ball. To look at the opposing line before a play might lead you to conclude that there are no openings, that every possible opportunity is covered. But a quarterback scours the defense looking for weaknesses on the other team or for matchups that might be favorable for the offense. That way, when the ball is snapped, everyone on the team knows where to go. They head for the places where gains might be made. If they are wrong, they better have a backup plan and the ability to change directions. But it is not until the ball is snapped and play begins that they really find out about the power of each side.

In my judgment, if we are to find our way out of the terrible polarizations and problems facing our society, if we are to address the long-term effects of the stagnation of real wages and the redistribution of wealth from the poor and middle classes to the wealthy, if we are to confront the materialism, greed, and selfishness unleashed by the enterprise economy of the eighties, we need to have the instincts of an organizer. That does not mean that wishful thinking or blind determination can change concrete material and historical circumstances. It does not involve believing that things are true because we would like them to be true. But it does mean that we have to arm ourselves with knowledge, assess our chances realistically, and investigate all possible places from which a change might come. For me, the labor upheavals of the forties—and the unresolved legacy of the changes they helped initiate—are one of those places worth another look.

NOTES

1. I have written about this insurgency elsewhere. See my articles "Beyond the Fringe Benefits: Rank and File Teamsters in St. Louis," *Liberation* (July–Aug. 1973): 31–53, and "Harold and Me: The Problem of the Progressive Union Leader," *New Politics* 3, no. 4 (1992): 150–54.

2. Robin D. G. Kelley, *Hammer and Hoe: Alabama Communists during the Great Depression* (Chapel Hill: University of North Carolina Press, 1990); Lizabeth Cohen, *Making a New Deal: Industrial Workers in Chicago* (Cambridge: Cambridge University Press, 1990); George Sanchez, *Becoming Mexican American: Ethnicity, Culture, and Identity in Chicano Los Angeles, 1900–1945* (New York: Oxford University Press, 1993); Vicki Ruiz, *Cannery Women, Cannery Lives: Mexican Women, Unionization, and the California Food Processing Industry, 1930–1950* (Albuquerque: University of New Mexico Press, 1987); Earl Lewis, *In Their Own*

Interests: Race, Class, and Power in Twentieth Century Norfolk, Virginia (Berkeley: University of California Press, 1991); Joe William Trotter, Jr., *Coal, Class, and Color: Blacks in Southern West Virginia, 1915–32* (Urbana: University of Illinois Press, 1990); Wendy Kozol, *Life's America* (Philadelphia: Temple University Press, 1994); Lynn Spigel, *Make Room for TV: Television and the Family Ideal in Postwar America* (Chicago: University of Chicago Press, 1992).

3. This is how Claude Debussy described the music of Richard Wagner, as a sunset that thought it was a sunrise.

4. Stanley Aronowitz, *False Promises* (Durham: Duke University Press, 1992), 396.

5. Toni Cade Bambara, "What It Is I Think I'm Doing Anyhow," in Janet Sternburg, ed., *The Writer on Her Work* (New York: W. W. Norton, 1981), 162.

6. Paul Buhle, *Marxism in the United States: Remapping the History of the American Left* (London: Verso, 1987).

7. "Social Protest in St. Louis," St. Louis University, St. Louis, Mo., Mar. 3, 1983.

8. I thank Stan Weir for his questions and answers about what it means when people assume that any positive judgments about the working class must stem from "romanticism."

PART ONE

Class, Gender, and Race
in Wartime, 1943–45

CHAPTER ONE

Tradition, Turmoil, and Transformation

Three Wartime Workers

EVERY HISTORICAL MOMENT contains elements of both continuity and change. Even in the most tumultuous times, ancient habits and traditions endure; in seemingly static periods, hidden and visible transformations still transpire. But there are some time periods so marked by rupture and upheaval that human nature itself can appear to be changing. Traditional ways of loving, playing, or worshipping can seem suddenly outmoded, while familiar sites like the city street, the factory floor, or the motion picture theater can percolate with an unfamiliar sense of possibility. What might have seemed impossible yesterday becomes possible today; what might have appeared inevitable and necessary yesterday becomes intolerable and unacceptable today. Often provoked by events of monumental global importance, these transformative eras ultimately challenge every aspect of how people live in the world, down to the most localized, personal, and intimate issues of identity, imagination, and desire.

Mobilization for World War II and postwar reconversion initiated an extraordinary era of transformation in the United States. Through intense conflicts and struggles on the home front as well as on the front lines of far-away battlefields, Americans in the forties forged fundamentally new political, cultural, and social relationships. After more than a decade of unemployment, of low wages and economic stagnation, defense spending brought full employment, high wages, and full production. The need for a cooperative effort against fascism provided an opportunity for women and racial "minorities" to struggle for rights and opportunities long denied them because of gender and racial prejudice. World War II permanently altered the relationship between government and business leading to a government infrastructure capable of sustaining an expanding corporate economy that became institutionalized in the postwar era. The horrors and sac-rifices of war forced people to confront difficult questions about religious faith and patriotism that could no longer remain remote or abstract. In the crucible of war mobilization and postwar reconversion, changing roles and expectations relating to ethnicity, race, age, and gender turned common and ordinary places like city buses, municipal parks, and housing projects into contested spaces where competing individuals and groups hammered out new ways of living.

Most important, wartime emergency and postwar turmoil produced an active movement for social change whose successes and failures have had an enormous impact on American society ever since. Mobilization for war reconstituted the American working class, bringing large numbers of rural, female, and black workers into mass production industries for the first time, disrupting traditional networks of paternalistic authority and control, and encouraging the growth of new cultural forms in facto-ries and in working-class neighborhoods. Strikes and mass demonstrations sought redress for immediate grievances, but they also expressed a sense of what Stanley Aronowitz calls "incipient class formation" emerging among workers—of a collective understanding of the possibility of producing political and social change out of the crucible of economic struggle.[1]

During and after the war, U. S. workers launched the largest strike wave in history. Their shop-floor struggles, picket-line clashes, and mass mobili-zations won a huge postwar wage increase and forced the implementation of a variety of government programs that created what we have come to call "the American standard of living." Because of these successes, many ordinary workers in the postwar years could routinely expect to own their own homes, to take vacations with pay, and to send their children to col-lege. They secured private pension and medical plans for organized workers and provided persistent pressure on government to provide extended assis-tance for housing, education, medical care, and pensions for the rest of the population. They disseminated democratic and egalitarian ideals all across the country, and they produced important new forms of popular culture characterized by prestige from below and pluralism.

Yet this movement had its share of defeats as well. In the thirties, grass-roots mobilization by workers had created primary work groups in factories that exercised important influence on the organization of work. General strikes in Minneapolis, San Francisco, and Toledo in 1934 induced leaders of business and government to implement a comprehensive federal social welfare program in 1935 with the legislation known as the "Second New Deal." But mobilization for war in the forties disrupted the informal net-works among workers that had flourished during the thirties, strengthening the hand of both management and labor unions in imposing harsher work-ing conditions on the rank and file.

Delighted by government-administered contracts that automatically made workers in war industries members of unions, the union leaders did not provide mechanisms for workers to make decisions about production or even forums for the discussion and resolution of grievances. Consequently, workers resorted to withdrawals of efficiency and "collective bargaining by riot."[2] These changes strengthened union, corporate, and government bureaucracies and left workers little recourse for fundamental change within the shops. In politics, workers and their allies failed to build a coalition capable of competing successfully for power with big business, leaving them with largely melioristic gains, not substantive social reforms. Counterattacks by government and business leaders frequently transformed working-class institutions into instruments of social control. Many of the gains won by better-organized workers came largely at the expense of the unorganized; concessions to white male workers often made things worse for women and members of aggrieved racial groups. Too often, labor militants of the forties settled for immediate and tangible economic gains that did little to address the broad range of social and cultural alienations that produced their movement in the first place.

Millions of workers took part in the upheavals of the postwar period, and they mobilized thousands of allies in the streets of industrial cities. Such a mass movement cannot be judged only by its tangible accomplishments. Movements for social change may coalesce openly around concrete and practical goals, but their underlying aims are often more ambitious— to change social relations, to break down the barriers that divide people from one another, and to create a new public culture and new social institutions. Frequently the risks incurred through political activism outweigh by far its potential achievements, but taking direct action to fight for a better future can be a rewarding end in itself. The millions of people in the forties who joined union picket lines or wildcat strikes, who participated in the mass demonstrations or general strikes of the postwar era expressed their support for specific demands and policies, but they also created a new public sphere and affirmed a collective solidarity more important than the specific goals of any particular struggle.

Workers and their allies in the postwar era fought for themselves and for their own interests, to be sure. But they also made sacrifices for one another, embracing the grievances and aspirations of strangers as fervently as they did their own. This mutuality and collectivity served as an important weapon of social contestation, but it also created a social reality that may very well be an even more important legacy of this movement than its concrete economic and political accomplishments. Through disciplined collective political work, but also through the rambunctious "aggressive festivity" of general strikes and carnival-like disturbances, the movement for social change during the forties nurtured and sustained a culture of opposition to exploitation and hierarchy whose impact is still felt to this day.

Instances of local direct-action protests at the grass roots provided the driving force propelling the social movements of the forties. Incidents that might seem trivial and insignificant in isolation can assume great importance when understood as part of an aggregate struggle for change. For example, a few days before Christmas in 1943, gangs of workers armed with scissors and matches roamed through one of Detroit's largest aircraft factories, cutting off their supervisors' neckties and placing lighted matches in the shoes of fellow workers.[3] St. Louis bus drivers staged a surprise strike on Memorial Day 1944, congregating jovially around the bus barns by day, but disrupting a government-sponsored back-to-work meeting at night as they drank, played cards, and heckled antistrike speakers.[4] Three hundred welders employed by Cadillac in Detroit walked off the job in December 1944 to protest restrictions against smoking at work.[5] In a Detroit auto plant shortly before the end of World War II, workers walked off the job in protest against a company order banning checker games during lunch.[6] Less than a year later, striking steelworkers in Fairfield, Alabama, filled the street in front of the mill and "demonstrated" by holding a jitterbug dance.[7] These bizarre and seemingly trivial outbursts, along with thousands of other disruptions, demonstrations, and strikes like them, expressed an important rebellion against work, authority, and hierarchy. They expressed the anger, anxiety, and aspirations of ordinary workers in the face of the radical changes in U.S. society engendered by World War II and its aftermath.

Resentful of wartime sacrifices, eager to control their own destiny, and determined to shape the postwar world in keeping with their own aspirations, American workers devised plans and methods to help them wage real and symbolic struggles for power in these outbursts. More than just a response to wartime overcrowding and overwork, these instances of voluntary self-directed action demonstrated a collective understanding by workers that the war emergency and its aftermath offered an opportunity to fulfill some very old hopes. Workers brought challenges to authority into union halls in tumultuous faction fights; into the courts as they broke the law and defied legally constituted authorities; and, most important, into the streets of American cities in a series of general strikes. In so doing, they advanced their own immediate interests concerning the nature and conditions of their work, but they also gave political leadership to resentments against the centralized power that emerged from the war experience among the public at large.[8]

The momentous changes engendered in American life and culture by wartime mobilization and postwar reconversion made themselves felt in many ways, but few of them are immediately visible in the present. During the late forties, union membership had reached unprecedentedly high numbers, and workers deployed their political power to win national commitments to full employment, a decent home and living environment for every person, and a more egalitarian distribution of the nation's income. The traces of these struggles are not immediately evident in the status of contemporary trade unions or government policies. But perhaps some examples from popular culture can help us begin a process of historical archaeology that will connect the present with the past.

In the nineties, popular culture includes representations of and reflections on three figures from the forties—the singer Hank Williams, the actress Marilyn Monroe, and the writer Chester Himes. The life of Hank Williams has been reenacted in contemporary theater productions, in a music video featuring Hank Williams, Jr., singing a duet with an old film of his father, and in innumerable country-and-western songs, the latest of which has been Alan Jackson's "Midnight in Montgomery." Marilyn Monroe appears even more ubiquitously, in Madonna videos, on the cover of *Life* magazine commemorating her death thirty years ago, and as an icon in assorted films, silk screens, and songs including Elton John's "Candle in the Wind." Contemporary writers Simon Njami and Walter Mosley write postmodern fiction evoking Himes's detective novels, while Robin Givens stars in a major studio film version of Himes's book *A Rage in Harlem*. But in addition to their other identities, Williams, Monroe, and Himes were all industrial workers during World War II whose work experiences helped shape the perspective they brought to their arts later on. Perhaps by examining their origins, we can see some firm cultural connections between the present and the social upheavals of the forties.

Williams, Monroe, and Himes were not "typical" workers, shop-floor militants, or union activists, but nonetheless their histories tell us much about working-class life and culture in the forties. Of course much of the popularity and renown secured by Williams, Monroe, and Himes over the years has been because of their individual talents, but to see them as part of the wartime working class is to understand something important about the formative influences that shaped their beliefs, aspirations, and values. All three have also attracted attention not just because of their talents but also because of their lives, their problems, and their contradictions, all of which resonated with the unresolved tensions and conflicts of working-class life in the forties.

Williams's music and lyrics expressed a loneliness and alienation rarely heard in mainstream U.S. culture. Monroe's efforts to grow as an actress and as an intellectual struggling against her objectification as a sex symbol took on iconic status for many women over the years. Himes's fiction delved into realms of hate, hurt, and fear so powerfully that it illumined the pathology of American racism in a way that has seemed prophetic to many of his subsequent readers. To see how working-class life during and after the war shaped all three of these individuals helps us to understand better the alienations and indignities of social class in the United States, but it also enables us to see the powerful impact that working-class voices, images, and ideas have had in fashioning and refashioning the core concerns of American popular culture.

Born in 1923, Hank Williams grew up in a white working-class family in rural Alabama during the Great Depression. He starting selling peanuts to workers in a logging camp when he was only three, and throughout his childhood he worked hard, shining shoes and delivering groceries. His father, who had suffered from shell shock during World War I, drove locomotives for the W. T. Smith Lumber Company for a while, but then drifted from job to job. "That's the way I wanted it," Lon Williams later explained defensively. "A company gets to feel that it owns a man. I always felt I was a free man and could go off and work somewhere else."[9] Lon Williams was committed to the Veterans Administration Hospital in Biloxi in 1930 and remained there for ten years. His family picked strawberries for a living until Hank's mother, Lilly, secured employment in a cannery run by the New Deal's Works Progress Administration (WPA). At fourteen, Hank made his first musical appearance at an amateur night show at the Empire Theater in Montgomery, singing his own composition about working for the WPA.[10]

Hank Williams's body paid a price for the deprivations of his working-class upbringing. He suffered so severely from hookworm that it injured his vision, and a childhood of malnutrition left him perpetually underweight later in life. He suffered chronic backaches caused by an accident while trying to become a rodeo performer and aggravated by an untreated form of spina bifida.[11] He started drinking alcohol at the age of eleven, and like many working-class musicians, he pursued a career in music in part because it appeared the only feasible alternative to a life of underpaid arduous labor. Unable to afford medical treatment as a child, he remained suspicious of physicians later in life and secured one of his greatest professional triumphs singing as part of a traveling caravan sponsored by Hadacol, a "quack" medicine that promised to cure arthritis, ulcers, asthma, tuberculosis, epilepsy, paralytic strokes, high and low blood pressure, and gallstones.[12]

In 1942, Williams dropped out of high school (he was a nineteen-year-old sophomore) and traveled to Mobile in hopes of enlisting in the military. When he failed his physical exam (as he had a year earlier when called by his draft board) Williams took a job for sixty-six cents an hour as a shipfitter's helper at the Alabama Drydock and Shipbuilding Company. He worked there for nearly two years, eventually becoming a welder, which increased his pay to ninety-seven cents an hour.[13]

Even when he later attained wealth and fame as a performer, Hank Williams continued to look at the world from the standpoint of a worker. He presented a Saturday afternoon radio program sponsored by Duckhead Work Clothes in 1950, and his last live performance in 1952 came at a musician's union dinner in Montgomery.[14] In addition, class resentments pervaded Hank Williams's songs. In "Be Careful of Stones That You Throw," "Mansion on a Hill," and "Men with Broken Hearts" he condemned "respectable" people for thinking themselves superior to poor people. Speaking to a reporter about "Men with Broken Hearts" Williams explained, "Don't know why I wrote that thing. Except somebody that's fell, he's the same man ain't he? So how can he be such a nice guy when he's got it and such a bad guy when he ain't got nothing?"[15] The singer carried those sentiments over into his own personal behavior, refusing an invitation to dinner with a wealthy Montgomery banker because "when I was starving in this town, the son of a bitch wouldn't buy me a hamburger. Now there's nothing too good for me. What's the matter, ain't I the same guy?"[16]

Frequent acts of personal generosity demonstrated Williams's sensitivity to the injuries of class. He routinely brought sacks of groceries to his second wife Billie Jean's grandparents, who were on welfare. "He did that with everybody poor who gave him a sob story," she explained. "I think he gave everybody down here a gun. He gave away some [performing] uniforms too. 'You like this one?' he'd say to somebody. 'Here, take it.'"[17] Williams secretly gave $400 a month to a Catholic orphanage even though he was not a Catholic himself.[18] Lum York, who played bass fiddle behind Williams, later recalled that when the band went on tours, "We'd be ridin' around and he'd see a black guy playin' a guitar and singin' and he'd always stop and pick him up and ride him around and let him play for us a couple of hours and then he'd give him some money when he let him out. Anybody playin' on the street like that he'd usually give them a little money."[19]

If his working-class upbringing marked Hank Williams in one way, his racial identity as a white southerner shaped him in another.[20] As a child growing up in Ku Klux Klan territory in the Alabama black belt, he was no stranger to white racism and terrorism. In his hometown, Jim Warren, a white store owner who maintained a friendship with a black family and rented a house to them, incurred the wrath of the Klan. They beat him up and demanded that he leave town, but while Warren sent the family to live elsewhere, he "stuck it out in Georgiana, even though the town was ashamed of him."[21] The young Hank Williams knew about Warren's reputation, but visited his store often to talk and to get lessons from Warren on the guitar.

He also admired a black street singer, Connie McKee, known as "Big Day," and received his first music lessons from another black singer, Rufus Payne, known as "Tee-Tot." The black street singer gave lessons to local children, including Williams, in exchange for money and meals, and his artistry shaped Williams's subsequent approach to music. The blues guitarist and singer B. B. King once recalled the familiarity he felt toward Williams's music when he first heard it on the radio: "Like Hank Williams, man, when he wrote 'Cold, Cold Heart,' tunes like that, that carried me right back to my same old blues about 'don't answer the door' and all that kind of stuff. 'Cause this is a guy hurting. He's hurting from inside. And 'Your Cheatin' Heart,' many things of this sort are just to me another form of blues sung by other people. And they call it country and western." [22] When Williams performed on the Louisiana Hayride country music radio show in Shreveport in the early fifties, blacks flocked to the show, and they also turned out in large numbers for his funeral in Montgomery in 1953. [23]

When Williams began his job as a shipfitter's helper in 1942, the Alabama Drydock and Shipbuilding Company in Mobile segregated its employees, assigning black workers to separate sections of the shipyard. Many white workers resented the relatively high wages paid to blacks and they feared that the company would have to comply with federal law and desegregate the yards. When protests by black workers secured the right to work at job categories previously denied to them, more than five hundred white workers responded violently, attacking black men and women throughout the shipyards with "pipes, tools, and fists." [24] Company security guards did nothing to stop the violence; some participated in it. Police officers and national guard units eventually restored order, but not before fifty black men and women had been badly injured. Employers throughout Mobile dismissed black workers for the day, sending them home without pay, while black organizations asked the president to declare martial law to ensure their safety. [25]

Williams's biographers have offered no information about his response to the shipyard attacks on black workers, but they have informed us of an intense series of interactions with black people throughout his life. Perhaps one source of the inner pain that Williams expressed so poignantly in his songs came from conscious or unconscious recognition of the contradiction between white racist treatment of African Americans and the very real debts owed to them by white working-class people like himself. Or perhaps he resented the new roles assumed by blacks during the war, threatened by the peril they posed to white supremacy and the security it offered to white workers like himself. Either way, the changing state of race relations in the United States had to affect Williams and add further complexity to negotiating his identities as a white male worker.

No less than class and race, tensions relating to gender defined the music of Hank Williams. Kent Blaser points out that forty-five of Williams's fifty most important songs dealt with relations between men and women, and that fifteen of these complain about abandonment by one's partner.[26] From "Lovesick Blues" to "Your Cheatin' Heart," his most popular songs articulated loneliness, frustration, and despair as routine features of the search for love and affection. His pessimism made a noticeable break with the traditional romantic optimism purveyed through popular music in the United States, especially in the early fifties.

Williams's own life experiences allowed him precious few illusions about the nuclear family, and in that respect his experiences were those of his class. Unemployed fathers deserted their families in large numbers during the depression; by 1940 more than 1.5 million married women lived apart from their spouses. Many families formed extended households by moving in with relatives, but by the midthirties an estimated 200,000 vagrant children roamed the country. Women and children entered the labor force in large numbers, and their earning power undercut the authority and self-image of many male breadwinners.[27] During World War II, 6 million women workers entered high-paying production jobs in industry. Sixteen million Americans left their homes to join the armed forces, and another 15 million traveled to new jobs in war production centers. Under these conditions, established forms of family and community life broke down, and workers experienced new gender and family roles.[28]

Hank Williams's father spent the entire decade of the thirties in the Veterans Administration Hospital in Biloxi. From the time he was six until he was sixteen, Hank was raised by his mother, Lilly, who assumed an awesome presence in his life. Like many working-class children, Hank also spent considerable time with relatives outside his nuclear family, living for a year when he was six with his cousin J. C. in nearby Monroe County, Alabama, so that J. C.'s sister could go to school in Georgiana by living with Hank's mother and sister.[29] Lilly Williams moved her family to Montgomery in 1937 when Hank was fourteen, and she ran a boarding house there that exposed her son to a new extended "family."

For Hank Williams, shipyard work in Mobile provided an opportunity to escape the surveillance of his mother and to fashion a new identity. It also opened up more opportunities for a career in music, entertaining well-paid war workers in taverns and night clubs. Several months after he began work there, he played for a "medicine show" in Banks, Alabama, where he met Audrey Mae Sheppard, a married woman with a daughter at home and a husband (who had deserted the family at their daughter's birth) overseas. They started dating and lived together in Mobile, where they worked "side by side" in the shipyards. Audrey later recalled to her daughter, Lycrecia, that "In the evenings we'd go back to this terrible little old hotel room and I'd wash out our clothes for the next day. Finally, one day I told him, 'This is just not it, Hank. I want to go back to Montgomery. I want to get a band together for you and get you back on a radio station and start working shows.' " [30]

Sheppard's father threatened to kill Hank because his daughter was still legally married to her first husband. When Williams first brought Audrey home to meet his mother, Lilly asked, "Where'd you get this whore?" a question that provoked a fistfight between mother and son. [31] In a culture that increasingly idealized motherhood in the abstract while imposing ever-greater burdens on it in practice, not every son could use the words that Hank Williams employed in describing his mother to the comedienne Minnie Pearl: "Minnie, there ain't nobody in the world I'd rather have alongside me in a fight than my mama with a broken beer bottle in her hand." [32]

Hank married Audrey in 1944 before a justice of the peace in a Texaco station in Andalusia, Alabama, but the marriage was soon declared illegal because it came too soon after Audrey's separation from her husband to satisfy the requirements of Alabama law. [33] Hank and Audrey were divorced in 1948, but reconciled and remarried after the birth of their son Randall Hank (Hank Williams, Jr.) in 1949. [34] Their tempestuous relationship led to another divorce, and his marriage (in 1952) to Billie Jean Eshlimar (who had been abandoned by her first husband) led to constant bickering among Williams, his mother, and both of his wives. [35]

The instability of Williams's home life and love life formed an important focus for his song lyrics, and elements of instability characterized his life on and off stage. He named his backup band the Drifting Cowboys and recorded a series of recitations under the pseudonym "Luke the Drifter." In 1944, while still working at the Alabama Drydock and Shipbuilding Company in Mobile, he took a trip to Portland, Oregon, to work for a time in that city's Kaiser shipyards, without informing his friends or family. [36]

Success as a performer hardly resolved Williams's sense of alienation. Addicted to alcohol and to pain-killing drugs, he neglected his diet and went for long periods without sleep. His excessive drinking often made him unable to fulfill his performing commitments, but sometimes he used alcohol deliberately to insulate himself from aspects of show business that he despised. As one musician who knew him well claimed, "I think the man was scared. Hank was a genius. But he began to see that he was becoming a thing, a salable product, and he didn't know how to handle it. 'They're slicing me up and selling me like baloney,' he complained to me." [37]

The unstable relationships in Hank Williams's songs resonated with the instabilities of working-class life that he knew so well. As one of his most perceptive critics has noted, part of his appeal to audiences came from his ability to infuse songs about failed romance with the injuries of class. "A tragic love affair, then, is the final insult—and perhaps the focus for economic and social frustrations it would be unmanly to admit," argues Dorothy Horstman.[38]

The lyrics of Hank Williams's songs expressed an egalitarian, forgiving, and fatalistic worldview; they make no direct references to politics. Yet the contradictions of class, race, and gender so painfully present in his songs reflected the historical context in which they were created as well as the personal history of Williams himself. He created a music that underscored the connections between whites and blacks, that lamented the schisms between men and women, and that cried out for a more just and more loving existence for ordinary men and women.

Like Hank Williams, Marilyn Monroe entered the wartime work force while still a teenager. Born in Los Angeles in 1926, Monroe and her family had already been abandoned by her father. She was raised by her mother, who worked in the motion picture industry as a negative cutter and film processor until mental illness led to her commitment to the Norwalk State Hospital. After that, Monroe (then Norma Jean Baker) spent much of her childhood and adolescence in orphanages, foster homes, and the houses of relatives in working-class districts of Los Angeles.[39]

Even as a child, Monroe took to acting as an escape from the harsh realities of her life. In her last interview she recalled, "When I was five—I think that's when I started wanting to be an actress—I loved to play. I didn't like the world around me because it was kind of grim—but I loved to play house and it was like you could make your own boundaries."[40] Like many people during the Great Depression, she looked to Hollywood films for a better, happier world. "Some of my foster families used to send me to the movies to get me out of the house," she recalled, "and there I'd sit all day and way into the night—up in front, there with the screen so big, a little kid all alone, and I loved it. I loved anything that moved up there and I didn't miss anything that happened—and there was no popcorn either."[41]

Monroe quit high school at the age of sixteen to marry Jim Dougherty, a twenty-one-year-old sheet metal shaper at the Lockheed plant in Burbank. He routinely brought "pin-up" pictures of his wife to the job to show to his work partner, an ex-convict from Georgia who later became a film star himself, Robert Mitchum. Exempt from the draft because of his marriage and because of his status as a defense worker, Dougherty nonetheless felt embarrassed to be a factory hand rather than a soldier. In addition, the presence of women workers on the shop floor upset him. He felt that they endangered his safety by not having enough physical strength required to tighten the clamps they handed him, but his efforts to find work more to his liking away from women in the plant proved unsuccessful. In 1943 he joined the merchant marine, and in 1944 by his request he shipped out on a freighter to Australia.[42]

When her husband went to sea, Norma Jean Dougherty joined her mother-in-law on the assembly line packing parachutes at the Radio Plane Company in Burbank. She hated the monotony of the job from the start and quickly secured a transfer to the "dope room," where she sprayed liquid plastic on the fuselages of planes. She won a commendation from the company for excellence on the job, but seems to have been resented by other employees who felt that her pace set an unrealistic standard for the rest of them. They muttered hostile remarks during the ceremony where she received her award, and later one woman bumped into her in what she interpreted as a deliberate effort to make her spill a can of liquid plastic. She vowed to herself that she would find a way to leave the shop and got her opportunity in June 1945 when a photographer taking "glamor" pictures of women war workers for military magazines discovered her and took photographs that helped launch her career as a model.[43]

Monroe went on to even more success and fame than Hank Williams, but like him, she carried her working-class past with her. Reflecting on the high-stakes card games she saw in Hollywood, she registered her disgust by recalling, "When I saw them hand hundred and even thousand-dollar bills to each other, I felt something bitter in my heart. I remembered how much 25 cents and even nickels meant to the people I had known, how happy ten dollars would have made them, how a hundred dollars would have changed their whole lives."[44] Another time, she complained about the absence of monuments or museums about the film industry in Hollywood. "Gee, nobody left anything behind, they took it, they grabbed it and they ran—the ones who made the billions of dollars, never the workers."[45] When studio officials accused her of ingratitude for their efforts to make her a star, she replied, "If I am a star—the people made me a star—no studio, no person, but the people did. There was a reaction that came to the studio, the fan mail, or when I went to a premiere."[46] Recalling her feelings about singing "Happy Birthday" to President Kennedy at a Madison Square Garden rally, she stressed her working-class origins, noting, "I looked all the way up and back and I thought, 'That's where I'd be—way up there under one of those rafters, close to the ceiling, after I paid my $2 to come into the place.'"[47]

In making the transition from war worker/model to film star, Norma Jean Dougherty acquired the name "Marilyn Monroe" and an appearance that owed as much to careful construction as it did to nature. Preparing her body for scenes in films could take as long as six hours. She blended together three shades of lipstick to give her lips a distinctive look beneath the Vaseline and wax gloss applied by makeup artists for her screen appearances. Studio personnel made her hair platinum blonde by dying it with a special blend of peroxide, bleach, and de-yellowing agents every four days during filming. Other makeup artists painted platinum polish on her finger-nails and toenails, while seamstresses sewed her into form-fitting evening gowns. As Graham McCann notes perceptively, the circulation of images of Monroe's objectified body in the postwar era served as a perpetual ad-vertisement for consumer culture and the "looks" that it promised through purchases of cosmetics and clothing.[48]

Yet if Hank Williams's voice expressed the toll that working-class life took on his body, Marilyn Monroe's body provided her with an opportunity to give voice to her feelings, to trade the dreariness of factory and house-work for a life of glamor and fame. To be sure, the pin-up photographs that got her out of the factory led to the commercialization and commodifica-tion of her face and body by Hollywood as a depersonalized icon of male lust. But her struggles to assert her own identity as an actress and as a per-son repeatedly pitted her real body and its history against the fetishized body that Hollywood created and celebrated.

For all of her resentment against being turned into a "thing," Mon-roe never rejected sex itself. "That's the trouble, a sex symbol becomes a thing," she explained. "I just hate to be a thing. But if I'm going to be a symbol of something I'd rather have it sex than some other things they've got symbols of."[49] In response to charges that she had slept her way to suc-cess, she replied frankly, "I was never kept; I always kept myself. But there was a period when I responded too much to flattery, and slept around too much, thinking I would help my career, though I always liked the guy at the time. They were always so full of self-confidence and I had none at all and they made me feel better. But you don't get self-confidence that way. You have to get it by earning respect. I've never given up on anyone who I thought respected me."[50]

Monroe labored to be more than a sex symbol—to be an actress, a wife and mother, and an informed citizen, but at every turn she confronted the constraints of prevailing definitions of gender roles and the inability of men to see her as anything other than an eroticized body. Studio executives and fellow actors frequently derided Monroe's "temperament" because she often reported to work late and interrupted the filming of scenes, claiming that she felt ill. Fans and friends portrayed her as tragically unlucky when her efforts to bear children led to miscarriages. Journalists complained that she had "let herself go" when her figure no longer conformed to their ex-pectations. But Monroe suffered from a then-undiagnosed case of endo-metriosis, a condition where the lining of the uterus spreads throughout the stomach, causing menstrual pains and cramps that often accounted for her absences from work. Endometriosis also renders attempts at childbear-ing particularly dangerous and painful. Perhaps she would have been more willing to adopt a child and less eager to bear one herself had she known the full import of her condition. The medical profession's historic disinterest in and ignorance of "female problems" combined with the overwhelming cultural expectations in the fifties about the "natural" imperative for women to bear children contributed to representations of Monroe's serious medical problems as a character flaw or metaphysical tragedy.[51] Similarly, complaints about her "weight" problem revealed more concern for the fantasy lives of male voyeurs than for the health of the actress herself.

In her battles with stereotypical societal expectations about women, Monroe hardly encountered something new in her life. Her first marriage originated as much from the desire of her relatives to get her out of the house than from any particular passion of her own for James Dougherty. "My marriage brought me neither happiness nor pain," she reminisced. "My husband and I hardly spoke to each other. This wasn't because we were angry. We had nothing to say."[52] For his part, Dougherty found his wife's idea of housekeeping exasperating, especially her ideas about cooking—like serving a dinner consisting of only peas and carrots every night.[53] Her subsequent marriages to the baseball star Joe DiMaggio and the playwright Arthur Miller attracted enormous attention because of the fame of her husbands as well as because the divorces that followed them seemed to confirm to most of the mainstream press Monroe's deficiencies as a woman. But she defended her marriages by placing them within the context of her working-class female experience. "I was never used to being happy," she explained, "so that wasn't something I ever took for granted. I did sort of think, you know, marriage did that. You see, I was brought up differently from the average American child because the average child is brought up expecting to be happy—that's it, successful, happy, and on time. Yet because of fame I was able to meet and marry two of the nicest men I'd ever met up to that time."[54]

The actress studied her craft with Lee Strasberg after she had already been established as a hit with the public, and she quietly attempted to take adult extension classes at UCLA in art appreciation and literature. Yet even her efforts at self-improvement and her marriage to Arthur Miller offended people who viewed her aspirations to be something other than a sex symbol as inappropriate.

The television personality Jack Paar revealed more about his own class biases than about Monroe's character when he quipped, "I fear that beneath the facade of Marilyn Monroe there was only a frightened waitress in a diner."[55] In truth, she wore her working-class identity proudly. In her first screen appearances, Monroe played a switchboard operator and a secretary, and she gave two of her best performances as a cannery worker in *Clash by Night* and as a saloon singer pursued by a cowboy in *Bus Stop*. Monroe repeatedly told interviewers how highly she valued her work, telling one, "I guess I've always had too much fantasy to be only a housewife."[56] Those who knew her best admired her work ethic enormously, but she talked about acting in a way that revealed traces of her previous experience as a parachute packer (and her alienation from that job) when she claimed, "I'm not an actress who appears at the studio just for the purpose of discipline. This doesn't have anything to do with art. I would like to become more disciplined within my work. But I'm there to give a performance and not to be disciplined by a studio! After all, I'm not in a military school. This is supposed to be an art form, not just a manufacturing establishment."[57]

Monroe's struggles with prevailing definitions of acceptable gender and class roles led her to take critical positions on other social issues. According to one acquaintance, "she told us of her strong feelings for civil rights, for black equality . . . her admiration for what was being done in China, her anger at red-baiting and McCarthyism, and her hatred of J. Edgar Hoover."[58] When a Los Angeles night club turned down the opportunity for a performance by the jazz singer Ella Fitzgerald because of the club's policy against hiring blacks, Monroe protested and promised the establishment's owners that she would sit in the front table every night if they let Fitzgerald perform there. "Marilyn was there, front table, every night," Fitzgerald later recalled. "After that, I never had to play a small jazz club again."[59] When asked about her surprisingly high popularity among black women, Monroe talked about her own resentments about being judged by her appearance— implying that black women knew what she was going through. "Negroes can sometimes see through appearances better than whites," she claimed.[60]

Hank Williams turned to black culture for a musical and discursive vocabulary capable of voicing the alienations and oppressions of class. Marilyn Monroe found among black people a disposition against visual stereotypes that resonated with her own resentments against her treatment as a woman. But for Chester Himes, race offered more than a rich metaphor illumining his class or gender identities. As a black man in the United States, race provided a relentless oppression all its own, even as Himes struggled with the ways in which it also inflected and determined his experiences as a man and as a worker.

Before he entered the wartime work force in 1942, Chester Himes had been a college student and a prison inmate, an unskilled laborer and a published author. Born in 1909 in Jefferson City, Missouri, where his father taught blacksmithing and wheelwrighting at Lincoln Institute, he grew up in a family highly conscious of racial issues. His father taught technical courses at black colleges in Missouri, Mississippi, and Arkansas, in keeping with the conservative black nationalist teachings of Booker T. Washington, who urged African Americans to obtain useful skills in order to carve out a modest niche for themselves within a white-dominated society. But his mother had a very different attitude, expressing freely to her children her hatred of condescension from white people and her belief in the importance of fighting back. When Professor Himes served on the faculty of Alcorn A&M in Mississippi, the Himes family owned the first private automobile in their remote rural county. Local mule drivers claimed that the car frightened their animals, and they threatened to shoot at it when it came by. But Himes's mother routinely took her children for rides, bringing along a pistol, which she drew whenever she saw a mule driver reach for his rifle. This transgression of local norms drew numerous complaints from white people, eventually leading to the dismissal of Himes's father from his job. Yet Himes's mother continued to display the same sense of entitlement and militancy wherever they moved.[61]

The Himes family eventually settled in Cleveland, where Chester graduated from East High School. Eligible to attend Ohio State University as a graduate of an Ohio public high school, Himes took a job as a busboy at the Wade Park Manor Hotel during the summer after his graduation in order to earn money to pay for his college education. While working at the hotel he fell into an open elevator shaft, breaking two bones in his arm, fracturing three vertebrae in his spine, and breaking his jaw. The Ohio State Industrial Commission awarded medical expenses and a small disability allowance to Himes because it found the hotel negligent about the conditions that caused his accident, and in the autumn of 1926 he entered Ohio State.[62]

Despite the nominal integration of the university, and despite Ohio's strict antidiscrimination laws, Himes found the school and the surrounding community in Columbus hostile to the presence of black students. Even among other African Americans he found an unpleasant color consciousness whereby light-skinned blacks disdained those with darker complexions. Himes did badly in his school work, and when he returned to Cleveland during school vacations he began spending considerable time at local gambling establishments and houses of prostitution. He got caught passing bad checks in Columbus during his junior year and had to leave school. In November 1928, he left the university, and later that month police officers arrested him for burglarizing a suburban home; he would spend the next seven years at the Ohio State Penitentiary.[63]

Chester Himes first became a published writer in prison, selling short stories to national magazines. He later claimed that he did so in order to save his life, reasoning that the guards would be less likely to kill him if people outside of jail knew his identity. After his parole, he spent the late thirties working first as a laborer, bellhop, and waiter, then as a research assistant at the Cleveland Public Library and as a writer with the WPA

Ohio Writers' Project. He began writing for the labor newspaper *Union Leader* and participated in CIO organizing drives.[64]

When defense orders for World War II began creating new opportunities for employment, Himes applied for work at several of Cleveland's biggest factories, but when he saw that the jobs went almost exclusively to whites, he became discouraged and disillusioned with life in Cleveland and decided to see if his prospects might not be better in Los Angeles.[65]

The Selective Service called Himes for a preinduction physical in 1943, but they gave him a medical deferment when they discovered an un-united fracture of the vertebrae and his twisted pelvic structure—the results of his hotel accident in 1926.[66] Partially because of learning from his father's jobs in mechanics departments at black colleges, Himes could read blueprints, do construction work, operate machine tools, and repair combustion engines. Labor shortages and pressure by civil rights activists had forced California employers to drop barriers against black employment, and Himes found that his skills made him employable for the first time. He held twenty-three different jobs during the war, a mobility made possible by his intelligence and skills—but made desirable to him largely because of his resentments against racism on and off the job.[67] His real ambition was to become a writer in Hollywood, but even though he had been promised a job at Warner Brothers Studios, it reportedly fell through when studio boss Jack Warner warned a subordinate, "I don't want no niggers on this lot."[68]

Instead of writing for Hollywood, Himes produced essays and short stories about racial issues for *The Crisis,* the monthly publication of the National Association for the Advancement of Colored People.[69] Although he saw some hope in the way that wartime Los Angeles provided new opportunities and brought African Americans, Euro-Americans, Mexican Americans, and Asian Americans into close proximity with one another, he found racism in Los Angeles to be deep-seated and offensive. "Los Angeles hurt me racially as much as any city I have ever known—much more than any city I remember from the south," he later recalled. "It was the lying hypocrisy that hurt me. Black people were treated much the same as they were in an industrial city of the South. They were Jim-Crowed in housing, in employment, in public accommodations, such as hotels and restaurants."[70]

While working in Los Angeles war plants, Himes conceived *If He Hollers Let Him Go* and *Lonely Crusade,* two novels published during the postwar period that offer exceptionally important insights into working-class life. He later stressed how hard he tried in these books to evoke a sense of the actual social tensions that he had seen as a war worker. In *If He Hollers Let Him Go* and *Lonely Crusade,* Himes details the sense of shared purpose and accomplishment that binds together small groups of workers at the point of production. He also describes many of the frustrations of waged work—the unrealistic production quotas, involuntary overtime, and dangerous safety conditions on the shop floor, as well as the overcrowded, inadequate, and inaccessible housing, transportation, and medical services of the industrial city. Yet for Himes, all of these class concerns could not be disassociated from issues of white supremacy and antiblack racism.

In his fiction about wartime Los Angeles, Himes dramatizes actual historical events like the internment of more than one hundred thousand Japanese Americans in camps, the "zoot suit" riots when sailors attacked Mexican-American youths, and numerous incidents of interracial violence in Los Angeles during the war years. A character in *Lonely Crusade* picks up newspapers and reads about "the growing racial tensions throughout the city—a Negro had cut a white worker's throat in a dice game at another of the aircraft companies and was being held without bail, and a white woman in a shipyard had accused a Negro worker of raping her. A group of white sailors had stripped a Mexican lad of his zoot suit on Main Street before a host of male and female onlookers. Mistaken for Japanese, a Chinese girl had been slapped on a crowded streetcar by a white mother whose son had been killed in the Pacific."[71]

Yet for all of their illumination of public events like the Japanese-American internment and the zoot-suit riots, perhaps the most stunning accomplishment of these two novels lies in their illustration of the pervasive pressure exerted on individuals by racial antagonisms in wartime and postwar Los Angeles. In one telling passage, the narrator of *If He Hollers Let Him Go* explains that even more than not getting a job or being denied service in a restaurant what bothered him most was "the look on the people's faces" when he showed up to apply for a job: "They just looked so goddamned startled that I'd even asked. As if some friendly dog had come in through the door and said, 'I can talk.' It shook me."[72] Yet white racism was neither uniform nor static. In another section of the same book, the narrator ruminates about "when white people started getting white—or rather, when they started losing it. And how you could take two guys from the same place—one would carry his whiteness like a loaded stick, ready to bop everybody else in the head with it; and the other would just simply be white as if he didn't have anything to do with it and let it go at that."[73] But blacks do not escape from white racism without their own contradictions and scars, without prejudices and hatreds of their own, according to Himes. In one of his stories published in *The Crisis*, a black man asserts that "he needed all of his crazy, un-called-for and out-of-place defiance, his lack of civility and rudeness; . . . he needed every ungracious thing he ever did."[74]

In his probing of the causes and consequences of white racism, Himes placed great importance on sex and gender. In his analysis of the zoot-suit riots for *The Crisis*, he placed the blame for the riots on efforts by white sailors to have sex with Mexican-American young women and the sailors' subsequent need to symbolically "emasculate" Mexican-American males.[75] "There is some rare and inexplicable [not only inexplicable but incomprehensible] ego in the average southern white man which makes him believe he can have an affair with any dark-skinned woman anywhere on earth—Los Angeles being no exception," Himes argued. He noted that in his neighborhood, he had never seen a white woman molested by Mexican-Americans and that while he had seen black youths occasionally make comments to white women, "they will never go as far as white men toward Negro women in a white district."[76]

These issues about the connections between masculine self-affirmation, racial identities, and control over women affected Himes personally. When he moved to Los Angeles, his wife secured a good job as codirector of women's activities for the United Service Organizations. His wife's success made Himes jealous, hurt, and fearful. He later recalled, "It hurt me for my wife to have a better job than I did and be respected and included by her white co-workers, besides rubbing elbows with many well-to-do blacks of the Los Angeles middle class who wouldn't touch me with a ten-foot pole. I found that I was no longer a husband to my wife; I was her pimp. She didn't mind, and that hurt all the more."[77] The crowning blow of racial prejudice in Los Angeles for Himes came from "finding myself unable to support my black wife, whom I loved desperately."[78]

Himes worked these concerns about patriarchy and masculine identity into his fiction. The shipyard worker Bob Jones in *If He Hollers Let Him Go* describes his girlfriend in terms of the pride he feels "to have a chick like her" because her position and appearance demanded respect from whites and blacks alike and because he knew that other workers respected him when they saw them together. When this relationship becomes imperiled, he seeks compensation through a sexual conquest of a racist white woman worker. Union organizer Lee Gordon in *Lonely Crusade* feels overwhelmed by "the fear of being unable to support and protect his wife in a world where white men could do both."[79] This fear shaped his sexuality, making him want to be the "man" in bed that he could not be in a war plant, but that very pressure "reduced him to sterility as if castrated by it."[80]

Himes understood how the failure to address and resolve racial tensions would doom any efforts at classwide solidarity within the working class. Furthermore, he saw how racist hierarchies and antiracist resentments became transposed onto issues of sexuality and gender. Yet his uninterrogated assumptions about the need for men to possess and protect women undermined any possibility of his formulating an effective oppositional critique of the ways in which racism becomes sexualized, how it becomes rendered a product of "nature" rather than of history. Nonetheless, Himes did have some important insights into the positive uses to which the hate, hurt, and fear he witnessed might be put.

Himes's heroes live in fear; fear that they will give up the struggle and resign themselves to white supremacy, but also fear that they will not be able to take any more and will lash out violently—an effort doomed to failure by the power realities of the country in which they live. But Himes also sees a redeeming virtue in this fear, because it honestly addresses the unresolved contradictions of race and class. The first step, in his view, was to admit the ugliness of the situation. "To hate white people is one of the first emotions an American Negro develops when he becomes old enough to learn what his status is in American society," Himes told a Chicago audience in 1948. "He [the Negro] must, of necessity hate white people. He would not be—and it would not be human if he did not—develop a hatred for his oppressors. At some time in the lives of every American negro there has been this hatred for white people; there are no exceptions. It could not possibly be otherwise."[81] Honesty would reveal unflattering things about blacks as well as whites, in Himes's judgment, but it provided a necessary first step toward facing the magnitude of the race problem. But his point was not simply to open up racial wounds, but rather to see how they and their underlying causes might be healed and transformed.

In the May 1944 Crisis, Himes called for "Negro martyrs" to lead an American revolution whose aim was nothing more than the democratic society that the United States already claimed to be. He welcomed participation in this revolution from all quarters, arguing that if, in fact, a majority of the people actually believe in democracy and would fight for it, "a Negro American revolution will cease to be a revolution and become a movement of people to stamp out injustices, inequalities, and violations of our laws."[82] For all his bitterness, Himes at that point could see the possibility of positive radical change in America. As his fictional character Bob Jones explained in If He Hollers Let Him Go, "I'd learned the same jive the white folks had learned. All that stuff about liberty and justice and equality. . . . That was the hell of it; the white folks had drummed more into me than they'd been able to scare out."[83]

Chester Himes hoped to derive some useful lessons from the hate, hurt, and fear that he saw all around him in wartime Los Angeles. The political scientist Thomas Dumm points out that the word fear in Teutonic languages draws its root meaning from "the experience of being in transit," of removing oneself from protection. This has its obvious negative aspects, but being "in transit" and making transitions also opens up the possibility of transcending the oppressions of the past.[84] For Himes, and for many others, World War II and the social changes that it engendered provided the promise and peril of being in transit. In his 1948 Chicago speech, Himes outlined a dangerous journey that offered a promise of transcendence: "It is a long way, a hard way from the hatred of the faces [of another race] to the hatred of evil, a longer way still to the brotherhood of men. Once on the road, however, the Negro will discover that he is not alone. The white people whom he will encounter along the way may not appear to be accompanying him. But all, black and white, will be growing. When the American Negro writer has discovered that nothing ever becomes permanent but change, he will have rounded out his knowledge of the truth. And he will have performed his service as an artist."[85]

Although *If He Hollers Let Him Go* received generally favorable reviews, Himes chafed at what he viewed as condescending and uncomprehending comments by the reviewers. He tried to be more direct about his political views in *Lonely Crusade*, but in the process he created a book that "everybody hated." As Himes recalls in his autobiography, "The left hated it, the right hated it, Jews hated it, blacks hated it." Within a few years, Himes left the United States for a self-imposed exile in France and Spain, where he wrote action thrillers about black life in America largely for appreciative if somewhat uncomprehending European readers.[86]

Like Hank Williams and Marilyn Monroe, Himes spent only a brief time as an assembly-line worker. Like them, his time as a production worker sparked both utopian hopes and existential despair. His pessimism about the prospects for radical change resonated with sentiments similar to those of Hank Williams, who interrupted a rendition of his gospel song "I Saw the Light" for his friend Minnie Pearl by saying, "But that's just it Minnie, there ain't no light."[87] Himes's decision to move to Europe reflects some of the weariness with fighting entrenched social barriers that motivated Marilyn Monroe to tell an interviewer shortly before her suicide that "it might be nice to be finished."[88] Williams's death from a heart attack at the age of twenty-nine, Monroe's suicide at the age of thirty-six, and Himes's exile starting when he was forty-four until his death at seventy-five reveal some of the personal costs of their unmet needs and desires. Yet the enduring impact of their lives and art indicate that they also gave eloquent voice to collective hopes and aspirations as well as resentments and fears.

Chester Himes titled his second book *Lonely Crusade*. Hank Williams wrote "I'm So Lonesome I Could Cry." According to one friend, Marilyn Monroe "was not a loner, she was just alone."[89] The loneliness that they felt in their lives and inscribed into their art touched a resonant chord for listeners, readers, and viewers in the postwar era. It reflected some of the degree to which wartime mobilization and postwar reconversion disrupted old communities and consolidated new forms of bureaucratic power. One

way to understand their "loneliness" is to comprehend the gap between
the utopian hopes of the forties, the rise of an enthusiastic and tumultuous
public sphere among the working class, and the atomization and individualism of fifties consumer-commodity society.

Yet at the same time, the sense of entitlement expressed by Hank Williams, Marilyn Monroe, and Chester Himes reflected some of the degree to
which wartime and postwar working-class self-activity emboldened individuals and groups, placing an egalitarian and emancipatory agenda before
millions of people. The strikes waged by workers in the forties responded
to both the apocalyptic and the utopian possibilities emerging all around
them. Most important, their strong sense of collectivity, mutuality, and
reciprocity countered the painful loneliness addressed so eloquently by
Williams, Monroe, Himes, and many other artists of the era.

The interconnected issues of class, gender, and race that absorbed the
energies of Hank Williams, Marilyn Monroe, and Chester Himes grew directly from the crucible of incipient class formation in the forties. It is
not just that the working class was reformed by adding rural, female, and
black workers to its numbers, but also that it became transformed into
a public force fighting for its own interests and offering the possibility of
radically reforming society. The transformations that Williams, Monroe,
Himes, and millions of other workers experienced during and after World
War II exposed class, gender, and race as complicated and mutually constitutive identities to be made or remade, defended or attacked in all spheres
of life. Williams confronted class issues with certain self-definitions about
what it meant to be a white man. Monroe engaged dominant definitions of
gender in ways that revealed great self-consciousness about class and race.
Himes waged his battle against white supremacy in the context of how
racism shaped and determined his life chances as a worker and as a gendered subject.

Unresolved in their lifetimes, these issues of class, gender, and race remain unresolved today. But the utopian spirit that enabled Hank Williams,
Marilyn Monroe, and Chester Himes to dream of a better world than the
one they had been given had everything to do with changes in working-
class life and culture at critical times in their lives. They belonged to segments of the work force underrepresented in the high-paying skilled jobs
normally represented by trade unions; but like many other rural white
males, urban housewives, and underemployed black workers, Williams,
Monroe, and Himes secured high-paying jobs and participated in the creation of a new working-class public culture during World War II. The
struggles they waged were not theirs alone as individuals, but rather were
a part of the collective insurgencies and upheavals in the forties that raised

significant challenges to exploitation and hierarchy whose effects are still being felt today.

NOTES

1. Stanley Aronowitz, *Working Class Hero: A New Strategy for Labor* (New York: Pilgrim Press, 1983), 109–10.

2. Stan Weir supplied me with the phrase "collective bargaining by riot" as well as with information about the ways in which the war undermined the power of the rank and file on the factory floor.

3. *Business Week*, Mar. 18, 1944, 88; *Detroit Free Press*, Dec. 25, 1943, 1, Dec. 27, 1943, 1.

4. *St. Louis Post-Dispatch*, June 2, 1944, 31, June 3, 1944, 1.

5. *Detroit Times*, Dec. 17, 1944, 3.

6. *Business Week*, June 30, 1945, 100.

7. Ibid., Feb. 16, 1946, 98; *Birmingham Post*, Feb. 1, 1946, 10.

8. General strikes took place in Stamford, Connecticut; Lancaster, Pennsylvania; Rochester, New York; Pittsburgh, Pennsylvania; and Oakland, California.

9. Roger M. Williams, *Sing a Sad Song: The Life of Hank Williams* (New York: Ballantine Books, 1973), 5–6.

10. Ibid., 31.

11. Chet Flippo, *Your Cheatin' Heart: A Biography of Hank Williams* (New York: St.Martin's Press, 1981), 45, 50; Roger M. Williams, *Sing a Sad Song*, 53, 54; George Koon, *Hank Williams: A Bio-Bibliography* (Westport, Conn.: Greenwood Press, 1983), 50.

12. James Harvey Young, *American Health Quackery* (Princeton: Princeton University Press, 1992), 6–7.

13. Roger M. Williams, *Sing a Sad Song*, 54.

14. Lycrecia Williams and Dale Vinicur, *Still in Love with You: The Story of Audrey and Hank Williams* (Nashville: Rutledge Hill Press, 1989), 65, 110.

15. Roger M. Williams, *Sing a Sad Song*, 128.

16. Ibid., 175.

17. Ibid., 205.

18. Ibid., 139.

19. Lycrecia Williams and Dale Vinicur, *Still in Love with You*, 30.

20. In her unfinished memoir, Audrey Williams describes Hank Williams as "part Indian." My description of him as a white southerner refers to his social role, how his was perceived by his public. Any ambiguity in his own racial identity would only strengthen my feeling that what makes Williams interesting is his split subjectivity—his sense of being "hailed" by many different identities. See ibid., 6.

21. Former Georgiana mayor Herman Pride quoted in Roger M. Williams, *Sing a Sad Song*, 21.

22. Lawrence Redd, *Rock Is Rhythm and Blues* (East Lansing: Michigan State University Press, 1974), 97. See also the excellent discussion by Richard Leppert

of the musical traits linking Williams's singing to black styles in our co-authored article " 'Everybody's Lonesome for Somebody': Age, the Body, and Experience in the Music of Hank Williams," *Popular Music* 9, no. 3 (1990): 269–70.

23. Roger M. Williams, *Sing a Sad Song*, 74.

24. James Burran, "Racial Violence in the South during World War II" (Ph.D. diss., University of Tennessee, 1977), 113.

25. Ibid., 104–28.

26. Kent Blaser, " 'Pictures from Life's Other Side': Hank Williams and Popular Culture in America," *South Atlantic Quarterly* 84, no. 1 (Winter 1985): 23.

27. Steven Mintz and Susan Kellogg, *Domestic Revolutions: A Social History of American Family Life* (New York: Free Press, 1988), 137–38.

28. Ibid., 155.

29. Jay Caress, *Hank Williams: Country Music's Tragic King* (New York: Stein and Day, 1979), 12.

30. Lycrecia Williams and Dale Vinicur, *Still in Love with You*, 6, 14. Audrey Williams's account is clearly self-serving; she gives herself credit for Hank's entering show business as does Hank's mother, Lilly, in her accounts.

31. Caress, *Hank Williams*, 35–36, 38.

32. Minnie Pearl with Joan Dew, *Minnie Pearl: An Autobiography* (New York: Simon and Schuster, 1980), 213.

33. Koon, *Hank Williams*, 19.

34. Ibid., 29–30.

35. Caress, *Hank Williams*, 189.

36. Ibid., 47; Koon, *Hank Williams*, 34.

37. Danny Dill, quoted by Lycrecia Williams and Dale Vinicur, *Still in Love with You*, 100–101.

38. Dorothy Horstman, *Sing Your Heart Out, Country Boy* (New York: Dutton, 1975), 140.

39. Maurice Zolotow, *Marilyn Monroe* (New York: Harcourt Brace, 1960), 3; Fred Lawrence Guiles, *Legend: The Life and Death of Marilyn Monroe* (New York: Stein and Day, 1984), 44, 46.

40. Richard Meryman, "Marilyn Monroe: The Last Interview," *Life*, Aug. 1992, 75.

41. Ibid.

42. Mike Tomkies, *The Robert Mitchum Story* (New York: W. H. Allen, 1972), 58, 141; Graham McCann, *Marilyn Monroe* (Cambridge: Polity Press, 1988), 40; Guiles, *Legend*, 77, 80.

43. Guiles, *Legend*, 84–85, 89–90.

44. Gloria Steinem, *Marilyn* (New York: H. Holt, 1986), 63.

45. Meryman, "The Last Interview," 77.

46. Carl E. Rollyson, *Marilyn Monroe: A Life of the Actress* (Ann Arbor: UMI Reprint Press, 1986), 208–9.

47. Meryman, "The Last Interview," 77.

48. Graham McCann, *Marilyn Monroe* (Cambridge: Polity Press, 1988), 64–65, 67.

49. Rollyson, *A Life of the Actress*, 211.

50. McCann, *Marilyn Monroe*, 42.

51. Ibid., 47.

52. Zolotow, *Marilyn Monroe*, 31–32.

53. Ibid., 35–36.

54. Meryman, "The Last Interview," 78.

55. McCann, *Marilyn Monroe*, 45.

56. Meryman, "The Last Interview," 75; McCann, *Marilyn Monroe*, 91.

57. Meryman, "The Last Interview," 77.

58. McCann, *Marilyn Monroe*, 51, quoting Frederick Vanderbilt Field, *From Right to Left: An Autobiography* (Westport, Conn.: Lawrence Hill, 1983), 302.

59. McCann, *Marilyn Monroe*, 51.

60. Ibid.

61. Chester Himes, *The Quality of Hurt* (New York: Paragon Press, 1990), 4, 8, 22.

62. Ibid., 20.

63. Ibid., 25, 29, 46, 59.

64. Robert E. Skinner, "The Black Man in the Literature of Labor: The Early Novels of Chester Himes," *Labor's Heritage* 1, no. 3 (July 1989): 54.

65. Himes, *The Quality of Hurt*, 70–73.

66. Ibid., 74.

67. Ibid., 4, 74–75.

68. Gilbert Muller, *Chester Himes* (Boston: Twayne, 1989), 21.

69. See the correspondence between Himes and Roy Wilkins, then editor of *The Crisis*, in Box 16, the NAACP Papers, Library of Congress, letters of Oct. 21, Nov. 9, Nov. 11, and Nov. 18, 1943, especially.

70. Himes, *The Quality of Hurt*, 73.

71. Chester Himes, *Lonely Crusade* (New York: Thunder's Mouth, 1986), 207.

72. Chester Himes, *If He Hollers Let Him Go* (New York: Thunder's Mouth, 1986), 3.

73. Ibid., 41.

74. Chester Himes, "All God's Chillun Got Pride," *The Crisis* (June 1944): 188.

75. In this analysis, Himes makes an argument similar to that recently advanced by Mauricio Mazon, whose excellent study interprets the attacks on zoot-suiters as symbolic castration and who understands the motivations of the zoot-suiters to stem mostly from their desire to protect their community from outside attacks. See Mauricio Mazon, *The Zoot-Suit Riots: The Psychology of Symbolic Annihilation* (Austin: University of Texas Press, 1984).

76. Chester Himes, "Zoot Riots Are Race Riots," *The Crisis* (July 1943): 201.

77. Himes, *The Quality of Hurt*, 75.

78. Ibid., 76.

79. Himes, *Lonely Crusade*, 39.

80. Ibid., 48, 7.

81. Chester Himes, "Dilemma of the Negro Novelist in U.S.," in John A. Williams, ed., *Beyond the Angry Black* (New York: Cooper Square Publishers, 1966),

56. I thank Wendy Walters for supplying me with a full copy of this text and for her many insights into Chester Himes in her unpublished papers, especially "A Landmark in a Foreign Land: Chester Himes and Simon Njami."

82. Chester Himes, "Negro Martyrs Are Needed," *The Crisis* (May 1944): 159.

83. Himes, *If He Hollers Let Him Go*, 151.

84. Thomas Dumm, *Democracy and Punishment* (Madison: University of Wisconsin Press, 1987), 148.

85. Himes, "Dilemma of the Negro Novelist in U.S.," 58.

86. Himes, *The Quality of Hurt*, 100–101.

87. Pearl and Dew, *Minnie Pearl*, 266.

88. Meryman, "The Last Interview," 78.

89. The quote is by Joe Mankiewicz, in McCann, *Marilyn Monroe*, 200.

CHAPTER TWO

"A Rainbow at Midnight"

Women, Work, and
Corporate Liberalism

AT THE END of World War II, many people in the United States faced the future with a combination of exuberant optimism and nervous anxiety. Four years of battlefield deaths and civilian sacrifices left the nation eager to realize the utopian promises of peace and prosperity made to them throughout the conflict by their leaders. But the war also made Americans apprehensive about all they had lost—not just lives in combat—but also time, opportunities, and perhaps a simpler and more innocent way of life. World War II revealed horrifying aspects of human behavior on all sides, and it left no one untouched by its all-encompassing imperatives.

The entry of large numbers of women, racial "minorities," and unskilled laborers into the work force transformed social life inside American factories as well as in the communities outside them. Wartime government secrecy, centralized decision-making, and economic regulation had transformed the nation's politics in lasting ways, and people had to wonder what kind of a country would emerge from the conflict once the necessity for wartime unity disappeared.

A former road construction worker from Texas captured some of that national ambivalence between fear and hope in a song that he recorded in 1946. Ernest Tubb's country-and-western hit, "A Rainbow at Midnight," recounts the feelings of a soldier returning home from overseas on a troop ship. His vision of a rainbow in the night sky reminds him of the woman he left behind when he went to war, and it makes him think of her love, to which he is returning. He anticipates a future filled with the warmth of domestic life and looks forward to having "a baby or two." A distinctly male fantasy, "Rainbow at Midnight" offers the possibility of restored patriarchal authority as the penultimate reward for wartime sacrifice. World-weary and somber despite its optimism, Tubb's song conveyed a promise that the dark and trying present might merely be a prelude to an idyllic, romantic future.

The ambivalence in Tubb's song reveals an important personal dimension to the geopolitical and military conflicts of the forties. In fighting against fascism, U.S. soldiers and civilians confronted a monstrous and evil system; the villainy of the enemy and the threat that it posed to people all over the globe sufficed to persuade millions to put aside their personal concerns to support the war effort. Yet while nations fight wars for clearly defined strategic and political goals, individuals often act from more personal motives. Promises by politicians, propaganda posters, and advertisers about a postwar world free of fear, filled with material abundance and comfort, and firmly grounded in family ties and romantic affection helped many endure the horrors and sacrifices of war. Much of the turmoil and tumult of the postwar period can be read as a battle over those promises in virtually every area of life and culture in the United States—from partisan politics to poetry, from church pulpits to popular culture.

Of course, a popular song like "A Rainbow at Midnight" is not a policy statement; any given song or popular film might have very different meanings for different audiences. We can never know for certain all the uses and effects of a piece of popular culture. But we can reasonably assume that widely circulated images and ideas in popular culture in some way reflect and shape the times in which they appear. As the products of a complex interaction between the subjective perceptions of cultural consumers and the historical circumstances in which they find themselves, popular culture artifacts contain clues about dispositions, moods, and feelings among the populace that might otherwise elude us. They enable us to make reasoned speculations about the ways in which products bought and sold as commercialized leisure might have functioned for people as they interpreted and analyzed the world and their place in it.[1] For a period like the forties, they enable us to see how structural social problems might have interacted with the intimate personal perceptions of individuals.

As a cultural symbol, Ernest Tubb's "rainbow at midnight" might have had multiple meanings. In folklore, a rainbow often points the way to the pot of gold waiting at its end. In literature, a rainbow can serve as a metaphor celebrating diversity, emblematic of the harmonious coexistence of different but compatible colors. In the Bible, the rainbow symbolizes deliverance from the perils of the great flood, but also communicates a dire warning about "the fire next time" that might destroy the world. As they looked forward to the postwar era, listeners to "A Rainbow at Midnight" might have employed any or all of these meanings. Their recent experiences made it possible for them to imagine the future as a time of material abundance, as a time of cross-cultural cooperation, or as a time of deliverance from the trials of war. But they also might have viewed the future as a time of peril, encapsulated in the existence of the atom bomb and exacerbated by the uncertainties of postwar politics and social conflicts.

The utopian expectations and dystopian fears encoded in "Rainbow at Midnight" appeared in other postwar products of popular culture as well. In popular music, Perry Como's "Dig Ya' Later, Hubba Hubba" announced the end of the war in the Pacific, while his subsequent "Till the End of Time" borrowed the melody of Fredric Chopin's Polanaise in A-flat Major to celebrate the luxury of time together afforded lovers by the cessation of hostilities and the return to civilian life. In their songs, Ernest Tubb and Perry Como sang about the love of women as the ultimate postwar reward for men, a view encouraged at the highest levels of government. As Robert Westbrook argues, the government endorsed the dissemination of "pin-up" pictures of Betty Grable and Rita Hayworth during World War II as part of a strategy to present participation in the war as a matter of fulfilling private gender-specific obligations (to wives, sweethearts, sisters, and mothers), rather than as a matter of political principle.[2] In their songs, Tubb and Como laid claim to the patriarchal promises made by government and advertisers during the war.

In contrast, a series of Hollywood films employed what Lisa Lewis calls "female address" to articulate wartime anxieties and postwar expectations in a significantly different fashion.[3] These films also expressed longings for reunification with distant romantic partners, but at the same time they displayed a recognition of a growing chasm between men and women in respect to their expectations about the future. Exemplified in a series of wartime musicals, including MGM's 1943 Cabin in the Sky and 1944 Meet Me in St. Louis, these "women's" films incorporated important messages about wartime tensions within plots and settings far removed from the war itself.

For example, Cabin in the Sky presented an all-black cast in a stylized representation of the battle between good and evil in a rural black community. Reminiscent of Green Pastures (1936) and other condescending minstrel-like evocations of African-American life and culture, the film's core tension stems from the imperiled relationship between Petunia (Ethel Waters) and Little Joe (Eddie Anderson). In this film, a strong, competent, and moral female tries to reform her weak, irresponsible, and amoral husband. In the title song, sung as a duet between the two stars, Little Joe expresses his desires for immediate gratification, for pleasure now because he does not know what will happen in the future. We later learn that his uncertainty even undermines his fidelity and commitment to his wife. Little Joe appears as well-intentioned but weak. On the other hand, his wife, Petunia, answers with a call for faith in the future, with utopian

descriptions of domestic bliss in a "cabin in the sky." Her idealism comple-
ments her competence in other areas; even though her goal is to preserve a
distinctly subservient relationship with her husband, she appears as strong
and intelligent in marked contrast to him.

The duet in *Cabin in the Sky* takes on greater meaning if we connect it
to the experiences of audiences outside motion picture theaters in 1943—
to wartime separations, to the possibility of the imminent death of loved
ones, but also to the growing self-confidence of women as they worked
outside the home for pay in increasing numbers. The repeated references
in *Cabin in the Sky* to the pervasiveness of evil forces in the world and the
film's apocalyptic scene in which an entire town is destroyed by the wrath
of God clearly resonate with the concerns of a country at war.

Similarly, *Meet Me in St. Louis* slips in horrifying moments in the present
and anxieties about the future within the context of a story that looks
back nostalgically to the innocence and comfort of upper middle-class life
at the turn of the century. The plot concerns the possibility that a family
might have to leave their St. Louis home and move to New York because
of the father's transfer to a new job by his employer. But as Serafina Bathrick demonstrates in her thoroughly persuasive analysis, this "historical"
film addressed quite contemporary concerns for its audience.[4] It shows a
female-dominated household finding the strength to face the future in a
time of great danger. The women display affectionate solidarity and draw
on each other's strengths to solve common problems. Within the Victorian
home (whose stately exterior is depicted often in the film), the women
display mastery over the problems that confront them. Social changes outside the home—new technologies and new social relations in the world
run by men—pose dangers that threaten to undermine the happy mutuality within this household.

At one key point in the narrative, the family's youngest daughter, Tootie
(Margaret O'Brien), learns that they may have to leave St. Louis. She angrily destroys snowmen that she has built in their backyard, knocking off
their heads and dismembering their bodies with sadistic ferocity. In an
emotionally powerful scene, her sister Esther (Judy Garland) sings "Have
Yourself a Merry Little Christmas" to her. The song's lyrics predicting that
"we'll all be together" next year "if the fates allow" don't completely make
sense within the plot of the film, because even if the family does move
to New York they will be together nonetheless. But in the context of the
United States in 1944—in the midst of popular impatience about the war's
duration—the scene serves to strengthen resolve about the future in the
face of frustrations and disappointments, especially those imposed on the
household by the affairs and ambitions of men. *Meet Me in St. Louis* and
Cabin in the Sky resolve their problems in typical Hollywood fashion—the

women protagonists learn that they can face the challenges of their day without sacrificing romantic love. But other mass-media representations reflected a far less utopian sensibility.

Many popular culture products of the postwar era projected dystopian images of relations between men and women. Film comedies ridiculed working females, while science fiction, mystery, and crime pictures presented a new breed of strong-willed women villains.[5] On the other hand, Gothic romances repeatedly portrayed young women married after whirlwind courtships who begin to entertain deep suspicions about the men they married. They fear that these men are not the charming and loving individuals they appeared to be, but rather cunning manipulators who hate women. The cinema scholars Diane Waldman and Andrea Walsh have observed that in the films of the early forties these women's suspicions are generally found to be false, that their doubts about their husbands prove baseless. But in films released between 1943 and 1948, Gothic heroines find that their fears *are* well founded, that the husbands do hate them and frequently want to kill them![6] Reflecting more than just changes in the conventions of individual genres, the antagonisms between men and women in these films stem in part from the very real redefinitions of gender roles taking place in society in the forties.

Wartime labor shortages brought large numbers of women into new positions within the work force. Although this continued a trend that began in the thirties toward greater numbers of women working, the nature and extent of changes in workplace gender roles in the forties played a crucial role in shaping the incipient class formation of that decade. The percentage of women in manufacturing jobs in the United States increased 140 percent between 1940 and 1944. The number of women in trade unions tripled during those years, as females who had been homemakers, students, or service workers secured high-paying jobs in heavy industry.[7] Although direct discrimination and segregation of job descriptions by gender left women war workers averaging only sixty-five cents for every dollar earned by men, they nonetheless experienced a significant increase in wages and opportunities.[8]

Two-thirds of the females working in eating and drinking establishments when the war began secured other jobs by the time it ended. Nearly half of the women employed in factories in 1945 had held other employment in 1940.[9] Before the war, almost 60 percent of employed black women worked as domestics while little more than 6 percent labored in factories; by 1946, only 48 percent of black female workers held jobs as domestics while 18.6 percent worked in factories.[10] National surveys demonstrated that many of these women first viewed their sojourn as laborers to be temporary, but by the end of the war, 75 percent of all women workers (and 80 percent of those over the age of forty-five) wanted to continue their wartime employment.[11] The New York State Department of Labor surveyed female workers in forty-seven factories in 1944 and 1945 and found that 81 percent planned to remain workers after the war and that 84 percent of that group hoped to stay in the same job or to secure similar factory employment.[12]

Working women during World War II often had to fight for the right to enter factories, and then they had to fight to transform the workplace to suit their needs once they gained access to production jobs. In October 1941, male workers at a Kelsey-Hayes Wheel Company plant in Plymouth, Michigan, walked off the job to protest the assignment of two women to what had previously been "men's jobs." Since the maximum wage paid to women in this plant fell fifteen cents short of the hourly rate paid to men, male workers worried about losing their own jobs to women could complain that the company might use women workers as an excuse to lower wages. But they showed no interest in fighting for higher wages for women as a way to defeat that strategy. Because of the walkout by men at Kelsey-Hayes, company and union officials agreed to limit the number of women workers in the plant to 25 percent of the total work force and to deny women jobs as machine operators.[13]

Like other black workers, black women often found themselves confronted with "hate strikes"—white walkouts protesting against the presence of blacks on assembly lines.[14] Karen Tucker Anderson notes that white male workers directed hate strikes against black men to preserve white male monopolies over skilled jobs and their higher rates of pay. But white female workers generally resisted the entry of black women into the work force as a means of maintaining social distance, even when it gave them no economic advantage.[15] Although white male workers rarely took direct action to assist women, racial solidarity sometimes motivated black men to use their power at the point of production to secure gains for black women. For example, at the Highland Park Chrysler plant near Detroit, black male janitors staged a strike to protest against the working conditions and constrained opportunities for advancement confronting black women in their plant.[16] Similarly, black male workers at the General Steel Castings plant near St. Louis staged a walkout in order to pressure their employer into hiring black women at positions higher than custodial work.[17]

Facing demands slightly different from those confronting male employees, women workers during World War II found that they had to transform the workplace to meet their needs. Unlike male workers they faced a "double day" of waged labor coupled with primary responsibility for household chores and child-raising. Largely because of these demands, which often called them away from the factory for personal and family responsibilities, women workers found it harder than men to remain at one job; throughout the war their rate of labor turnover more than doubled that of men. In addition, absenteeism rates among women exceeded those of male workers by about 50 percent.[18]

Yet adaptive strategies inside and outside of the factory helped women cope with their multiple responsibilities. In his excellent book *Wartime Strikes*, Martin Glaberman recalls how women in one factory figured out how to do their production work and still run errands for themselves and their families: "They all chipped in to do the work of the restroom matron, while she went downtown during working hours with a long shopping list and did the shopping for the whole department."[19] Glaberman notes that women in other plants often had similar arrangements, sometimes pooling their own labor to share other tasks not directly related to work, like cutting each other's hair or assisting one another on sewing projects.

Women workers at the Highland Park Ford plant in 1942 faced another unusual problem related to their gender. Company officials claimed that brightly colored garments on women would inflame the passions of their male counterparts, so supervisors insisted that women wear only a two-piece navy blue gabardine work suit on the job. When twenty of them came to the plant wearing their own work clothes, management sent them home. Their spokesperson explained, "We object to throwing away our clothes and we think it is silly to lose valuable hours over the color of our clothes. After all, the men in the plant have no regulations as to what they shall wear." Faced with direct defiance of their orders, company supervisors relented and the women won the right to wear their own clothes to work.[20]

Labor leaders feared, and company officials hoped, that women workers might be less militant on shop-floor "control" issues than men. Yet women played a prominent role in wildcat strikes during the war, accounting for 19 percent of the workers involved in wildcat strikes during the turbulent year 1944 alone.[21]

During the reconversion period, women workers fought hard to retain their wartime gains against management and union efforts to give their jobs to men. In the first year of peace, nearly 3.5 million women workers left their jobs, although another 2.75 million started new employment during the same period. Most women remained workers because they needed to work and they liked to work. They pursued factory employment whenever possible because it offered better working conditions, higher pay, and more opportunities for advancement. By July 1946, the U.S. Employment Service's Detroit office had more applications on file for manufacturing jobs from women than from men and more applications for clerical and service work from men than from women. But contrary to the wishes of their workers, most employers attempted to resegregate jobs by gender after the war.[22]

Companies fired women because they were women, but not without a fight. Twenty-four fired female employees picketed the Lindstrom Tool and Toy Company in Bridgeport, Connecticut, on September 19, 1945, after the firm decided that the women now lacked the physical strength to perform jobs they had carried out with no problems during the war.[23] Three hundred women fired as drivers for the city of Detroit's street railway system demonstrated at city hall in August 1946, demanding full reinstatement, seniority credit for work they had already performed, and recognition that women had a right to hold those jobs.[24] Female workers staged a demonstration at the Tennessee Coal and Iron Company in Bessemer, Alabama, in October 1946 to protest against the company's outright dismissal of 430 women whom the company judged to be either married or "inclined to marry."[25] Supervisors at the General Motors plant in Pontiac, Michigan, suddenly fired six women in May 1947, alleging that females in the plant now constituted a "distracting influence."[26]

Trade unions generally ignored the seniority rights of wartime women workers, allowing employers to replace experienced female operatives with inexperienced men.[27] When management officials at Ford's Highland Park plant fired 103 women in direct violation of seniority rules in April 1945, a union committeeman refused to write up grievances on behalf of those laid off. When the women complained to higher officials in the union, the local's president did write up their grievances in triplicate. But then he claimed that the forms had "mysteriously disappeared." Amid rumors that union committeemen had phoned supervisors to tell them that the union would not contest the firings, the union's women's committee called for a plantwide meeting to discuss the issue, but male union members removed notices of the meeting from plant bulletin boards. After a long struggle, women succeeded in getting four hundred women workers recalled to work at the factory in 1946 and 1947, but this was only after more than five thousand women workers had been laid off at this facility.[28]

Delegates to the 1946 UAW convention warned the auto workers' union against abandoning women workers. A delegate from a local in Detroit told the conclave how she had been discouraged from participating in union picket lines by other union members and by elected union officers, who told her and other women to "go home and cook on your stoves." She replied, "Some of us don't have a stove to cook on, our husbands have died overseas. We have orphaned children to support and we are entitled to a decent wage and a decent living. . . . Certainly we are not going to work to organize the union and then go back to work for $15 a week."[29]

Women workers wanted to retain wartime gains in wages, but their concerted efforts to remain in manufacturing positions after the war also reflected an effort to preserve the social world of work that women had created in the preceding years. Surveys by social scientists about job attitudes among workers during and after World War II found that women workers consistently placed greater value than men did on the social aspects of the job—pleasant work, fellowship of co-workers, and independence from supervision. For example, a survey of job applicants to the Minneapolis Gas Light Company revealed that men expressed greatest interest in security, advancement, and benefits, while women tended to be more concerned with the nature of work, attitudes of co-workers, supervision, hours, and conditions.[30] In their study of psychology and the paycheck, LeBaron O. Stockford and K. R. Kunze found wages more important to men than to women.[31] Retired men and nonworking women surveyed in Norristown, Pennsylvania, emphasized issues relating to the quality of life to a greater degree than other groups, and women workers in the same survey expressed more concern for those issues than did men.[32]

What accounts for the sensitivity among women to the quality of life on the job? Women filled many of the worst jobs in war industries, and they received lower pay than most men. Half the women holding factory jobs in 1945 held other industrial employment before the war, and many were the sole support of their families. By the standards of self-interest alone, higher wages and job security should have been as important to women workers as to men. Yet their consciousness of themselves as workers *and* women militated against a purely self-interested economic approach.

Like any group of first-generation industrial workers, the women who entered the labor force during World War II carried attitudes and values designed for another kind of life. The unjust and inexcusable history that confined women to secondary sectors of the labor market or to unwaged work in the home also helped to shape values among women who recognized the legitimacy of cooperation and personal happiness. Men also valued these qualities, but were likely to view them as illegitimate in the world of work. The presence of women at the workplace during the forties not only challenged the sexual division of labor but also served to accent and emphasize the desires for community and cooperation already present among male workers (but generally acknowledged only in covert ways). In a work force already interested in freedom from supervision, closeness with fellow workers, and dignity on the job, an influx of women workers lent legitimacy to those goals.

In some cases, women workers became militant out of self-defense. Sexual harassment from fellow employees and supervisors often worked to create an intimidating and hostile atmosphere on the shop floor. In some industries, supervisors used harassment as a form of organizing production, demanding sexual favors from women workers in return for better work assignments on the job.[33] Women sometimes responded to "wolf whistles" by whistling back at men and exchanging wisecracks. In plants with large numbers of female workers, they sometimes held "indignation meetings," where they encouraged each other to speak out against harassment.[34] One reason for the popularity of trade-union representation among women came from the ways in which "bureaucratic" union regulations took favoritism out of hiring and promotion policies, imposing a major obstacle to sexual harassment of individuals by supervisors.[35]

At the same time, women workers found new respect and rewards from labor once they started working for wages in skilled jobs. The factory setting encouraged a sense of interdependence and mutuality that lent itself easily to direct-action protests as well as to covert reorganizations of labor at the point of production. In the process, women workers not only played an important role in redefining the relationship between labor and management during the war but they also worked with one another to redefine gender roles in society at large based on the new opportunities open to them from participation in the work force.

Management representatives often attempted a paternalistic control over the lives of women workers that they would rarely attempt with men. Management "expert" Donald Laird's sexist and homophobic *The Psychology of Supervising the Working Woman* counseled executives that "those wonderful 'friendships' which spring up quickly are usually crushes between the girls. They walk around together during the lunches . . . buy birthday presents for each other, temporarily lose interest in boys. When a crush is just starting the alert executive will transfer one of the girls."[36] Union leaders often displayed their own version of this kind of condescension toward women, treating them as temporary workers and a threat to male wages and privileges, rather than with the class solidarity on which successful unionism depends. But the new gender roles fashioned inside factories also found powerful reinforcement from the new public sphere for women being constructed outside the plants.

With large numbers of males in the military service and with many females taking on new posts in factories and workshops, women began to experience a new relationship to public space in war production centers. Across the country women aged twenty to twenty-four outnumbered men in the same cohort by a two-to-one margin. In Detroit and other industrial cities the ratio was three to one.[37] Some seven million women migrated to war-boom areas, escaping traditional constraints and surveillance, particularly in respect to their dating and sexual behavior.[38] Experts noted a new openness about sexual behavior, an increase in illegal abortions, and the emergence of lesbian and gay countercultures creating space for nontraditional definitions of gender roles.[39]

Even traditional gender roles took on new meaning in the context of war mobilization and reconversion to peacetime production. Prosperity created by defense spending ended the low levels of marriages and childbirths that had been characteristic during the depression. During the thirties, the complexion of the family changed. Economic hardship led fathers to desert their families in record numbers. Many people formed extended families in an attempt to cope, but hundreds of thousands of children were left to roam the streets.[40] In the forties, on the other hand, people in the United States formed families at younger ages and had more children than they had in previous decades.[41] In the years between 1940 and 1943, a million more marriages took place than would have been predicted by prewar standards.[42] But the very economic and social forces that enabled these families to form in the first place also determined that they would involve fundamentally new relationships between men and women.

During the war, the number of married women workers doubled. The percentage of married women working for pay outside the home rose from 15.2 percent in 1940 to about 24 percent by 1945.[43] At the same time, the divorce rate also rose during the war, from 8.8 per 1,000 marriages in 1940 to 14.4 per 1,000 marriages by 1945.[44] Wartime production for defense not only realigned the economy, it brought dramatic changes as well in gender roles, the family, and in the power realities that framed relations between men and women.

Thus, the tensions that provided songs like "A Rainbow at Midnight" and "Till the End of Time" with very different notions of the future from those articulated in films like *Cabin in the Sky* or *Meet Me in St. Louis* stemmed from structural changes in society during the war years. As the anthropologist Margaret Mead observed, "In wartime, men and women get out of step and begin to wonder about each other. What will he be like after all those years in the Army? What will she be like after all those years at home? Will he be harder on the children and want them to toe the line too hard? After all that's all he's seen for years. Will she have learned to be so independent that she won't want to give up her job to make a home for me. . . . What's happened to his morals? What's happened to her morals?"[45]

As people projected their rainbows in the midnight of postwar uncertainty, personal happiness certainly loomed large in their hopes. The romantic fulfillment and economic abundance promised them by commercial advertising, Hollywood films, and popular songs at last lay within arm's reach. Unfortunately, many of those utopian hopes clashed with immediate realities. These personal desires had been generated in part by social change; they would have to be met or frustrated not just on the personal level, but in social terms as well. Desires for romance, sexual pleasure, and family formation sustained individuals in personal ways during the war, but they would have to be realized in the context of bitter fights over the nature of the postwar economy and of acceptable gender, class, and racial roles within it. To further complicate matters, ordinary workers and citizens might have precious little voice in shaping that world, because they held too little power over the main institutions within U. S. society.

In an ideal capitalist world, economies would have no room for categories like class, gender, and race. Capitalist theory holds that people's fortunes should rise or fall based on their own merits as individuals. A world of free and open markets operating under principles privileging personal economic self-aggrandizement is supposed to give everyone the same opportunities. But people do not live in ideal theoretical worlds. They must make their way under historically and socially specific circumstances that include legacies of racism and sexism, their society's past and present experiences with collective activity by elites, and the political and cultural struggles for power that shape their world. Real human beings never live their lives as pure instruments of economic accumulation. Rather, they pursue economic goals in the context of their many other identities and aspirations—as gendered subjects and citizens, as members of communities, as creative individuals, as sexual beings, and as social actors.

Ideally, capitalists would like to have all people buying as many products as possible at all times, to colonize every aspect of mind, body, and spirit as sources of capital accumulation. But their efforts meet with resistance; economic interests are not all-consuming or all-important to most people. To the contrary, the materialism, greed, selfishness, and hierarchy of the economic sphere conflicts with many people's most profound, personal, philosophical, and religious beliefs. Capitalism's efficiency as an economic order and its legitimacy as a way of life often depends upon convincing people that material goals do not conflict with moral goals, that personal happiness can be best achieved in the context of capital accumulation.

Under these circumstances, capitalists can capitalize (literally and figuratively) on division and discrimination among groups, as well as on the fears and frustrations of individuals. Advertisers exploit loneliness and alienation, promising us that products will provide us with enhanced identities that will evince admiration and affection from others. Their mode of address turns families into consumption units and market segments; it encourages individuals to own more and better things than their neighbors. In the workplace, employers utilize hierarchies of race and gender to pit workers against each other, to "naturalize" discriminatory job segregation as well as to reinforce biased hiring and promotion policies that enable management to pay lower wages and impose harsher working conditions on aggrieved groups. In a society like the United States in the forties, the real and potential power of capitalists meant that no decisions about love, romance, sexuality, family formation, or gender and racial identity could be made independently of the economy and of struggles for power and authority over it. In fact, one reason why gender, sex, and race emerged as contested categories in the postwar era stemmed from the ways in which extraordinary changes in the economy during and after the war created a completely new context for cultural and social identity—the context of monopoly capitalism.[46]

Mobilization for war and postwar reconversion during the forties permanently altered economic and political power relations within American society, producing a potentially totalitarian oligarchy of the major interest groups—big business, government, and labor. In projecting their aspirations onto the postwar world, ordinary workers and citizens had to contend with the ways in which wartime spending and economic consolidation strengthened the power of executives running large corporations, giving them unprecedented control over economics, politics, and communication in society at large and over the everyday experiences of production, consumption, and play in the lives of individuals.

Direct government military spending during the war provided the nation's wealthiest firms with a steady influx of capital, with secure and ever-increasing markets for their products, and with expanded facilities that made increased production more profitable. New tax incentives, subsidies for research and development, and close cooperation between leaders of business, labor, and government contributed to the increased power of the nation's largest businesses.

Yet, a relatively small number of companies derived most of the benefits from federal expenditures during the war. Between June 1940 and September 1944, the government paid $175 billion to over 18,000 businesses in the form of direct military contracts. Two-thirds of this money ($117 billion) went to just 100 companies. The top ten defense contractors received 30 percent of these funds, while more than half went to just 33 corporations.[47] Such concentration gave the largest firms enormous advantages over their competitors, particularly in view of the volume of military spending and its relation to the expansion of the economy as a whole.[48]

The nation's largest businesses clearly reaped the greatest benefits from one of the largest welfare projects in history—wartime industrial expansion. America's 250 largest corporations operated 79 percent of all new, privately operated plant facilities built with federal funds during the war. The facility holdings of these few corporations by 1945 equaled the facility holdings of *all* corporations in 1939.[49] Thus, government decisions about the expenditure of tax dollars practically doubled the size of the American economy during the war and then handed over the profits from that increase to those who already had the greatest share of the nation's wealth.

Government taxation policies also assisted economic concentration. The wartime Five Year Amortization Plan turned over to contracting companies all assets of commercial value leased from the government after five years. The plan permitted defense contractors to deduct 20 percent of the installation costs of these buildings from their taxes each year. Consequently, companies paid reduced taxes on factories that would last twenty, thirty, or more years, as if they would be obsolete in five. Corporations lowered their taxable earnings during years of high wartime taxation, but in the process received enhanced earning power for later years when lower taxes could be expected.

To lessen complaints about corporate war profiteering, Congress passed an excess profits tax, setting a limit on wartime profits. The tax required deposit of excess profits with the government, to be returned to the companies as a means of defraying the costs of reconversion to peacetime production when the war ended. More a forced savings plan than a true excess profits tax, it guaranteed that money would be available to industries when they needed it most. American businesses made many genuine sacrifices when they converted to war production, but government spending and tax incentives also provided them with the greatest capital expansion in American history.[50]

Government spending also underwrote the costs of research and development for industry during World War II. "Cost-plus" contracts paid companies the expenses of developing and producing defense material— no matter how inefficient or costly—plus a guaranteed profit regardless of the costs incurred. The army alone spent more than $50 billion on these contracts, a sum in excess of one-third of all army purchases.[51] Cost-plus contracts absorbed all the risk involved in research and also stimulated an increase in total research efforts. Before the war, research expenditures in American industry ran between $300 and $400 million per year. During the war, that figure escalated to better than $800 million every year, as the federal government absorbed the risks for a wealthy handful of companies. Private research spending fell to about one-half of prewar levels, while government research costs increased tenfold. The sixty-eight top contractors received two-thirds of the value of government research spending during the war, while the top ten received nearly 40 percent.[52]

These expenditures all helped to win the war, and they made sense as a means of mobilizing the nation's resources quickly and efficiently; yet they also involved subsidies to big business above and beyond the scope of wartime necessity. Taxpayers financed the costs of industrial expansion, but business kept all of the profits and all of the increased money-making opportunities from new plants, equipment, and research. Consumers endured shortages of food and other necessities while government planning guaranteed abundant resources for large corporations. Unions vowed not to strike and workers put in long, hard, dangerous hours on the job, only to find the government freezing their wages while profits and prices continued to climb. Small business owners enjoyed none of the favored treatment shown more monopolistic competitors, yet they had to continue competing with big business for markets and capital.

The inequalities of sacrifice and disproportionate rewards for big business during the war had chilling implications for economic and political freedom in America. Previously, government had never been completely neutral in the struggle between labor and capital, but it had often taken on the role of a broker between interest groups in order to sustain social peace. Never before had it been as important an instrument of capital accumulation, and never before had it so directed its foreign and domestic policies to stimulate expansion and growth. As corporate wealth increasingly depended on decisions made in the political arena, corporate leaders played an even larger role in politics. Economic and political power merged closer together than ever before, and the individual worker, consumer, or citizen had little recourse if he or she objected to the priorities set by big business.

As they looked to the future, leaders of American industry hoped for a continuation of the close cooperation between business, government, and labor-union leaders that did so much to protect their interests during the war. Government bureaucrats, some of whom had previously worked in industry, channeled precious supplies and raw materials to the largest and most monopolistic manufacturing firms. Government construction and transportation projects paid many of the indirect costs of production and distribution of industrial products for big corporations. Tax dollars financed vocational schools to train war workers, while military conscription policies helped manufacturers fill their needs for employees. Government agencies directly promoted labor-management cooperation by setting up committees in factories to stimulate productivity and reduce absenteeism.

Projected into the postwar years, these policies might involve employing the power of government to guarantee access to raw materials, stable markets, uninterrupted production, and adequate capital for big business, thus completing the identification of the national interest with corporate interests, as long envisioned by key leaders of the business community.

Intelligent and visionary leaders of big business and government had for years recognized the desirability of government action to prevent economic instability, to help raise capital for private enterprise, to secure new areas of investment, to limit competition, to mediate between capital and labor, and to lend legitimacy to the inequities and sacrifices demanded by such a system. Historians have appropriately employed the term *corporate liberalism* to this philosophy of using state power energetically to balance the power of major interest groups and to ensure long-range stability. *Cor-*

porate both because it reflects the interests of large corporations, but also consistent with the older meaning of the word *corporate*, which used the human body as a metaphor for a body politic united by a common purpose. In this usage *liberalism* does not mean support for laissez-faire capitalism, although it did imply support for free trade, comparative advantage, and economies of scale.[53] Neither does it mean opposition to the prerogatives of management or the imperatives of capital accumulation. Rather it means a kind of neopaternalism in which those in power seek popular legitimacy by making some concessions to potentially dissident groups in order to give them a stake in preserving the system. Monopolistic corporations interested in long-range stability wanted to avoid conflict and create a climate for stable investments and earnings and would, when necessary, endorse concessions to bring about that result.[54]

Although federal legislation as early as the nineteenth century reflected some of these principles, corporate liberals could not easily translate their complete vision into reality. Executives representing small competitive firms often correctly recognized that government intervention to promote "stability" could aid the largest and most monopolistic firms at the expense of others. Workers recognized that stability did not necessarily bring justice, and they demanded better wages, working conditions, and participation in decisions about production that corporate liberals could not or would not grant. Even among the large corporations themselves, economic and political competition militated against full-scale cooperation, as the lure of immediate profits often overshadowed long-range considerations of stability. Corporate-liberal principles had prevailed successfully during the economic boom of World War I, but American business emerged from the war sufficiently competitive, and sufficiently optimistic about the future, to dismantle many of the system's features once the war ended. Not until the Great Depression of the thirties exposed the weaknesses of the existing economy and hurt the political reputation of American capitalism, and not until World War II spending demonstrated the viability of large-scale corporate liberalism as a solution to the depression, could corporate liberalism be implemented in a comprehensive way.

Corporate liberals projected the short-term adjustments made during World War II into the permanent contours of the future American economy. Corporate liberalism won gains for large corporations at the expense of workers, citizens, and consumers, but it exacted a particular price from its traditional enemy: competitive small business. As defined by James O'Connor in his path-breaking *The Fiscal Crisis of the State*, competitive businesses are those in fields that require relatively little capital to enter and thus tend to be overcrowded, which cater to local or regional markets, and which rely on hiring more workers in order to increase production.[55]

Historically characterized by low wages, low productivity, and a limited investment in machinery, these firms traditionally pursue anti-union policies, risking shutdowns of plants and machinery as a way of limiting their all-important labor costs. Their local constituency, susceptibility to increased labor costs, and their generally narrow profit margins all make them hostile to corporate-liberal principles.

By contrast, those enterprises in fields that require large amounts of capital to enter, that rely mainly on machinery to increase production, and that cater to national or international markets comprise the monopolistic sector. Fearful of unused capacity, dependent on steady and predictable output, and concerned with long-term security for their investments, these companies generally recognize unions, pay higher wages, and support vigorous government action to bring stability. As ideal types, competitive and monopoly enterprise may imperfectly describe the reality of any one firm. A company with a local market might have high labor costs, some highly automated firms suffer from low productivity, and a diversified business could encompass features of both. Executives of a competitive firm might hold political beliefs more in keeping with the interests of the monopoly sector and vice versa. Yet a model of the American economy that distinguishes between the interests of competitive and monopolistic sectors does much to unravel the economic and political mysteries of the postwar era.

Changes in the American economy during and after the war facilitated the rise of corporate liberalism by offering gains to monopoly enterprises at the expense of competitive ones. Firms with less than 500 employees hired 52 percent of the workers in manufacturing in 1939, but only 38 percent by 1944. On the other hand, businesses with 10,000 or more employees accounted for 13 percent of total employment in 1939, but more than 31 percent by 1944. Other figures confirm the demise of small enterprise and the growth of large companies during the war. Businesses with more than 1,000 employees held 30 percent of total employment and paid 36 percent of the nation's total payroll in 1939, but firms of that size increased their share of employment to 43 percent and their payroll responsibilities climbed to 53 percent by 1943.[56]

During the war, more than a half million small retail, service, and construction companies went out of business.[57] Some of these fell victim to the better than 1,600 mergers during the war, nearly one-third of which involved corporations with assets of $50 million or more taking over smaller enterprises.[58] Adjustments in the economy often require inefficient producers to fail, but the number of failures, coupled with small business's declining political power, marked the war experience as exceptional. One government official involved in industrial mobilization lamented "the reduction of much small business to a condition of semi-feudal dependence upon big and middle sized businesses."[59] He attributed that dependency to the reliance of small firms on subcontracting parts of larger contracts from monopolistic firms in defense work, but in reality, the amount of subcontracting open to small business was minimal, with most subcontracts from large firms going to other large companies.[60]

The deterioration of the small-business sector during the war had important social consequences. Economically, the failures of small business helped redistribute wealth upward into the hands of those who controlled the nation's largest corporations, further accelerating the drift toward monopoly. Psychologically, the ideal of small-business ownership constituted a popular symbol of freedom in the United States, and its increasing impracticality forced many Americans to face a life of working for others. Politically the war experience and the decline of small business enabled the monopoly sector to complete its translation of economic wealth into political power and its transformation of government into the key instrument for asserting the hegemony of large corporations over American society.

Yet both the monopoly and the competitive sectors of American business had to contend with the ways in which World War II had strengthened organized labor. The proportion of the work force belonging to unions grew during the war from 12.7 percent to 22.2 percent, changing from 7.2 million workers in 1940 to 12.6 million by 1944.[61] Fifteen million workers (about one out of every three) secured significantly better jobs in the war years, and the Congress of Industrial Organizations doubled in size as a result of war mobilization.[62]

Emboldened by the wartime labor shortage, workers also displayed increasing shop-floor militancy in the first half of the forties. Through wildcat strikes, direct negotiations, and covert reorganization of work at the point of production, workers steadily chipped away at management prerogatives and secured more control over their daily routine. An executive in the auto industry felt the situation had gone so far that "if any manager in this industry tells you he has control of his plant he is a damn liar."[63]

Just as the entrenchment of corporate-liberal power constituted the logical expression of the needs of big business, working-class strategies of independence gave voice to popular aspirations for democratic and egalitarian social relations. Capable of collective action, strategically important to the economy, and willing to go outside legitimate channels to pursue their interests, the working class after the war emerged as the most significant opponent of corporate liberalism. Workers saw the best and the worst that the future had to offer during the war, and their postwar activity drew on both sides of their experience.

Military spending ended the depression, provided jobs for almost all who wanted them, opened up many high-paying skilled positions to women and blacks, increased take-home pay, and accelerated organization of unions in heavy industry. On the other hand, workers also faced limits on wages while prices continued to climb. They experienced unsafe working conditions and speedups and endured union-management-government collusion in the interest of uninterrupted production. In their efforts to preserve the gains of the wartime economy while shedding its burdens, American workers posed the only significant alternative to the corporate-liberal vision, and they embodied the best possibilities of resistance against the centralization of power and wealth brought on by the war.

Wartime production and corporate-liberal power disrupted working-class communities, increased the regimentation of work, expanded bureaucratic power, and put the combined forces of government, business, and unions behind the imperatives of social harmony. Centralized economic power, collaboration between unions and employers, and the transformation of the state into a force for labor peace left workers with few legitimate channels—forcing them to explore their own resources via mass demonstrations and strikes. These direct-action protests challenged corporate-liberal presumptions about the congruence between the national interest and the interests of the big corporations. They directly threatened the political stability and uninterrupted production that had been the goal of corporate liberalism from the start. Even strikes that began with only defensive intentions sometimes grew into broader struggles uniting workers and their allies in a collective effort to change their destiny. Grass-roots activism helped create a new workers' public sphere, threatened the legitimacy and efficacy of bureaucratic power, and offered a tantalizing harbinger of future possibilities.

The same forces that so transformed shop-floor politics during the war and postwar periods had also brought unprecedented numbers of women and black workers into key jobs in heavy industry. The particular concerns of those groups had been ignored by those in power when they performed less essential labor, but when they became central to the dynamics of the industrial workplace they gained new economic and political power. The concern for equality voiced by women and black workers became a central issue in workplace struggles and lent greater emphasis than ever before to questions of human dignity within the productive process. White male workers with little previous contact with black or women workers now had to respond to their presence and to their aspirations. Finally, the spread of bureaucratic power and the increasing regimentation of work gave diverse groups the same enemy, allowing unity about oppressions experienced separately as well as those stemming from shared experiences.

At the very moment that it achieved its greatest triumph, the corporate-liberal system began to create forces capable of destroying it. For nearly a century, monopoly capitalists had battled with workers and competitive-sector business owners for control of the state and the economy. For most of that time, workers attempted to defeat the system on its own terms by battling for control of key institutions. When institutionalized religion seemed to favor capital, workers built churches that reflected their own class position. When the major political parties catered to the whims of the powerful, laborers dreamed of their own independent parties. When business centralized economic wealth, working-class people struggled to build economic cooperatives to aid them in their struggle against scarcity. All of these steps involved necessary defenses against superior power and held open hopes for a future society based on cooperation rather than class oppression. Yet, as defensive measures, they remained subordinate adjustments within the structure of capitalism. Workers had never successfully presented their interests as identical to the interests of all of society, nor did they build a coalition for change capable of winning substantive power.

Prior to the emergence of corporate liberalism in the forties, fights between workers and employers, between rich and poor, between men and women, and between blacks and whites could be made to appear private issues to be settled on a case-by-case basis. But with the triumph of corporate liberalism, those same fights threatened the illusion of consensus needed to compel national unity, and they automatically became issues of state power. As the government attempted to stabilize and control more aspects of American life, even reformist efforts had to be directed at the power of the state. Previously private conflicts automatically assumed a political dimension.

In addition, since the state took upon itself the role of preserving social harmony, workers and others opposed to the status quo found themselves fighting the government. Bureaucratic power turned legislative representatives and trade-union leaders into agents of social peace, forcing workers to go outside the system, creating their own instruments of direct democracy and political power. Demonstrations and mass strikes were not new, but they became more necessary to workers and more threatening to capital under conditions of corporate liberalism. In their resort to mass demonstrations and strikes, workers relied on microsocial forms like neighborhood or shop-floor groups too small to be monitored and controlled by those in power, as well as on macrosocial forms like huge demonstrations that were too large and too unstructured to be controlled by the state. Workers created the forms most likely to advance their interests in the present and most capable of building the nucleus of a future society based on their hopes and aspirations.

Intended to ensure stability, predictability, and security, corporate-liberal strategies instead unleashed utopian aspirations for direct democracy that took shape in the disruptions and chaos of mass demonstrations and strikes. Independent attempts to reshape reality by American workers after the war presented the possibility of a significant break with the past and inaugurated a struggle that attempted to make a tangible reality out of traditional American promises about freedom and democracy.

The working class did not secure the utopian goals envisioned in its rainbow at midnight by the end of the war. The concentrated power of its opponents, physical and legal repression, division among workers, confusion about its own vision, an inability to translate momentary victories into permanent gains, and even the audacious and grandiose scope of its own aspirations all undermined the strategies of independence that flourished in the postwar years. Yet the experiences of that struggle became entrenched in working-class life, culture, and politics, and they remain important forces to this day. Even in defeat, workers placed democracy, equality, and the right to dignity squarely in the middle of the American agenda. Their struggle was itself a rainbow at midnight—an inspiring symbol of great hopes in the midst of a dark period.

NOTES

1. For a more thorough explanation of the methods I employ in this book in respect to popular culture see my *Time Passages: Collective Memory and American Popular Culture* (Minneapolis: University of Minnesota Press, 1990), as well as the discussion of discursive transcoding in Douglas Kellner and Michael Ryan, *Camera Politica* (Bloomington: University of Indiana Press, 1988).

2. Robert Westbrook, "'I Want a Girl, Just like the Girl That Married Harry James': American Women and the Problem of Political Obligation in World War II," *American Quarterly* 42, no. 4 (Dec. 1990): 587–614. I thank Wendy Kozol for directing my attention to the importance of this theme, which she develops more fully in *Life's America* (Philadelphia: Temple University Press, 1994).

3. See Lisa Lewis, *Gender Politics and MTV* (Philadelphia: Temple University Press, 1990). These concepts of "female address" and "male address" are ideal types; of course, people of either gender often have important investments in cultural products "addressed" to the gender to which they do not belong as well as to the one to which they do.

4. Serafina Bathrick, "The True Woman and the Family Film: The Industrial Production of Memory" (Ph.D. diss., University of Wisconsin, 1981). See also Serafina Bathrick, "The Past as Future: Family and the American Home in *Meet Me in St. Louis,*" *Minnesota Review* nos. 5–6 (Spring 1976): 132–39.

5. Andrea Walsh's *Women's Film and Female Experience, 1940–1950* (New York: Praeger, 1984) provides an excellent discussion of maternal dramas, career woman comedies, and films of "madness, suspicion, and distrust." See, for example, *His Girl Friday* (1940), *Woman of the Year* (1942), *Swing Shift Maisie* (1943), *Cat People* (1942), *Calling Dr. Death* (1943), *Scarlet Street* (1945), and *Detour* (1945). For a

brilliant analysis of films throughout the decade see Dana Polan, *Power and Paranoia: History, Narrative, and the American Cinema, 1940–1950* (New York: Columbia University Press, 1986), and Diane Waldman, "'At Last I Can Tell It to Someone!': Feminine Point of View and Subjectivity in the Gothic Romance Film of the 1940s," *Cinema Journal* 23 no. 2 (Winter 1984).

6. Waldman, "'At Last I Can Tell It to Someone!'" 29–30.

7. Walsh, *Women's Film and Female Experience*, 54, 57.

8. Ibid., 58.

9. Anna Long, "Women Workers after the War," *Political Affairs* (Mar. 1945): 258; William Henry Chafe, *The American Woman* (New York: Oxford University Press, 1972), 142.

10. Long, "Women Workers after the War," 258; Chafe, *The American Woman*, 142; Karen Tucker Anderson, "Last Hired, First Fired: Black Women Workers during World War II," *Journal of American History* 69, no. 1 (June 1983): 83.

11. Chafe, *The American Woman*, 178–79.

12. Ronald W. Schatz, *The Electrical Workers: A History of Labor at General Electric and Westinghouse, 1923–60* (Urbana: University of Illinois Press, 1983), 121.

13. Ruth Milkman, *Gender at Work: The Dynamics of Job Segregation by Sex during World War II* (Urbana: University of Illinois Press, 1987), 69.

14. White women walked off the job to protest the presence of black women at the U.S. Rubber Plant in Detroit in March 1943, at the Western Electric factory in Baltimore during the summer of 1943, and in a Dan River, Virginia, textile factory in 1944; see Anderson, "Last Hired, First Fired," 86, 87.

15. Ibid., 86.

16. *Michigan Chronicles*, Mar. 16, 1954, p.1, box 54, Civil Rights Congress of Michigan Papers, Labor History Archives, Wayne State University, Detroit Mich.

17. "March on Washington Movement," Aug. 16, 1943, General Castings folder, box 9, St. Louis Urban League Papers, Special Collections, Washington University Libraries, St. Louis, Mo.

18. Milkman, *Gender at Work*, 124.

19. Martin Glaberman, *Wartime Strikes: The Struggle against the No-Strike Pledge in the UAW during World War II* (Detroit: Bewick, 1980), 23.

20. *Detroit News*, Nov. 24, 1942, 1.

21. Milkman, *Gender at Work*, 87.

22. Ibid., 102.

23. *New York Times*, Sept. 20, 1945, 18.

24. *Daily Worker*, Aug. 29, 1946, 5.

25. Ibid., Oct. 15, 1946, 12.

26. *Pontiac Fair Practice News*, May 9, 1947, 4.

27. Anderson, "Last Hired, First Fired," 96.

28. Milkman, *Gender at Work*, 137, 140.

29. Ibid., 138.

30. Clifford E. Jurgensen, "Selected Factors Which Influence Job Preferences," *Journal of Applied Psychology* 31 (Dec. 1947).

31. L. O. Stockford and K. R. Kunze, "Psychology and the Paycheck," *Personnel* 27, no. 2 (Sept. 1950).

32. Gladys Palmer, "Attitudes toward Work in an Industrial Community," *American Journal of Sociology* 52 (July 1947).

33. For a brief history of these practices see Mary Bularzik, "Sexual Harassment at the Workplace: Historical Notes," in James Green, ed., *Workers' Struggles, Past and Present: A "Radical America" Reader* (Philadelphia: Temple University Press, 1983), 117–35.

34. D'Ann Campbell, "Wives, Workers, and Womanhood: America during World War II" (Ph.D. diss., University of North Carolina, 1979), 191, quoted in Walsh, *Women's Film and Female Experience*, 84.

35. Vicki Ruiz, *Cannery Women, Cannery Lives: Mexican Women, Unionization, and the California Food Processing Industry, 1930–1950* (Albuquerque: University of New Mexico Press, 1987), 34, 73.

36. Quoted in Walsh, *Women's Film and Female Experience*, 60.

37. Karen Tucker Anderson, *Wartime Women: Sex Roles, Family Relations, and the Status of Women during World War II* (Westport, Conn.: Greenwood Press, 1981), 94, quoted in Walsh, *Women's Film and Female Experience*, 65.

38. Walsh, *Women's Film and Female Experience*, 65.

39. Ibid.

40. Steven Mintz and Susan Kellogg, *Domestic Revolutions: A Social History of American Family Life* (New York: Free Press, 1988), 137–38.

41. Susan Hartmann, *The Home Front and Beyond* (Boston: Twayne, 1982), 164–65.

42. Walsh, *Women's Film and Female Experience*, 66.

43. Chafe, *The American Woman*, 182.

44. Walsh, *Women's Film and Female Experience*, 67.

45. Quoted in ibid., 77.

46. *Monopoly capitalism* does not mean that individual firms are allowed to have legal monopolies, but rather that oligopolies so control the state that they insulate themselves from any semblance of genuine competition.

47. John Blair et al., *Economic Concentration and World War II*, Report of the Smaller War Plants Corporation to the U.S. Senate Special Committee to Study Problems of American Small Business (Washington, D.C.: GPO, 1946), 29.

48. The construction cost of all existing manufacturing facilities in 1939 totaled $40 billion. During the war, new plant and equipment construction costs exceeded $26 billion, two-thirds of which came from federal funds. See Blair et al., *Economic Concentration and World War II*, 37. Total authorized construction in all fields in 1942 amounted to $23 billion, with $15.6 billion of that financed by the government. See Civilian Production Administration, *Industrial Mobilization for War: History of the War Production Board and Predecessor Agencies* (Washington, D.C.: GPO, 1947), 1:385. Machine-tool construction and installation, a particularly important indicator of economic growth, also demonstrates the same pattern. An inventory of American factories in 1940 revealed 827,000 machine tools in place. In the next five years alone, U.S. industry built and installed 747,000 new machine tools, most of which exceeded the old in size, speed, and capacity to hold a fine tolerance. See Blair et al., *Economic Concentration and World War II*, 39.

49. Blair et al., *Economic Concentration and World War II*, 40.

50. R. Elberton Smith, *The Army and Economic Mobilization* (Washington, D.C.: U.S. Army, 1959), 475.

51. Ibid., 280.

52. Blair et al., *Economic Concentration and World War II*, 51.

53. Thomas J. McCormick, *America's Half-Century: United States Foreign Policy in the Cold War* (Baltimore: Johns Hopkins University Press, 1989), 50.

54. Many historians have employed the concept of corporate liberalism. Most owe their insights to the pioneering work of William Appleman Williams, whose *Contours of American History* (Chicago: Quadrangle, 1966) provides one of the best analyses of this system, particularly in chapter 4.

55. James O'Connor, *Fiscal Crisis of the State* (New York: St. Martin's, 1973).

56. Blair et al., *Economic Concentration and World War II*, chap. 3.

57. Ibid., chaps. 1, 3.

58. A. D. H. Kaplan, *Big Enterprise in a Competitive System* (Washington, D.C.: Brookings Institute, 1954), 32–33.

59. Donald M. Nelson, *Arsenal of Democracy: The Story of American War Production* (New York: Harcourt Brace, 1946), 270.

60. Blair et al., *Economic Concentration and World War II*, 32–33. The 252 largest corporations subcontracted 34 percent of their prime contracts in 1943, but three-fourths of the dollar value of those subcontracts went to other large firms. Small companies conducted only 30 percent of that year's total war production, accounting for 22 percent of prime contracts and only 7 percent of first-tier contracts.

61. Milkman, *Gender at Work*, 85.

62. Nelson Lichtenstein, *Labor's War at Home* (Cambridge: Cambridge University Press, 1982), 111, 203.

63. Rick Fantasia, *Cultures of Solidarity: Consciousness, Action, and Contemporary American Workers* (Berkeley: University of California Press, 1988), 54. Nelson Lichtenstein describes some of these struggles for control in a revealing passage in his excellent book *Labor's War at Home*, where he notes, "At Dodge Main in Detroit aggressive stewards turned the union's formal right to observe company time-study procedures into the power to set jointly all new rates. At Packard, union committeemen prevented managers from making any new time studies in the naval engine department and reached an agreement with foremen in the overstaffed aircraft division that once the work quota for the day had been fulfilled, the men could doze or play cards until quitting time" (118).

CHAPTER THREE

"Till Then"

Hate Strikes, Black Self-activity, and Wartime Wildcats

A FEW MONTHS after the bombing of Pearl Harbor, Walter Jackson came face to face with the enemy and prepared to die. As he contemplated the firepower and numbers of the foe, the thirty-five-year-old father of five children quietly resolved to "let the bad luck happen," vowing that "I have only got one time to die and I'd just as soon die here." The outbreak of war inevitably compels individuals to confront violence, but Jackson's brush with death came on the streets of Detroit, not on a distant battle-field. His enemy consisted of fellow defense workers, not German or Japa-nese soldiers. Although far removed from the main theaters of combat, the heroic struggle of Walter Jackson held as much significance for the future of American freedom as any engagement of the war.

A law-abiding citizen, parent, union shop steward, and veteran of the sit-down strikes of 1937, Walter Jackson faced danger in 1942 because he was a black man attempting to move his family into a federally funded housing project in a white Euro-American ethnic neighborhood. Faced with the same difficulties of finding a place to live as other defense workers, but bearing the added burden of discrimination, blacks in Detroit had waged a long political battle to guarantee themselves access to apartments in the Sojourner Truth project. Black churches waged a mass campaign for fair housing that drew from three hundred to three thousand people to weekly meetings, and they secured extensive financial assistance from sympa-thetic liberals like the Jewish merchant Samuel Lieberman.[1] On the night of February 27, white protesters burned a cross on the project grounds in an attempt to intimidate black families from moving into the Sojourner Truth apartments the next day.[2]

When the Jacksons and other black families attempted to enter their new dwellings on February 28, a mob of 700 armed whites stopped the moving vans and attacked the 300 blacks massed behind them. Although outnumbered and outgunned, blacks fought back against their assailants and defiantly asserted their determination to live in the Sojourner Truth apartments. City police ignored white rioters, but arrested young blacks who flocked to the scene. The New York newspaper *PM* reported that 101 out of the 104 persons arrested during the disturbance were black.[3] According to Gloster Current of the Detroit branch of the National Association for the Advancement of Colored People, "Negroes quickly perceived that the police had no intention of protecting them nor of restraining the immigrant group."[4] White vigilante violence worked, at least in the short run, as federal officials retreated from their previous resolve and announced a "reevaluation" of their decision to designate the project as housing for blacks.

Like Walter Jackson, other blacks expressed a grim determination to see the matter through to its conclusion, regardless of the personal risks involved. One African-American participant in the February confrontation vowed, "The army is about to take me to fight for democracy, but I would as leave fight for democracy right here." In that spirit, blacks insisted that the government stand by its commitment, and on April 29, 1942, fourteen black families, including the Jacksons, began moving into the Sojourner Truth apartments under the protective eye of one thousand state troopers.

Making no apologies and asking for no favors, the black people who fought for the right to live in decent housing in Detroit in 1942 did so as citizens laying claim to what they legitimately deserved. That sense of legitimacy manifested itself in the legal defense offered by two blacks charged with possessing weapons during the first attempt to open the project. They demanded dismissal of the charges against them on the grounds that they "acted as citizens of the U.S. and as members of the unorganized militia of the U.S. seeking to put down a state of rebellion against the duly constituted authorities." Their argument not only claimed the right to armed self-defense but actually presented it as a matter of patriotic obligation. Government officials could find many good reasons for and against black occupancy of the Sojourner Truth apartments, but the determined resolve of black people themselves forced the issue and left the government no alternative but to allow black families to take residence in their new homes.

The victory at the Sojourner Truth project constituted a part of a larger struggle. Throughout the country, black people responded to the imperatives of war with a determination to pursue "victory" at home as well as overseas. Discrimination in housing, employment, and citizenship rights seemed even more outrageous in the midst of war propaganda demanding sacrifice in the name of a war against fascism, in the midst of slogans

touting the merits of freedom and democracy. War mobilization and its ensuing labor shortages underscored the waste of resources caused by racism
and enabled blacks to present discrimination as not only injurious to their
group but as inefficient and a detriment to the interests of all. Most important, black citizens all across the nation understood that the enormous
changes taking place in society because of war mobilization allowed for the
possibility of completely different social relations once the war ended. In
their demands for fair housing, equal employment opportunities, and full
citizenship rights, blacks responded to the needs of the present, but they
consciously moved to help shape the future as well.

Black demands for a better life coincided with serious reappraisals of
U.S. society by many individuals and groups. The same forces that created
new possibilities and new problems for blacks enabled others to project
their own hopes and aspirations into the future as well. Once people detect
a change in prevailing power relations, and once they start insisting that
real life conform to their own expectations, they place social change on
the public agenda. Under those circumstances, even those intent on preserving the status quo must formulate some response and articulate some
competing principles of social organization.

Black protest during World War II contributed to politicizing the home
front by examining social practices previously taken for granted, by subjecting them to heated struggle and debate. Demands for equal treatment by blacks inevitably led to a discussion about what constituted a
good life for anyone. Campaigns to secure access to housing and employment for blacks compelled others to reflect on their own needs and aspirations. By challenging employers, landlords, and government officials,
black protest challenged traditional authority figures and revealed effective ways through which the "weak" could pressure the powerful. Important in themselves, black struggles against exploitation and hierarchy took
on even greater significance as they merged with challenges to authority
raised by other groups, particularly white workers.

This is not to allege that white Americans welcomed black protest. Indeed, the history of the home front during World War II contains horrifying examples of racist reactions to black initiatives. People accustomed
to relying on outside authorities to make decisions for them often make
vicious and contemptible choices when suddenly forced to act, but even
their worst mistakes can inaugurate a process in which they take control
of their own destinies. Black protest movements provoked hatred, anger,
and violence from whites, but they also stimulated protest movements
against hierarchy and exploitation throughout American society at large.
Mass demonstrations and wildcat strikes proved to be effective tactics of
publicizing and advancing the goals of the black movement, but they also

emerged as liberating experiences in themselves, providing a small but tangible example of what it felt like to shape one's own future. By the end of the war, the wildcat strike had become the main resource of workers in their efforts to build a secure future for themselves. In the postwar era, the mass demonstration and the wildcat strike combined to form the main popular response to concentrated economic and political power. By that time, they had involved millions of people from diverse backgrounds, but the essential groundwork in building that strategy of popular power came from the efforts of black people during the war.

Black protest in America started on the day that the first African arrived in chains on this continent. Over several centuries millions of black people have struggled against a society that exploited their labor, abused their culture, and denied them political power. Black resistance tempered some abuses, maintained solidarity and dignity in the face of oppression, and preserved the hope of future freedom, but it could not end white racism. In the historian Eugene Genovese's eloquent formulation, blacks in the United States have faced the impossible dilemma of trying to integrate into a country that would not accept them or trying to separate from a country that found it too profitable to let them leave. During World War I, some black leaders hoped that the emergency of war might provide opportunities for blacks to win full citizenship rights by demonstrating their courage, loyalty, and capabilities. But they found their efforts rewarded only by renewed racism once the conflict in Europe ebbed. Twenty years of relentless and heroic struggle against racism followed, but on the eve of World War II blacks remained superexploited workers, second-class citizens, and a cultural group despised and reviled by the white majority. Yet the outbreak of another war and its attendant needs combined with the traditions of resistance in the black community to create an opportunity for a breakthrough in the black liberation struggle.

Conscious of the government's need for domestic tranquility and for unanimous support for the impending war effort, black organizations launched a strategy of "double victory" that linked their support for the war to demands for an end to discrimination. They understood that even the smallest disruptions threatened the war consensus and that discrimination tolerated in the past now undermined the rhetoric of liberty and democracy so essential to the war effort. Their struggles seemed spontaneous in that they were self-directed, inwardly controlled, and voluntary. But they also reflected a carefully constructed, disciplined movement intent on using the war emergency to realize long-frustrated hopes. Black people who had lived through the lynchings and race riots that accompanied the end of World War I, who experienced the exhilarating vitality of black nationalist movements like Marcus Garvey's Universal Negro Improvement Association in the twenties, and who organized themselves in thirties grass-roots "Jobs for Negroes" campaigns could not uncritically join in a war to "save democracy" without assurances of a commitment to democratic principles within the United States as well. They wanted to avoid past mistakes, but they also wanted to create a very different future.

Under the leadership of A. Philip Randolph, the brilliant veteran of socialist, trade-union, and civil rights struggles, black men and women built the March on Washington Movement in 1941. Starting with local rallies in cities across the nation, the movement announced its intention to conduct a gigantic mass demonstration in the nation's capital to demand that President Roosevelt order fair employment practices in all defense industries. Faced with the specter of hundreds of thousands of demonstrators on the streets of Washington at the very moment that he was trying to build national solidarity in anticipation of the U.S. entry into the war, Roosevelt capitulated and signed an executive order banning discrimination in defense plants. Although the march never took place, black people had taken control of their own destinies and discovered a powerful tool for changing power relations in American society.

Neglecting "legitimate channels" like appeals to elected representatives or trade unions, black protesters took their grievances directly to the streets in an attempt to force a response. They understood that a power structure that obscures real conflicts through false claims of consensus makes itself vulnerable to even a small group of demonstrators because their actions shatter the illusion of unanimity. The presumed "national interest" in reality masks serious divisions by class, race, ethnicity, and gender (among others). Mass demonstrations and disruptions expose real inequities and transform even a minor redress of grievances into issues of state power. In the March on Washington Movement, the threat of mass protest and disruption opened the gates for improving the lives of black people, and they relied on continued direct action to secure those gains in the ensuing years.

Between 1940 and 1944 blacks entered industry in unprecedented numbers. According to Robert C. Weaver's careful study, blacks comprised 3 percent of war workers in 1942, but 8 percent by 1944. Twice as many blacks held skilled positions at the war's end than did so when it started. In all, over one million black workers became part of the industrial work force during the war years. Because of their increase in numbers as well as their strategic location in industry, black workers turned to wildcat strikes and mass demonstrations as their most important weapons for social change during the war.[5]

Although virtually every union leader vowed to ban strikes as long as the war lasted, rank-and-file black workers understood the wildcat to be their best means of ensuring that employers and unions alike would comply with the fair employment practices pledge secured by the March on Washington Movement. They went on strike to get more blacks hired, and they went on strike to get blacks upgraded to higher-paying skilled jobs. Often led by blacks with industrial experience as janitors or foundry workers, these strikers understood one of the oldest principles of labor-management relations—that stopping production provides one of the best tools for workers to win the attention of management.

Black foundry workers at the Dodge Motor Company in Detroit staged two separate wildcat strikes in August 1941, to protest the company's practice of transferring only white employees to high-paying skilled jobs in defense work. Dodge executives stubbornly defended the transfers as part of traditional management prerogatives, but the black workers refused to back down. Complaints to government agencies responsible for supervising war production brought an official investigation into charges of racial bias. Management claimed that the local union condoned its policies, compelling the United Auto Workers International leadership to intervene in keeping with its public commitment to fair employment practices. As leaders from government, business, and labor negotiated the issues, rank-and-file black workers threatened another strike when Dodge began to transfer white janitors instead of blacks with more seniority and more varied work experience to defense work. Although some white workers expressed a willingness to strike in support of the black demands, the insurgents perceived opposition from other whites sufficient enough to keep production running, so they called off a third strike. Yet their willingness to act forced the issue, produced earnest negotiations aimed at correcting the injustice, and eventually led to the upgrading of black workers from Dodge Main to defense work at the Chrysler Tank Arsenal and other plants.[6] Black workers at Dodge served notice that they would defy management to win fair treatment, and their example shaped the behavior of workers, unions, and companies in other plants.

The indifference or hostility of white workers provided the main obstacle to direct action at Dodge, and it became even more important elsewhere, most notably at Packard Motor Company's Main plant in Detroit. Indifference on the part of local union officials about violations of fair employment practices caused black auto workers at Packard Main to complain to their international executive board early in 1941. When union officers finally protested against company practices, Packard officials reluctantly agreed to upgrade black employees. But personnel officers warned blacks that bloodshed might ensue if they accepted transfers to higher-paying defense jobs. After consulting with union shop stewards, the blacks accepted transfers, and in September 1941, 2 blacks formerly employed as metal polishers accepted skilled jobs on defense work. As soon as they appeared at their new posts, 250 white workers staged a forty-minute wildcat strike that persuaded management to remand the matter of upgrading to further negotiations. Just as blacks employed disruption and direct action to enter the workplace, racist whites retaliated with the same tactics in an effort to keep them out.

For the next three years, Packard Main became a battleground between wildcat strikes by blacks trying to win upgrading on the one hand and "hate strikes" by whites aimed at maintaining a white monopoly over high-paying defense jobs on the other. Special circumstances in this particular plant aggravated the racial tensions felt elsewhere over the entry of blacks into new jobs, and they fomented a bitter struggle. Management officials quietly encouraged the white hate-strikers because they wanted to undermine the UAW International officers. At the local level, Ku Klux Klan members exerted an inordinate influence through their covert and overt mobilization inside the local union that represented Packard's workers. In addition, company and union efforts to increase production by speeding up machines and limiting the time allowed for lunch made workers angry and tense. Despite all these obstacles, blacks at Packard Main tenaciously resorted to direct action as a means of gaining and securing good jobs in the plant.[7]

Almost two years after negotiations began between the company and the union on the issue of upgrading, 4 black women received assignments to skilled work in March 1943. Immediately, 2,300 workers walked off the job, and another 700 joined them in a few days to protest the transfers. In retaliation, one month later 100 black workers stopped production until the union promised to respect black seniority rights when making promotions.[8] When 3 more blacks began to do skilled work, Klan leaders instigated a hate strike in the plant involving 800 workers. Blacks responded with another strike of their own, this time getting 2,000 workers to leave the job for twelve hours and return only after receiving assurances that blacks would continue to have access to skilled work.[9]

Packard's general supervisor and personnel director exploited the racial tensions inside the Main plant, telling white workers that they could, and should, defy their union and refuse to work with blacks.[10] Although the protests eventually brought gradual improvements for blacks, hard feelings continued to fester. Several hundred white workers staged a hate strike in October 1944 over the upgrading of four black workers. When the wildcat forced the company to remove the four from skilled jobs, black workers retaliated with direct action of their own. More than three thousand workers walked off the job in retaliation for the white walkout, and they did not return to production until they secured a series of concessions stipulating that any black worker who could prove discrimination would win the desired job and all due back pay, that the company warn all supervisors and inspectors against racism, that all new employees receive training on skilled jobs, and that all employees could return to work without punishment for their walkouts.[11]

The hate strikes at Packard Main represented a vicious, destructive, and foolish response by white workers to the justified aims of blacks. White workers allowed their racism to make them view fellow workers as their enemies, while management and union collaboration undermined working conditions inside the plant. Yet these workers did undertake direct action designed to challenge management. Even the racist strikes dramatically upset the status quo on the shop floor. The same pressures that could provoke hate strikes—long hours, unsafe working conditions, resentments against inefficient production and insensitive supervisors—also provoked some white workers to question their own racism and to unite with blacks against a common enemy. For example, in the heat of one of the controversies over upgrading black workers at Packard Main, some whites from the plant took exemplary action along these lines in March 1943.

As they ate lunch in Crisfield's Restaurant, across the street from the plant, a group of white workers heard the proprietor refuse to serve a meal to their black fellow worker and union chief steward Chris Alston. A veteran of years of civil rights and trade-union activism, Alston had been a prominent leader of the campaign to upgrade black workers at Packard Main. Initially, his fellow workers made no collective response when restaurant personnel refused him service, but then an elderly white woman loudly denounced the restaurateur and walked out. Galvanized by this gesture, the workers demanded that Alston be served. Ultimately, police officers arrived and evicted them from the establishment.

Upon their return to the factory from Crisfield's, the workers immediately called a meeting in the plant. They collected money for a fund to fight discrimination and approved a resolution that stated:

> Whereas: the white workers of the core room of the foundry know that discrimination against any other people is a weapon in the hands of Hitler and
>
> Whereas: the incident at the Crisfield restaurant in which our union representative "Chris" Alston was discriminated against is as much a part of the war as the offensive in Africa against Rommel,
>
> We therefore want it known that the white workers of the core room can be counted on the side of democracy, at home and abroad. And that this committee of white workers have raised a collection to aid our representatives in this fight.[12]

Black protest only rarely provoked such high-minded responses from whites, but the fact that it did so even once testifies to the persuasive power of direct action. Even when whites responded with hatred and violence, black workers continued to press their demands and pursue their goals. That determination helped win major gains, but it ran the risk of provoking hate strikes similar to those at Packard Main. For instance, at the Hudson Naval Ordnance Plant in Detroit, two hundred white workers staged a wildcat strike in January 1942 to prevent the transfer of two blacks to jobs as machine operators. Management returned the two to their former employment as janitors, and the union suggested that future upgrading be conducted by creating all-black departments on some skilled work. Blacks in the plant refused to accept either "solution" and continued to pressure the government, company, and union to live up to their commitments. Although that insistence led to another hate strike in June, by midsummer blacks at Hudson Ordnance had secured the right to run machines and perform other skilled jobs.[13]

In plants all across the country, white workers engaged in sporadic hate strikes against the hiring and promotion of black workers. Transfers of black workers to defense jobs at the Dodge Truck plant in Detroit caused 350 white workers to walk off the job in June 1942, and 18 white workers at the city's Timken Axle Company paralyzed production a month later to avoid working with blacks assigned to replace absent white machine operators.[14] A black woman upgraded to work on a hand milling machine at the Detroit Aluminum Brass Company in January 1943 watched her entire department quit rather than work with her.[15] In the same month, workers at the Duplex Printing Press Company in Battle Creek, Michigan, instigated a wildcat strike when a black welder trainee showed up on the job.[16] More than 50 percent of the work force at a U.S. Rubber Company factory in Detroit refused to work when they saw black women operating machines in the plant in March 1943. The strikers demanded that the women be transferred or that the company construct separate toilet facilities for blacks.[17] These hate strikes slowed down, but did not stop, the entry of blacks to better jobs. Most of the strikes ended quickly, and black workers eventually won the contested jobs because they did not back down, because they continued to fight for them.

In places where their numbers and role in production made such action effective, blacks conducted strikes of their own. Forty black night-shift janitors at the Highland Park Chrysler Plant near Detroit wildcatted in March 1943 in protest against the company's failure to promote blacks and to pay them adequate wages. One month later they walked off the job again because management demoted a black supervisor and placed the janitors under the authority of a white man.[18] Black workers in a steel mill in Ford's River Rouge complex in Detroit went on strike in April 1943 because the company handed out suspensions to three black workers defending themselves against an attack by company guards who mistook their horseplay for a real fight. When white workers at a Republic Steel Plant in Youngstown, Ohio, prevented two blacks from changing clothes in a previously all-white locker room in June 1943, fifty blacks went on strike in protest, and fifty more joined them on the next shift.[19]

In some cities, entire African-American communities mobilized to secure fair employment opportunities in defense work. The St. Louis March on Washington Committee mobilized 500 demonstrators outside the United States Cartridge Company on June 20, 1942, to protest against discriminatory hiring. Pointing out that the plant's 21,000 workers included only 600 blacks (most of whom were employed as porters and laborers) and that there were no blacks among the 9,000 women employed by United States Cartridge, the demonstrators demanded that the firm hire and upgrade African-American workers. Within a week of the demonstration, management raised the wages of its porters, hired 72 black women, and announced plans for integrating blacks into skilled production jobs. But when these concessions failed to win actual spots on the assembly line for black workers, the committee sent a telegram to United States Cartridge management charging that "your discriminatory practices forced us to take this issue into the streets. We propose to keep it in the streets until it is settled and settled right."[20] In Detroit, more than 10,000 black and white workers conducted a march on downtown Cadillac Square on April 17, 1943, to protest job discrimination, police brutality, and refusals by local restaurants to serve black customers.[21]

Hate strikes often masked other issues. Many of the plants hit by hate strikes also suffered from rivalries between union factions, anxiety over losing seniority rights, concern about company discipline procedures, and anger over unsafe and unpleasant working conditions. Racial tension proved to be the stimulus that made the frustrations explode. In Cincinnati, Philadelphia, Toledo, and Detroit complicated disputes over diverse grievances erupted into hate strikes in 1944.

When management at the Curtiss-Wright plant in Lockland, Ohio (near Cincinnati), transferred 7 black workers to skilled jobs alongside whites in June 1944, it provoked a hate strike that idled 9,000 employees. Behind the seemingly spontaneous outburst of race hatred lay a long and complex struggle. As a manufacturer of airplane engines, Curtiss-Wright based its operations on the automobile motor industry, which traditionally employed many blacks in foundry work. The company counted 500 blacks among its 5,000 employees in 1941, and that number increased in succeed-

ing years. Curtiss-Wright employed more blacks than any other area manufacturer, but its refusal to mix black and white workers drew repeated
protests and complaints to federal agencies from blacks. White workers in
the plant attempting to win union recognition for the United Auto Workers
supported the black demands for fair employment practices. They viewed
blacks as the key to the unionization effort because of their numbers and
strategic location in the foundry (which supplied parts to the rest of the
plant). A strike by blacks could paralyze production, and union organizers
made special efforts to win their support. Once the union won bargaining
rights in the plant, its enemies attempted to use its support for black rights
as a means of discrediting it with white workers.

The hate strike at Curtiss-Wright took place after months of racial tension, union rivalries, and company assaults on working conditions. Union
dissidents who wanted to align with the United Mine Workers' industrial
auxiliary attacked the Auto Workers' sympathy for blacks, but even the dissidents complained that company supervisors deliberately promoted violence and encouraged the hate strike. Once the strike began, worker complaints shifted away from the question of race and focused on the union's
inability to win grievance disputes and on the company's attempts to combat "malingering" by placing transparent glass on the doors of men's rest
rooms.[22] Race hatred provoked the walkout, but Cincinnati's hate strike
stemmed from complex and partially hidden causes, as did a racially motivated wildcat strike by Philadelphia transit workers two months later.

The struggle to win better jobs for blacks at the Philadelphia Transportation Company (PTC) extended back to the summer of 1941, when a rank-
and-file committee of black workers led by a welder from the maintenance
department complained to management about the firm's discriminatory
hiring policies. When the company ignored that protest, the workers approached their union—the Philadelphia Rapid Transit Employees Union
(PRTEU)—but received no satisfaction. With the assistance of black civil
rights organizations, they filed complaints with government agencies demanding federal intervention to ensure fair employment practices at the
PTC. As the case worked its way through bureaucratic channels for two
years, blacks experienced no improvement in promotion possibilities at
the company.

Plagued by shortages of trained labor, the PTC advertised openings for
100 white workers to serve as drivers in November 1943. The War Manpower
Commission ordered them to employ blacks, but PTC management refused
and launched a campaign approved by the PRTEU to recruit white women
for the jobs. Only after the Transportation Workers Union (TWU) of the
CIO wrested bargaining rights at the PTC away from PRTEU—partially because of their promise to promote fair hiring—did the company seriously

consider upgrading black workers. When the War Manpower Commission issued a directive on July 1, 1944, forbidding employers in essential industries to discriminate in hiring and promotions, the PTC reluctantly agreed to train eight black workers for jobs as drivers.[23]

The former president of the PRTEU and other disaffected workers loyal to the old union held a meeting in one of the company car barns in late July and voted to "call in sick" if blacks began work as drivers. Aided by priests affiliated with the anticommunist Association of Catholic Trade Unionists, the dissidents attempted to exploit racial tensions in order to discredit the leftist leadership of the union.[24] Despite the fact that the trainees experienced no hostility from fellow workers, and despite the opposition to a strike by the TWU (or perhaps because of it), the seventy-five people present at the meeting agreed to walk off the job as soon as blacks appeared at their new posts. The strike leaders maliciously spread word that employment of blacks would eliminate white seniority rights—an outright lie, but one calculated to arouse the insecurities of war workers apprehensive about employment prospects once the war ended.

The strikers shut down streetcar service in Philadelphia on August 1, 1944, and they mobilized 3,500 workers to a mass meeting at a company car barn that day. Military authorities condemned the strike for its interference with war production, and they tried without success to persuade the strikers to return to work. Blacks in the maintenance department stayed off the job for one day, but returned on August 2 and remained there for the duration of the strike. Although the NAACP distributed leaflets in the black community urging moderation and restraint, some blacks could hardly contain their bitterness over the strike. One black war worker threw a paperweight at the Liberty Bell and exclaimed, "Liberty Bell, liberty— that's a lot of bunk."[25]

Arrests of key strike leaders, the presence of five thousand soldiers to help run the cars, and threats of severe penalties for continued strike activity ended the walkout by August 7. Ugly manifestations of race prejudice permeated the strike, but it had other roots as well. The PRTEU used racism to win support in its factional strife with the TWU, and its false claims of a threat to the seniority system panicked workers who feared that desegregation would deprive them of hard-won gains. The PTC also had a hand in provoking and perpetuating the strike. Management's resistance to upgrading black workers divided the employees and gave encouragement to racists in the three years preceding the work stoppage, and the company acted even more reprehensibly once the walkout started. Strikers who supported the PRTEU held meetings in company buildings at will, but TWU loyalists attempting to organize a back-to-work movement found themselves locked out of the car barns. When the strike leaders appeared in court nearly a year later to answer charges connected with the disturbance, the presiding judge indicated his surprise that the company did so little to halt the disruption, and the defense attorney contended that his clients could not have planned a strike that well on their own.[26] If management did not instigate the Philadelphia hate strike, it certainly demonstrated a fine understanding of how to take advantage of it.

A heated rivalry between contesting unions, job insecurity, and management manipulation helped to fan the flames of race hatred in Philadelphia. Once the strike ended, blacks began work as drivers without further incident, suggesting that the racial issue may well have been a symbolic focus of diverse frustrations rather than the cause of the unrest itself. The complex relationship between racial antagonisms and work-related grievances complicated other strikes in 1944 in a similar manner, particularly in Toledo and Detroit.

A walkout by 1,400 General Motors workers in Toledo, Ohio, in April had all the appearances of a hate strike. When the U.S. Employment Service sent 4 black women to work in the plant, 2 whites refused to teach them how to do their jobs, and others simply walked out. Management disciplined some of the employees who refused to work, causing 106 others to stage a temporary walkout. The factory maintained production as usual for one day, but the entire plant walked off the job when some of the workers set up a strong picket line demanding reinstatement for those who had refused to work with blacks. The first strike clearly started as a conscious effort to keep blacks out of skilled jobs, but the second involved no such demand; it aimed instead at combating management discipline. The issue of discipline produced a similar strike, albeit with seemingly opposite motivation at the Graham-Paige Motor plant in Detroit in June, 1944. When management disciplined 8 black workers for leaving the job without permission after eight hours of work, more than 1,800 white workers launched a wildcat strike in protest. Eventually nearly 3,700 employees from all shifts joined the strike to demand reinstatement of those punished.[27]

The determination by black people to secure fair employment opportunities for a better life enabled them to emerge from most of the hate strikes as victors. But desegregation of the factories also involved the creation of new face-to-face relations on public transportation vehicles, shopping areas, and recreation sites. In the spring and summer of 1943, racial tensions in industrial centers across the nation led to violent outbursts.

One month after the Mobile, Alabama, shipyard riots (see chap. 1), white attacks on blacks in Beaumont, Texas, led to the declaration of martial law after rioting killed two and wounded eleven. When blacks began working at high-paying jobs in that city's shipyards during the spring of 1943, white workers greeted them by arranging a series of "mysterious" accidents, which including dropping hot rivets on them. Early in June, Beaumont police officers shot and killed a black man accused by a white woman of having raped her near the downtown district. The prisoner died of his wounds before a crowd intent on lynching him could make its way to the jail. About one week later, word spread through the shipyards that another white woman had been raped the previous day by a black man who had subsequently been arrested and brought to the city jail. Although a physician later determined that the woman had not been raped and that her report was false, in the tense atmosphere that prevailed in Beaumont in the summer of 1943, her charges led to mob action.

In the early evening of June 15, more than two thousand workers put down their tools and walked off the job with the intention of lynching the suspect. They made several efforts to enter the jail and pull black prisoners from it. Even when the woman who filed the rape report told the crowd that none of the jail prisoners resembled the man who had raped her, thousands of angry white workers remained outside the jail.

Shortly after midnight, a member of the crowd yelled, "Let's go to nigger town." For the next six hours, whites roamed through black neighborhoods, attacking blacks and vandalizing their homes and property. Rioters broke into more than one hundred black homes, and they destroyed close to two hundred buildings, burning twelve of them to the ground. The army declared Beaumont off-limits to its personnel; bus-line clerks in other Texas cities refused to sell tickets to Beaumont to blacks, and the U. S. Post Office canceled two-thirds of its deliveries in the city. Texas Rangers, local police, and soldiers from the state national guard eventually enforced an 8:30 P.M. curfew that restored order, but not before they forced the cancellation of African-American "Juneteenth" celebrations and ordered all blacks to stay at home.[28]

Desegregation of shop-floor jobs sparked the violence in Mobile and Beaumont, but overcrowding and drastic changes in social relations away from work also lay beneath the outbursts. More than 80,000 of the Mobile area's 260,000 residents in 1944 had moved there since 1940, while Beaumont's population grew from about 60,000 to more than 80,000 during the same period.[29] Inadequate housing supplies in both cities left thousands of people living in makeshift shacks and abandoned autos, while consumers faced shortages of food and ice. Population increases so strained municipal services in Beaumont that authorities there released hogs in an exposed garbage dump in an unsuccessful effort to find an affordable way of disposing of the city's refuse.[30] In addition, fights between blacks and whites on city buses and trolleys, black efforts to vote in all-white primary elections, and white fears of "a black uprising" fueled racial tension in both cities.[31]

A race riot convulsed the city of Detroit in June 1943, and a similar outbreak of racially inspired violence worked its destructive effects in New York in August.[32] In each of these disturbances, the tensions of wartime urban life found expression in race hatred, as whites demonstrated a deep-seated resentment of the self-activity and newfound economic status of blacks. This assertion of white male power took on another significant, if bizarre, cast during the "zoot suit" riots in Los Angeles.

On the night of June 4, 1943, two hundred cars and taxis filled with sailors roamed the streets of East Los Angeles in search of young Chicanos and blacks dressed in zoot suits—outfits consisting of long, draped coats and pegged pants extremely full at the knees and narrow at the ankle, often worn with pancake hats. Over a period of several days, sailors attacked young men dressed in that style. In Long Beach, four hundred sailors terrorized and chased zoot-suiters at random. One group pursued a youth into a movie theater and removed his pants while the audience cheered. Military and civilian authorities acted to curtail the riots by making many sections of the city off-limits to military personnel, but not until a group of Mexican-American youths fought back by hitting one sailor with a black-jack and slashing him across the chest with a knife. Although they had clearly been the aggressors, few sailors received any punishment for their acts. In fact, the press tended to cheer them on; the Los Angeles City Council passed a resolution making it a criminal offense to wear a zoot suit, and Los Angeles police officers did their part by slashing the clothing of the zoot-suiters they arrested. A federal judge even issued a restraining order—not against the attacks themselves, but to forbid one clothing store proprietor from selling the suits.[33]

Sailors and navy officials justified these attacks on Chicano youths by arguing that masculine honor was at stake. Members of the navy claimed that they had repeatedly been embarrassed and humiliated by young hoodlums in zoot suits. They charged that the youths insulted their dates and mugged them while they were drunk. Yet no attempt was made to tie specific individuals to specific crimes. The sailors committed violence of their own against people whose only misdeed had been to wear clothing of which the members of the navy disapproved. To the sailors, the city council, and the police, the zoot suit represented more than a fashion—it encoded the disturbing changes in society brought on by the war. They were not entirely wrong in that judgment.

In his interesting analysis, Mauricio Mazon explains how a war-inspired crisis of masculinity lay behind the zoot-suit riots in many ways. Nervous navy recruits purged their fears through ritualized violence against a demonized dark "other," symbolically castrating their foes by taking off their clothes. At the same time, zoot-suited "pachucos" could see themselves as defenders of the females in their community against the predatory sexuality of sailors. A crisis of femininity also pervaded the riots, as city officials expressed particular distress about the "slick chicks" who associated with male street gangs and whose long coats, draped slacks, huarache sandals, and pompadour hairdos constituted the female version of the zoot-suit style. Police officers questioning two young men in zoot suits after the riots arrested one twenty-two-year-old woman when she came out of her house carrying brass knuckles and shouted at them to "leave the zoot suiters alone."[34] But while deeply embedded in issues of gender and sexuality, the zoot-suit riots also had clear class and racial implications as well.

Unlike most other American fashions, the zoot suit originated with poor people and made no attempt to copy the dress of the rich. The *New York Times* reported that Clyde Duncan, a black dining room attendant in Gainesville, Georgia, invented the zoot suit in 1940 by insisting that a local clothing store order a suit tailored to his specifications. The store owner found Duncan's design to be absolutely ridiculous, but unable to dissuade his customer, he sent off to Chicago to have the suit made. As a joke, he took a picture of Duncan in his outlandish outfit and sent it to a men's apparel magazine, which inadvertently publicized the look. But a fashion like the zoot suit had no single inventor; it emerged from the collective imagination and dynamic stylization of young people from diverse communities as they confronted the changes of the forties. The "outlandish" fashion enjoyed popularity with southern blacks at first and later spread to black and Chicano communities all across the country. In northern cities, young whites even began to journey to black neighborhoods to buy zoot suits because they spoke to their own tastes and needs for self-expression.[35]

Created and popularized by people from poor communities constrained by external racism, the zoot suit expressed a worldview rooted in that experience. In its exaggeration and flamboyance, the zoot suit conveyed a bold sense of self-assertion that reflected the social struggles waged for equal rights and fair employment practices. Wide-brimmed hats and draped coats literally claimed space on city streets for poor and working-class youths. The zoot suit made a virtue out of being different; it flaunted, celebrated, and exaggerated those things which prevailing social norms condemned. It brought to male dress an ornamentation traditionally associated only with women's clothing, expressed an individualistic disdain for convention while hiding the face and body beneath an identity-absorbing mass of cloth, and provided a means of creating a community out of a disdain for traditional "community" standards.

In Los Angeles, zoot suits held particular appeal among young Chicanos who called themselves "pachucos." Originating in a Spanish slang expression for residents of the El Paso, Texas, area, the term *pachuco* came to symbolize an important rebellion against authority. A gang of criminals engaged in marijuana traffic in El Paso in the thirties had been known as pachucos, and their peculiar and colorful speech attained popularity among young Chicano slum dwellers who viewed them as heroes. Work-related migrations carried pachuco slang and the pachuco image throughout the Southwest, and the industrial boom accompanying the war brought the pachuco to Los Angeles.

During the war, the term became synonymous with allegedly secret societies of Chicano youths, identifiable by their tattoos (most commonly a cross between the thumb and forefinger), ducktail haircuts, and zoot suits. The young women who associated with these societies generally wore long coats, draped slacks, huarache sandals (known as "zombie slippers"), and pompadour hairdos. The pachuco image and speech won popularity in some sectors of the Chicano community, not just with gang youths, but with many other young people as well because the pachuco represented an important response to the realities of cultural oppression. Pachuco speech relied on exaggerated metaphors and attention-getting phrases to affirm group solidarity in the face of a threatening world. Like other linguistic codes, pachuco speech expressed the commonality of those who used it, as well as an understanding of outside hostility. Pachuco gangs maintained intense solidarity despite a loose and unorganized structure and no apparent leadership. Instead of trying to assimilate into the majority society, pachucos flaunted the things that made them different, cultivated an in-group psychology and language, and brazenly risked retribution from society by demonstrating scorn for its values. The zoot suit proved to be a perfect expression of that worldview.

Important as an icon of racial difference, the zoot suit also expressed the ways in which racial identity intersected with social class. In a perceptive analysis of the zoot suit as a rhetorical figure in *The Autobiography of Malcolm X*, Robin D. G. Kelley notes the opposition between play and work encoded in the clothing of young black workers like Malcolm Little. Kelley shows how the zoot suit provided a dramatic alternative to Malcolm's uniforms as a soda fountain clerk and pullman porter, how they reclaimed the work body for the pleasures of display and dance.[36]

In Los Angeles, in Malcolm Little's Boston, and in other areas of the country, the zoot suit emerged as an icon among black and white working-class and middle-class youths. Determined to defy popular conventions, and intent on celebrating the prestige from below associated with the zoot suit, young people turned the suit into a symbol of the new public sphere emerging in racially mixed urban areas. At the risk of persecution—or perhaps because of persecution—young people turned to the zoot suit as a symbol of alienation. Many of those who wore zoot suits had been poor and now had some money for the first time due to war production. They did not trust the present prosperity and retained a rage that transcended financial considerations. Bitter about discrimination, suspicious that the majority society might not be worth joining, and eager to affirm solidarity with people like themselves, the zoot-suiters represented not just a fad in fashion, but the politics of a spontaneous youth movement with a sophisticated understanding of the transitions and transformations of America instigated by the war.

The contradictions contained in the zoot suit reflected the contradictions present in the total wartime experience for people of color. In Los Angeles, the anti-Japanese internment, zoot-suit riots, and police brutality against black workers combined to send a message about the intensity of white supremacist attitudes and beliefs. Constantly reminded by white racism of the ways in which they differed from the rest of society, "minority" youths flaunted their marginality, making it visible and evident. They expressed pride in themselves in order to defy a world that constantly belittled them, but they also exaggerated their differences in order to carve out a space of their own as well as to provoke a response from white society. They dared society to victimize them or accept them, but they absolutely refused to either fade away or deny their own culture in order to be accepted. They understood what the novelist Ralph Ellison later articulated so eloquently in *Invisible Man*: that racism assaults its victims by obliterating their dignity. The zoot suit was nothing if not visible.

Even in the face of violent attacks, blacks and Chicanos continued to wear zoot suits. In Los Angeles, many Chicanos *started* to wear them only after the riots of 1943.[37] On June 12 in Philadelphia, twenty-five whites attacked four blacks wearing zoot suits. Two white members of Gene Krupa's band clad in similar attire met the same fate. Three weeks after those attacks, blacks wearing zoot suits in Evansville, Indiana, clashed with soldiers with the same intensity that had characterized the Los Angeles disturbances.

Like the wildcat strike for fair employment, the zoot suit provoked violent reactions from whites. But it also became a symbol of resistance to authority, of a desire for self-determination. Black strategies of independence made direct action a fact of everyday life in America's factories and cities, and they corresponded to similar strategies developed by white workers. Promises by union leaders to avoid strikes for the duration of the war, patriotic dedication to the war effort, and the elaborate bureaucracy created to administer peaceful labor relations might have implemented a period of unprecedented passivity by American workers. Instead, white workers drew on their own traditions of struggle to fashion a response to wartime regulations that eventually led to mass demonstrations and wildcat strikes over a variety of issues.

At the very time when war provided a rationale for sacrifice and unity, when defense spending guaranteed full production and full employment, and when labor leaders pledged an end to strikes, rank-and-file workers took the initiative to disrupt production in defiance of their unions, the corporations that employed them, and the government that claimed their allegiance. In the process, they advanced their own immediate interests concerning the conditions of work, and they resisted the increasing centralization of power and wealth characteristic of the war economy. In conjunction with other expressions of self-activity in economics, politics, and culture, these outbursts established direct-action protest as the key method for ordinary people to gain some control over the decisions that affected their lives in an increasingly constricted world.

Thousands of small strikes and work stoppages interrupted production throughout the war. Strikes in April 1943 cost American industry 675,000 person-days of production. By 1944, strikes numbered 1,455 in the first quarter alone, an average of 12 per day and a 42 percent increase over the previous year. In all of 1944, the total of work stoppages reached 4,956 and the record for 1945 almost matched that with 4,750. By comparison, the previous high total of strikes in the United States had been reached in 1919, when 3,630 strikes took place.[38] Unsettled grievances about working conditions, anxiety over the postwar world, and a desire by workers to assert some control over their lives account for the origins of most of these strikes, as some dramatic examples indicate.

Workers at Ford Motor Company's Willow Run bomber plant in Detroit staged a four-hour strike when the company discontinued telephone service in the factory in July 1942. Ford's personnel manager complained that one union shop steward instigated the walkout by 4,200 employees when he "just walked through the plant from department to department and told the men to sit down." Shop stewards in the same plant threatened a strike that same year unless they saw improvements in Detroit's transportation system to and from the plant, while workers in a General Motors plant in Flint, Michigan, went on strike over the right to smoke at work.[39]

A time study dispute at Republic Aircraft, reclassification of six workers at DeSoto, and disciplinary action against a steward at Kelsey-Hayes all instigated brief work stoppages in Detroit in May 1944. The firing of a blind man for allegedly failing to keep up with production standards at the Detroit Diesel Engine Company in May 1945 provoked a short strike involving more than 4,000 workers. Uncertainty about the postwar world accounted for many wildcat strikes. In St. Louis, union leaders at Emerson Electric attributed a five-day walkout in May 1944 to anxiety about postwar employment, noting that the strike took place in a plant with no pending civilian orders. Similarly, 16,000 Chrysler workers in Detroit went on strike in February 1945 over changes in production schedules, because they believed that the company intended to speed up the work to prewar levels—in anticipation of layoffs once peacetime production resumed.[40]

Business leaders voiced frequent exasperation with the seemingly trivial nature of many of the walkouts. A study of wartime work stoppages in St. Louis found that 2,500 workers walked off the job to protest the suspension of one individual; 4,000 struck for five days over the downgrading of another employee; and 1,800 stopped work for fourteen days in a jurisdictional dispute. An investigation into strikes in Detroit in December 1944 and January 1945 disclosed that only 4 out of 118 strikes involved disputes over money and that most started with disciplinary actions against workers by management. Workers at the Briggs Manufacturing Company in Detroit stopped production in June 1945 because they received no meat in plant meals.[41] Yet, the seeming triviality of these strikes tells a story in itself.

A strike can serve as a tactic to obtain specific ends, but it can also function as a symbolic demonstration of power on the part of the workers. Accumulated grievances and resentments appear in all strikes in submerged form; they may not become negotiating points, and they may never appear in print as "causes" of a strike, but any strike has a history hidden in past labor-management relations. And, of course, what seems trivial to management may have enormous importance for workers. During World War II, unsettled grievances perpetuated onerous and perhaps dangerous working conditions while leaving company profits secure. Layoffs and production changes threatened to reverse wartime gains in employment, exploiting labor's cooperation for the benefit of management. Eruptions of violence and displays of defiance released pent-up hostilities over the hours and conditions of work. Walkouts over disciplinary action expressed defiance of management prerogatives and voiced solidarity with other workers. Strikes to win the right to smoke on the job asserted the right to relax at work, and they denied to management the right to control personal habits. Demands for meat in cafeteria meals reflected anger over the inequalities of sacrifice that created huge profits for business but shortages of meat and consumer goods among workers.

Mischievous pranks like the ones perpetrated by gangs of workers armed with scissors roaming through one of Detroit's largest aircraft factories and cutting off the neckties of other workers, supervisors, and management personnel demonstrate another part of this reality (see chap. 1). Pranks that humiliate supervisors and connect the world of play to the citadel of work challenge the legitimacy of industrial discipline. Strikes that paralyze production graphically illustrate the importance of workers to society, and they provide an opportunity for a public rejection of work. On the factory floor and city streets, disciplined collective activity by workers expresses a sense of their own importance and a willingness to control their lives, even if it means defying authority to do so.

In a world that increasingly glorified stability, mass strikes and demonstrations championed the uncertainty of direct decision-making. In a world increasingly characterized by institutional and bureaucratic processes, workers identified each other as the main resource for solving their common problems. In a world designed to play oppressed groups off against each other, workers by necessity found that their own grievances brought them into conflict with the power elite but into congregation with other aggrieved populations. In small and large actions throughout the country, workers demonstrated their collective understanding of what only a few would articulate as individuals: that the emerging corporate-liberal state appeared particularly vulnerable to direct action and that workers had an outstanding capacity for such action. No plans for the postwar world could afford to ignore the power, consciousness, and activism workers displayed during the war, as leaders of unions and corporations both understood.

Working-class activism during the war constituted one of the few negative elements in an otherwise positive picture for labor leaders steeped in the corporate-liberal worldview. Although sympathetic to worker frustrations over increases in working hours, decreases in working conditions, and government limits on wages, union leaders also knew that part of the workers' discontent stemmed from the unions themselves, particularly the no-strike pledge.

As a gesture of national unity, and as the price of admission to the corporate-liberal elite, union leaders pledged to avoid strikes and to co-operate with industrial and government planners. Union participation in administration and planning of production made sense to business only if the union leaders could restrain the rank and file and guarantee uninterrupted production. In principle, workers generally supported the no-strike pledge, but as a practical matter, they refused to allow it to interfere with their struggles. As the war dragged on, workers perceived themselves to be making a disproportionate share of the sacrifices, and they became bolder about defying the pledge, as Martin Glaberman shows in *Wartime Strikes*.[42] In order to retain credibility with management and maintain their ability to win gains for workers through future bargaining, labor leaders frequently found themselves in opposition to their own rank and file. Of course, every wildcat strike involved a challenge to union authority, but in some, the conflict grew into open antagonism. For example, when black workers at Packard Main in Detroit went on strike in April 1943 to force the union to defend their seniority rights, a spokesperson for the group explained their action by saying, "We got tired of arguing back and forth with the union, trying to make it do something we are paying our dues to have done, so we called the strike."[43]

One of the most bitter conflicts between a union and its members took place at Detroit's Highland Park Chrysler plant in June 1943. When discharged wildcat strikers picketed the plant, United Auto Workers officials instructed their membership to cross the picket line. The union's attempt to fine those involved in the original wildcat caused thousands of others to stop work in protest. Richard Leonard, international regional director of the UAW, pleaded with nearby Highland Park Ford workers to end a different strike two months later, but they drowned out his appeal with heckling and catcalls. One worker shouted, "You are asking us to go back to work, but if we go back we will have conditions just as they are right now. What in the hell do you propose to do about it?"[44]

Union leaders frequently found themselves addressing hostile gatherings of wildcat strikers whenever they tried to ensure uninterrupted production. Their vision of labor's role in the corporate-liberal state placed them in an awkward position. They needed the threat of strikes to wring concessions from business and government, yet they needed to be able to prevent those strikes from actually occurring. Writing as a guest columnist in *Fortune*, the British writer Sherry Mangan understood the danger of their position when he wrote in November 1943 that "top labor bureaucrats like the ClO's Phil Murray . . . must more and more often knock on the White House Door to plead for concessions with which to quiet their increasingly discontented union members. But the closer they cling to Roosevelt the wider grows the gap between them and their rank and file."[45]

When union president R. J. Thomas delivered an impassioned speech in favor of the pledge to the 1944 UAW convention, delegates from Briggs Local 212 in Detroit pulled out little American flags, which they waved with one hand as they sarcastically wiped away mock tears with the other.[46] Even parliamentary victories could not change behavior. Predicting that a UAW referendum in 1945 would reaffirm the pledge, *Business Week* warned that "it will be increasingly difficult to hold the rank and file in line with a no-strike program."[47] In his extraordinary memoir of life as an auto worker, Matthew Ward illuminated the resistance by workers to the pledge by recounting an incident where

I had read a sign in a streetcar. A worker drew it and put it up. There was a lion and a tiger. The picture showed them meeting in the jungle and fighting each other. One picture showed them talking instead of fighting. The lion told the tiger that both of them should have their claws filed and their teeth drawn out. Then they wouldn't hurt each other. The tiger had his teeth drawn and his claws filed, the lion didn't. The next time they met, the tiger got killed. The idea was, that's what would happen if we took the no-strike pledge.

I took that position. I could see that we had to fight for keeping the strike. It poured into me that if we gave up the strike then we would have no teeth or claws.[48]

Labor leaders hoped that once the war ended and their position to deliver wage increases and employment security improved, they would be able to control rank-and-file insurgencies. A continuation of wildcat strikes and assertions of independence on the part of the rank-and-file workers would undermine labor's negotiating position, create dissension within unions, and lessen the political influence of labor leaders. On the other hand, rank-and-file militancy and struggle would be needed in the postwar era as companies endeavored to overturn the gains won by labor in the war years.

As they looked to the postwar economy, business leaders feared the perpetuation of wartime labor militancy even more than union leaders did. Wildcat strikes violated contracts, laws, and government directives, they demonstrated a contempt for authority, challenged management's basic prerogatives, and made it impossible for business to rationally anticipate future levels of production. Despite enormous profits and growth, business leaders felt they had made tremendous sacrifices during the war. Some abandoned production of consumer goods completely and retooled their factories to meet the military emergency. At the behest of government agencies, some changed their hiring practices, recognized unions, surrendered traditional areas of control to outside bureaucrats, and sometimes actually turned over ownership and operation of their facilities to the military. Yet they found organized labor unable or unwilling to abide by its own pledges of industrial peace, and they suffered repeated encroachments on traditional management rights by workers. Government spending and other subsidies compensated for those setbacks during wartime, but peacetime production threatened to bring shortages of capital, uncertain markets, and renewed competition.

Rank-and-file demands for full employment, wage increases, and more production of consumer goods portended disaster for business. Combined with the aspirations of labor leaders for political and economic power, they threatened business with the likelihood of a postwar depression that precluded implementation of the conventional remedies like cutting levels of production, employment, or wages. As a writer in the prestigious *Harvard Business Review* noted, wartime employment attained artificially high levels—employing teenagers, older people, and women—because one customer—the government—bought over half of the goods. A similar level of government spending after the war would likely produce runaway inflation and a huge national debt, but a drop in spending could leave business without adequate markets.[49] Yet attempts to cut production, wages, or employment could lead to political conflict with an angry working class. Union and government cooperation facilitated wartime growth and profits, but business leaders hoped for an end to the restrictions imposed on them by that cooperation, and they looked to a day when they could manage their affairs free from outside pressures and interference.

In the summer and fall of 1944, war-weary Americans found consolation in "Till Then," a dreamy ballad recorded by the Mills Brothers. Solemnly acknowledging the pain of wartime separation and sacrifice, the lyrics of "Till Then" envisioned a happier day when the suffering would cease and lovers would be reunited. Phrased in the terms of a homesick soldier's lament, the song's utopian hopes for the postwar world also reflected anxieties about the tremendous changes in American society on the home front. Workers hoped for a world with available jobs at high wages, but feared a return to the unemployment levels they experienced during the depression. Business owners sought increased profits and economic growth, but feared capital shortages and inadequate markets. Labor leaders hoped to expand their unions' wartime gains in membership and power, but feared that elimination of government controls would lead to an anti-union offensive similar to the one that characterized the period immediately after World War I. All had sacrificed for a war they would rather have avoided. They looked to the postwar world with mutually exclusive visions of the proper reward for wartime suffering. All of them could sing "Till Then," but it held a very different meaning for each. The single most unpredictable variable in the postwar world concerned the fate of the strategies of independence pioneered by blacks and utilized by rank-and-file workers to challenge entrenched power. Would that defiance and independence be moderated by the end of wartime conditions, or would peace unleash even more fervent movements for change? The answer came quickly, as rank-and-file workers took to the streets in the postwar years and launched the greatest strike wave ever in American history.

NOTES

1. Dominic J. Capeci, Jr., *Race Relations in Wartime Detroit: The Sojourner Truth Housing Controversy of 1942* (Philadelphia: Temple University Press, 1984), 84–85.

2. C. L. R. James, George Breitman, Edgar Keemer, and others, *Fighting Racism in World War II* (New York: Monad Press, 1980), 151.

3. Ibid., 152.

4. Capeci, *Race Relations*, 101.

5. Robert C. Weaver, *Negro Labor* (Port Washington, N.Y.: Kennikat Press, 1969).

6. Ibid., 68–71.

7. Ibid., 65; *Packard News*, May 3, 1942, May 6, 1942.

8. *Michigan Chronicle*, Mar. 27, 1943.

9. Ibid., May 29, 1943.

10. Ibid., June 5, 1943.

11. Ibid., Nov. 18, 1944.

12. Ibid., Mar. 13, 1943, 1. Packard Main was a center of support for UAW vice-president George Addes, who was held in high regard by members closest to the Communist party. The rhetoric of this proclamation is unmistakably influenced by the party and its wartime concerns. In the thirties, Alston had helped organize the Southern Negro Youth Congress. See Robin D. G. Kelley, *Hammer and Hoe* (Chapel Hill: University of North Carolina Press, 1990), 200.

13. New York *PM*, June 19, 1942.

14. *Detroit Free Press*, June 3, 1942; *Michigan Chronicle*, Aug. 1, 1942.

15. G. James Fleming, Senior Practice Examiner, President's Commission on Fair Employment Practices, Letter to Jack Raskin, July 20, 1943, box 54, Civil Rights Congress of Michigan Papers, Labor History Archives, Wayne State University, Detroit, Mich.

16. Ibid.

17. *Michigan Chronicle*, Mar. 27, 1943.

18. G. James Fleming to Jack Raskin; *Michigan Chronicle*, Mar. 27, 1943.

19. G. James Fleming to Jack Raskin.

20. James et al., *Fighting Racism in World War II*, 176–77.

21. Ibid., 235.

22. *Cincinnati Enquirer*, June 6, 1944, 1, June 8, 1944, 1, 6; *Business Week*, June 17, 1944; Weaver, *Negro Labor*, 120.

23. Weaver, *Negro Labor*, 162.

24. Steve Rosswurm, "The Catholic Church and the Left-Led Unions: Labor Priests, Labor Schools, and the ACTU," in Steve Rosswurm, ed., *The CIO's Left-Led Unions* (New Brunswick: Rutgers University Press, 1992), 129.

25. Allan M. Winkler, "The Philadelphia Transit Strike of 1944," *Journal of American History* 59 (June 1972): 87.

26. Weaver, *Negro Labor*, 165, 170.

27. *Michigan Chronicle*, Apr. 29, 1944, June 17, 1944.

28. *Houston Post*, June 16, 1943, 1, June 17, 1, 9; *Houston Informer*, June 19, 1943, 8, June 26, 1; *Beaumont Enterprise*, June 16, 1943, 1, 7.

29. Mary Martha Thomas, *Riveting and Rationing in Dixie: Alabama Women and the Second World War* (Tuscaloosa: University of Alabama Press, 1987), 13; James Burran, "Racial Violence in the South during World War II" (Ph.D. diss., University of Tennessee, 1977), 107.

30. Burran, "Racial Violence in the South," 166.

31. *Beaumont Journal*, June 5, 1943, 1, June 25, 1943, 1; *Beaumont Enterprise*, July 1, 1942, 1, July 3, 1942, June 6, 1943, 1–7; James Burran, "Violence in an 'Arsenal of Democracy': The Beaumont Race Riot of 1943," *East Texas Historical Journal* 14, no. 1 (Spring 1976): 39.

32. *New York Times*, May 26, 1943, 25, June 13, 1943, 30, June 17, 1943, 42, June 18, 1943, 7, June 23, 1943, 1.

33. *New York Times*, June 9, 1943, 23, June 10, 1943, 23. Beatrice Griffith, "Pachucos," quoted by B. A. Botkin, *Sidewalks of America* (Indianapolis: Bobbs-Merrill, 1954); Fritz Redl, "Zoot Suits: An Introduction," in Richard Polenberg, ed., *America at War: The Home Front, 1941–1945* (Englewood Cliffs, N.J.: Prentice Hall, 1968), 148–52; *Los Angeles Times*, June 13, 1943, 2; *Houston Chronicle*, June 13, 1943, 7.

34. Mauricio Mazon, *The Zoot-Suit Riots: The Psychology of Symbolic Annihilation* (Austin: University of Texas Press, 1984); *Los Angeles Times*, June 10, 1943, 1A.

35. *New York Times*, June 11, 1943, 22.

36. Robin D. G. Kelley, "The Riddle of the Zoot: Malcolm Little and Black Cultural Politics during World War II," ms., 1991.

37. George Barker, *Pachuco* (Tucson: University of Arizona Press, 1950); *Los Angeles Times*, June 13, 1943, 2; *Houston Chronicle*, June 13, 1943, 7.

38. *Monthly Labor Review* (Dec. 1946): 872, (May 1947): 780; Ralph Robey, "Real News on the Labor Front," *Newsweek*, June 14, 1943, 70, and "The No-Strike Pledge and the Record," *Newsweek*, June 12, 1944, 66. Howell John Harris cautions against overestimating the importance of wildcat strikes during the war, claiming that most occurred in Detroit and Akron. But as Rick Fantasia observes, many if not most wildcat strikes never get recorded. The Bureau of Labor Statistics counts as strikes only those walkouts that paralyze an entire eight-hour shift, and of course, the bureau only identifies strikes that have been reported to it by managers and union officials, who have little incentive to provide an accurate accounting. See Howell John Harris, *The Right to Manage: Industrial Relations Policies of American Business in the 1940s* (Madison: University of Wisconsin Press, 1982), 61; Rick Fantasia, *Cultures of Solidarity: Consciousness, Action, and Contemporary American Workers* (Berkeley: University of California Press, 1988), 64.

39. *Detroit Free Press*, July 17, 1942; *New York World Telegram*, July 16, 1942; *Detroit Times*, Dec. 17, 1944; *Detroit Free Press*, May 1, 1942.

40. *Business Week*, May 13, 1944, 20, Mar. 3, 1945, 101; *Detroit News*, May 21, 1945, 1; Arthur Hepner, "Wildcat Strikes," *Harper's*, Apr. 1945, 457.

41. Hepner, "Wildcat Strikes," 456; Jerome F. Scott and George C. Homans, "Reflections on the Wildcat Strikes," *American Sociological Review* 12 (June 1947): 279; *Business Week*, June 3, 1944, 12, June 30, 1945, 100.

42. *Business Week*, May 27, 1944, 102; Martin Glaberman, *Wartime Strikes: The Struggle against the No-Strike Pledge in the UAW during World War II* (Detroit: Bewick, 1980).

43. *Michigan Chronicle*, Apr. 17, 1943.

44. *Newsweek*, June 15, 1944; *Detroit Times*, Aug. 20, 1944.

45. Sherry Mangan, "State of the Nation," *Fortune*, Nov. 1943, 139.

46. Frank Marquart, *An Auto Worker's Journal* (University Park: Pennsylvania State University Press, 1975), 104–5.

47. *Business Week*, Jan. 27, 1945, 94.

48. Matthew Ward (Charles Denby), *Indignant Heart* (New York: New Books, 1952), 96.

49. Malcolm P. McNair, "The Full Employment Problem," *Harvard Business Review* 24, no. 1 (Autumn 1945): 1.

PART TWO

Reconversion and
General Strikes, 1945–46

CHAPTER FOUR

"A Few Selfish Men"

The 1945 Strike Wave

AS THE WAR in the Pacific ended, leaders of business, labor, and government looked forward to a cessation of hostilities on the home front as well. On August 17, 1945, President Truman saluted business and labor leaders for their efforts to secure industrial peace during the war, announcing that "a new industry-labor agreement to minimize interruptions of production by labor disputes during the reconversion period ahead of us is imperatively needed."[1] Yet the strikes continued.

Started with a series of small walkouts immediately after the war ended and propelled by especially dramatic insurgencies by auto workers in Detroit and by longshore workers in New York, more strikes took place in the twelve months after V-J Day than in any comparable period in American history. In thousands of small and large actions, culminating in simultaneous nationwide work stoppages in auto, steel, and electronics, rank-and-file workers served notice that they would continue their wartime fight for increased control over the pace, nature, and compensations of work while resisting corporate efforts to further control and contain them.

Workers suffered serious reverses as soon as the war ended. Cutbacks in production ended the opportunity for overtime work with its time-and-a-half bonus pay. Reduction in the normal work week from forty-eight to forty hours thus meant a 30 percent decrease in wages. Unemployment soared as factories retooled for peacetime production. In plants represented by the United Electrical Workers in 1945, employment fell from 700,000 to 475,000.[2] By the winter of 1945–46, one-quarter of all war workers had lost their jobs. Nearly 2 million workers found themselves unemployed by October 1, and real income for workers fell by an average of 15 percent in three months.[3] Prospects for the future offered little hope for improvement, as 10 million servicemen and women returned to civilian life to join the competition for jobs.[4] Fears of another depression, accumulated resentments over wartime sacrifices, and anger over postwar reverses in wages and working conditions ignited strikes and demonstrations from coast to coast.

In late August and early September 1945, thousands of CIO members in New York, Detroit, and San Francisco staged demonstrations calling for full employment.[5] Rubber workers at the Firestone and Goodyear plants in Akron, Ohio, demanded a thirty-hour work week with forty hours of pay as the only means to prevent the "worst unemployment crisis in history."[6] In Camden, New Jersey, 14,000 shipyard workers staged a four-day sit-down strike to protest against the dismissal of 25 welders.[7] Steel workers at SKF Industries in Philadelphia and machinists throughout the San Francisco Bay area initiated strikes spontaneously without bothering to comply with the legal strike notification procedures demanded by the Smith-Connally Act.[8] Workers in Detroit staged ninety unauthorized walkouts in September and October.[9]

By October, the strike wave assumed gigantic proportions. The strikers included 35,000 oil refinery workers from seven states; 6,000 GM Frigidaire employees in Dayton, Ohio; 16,000 elevator operators and building service workers in New York; 60,000 timber workers in the Pacific Northwest; 68,000 textile workers in the East; 45,000 coal miners across the country; and over 20,000 auto workers from various plants in the Midwest.[10] While lost wages and pent-up wartime frustrations played an important part in fomenting the strikes, workers also deliberately pursued policies designed to increase their control over production and to combat the centralized power of the corporate-liberal alliance. In the late summer and early fall of 1945, auto workers in Detroit and longshore workers in New York staged two widely publicized strikes that graphically demonstrated this resolve and in the process defined the key issues of labor-management conflict in the postwar era.

At the Kelsey-Hayes Wheel Company in Detroit, 4,500 members of the United Auto Workers Local 174 walked out of the plant on August 23, 1945, in a dispute over disciplinary firings. Thirteen workers had physically ejected a supervisor from their work area in April of that year; in retaliation, the company dismissed them. The War Labor Board (WLB) overturned nine of the firings, but upheld the company's right to discharge the other four, three of whom held posts as committeemen in the local union. Despite the walkout, management refused to reconsider the firings, maintaining that its right to discipline and control its workers had to be preserved.[11]

Local 174 endorsed the strike, but the UAW International officers called for acquiescence to the WLB decision. Union president R. J. Thomas personally appealed to the strikers to drop their protest, but they rejected his pleas and elected to continue the work stoppage by a vote of 1,036 to

212.[12] Deprived of the wheels and brakedrums normally produced at Kelsey-Hayes, other auto plants began to close, eventually idling 82,000 workers. Frustrated by the defiance of its authority and by the ability of one local to paralyze a sizable part of the industry, the UAW leadership declared the strike to be a wildcat and appointed an administrator to take over the local and end the dispute.[13]

On September 15, 100 workers in support of Local 174 drove from Detroit to Flint to picket the UAW Executive Board meeting. "An End to Your Strike-Breaking," read one sign. "Support the Kelsey-Hayes Strikers," proclaimed another. Thomas deplored the continuation of the strike, but moaned, "When you've got thousands of people, how are you going to force them to do anything?"[14] The union scheduled another back-to-work meeting for September 17, but their plans backfired when only 350 strikers showed up, and even *they* voted to continue the strike after applauding a rousing speech by one of the four dismissed workers who insisted that he be reinstated.[15]

Top management officials expressed great concern over the UAW's failure to end the Kelsey-Hayes strike. Manufacturers in the auto industry increasingly looked toward the federal government for a solution to labor problems, because of "the apparent inability of top union officials to cope with this situation [the Kelsey-Hayes strike] and similar ones."[16] Frank Riesing, general manager of the Automotive and Aviation Parts Manufacturers, Inc., released a memorandum in which he pointedly noted that management pays high wages because it expects the unions to guarantee "productivity and a sense of responsibility."[17]

George Kennedy, president of Kelsey-Hayes, took a more direct approach. He told the UAW that since the strike lacked proper authorization and since "you have failed to return the employees to work and admit you cannot control the actions of your representatives in our plants," he was canceling all written and verbal agreements with Local 174.[18] While less severe than it sounded—since the company and the union had never signed any actual contracts and operated by stenographic records of verbal agreements—the prospect of employers canceling contracts due to uncontrolled rank-and-file activity terrified union leaders and made them redouble their efforts to end the walkout.

Richard L. Frankensteen, UAW vice-president and labor's candidate for mayor in the nonpartisan Detroit election of 1945, complained that wildcat strikes hurt both the union and his chances to win the election. He vowed to end the strike at Kelsey-Hayes. "If I can settle it," Frankensteen asserted, "it might indicate that a Mayor from the ranks of labor might have something to offer the people of Detroit."[19] He met with company officials and strikers, but could make no immediate impact on the dispute. Another politician entered the fray when Michigan's governor Harry F. Kelly ordered an investigation into the walkout on September 21 allegedly because he heard that only 25 percent of the workers really wanted to strike. Terming the walkout a strike against the government (because it defied a WLB decision), Kelly exclaimed, "I just can't believe a majority of the Kelsey-Hayes strikers are ignoring the orders of their officials to go back to work."[20]

R. J. Thomas couldn't believe it either. On September 28 he appeared before a meeting of Local 174 to order an end to the work stoppage. As soon as Thomas took the floor, hundreds of the two thousand UAW members crowded into a Detroit high school auditorium began to boo. Men and women rose from their seats and began moving down the aisles shouting at the befuddled union officer. After trying unsuccessfully to be heard for a few minutes, Thomas relinquished the microphone to Chester "Moon" Mullins, one of the men fired by Kelsey-Hayes for the April incident. When Mullins spoke, the crowd applauded and cheered.[21]

In an attempt to bring the Kelsey-Hayes strike under control, the UAW Executive Board removed seventeen officials of Local 174 and ordered the strikers back to work on October 3. The union announced that the strike had ended, but only 200 of the plant's 4,500 employees reported for work. On October 7, the union and the workers finally reached a compromise whereby the strike would end, but the union would continue to press for reinstatement of the dismissed workers through negotiations.[22]

For forty-six days, Kelsey-Hayes strikers went without pay to challenge the company's right to discipline its work force and to pressure the international union to stand up for them. Some 100,000 auto workers lost close to $27 million in wages due to the strike.[23] Resisting threats from the company, from their union, and from elected officials, they demonstrated the explosive nature of rank-and-file challenges to company prerogatives, most notably in the way that hostility against management could be directed against apparently collaborationist union leaders. To corporate and union officials, the strike presented a horrible picture of their inability to control labor's rank and file. But to workers across the country it probably represented one more demonstration of the potential of rank-and-file militancy, as did a walkout conducted by New York longshore workers in October 1945.

Shortly after lunch on October 1, New York dockhands stopped loading cargo onto the Grace Line ship *Daulton Mann* at a pier in Manhattan's Chelsea district. They charged that the company had been steadily increasing the weight of the cargo in the slings (nets used for loading), which they had to push, and announced that any sling containing more than 2,420 pounds—one long ton—would not be loaded. When supervisors declined to recognize that limit, workers on six neighboring piers walked off the

job, contending that the company's refusal to abide by safe and reasonable limits on sling size constituted a lockout. By nightfall, 1,500 workers
with no centralized leadership spontaneously joined the strike all along
the Manhattan docks.[24]

The strikers belonged to Local 791 of the International Longshoremen's
Association (ILA). The ILA contract with the shippers had expired at the
end of September, and the Chelsea walkout came in the midst of negotiations for a new contract. Meeting in their local union hall on the first
night of the strike, the insurgents demanded that the new contract place a
limit on sling loads—which sometimes weighed as much as 7,000 pounds
under the old contract, which specified no weight limits.[25] But on October 2, delegates from all the ILA locals in the port voted unanimously to
accept the contract negotiated by the union's "president-for-life," Joseph P.
"King" Ryan. Praising wage increases in the new agreement while ignoring
the issue of sling loads, the delegates triumphantly announced the termi-
nation of the strike.[26]

When rank-and-file dockworkers learned that the settlement contained
no mention of their main grievance and that the delegates presumed to have
ended the strike, resentment quickly grew into retaliation. On the morning
of October 3, over 2,000 employees refused to work on the Chelsea docks.
Eugene Sampson, business agent of Local 791, pleaded with them to return
to work, but at a mass meeting in the union hall 1,500 workers voted to
continue the strike. As other longshore workers got word of Local 791's decision, the strike spread throughout the port. In Brooklyn, Hoboken, and
Staten Island, traffic on the piers came to a halt. Confusion reigned as the
spontaneous outlaw strike—in defiance of union regulations and contractual agreements—closed the entire harbor for the first time in twenty-five
years. Without apparent organization or leadership, 35,000 workers acted
in concert to pressure both their employers and their union.[27]

At meetings in local union halls, vacant lots, and church buildings, the
strikers began to formulate their demands. In a dynamic typical for wildcat
strikes, they first articulated their ideal list of demands, but then worked
their way down to what they might reasonably expect their employers to
concede. "At first everyone wanted the moon," rank-and-file spokesperson
William Warren later recalled, "regular wages, rest periods—but then we
got down to figuring what had a chance."[28] Their streamlined agenda still
asked for a lot. They demanded a one-ton limit for sling loads, a minimum of four hours guaranteed pay when called for work, a time-and-a-half
bonus for work done through the lunch hour, and a reduction in shape-ups
(lineups from which workers are picked) from three a day to two.[29]

Confident of his ability to control the workers, ILA boss Ryan resumed
negotiations with the shippers, boasting that if the strike didn't end within

days, "I will leave for Ireland." Ryan ordered a back-to-work election in Local 791, but only 276 of the local's 1,500 members voted, a turnout of 17 percent. Sampson, the business agent, contended that the low turnout signified rank-and-file endorsement of Ryan's negotiating, surmising that those who failed to vote must have been satisfied with the new contract. But the *New York Times* reported that other observers considered the vote to be an "eloquent expression of disinterest in the move to patch up the broken relations between 30,000 ILA members and the companies that employ them."[30]

Undaunted by the low turnout and narrow vote in favor of his contract (150 voted yes, 122 no, 4 ballots voided), Ryan told the press on October 6 that ILA members throughout the port supported his contract and would return to work shortly. They did not. At a mass meeting the next day, 2,000 workers from seven Brooklyn locals cheered Ralph Chettino of the newly formed rank-and-file negotiating committee and answered his inquiry as to whether they wanted to return to work with a rousing chorus of "NO!" On West Street in Manhattan, 200 workers appeared at the piers but remained on the far side of the street and refused to answer the shape-up whistle. One hundred longshore workers congregated in a vacant lot in Brooklyn at 6 A.M. to talk about the strike. Printed notices appeared all over the port asking dockworkers to stay away from their jobs until the rank-and-file demands became part of the contract.[31]

Rank-and-file complaints over excessive sling loads instigated the strike initially, and concern for working conditions remained the focal point of the walkout as it spread. Even Sampson admitted, "When the load is lifted by machinery from the dock and lowered into the hold the men have to push it around and guide it to the spot for depositing the sling. It is simply too much to push around. Do you think if it wasn't tough on the men they would be out on strike over such a thing?"[32]

Resentment over present working conditions mingled with long-standing grievances against Ryan and his dictatorial administration of union affairs. As early as 1942, 250 rank-and-file union members had staged a wildcat strike to protest the disciplinary firing of one worker, and by the end of that year thousands of ILA members had refused one or more orders from the international. Wartime labor shortages meant steady employment on the docks, enabling employees to form primary work groups capable of waging and winning wildcat strikes. Throughout the war, these militants won increased control over the nature and pace of work, and after the war their ranks were swelled by an influx of veterans determined to enjoy in peacetime the fruits of the victory they had helped fashion in the service. Together, they presented formidable obstacles to Ryan's collaboration with employers as the president for life discovered when he tried to address a back-to-work meeting in Brooklyn's Prospect Hall on October 10.[33]

Although many rank-and-file activists boycotted the meeting to hold their own rally that night, 2,500 others showed up to hear Ryan and other union officials urge them to end the strike and return to work. ILA officials even produced one Captain Sam Curpe, a former Brooklyn lawyer, who appeared in his army uniform to urge the crowd to return to work—invoking the spirit of the brave soldiers who followed orders to fight and die for their country during the war. Workers hissed, booed, and shouted Curpe off the stage, and then gave the same treatment to "King" Ryan. No union official could be heard above the din, and the only speakers allowed to finish were rank and filers speaking from the floor who delivered impassioned denunciations of Ryan in English and Italian.[34]

U.S. government officials hurried to Ryan's aid in an effort to open the nation's largest port to shipping. After a tour of the waterfront, John Andrew Burke of the U.S. Conciliation Service observed that the membership of the ILA seemed to have lost confidence in their leaders, and he announced that the government intended to take on the difficult task of restoring that faith *and* getting them back to work.[35] New York City's Mayor Fiorello La Guardia broadcast an appeal to the workers and their families, arguing that the tie-up could delay shipment of packages to many of their relatives in Italy. He asked them to end the strike "in the name of common sense." Newspaper stories emphasized the city's economic losses from the strike, as well as the potential posed by the dispute to delay dispatch of troop ships bringing home veterans from the war.[36]

Unable to negotiate an acceptable contract, embarrassed by his inability to control the ranks, and humiliated by hecklers at his own union meeting, Joseph Ryan resorted to one of his old tricks in maintaining control over the ILA. He now "discovered" that Communists had instigated and exploited the strike. To substantiate his claim, Ryan pointed to the active support lent to the strikers by the National Maritime Union (NMU) and the International Longshoreman's and Warehouseman's Union (ILWU), headed by his longtime foe Harry Bridges. As a member of the ILA in 1934, Bridges had led a successful maritime and general strike in San Francisco—despite Ryan's disapproval. Bridges led the entire West Coast membership of the ILA into the CIO's ILWU in the thirties, and the two unions nominally competed for recognition in ports across the country. Ryan had denounced Bridges as a Communist in San Francisco in 1934, and he regarded the NMU as a "Communist-dominated" organization in 1945.

In the early days of the New York strike, the NMU did distribute 25,000 leaflets supporting the "just and modest demands" of the rank and file. However, the leaflets urged the workers to remain in the ILA and "fight for your rights" with no mention of recruitment into the NMU. Bridges came to New York and urged the mayor to meet with representatives of the rank-and-file negotiating committee, while NMU members picketed in favor of the insurgents. But they confined their involvement to strike support. To surmise that Communists in the NMU played an active role in strike support would be perfectly accurate. To conclude that Communists fomented or controlled the walkout would be sheer fantasy. Yet the charges helped Ryan to explain his powerlessness to stop the strike, mobilized the press against the strikers, and helped divide the workers.[37]

Ryan's tactical anticommunism brought him some immediate rewards. Members of the anticommunist reform group the Association of Catholic Trade Unionists (ACTU) opposed the strike. A leader of the ACTU explained, "When it became clear that the choice was between Joe Ryan and the Communists, our members went back to work."[38] By October 15, small groups of longshore workers in Manhattan and Staten Island went back to work. Three thousand striking rank and filers demonstrated on the Brooklyn docks on the sixteenth, but throughout the harbor enthusiasm for the walkout diminished. Strikers divided into factions, some favoring continuation of the strike, others pushing for a National Labor Relations Board (NLRB) election for new officers.

Ryan exploited this confusion with another of his traditional weapons—physical violence. To combat the rank and file and the NMU, Ryan called upon the Seafarers International Union (SIU) for assistance. On October 17, a group of thugs from the SIU attempted to attack a rank-and-file meeting. Calling the strikers "Moscow-controlled lice," an estimated 150 attackers assaulted police lines in an unsuccessful attempt to break up the meeting. The SIU later issued a statement warning that "if the police are going to protect the Communists with their clubs and the law, we are going to have to take more drastic measures." That same day, with one-third of the strikers back on the job, unidentified persons brutally attacked and beat an anti-Ryan demonstrator.[39]

On October 18 the strike ended. The rank-and-file negotiating committee conceded defeat and told its followers to return to work. "We make this recommendation," the committee announced, "because the continuance of the strike in the face of Ryan's gangsterism, the strike-breaking of Lundeberg (President Harry Lundeberg of the SIU), the lies in the anti-labor press and the active collusion of the shipowners with Ryan and Lundeberg, convinces us that the unity of the ILA rank and file may suffer."[40] The committee's conclusion coincided with that of one dejected striker who complained, "That's the thanks one gets! I've been fighting Ryan's gang since the last war; so now they say I'm a Communist. Will it take another war to get him out?"[41]

One day after the strike's end, two reporters encountered rank-and-file activist William Warren on the Brooklyn docks. Warren stated that he hoped to find work that day, but because of his involvement in the strike he did not really expect to be hired. Suddenly a gang of fifty men appeared and began to savagely beat him and the journalists. Warren shouted to his attackers that the men with him were reporters, and they escaped with minor injuries. Warren was not as fortunate. That same day, another rank-and-file activist, Sal Barone, barely escaped a beating by running to his car and driving away. At ILA headquarters, Joseph Ryan announced William Warren's expulsion from the union for "failure to pay dues." [42]

On October 19, William Warren called a press conference to charge that trusted advisors had given him bad advice and "wrongly steered me into the communist camp." Stating that the rank-and-file negotiating committee's lawyer, Nathan Witt, had Communist leanings, Warren resigned from the committee and pledged to work constructively for change within the structure of the ILA. Almost immediately, the rank-and-file committee charged that Warren "sold out" and announced election of new officers at a press conference in Nathan Witt's offices. [43]

Despite the beatings and turmoil within the rank-and-file group, Ryan still had not secured a contract. On October 24 ILA members overwhelmingly rejected an agreement that made no mention of sling load size. Only 800 of the port's 35,000 workers approved Ryan's new settlement. One day later, the insurgents won a court order preventing Ryan from signing any contract pending an investigation into undemocratic procedures within the ILA. [44]

Once again the government stepped in, as Secretary of Labor L. B. Schwellenbach presented a proposal for arbitration that satisfied Ryan and the ship owners. On October 26 the rank-and-file negotiating committee denounced arbitration as "another deliberate attempt to sell out the longshoremen by violating our right to be consulted. . . . We do not oppose arbitration as such. We do oppose any attempt to settle the longshore situation without giving the longshoremen an opportunity to decide democratically and free from coercion what steps shall be taken in our behalf." [45]

Yet with the workers back on the job, with Ryan's power reaffirmed, and with arbitration taking place quietly and out of public view, the final settlement granted wage increases and some concessions on overtime hours, but left standards for sling load size completely up to the discretion of the companies. [46]

The longshore strike dramatized the strengths and weaknesses of rank-and-file insurgencies. Relying on their own means, rank-and-file workers closed the port of New York in defiance of the shipping companies, their union, and the government. Without any evident centralized leadership, they acted in concert to dramatize their grievances and to demonstrate their power. Informal and spontaneous methods rendered legitimate authorities powerless, eclipsing the channels of bureaucracy with the methods of direct action. The strike turned private complaints into public political issues. On September 30 few people in New York knew what a sling load was. Two days later nearly everyone did.

Yet while demonstrating the militance of the rank and file, the explosive potential of bottled-up grievances, and the inability of unions to adequately contain their memberships, the strike also exposed the limits of such outbursts. Spontaneous actions that proved so successful in dramatizing grievances proved ill-suited for fashioning secure solutions in the face of entrenched institutional power. Organized violent repression understandably intimidated individuals, while charges of Communist influence bred suspicion in the ranks and helped shatter the fragile unity formed in the first bursts of enthusiasm that ignited the walkout.

The New York ILA strike exacted a heavy toll in lost profits, lost work hours, and lost legitimacy for the union. Dockworkers made the threat of future strikes a credible weapon on their side, and along with the Kelsey-Hayes strikers demonstrated that any adjustment in labor-management relations in 1945–46 would have to acknowledge and contend with the militance of the rank and file. It was precisely such self-assertive behavior by workers that lay behind the strategies of business, labor, and government in the big nationwide strikes during the winter of 1945–46.

As auto, steel, and electrical workers voted overwhelmingly to strike in preparation for contract talks with the nation's largest corporations, leaders of government, business, and labor devised strategies to contain the rank and file. Although they were to fight bitterly with one another over the exact strategy to employ, they all agreed upon the necessity to limit rank-and-file activity. They sought secure labor-management agreements protecting the institutional power of corporations and unions while guaranteeing uninterrupted production. No strike better exemplified this struggle than did the 113-day walkout at General Motors (GM) by members of the United Auto Workers union.

The General Motors strike pitted one of the largest and most militant unions in the country against one of the nation's wealthiest and most powerful employers. It also featured a dialogue between two of the most sophisticated and visionary leaders of labor and management—Walter Reuther of the GM division of the UAW and C. E. Wilson of GM. Although on opposite sides, Reuther and Wilson shared so many concerns that they found themselves formulating a settlement that satisfied their own goals, an agreement that resonated powerfully with the aims of major leaders from other industries and labor unions, as well as from the federal government.

Reuther recognized that the unprecedented militance of the rank and file provided an opportunity for labor unions to emerge as full partners in the corporate-liberal system. Back in 1941, he had designed a defense mobilization plan for American industry that impinged on traditional management prerogatives by granting unions a major role in determining the nature and purpose of production. Although the specifics of his plan met with a hostile reception from manufacturers who had no intention of letting Walter Reuther tell them how to run their businesses, wartime labor-management-business cooperation did prove that high production, full employment, and labor peace could flow from application of Reuther's principles. His plans for postwar America represented an attempt to expand labor's involvement in helping to administer production in the name of industrial peace and the general welfare.

Defining the economy's major problem as the production of too many goods without adequate markets, Reuther recommended that wartime production levels be maintained, but converted to consumer items. He argued that a new depression could be avoided only by a 40 to 50 percent rise in consumer spending above prewar levels, and he favorably quoted a Federal Reserve System report that warned, "We must not accept the miserable alternative of having our products piling up as surplus for lack of markets and have their output shrink in consequence. We must not suffer our wealth to be the cause of our poverty, or permit the abundance of our resources to be the basis of our want."[47]

Although these sentiments would ultimately lead Reuther and other labor leaders into supporting an aggressive and expansive foreign policy, in the 1945 negotiations with GM he first hoped to secure prosperity through higher wages and the increases in purchasing power they would bring.

A series of wildcat strikes and local votes in favor of strikes indicated that GM workers expected large gains after the war. Demands percolating up from the ranks encouraged local unions to formulate militant demands for the abolition of bonus systems and piecework, for enhanced union power to influence the pace of production, for rules limiting the discretionary powers of supervisors to assign jobs and make transfers, and for increasing the role of union committeemen inside the plants.[48] Although these demands were fueled primarily by local issues relating to the pace, nature, and purpose of work, on a national level the UAW concentrated on winning wage increases. Union negotiators demanded a 30 percent increase in wages to help stimulate necessary consumer spending and to compensate for the loss of overtime work in the postwar period. GM executives knew they would have to grant some increases, but they had no intention of paying that much, arguing that a wage increase of 30 percent with no increase in productivity would be inflationary and necessitate price increases.

Reuther recognized the dangers of passing along to consumers the costs of higher wages for auto workers. Higher car prices might inhibit consumer spending and they would force unorganized workers and consumers to pay the price for any gains made by union members. Picking up a demand that originated among the rank and file, Reuther announced that he wanted to tie the union's demand for more wages to a stipulation that GM not increase prices. He reasoned that GM's fantastic wartime profits could more than cover the increase and that in the long run the company too would reap the benefits of increased consumer purchases. Reuther also understood that such a stipulation would set a precedent for labor participation in management decisions.

Despite his public pronouncements that GM could easily afford to raise wages immediately, Reuther had no intention of really challenging the company's traditional prerogatives or of interfering with its efforts to increase productivity. He saw his role as primarily winning wage increases for workers by helping the company increase production, and consequently he approved of management efforts to exert greater control over the workplace. Reuther gave voice to many rank-and-file frustrations, but his perspective reflected more the worldview of a sophisticated liberal manager of labor rather than that of a shop-floor militant. Reuther envisioned limits on workers' power at the point of production as an essential part of the final settlement of the auto workers' strike.

The UAW's emphasis on wages enabled the union to channel the 1945 strike toward the pursuit of demands that the company could easily afford to grant, while diverting attention away from more complex local grievances concerning working conditions.[49] By choosing to strike only at GM (ostensibly in the hope that competitive pressure from sales of Ford and Chrysler would force a settlement), the union gained a rationale for ending wildcat strikes at the other two companies on the grounds that such actions undercut strike strategy and ultimately punished the GM strikers. Most important, the UAW proposed to Ford and Chrysler (and ultimately to GM) that the new contract hold individual workers responsible for wildcat strikes, subjecting them to fines and dismissals. The union also proposed penalties for workers who failed to meet work and output standards or who engaged in slowdowns.[50]

GM eagerly agreed that containing the rank and file suited the interests of both the company and the union, but disagreed that granting more power to the union would produce the desired result. Industry officials felt that a 30 percent wage hike exceeded reasonable limits, but understood it as a negotiating ploy designed "to bring into line a rank and file that is getting out of hand" and, as such, a legitimate topic for discussion. Allowing the union to help determine price policy was another matter, as became evident in an exchange between Harry Coen, GM assistant director of personnel, and Reuther.

Coen: Why don't you get down to your size and get down to the type of job you are supposed to be doing as a trade-union leader, and talk about money you would like to have for your people and let the labor statesmanship go to hell for awhile?

Reuther: Translate it so that I can know what you mean.

Coen: If you come to us and say "We want X cents an hour" and we can talk to you about whether we can give you X cents, or half an X or quarter of X, or something like that. Instead of that you get off in your socialistic dreams, these Alice-in-Wonderland things of yours, and finally get off to where you don't even understand yourself.[51]

At first the corporation responded to the demand that no price increase accompany a wage hike by pleading poverty. Reuther shrewdly challenged GM to "open the books" and let the public decide whether the firm's profits could sustain a wage increase with no change in prices. A masterful propaganda stroke, Reuther's challenge presented the company with a difficult dilemma. To refuse to open the books would be to lose standing in the public eye and to appear to have something to hide. To open the books would be to concede that the union had a right to help decide how the company should allocate its resources, not to mention revealing the firm's rather secure financial position. The company chose to stand on its traditional privileges, branding the UAW demands as an assault on free enterprise. Although GM might be embarrassed by a strike prompted by their failure to "open the books," in actuality, the corporation had little to lose and much to gain from a work stoppage. The wartime Excess Profits Tax carry-back provisions guaranteed that any economic losses sustained in 1945 would be underwritten by the federal government as part of the costs of reconversion. Thus, GM could save money by not paying wages during the strike, while the federal treasury compensated them for any losses in sales income for 1945.

Bargaining over the terms of a wage increase they could well afford to grant, the company hoped to win contract language reaffirming its control over production and limiting the powers of both workers and their union. GM executives knew that a long strike might exacerbate rivalries within the union, lower worker enthusiasm for future strikes, and agitate public opinion against labor because of the resulting delays in conversion to peacetime production. With little or no financial risk, a strike might bring GM a contrite work force, a defeated union, and antilabor and antistrike legislation.

Although seeking as advantageous a settlement as possible, the company nonetheless had no intention of abandoning its relationship with the union. One month before the strike began, C. E. Wilson of GM expressed

satisfaction with labor-management relations in the auto industry, even
though he complained that "some of the men still thought the plants belonged to them."[52] Wilson defended the right of unions to pursue better
wages and working conditions for their members, but he assailed the ten-
dency of "monopolistic" unions to abuse those rights by promoting industrial strife. He told the *New York Times*, "The idea that a few thousand
truck drivers can shut off the gasoline supply of the people: that a few
thousand elevator operators can keep hundreds of thousands of New York-
ers from going to do their work: that the stockholders and management of
a big utility company and their employees could engage in economic warfare and shut off the light and power of one of our big cities certainly can
not be tolerated in modern society."[53]

Had Wilson been willing to ponder the democratic implications of the
concentration of wealth and power on the Board of Directors of General
Motors, he might have been more temperate in his denunciation of the
union's "monopoly," but nonetheless he did identify the major strength and
weakness of labor's position. Workers could legitimately claim public support when they disrupted the economy in the name of lower prices for all,
or for economic justice, but they would be susceptible to public pressure if
their disruptions could be portrayed as the narrow, self-serving strategy of
a minority building its power at the public's expense. Wilson cleverly refused to recognize the legitimacy of the UAW's social demands for lower
prices, but at the same time he lambasted the workers and the union for
their selfishness and defiance of the "public good." The company and the
union not only fought each other over issues of management prerogatives
but they also fought a public relations battle in anticipation of a political
struggle over the proper role to be played by government in protecting the
"public interest" in the strike.

Walter Reuther understood that fighting price increases not only guaranteed higher consumer spending but also built popular support for the
union and its image as a responsible public party. Capitalizing on public resentment over war profiteering, Reuther stressed the seemingly unchecked
wealth and power of the corporation in many of his public statements. In
a typical comment during the early stages of bargaining during the 1945
strike, he complained indignantly, "A corporation that has the money you
have, and you fellows sitting on top and enjoying every damn decent thing
of life, everything money can buy, and all the security. And when a bunch
of workers asks for their share of it you thumb your nose at them, tell them
to go to hell, refuse to conciliate, refuse to bargain, refuse to negotiate,
refuse to arbitrate."[54]

Reuther's strategy contained the possibility of translating popular resentments against big business into an antimonopoly coalition led by labor. Yet

Reuther's own ambitions and his commitment to corporate-liberal ideology made him wary of appeals to the public, compelling him to prove his "responsibility" to business and government by moderating his demands and limiting popular involvement in the strike. Like other labor leaders, Reuther realized that his aspirations for power depended more upon the good opinion of the corporate-liberal elite than on the wishes of the rank and file. Years later, Reuther's brother Victor recalled that "the GM strike was designed to take the ball out of the hands of the stewards and committeemen and it put it back in the hands of the national leadership."[55]

Just as Richard Frankensteen sought to be mayor of Detroit by ending the Kelsey-Hayes strike, CIO (and United Steel Workers) president Phil Murray sought the favor of the Truman administration by restraining rank-and-file militance during the big strikes of 1945–46. After a December meeting in which they bitterly disagreed over the propriety of asking GM to make public its financial records, Murray ordered Reuther to drop the demand that wage increases be tied to no increase in prices. Reuther complied and transformed the strike from a socially responsible assault on corporate power to a justified, but limited, exercise in self-interest. When CIO members in several states planned mass work stoppages in support of striking auto, steel, and electrical workers in February 1946, Murray canceled the demonstrations, warning that the CIO would not allow its members to violate existing contracts.[56] This moderation aimed at inducing federal officials to guarantee security for unions because of their contributions to the "public interest."

The federal government did play a major role in determining the outcome of the GM strike and others related to it. During reconversion, the federal government retained many of its wartime powers. Wage and price increases remained subject to federal supervision, and in fact, consumer prices rose when President Truman cooperated with business leaders in removing wartime price caps allegedly because of the strikes.[57] The WLB continued to regulate labor-management disputes, and the president maintained the power to seize vital industries in the national interest. Congruent with the goals of labor and business leaders, federal policy during reconversion emphasized the legitimacy of modest wage increases while strenuously attempting to contain rank-and-file militance.

Once they returned to work after the major sanctioned strikes of 1945 and 1946, workers faced renewed efforts by management to exercise greater control at the point of production. Westinghouse reduced rates paid to electrical workers in its main plant, and it encouraged "re-organization" of production at other locations. "Soon as we come back they cut us twelve or thirteen per cent off our base rate," complained one sheet-metal worker.[58] The president of one of the key locals for the United Electrical Workers told international officers, "The Company is changing long-established working conditions without consultation with the Union. It is intimidating officers, stewards, and ordinary members by sending them home and threatening them when they attempt to carry out their duly assigned union jobs."[59]

Government agencies, executive orders, and arbitrators repeatedly encouraged businesses to grant mild wage hikes consistent with their huge wartime profits in order to bargain for increased control over production. Government agencies directly assisted in the settlement of more than half of the labor-management disputes in 1945, and WLB recommendations for 14 to 20 percent wage increases provided the pattern for most of the settlements.[60] Yet while the Truman administration endorsed union wage demands, it also took extraordinary measures to limit strikes and curtail the power of workers and their unions. Secretary of Labor L. B. Schwellenbach told the nation in a network radio broadcast on Labor Day, 1945, "This nation has adequate machinery available to peacefully settle any labor dispute. To advance any demand to the point of stopping production instead of using machinery available for peaceful settlement is not in the national interest and will not be supported by public opinion. We must place the interest of the whole Nation above the interest of any individual or any group."[61]

When oil refinery workers went on strike in the fall of 1945, Truman seized the refineries and ordered the workers back on the job. In the face of the spreading strike wave of October 1945 he deplored the "few selfish men" standing in the way of reconversion and ordered workers to "cut out all the foolishness."[62] On November 21, 1945, the president took the time to upbraid transit workers in Washington, D.C., for a walkout that he claimed struck at "the very roots of orderly government."[63] In May 1946, Truman attempted to end strikes by railroad workers and coal miners by seizing the mines and railroads and ordering the strikers back to work. He demanded angrily that Congress pass an antilabor bill empowering the president to end work stoppages by drafting strikers into the army. The bill eventually failed when even public opponents of union power like Senator Robert Taft of Ohio objected to the chilling totalitarian implications of such legislation. Yet Truman demonstrated his clear intention to use the powers of government to ensure labor peace, a tactic that ultimately provided a key weapon in the war to restrain labor's rank and file.[64]

During the GM strike, business, government, and labor power combined to shape the essentials of the final settlement. From the beginning of the strike, GM demanded elimination of union security clauses, protection of management rights, and new powers to be used against wildcat strikers.[65] Chrysler and Ford enthusiastically supported GM's position, refusing to offer more in their negotiations and declining to build up their own sales to any significant degree at GM's expense. While encouraging the company to grant a 17 percent pay increase, government arbitrators pressured the strikers to lower their financial expectations and to make concessions regarding control over production. The UAW settled with Chrysler and Ford for less than they asked of GM and granted those companies contract language to punish wildcat strikers. Other unions followed similar procedures. The steelworkers settled for the recommendations of government fact-finding boards, and the electrical workers undercut the GM strike by settling with the electrical division of the company for less money than the UAW had asked.[66]

The final settlement of the auto workers' strike granted wage increases of 17 percent, hardly enough to keep up with lost income from cutbacks in overtime. Contract language regarding control over the workplace strengthened management at the expense of the workers, and wage increases with no bar against price hikes meant that unions' gains came at the expense of consumers. And, of course, economic losses to workers from lost wages were enormous.

During the 1945–46 strike wave, American workers lost over $1 billion in wages. Prices rose by 16 percent, while wages in durable-goods-producing industries increased by only an average of 7 percent. Strikes cost each coal miner $810, each steel worker $195, and each auto worker $850, while average wage gains from those strikes amounted to only $.03 per hour more than management offered before the strike.[67] Coupled with union commitments to increased productivity and contract provisions affirming management rights, these figures indicate a great victory for corporate-liberal strategies. Yet victory and defeat cannot always be measured in such formal terms.

Whatever else they may have won, leaders of labor, business, and government did not emerge from the 1945–46 strike wave with a docile working class committed to labor peace. Government efforts to put the power of law behind strikebreaking gave millions of workers a shared experience of defying the law and striking against the government. Business efforts to wait intransigently for workers to become demoralized only exacerbated tensions, strengthening rank-and-file commitment to the strikes. Union efforts to channel frustrations into wage demands left unresolved grievances and bitter feelings that surged to the surface once production resumed.

Most important, the efforts of business, labor, and government leaders to confine worker demands to questions of self-interest—while at the same time branding them as selfish—did not succeed. In city after city, workers and local unions appealed to public opinion and sought popular support on the grounds that their struggles promised gains for the many at the expense of the few. In many cases, the public responded enthusiastically. In Chicago, grocery store owners and druggists extended credit to packinghouse workers to help them wage their strike. Priests and neighborhood groups joined the picket lines, and small business owners supported the workers.[68] In Flint, Michigan, building owners refused to evict striking GM workers for nonpayment of rent, while grocers donated food to union strike kitchens.[69] Fifteen city governments across the country adopted resolutions in support of the electrical workers' strike in their towns, because they shared the view articulated by a citizens' committee in Essington, Pennsylvania, which proclaimed, "We feel that the unions are working in the best interests of the national economy in their efforts to maintain the country's pay envelopes."[70] In Jersey City, New Jersey, the mayor told his police force to ignore a court injunction and assist a strike by keeping nonstrikers from entering the plants.[71]

Despite enormous inconveniences caused by the strikes, despite the delay in production of consumer items, and despite worker defiance of laws and injunctions, a *Fortune* poll appearing in November 1946 revealed gradually *increasing* public support for labor. The poll asked people which side they would favor more often if they had been a referee in labor-management disputes. Those questioned between November 1945 and January 1946—at the beginning of the GM strike—divided, with 25.7 percent favoring labor and 44.7 percent siding with management. When asked between April and June 1946—at the peak of Truman's attacks on the coal and railroad strikes— 37.1 percent preferred labor and 36.6 percent took management's view. At the end of the major part of the first postwar strike wave—between September and November 1946—36.8 percent of those questioned chose to side with labor and 34.5 percent with management. In each poll, labor support increased or remained stable, while the number of people taking management's side declined. The poll also indicated sharp class divisions, as poor and lower-middle income groups grew particularly hostile to management in each of the three questioning periods.[72] But the most dramatic evidence of working-class gains from the first postwar strikes appeared in the real-life actions of workers across the country who transformed limited contract disputes into general strikes that paralyzed production and mobilized entire communities into public demonstrations in support of worker demands.

Bitter strikes involving machinists in Stamford, Connecticut, transit workers in Lancaster, Pennsylvania, municipal employees in Rochester, New York, electrical workers in Pittsburgh, Pennsylvania, and retail clerks in Oakland, California, erupted into general strikes when frustrated workers turned to mass demonstrations and collective pressure to advance their demands. Meeting the charge of selfishness head on, these workers placed their own grievances in a socially responsible context and forged alliances with other workers and citizens who saw the strikers' interests to be in harmony with their own. Recognizing the inherent limits of "legitimate" channels, they turned to mass disruptions and demonstrations as a means of continuing their fight for recognition, power, and control over their lives.

NOTES

1. *New York Times*, Aug. 17, 1945, 11.

2. Ronald W. Schatz, *The Electrical Workers: A History of Labor at General Electric and Westinghouse, 1923–60* (Urbana: University of Illinois Press, 1983), 121.

3. Nelson Lichtenstein, *Labor's War at Home* (Cambridge: Cambridge University Press, 1982), 221.

4. *Monthly Labor Review* (Dec. 1946): 872, (May 1946): 707, (Nov. 1946): 669.

5. *New York Times*, Aug. 30, 1945, 13; Art Preis, *Labor's Giant Step* (New York: Pathfinder, 1972), 4.

6. *New York Times*, Sept. 11, 1945, 5.

7. Ibid., 13; *Newsweek*, Oct. 8, 1945, 33.

8. *New York Times*, Sept. 30, 1945, 4; *Business Week*, Mar. 9, 1946, 92.

9. Lichtenstein, *Labor's War at Home*, 222.

10. *Newsweek*, Oct. 8, 1945, 33.

11. *Business Week*, Sept. 18, 1945, 110; *New Republic*, Oct. 1, 1945, 426.

12. *Business Week*, Sept. 8, 1945, 110, Sept. 15, 1945, 98.

13. *New York Times*, Sept. 16, 1945, 3.

14. Ibid., Sept. 17, 1945, 12.

15. Ibid., Sept. 18, 1945, 14.

16. Ibid., 1.

17. Ibid., Sept. 19, 1945, 20.

18. Ibid., Sept. 21, 1945, 13. This was not the first or last time Kennedy expressed such expectations about union discipline. Testifying before the Committee on Education and Labor of the House of Representatives on February 20, 1947, he related a history of labor troubles at Kelsey-Hayes, including how the company granted maintenance of membership during the war in hopes that it would stop "agitation and unrest" and how the union then asked for a union shop as a means of controlling the work force. By the time of that testimony, Kennedy was urging federal legislation to help him regain control of his factory. See Hearings before the House of Representatives Committee on Education and Labor, 80th Cong., 1st sess., Feb. 20, 1947.

19. *New York Times*, Sept. 19, 1945, 1.

20. Ibid., Sept. 25, 1945, 1.

21. Ibid., Sept. 29, 1945, 2.

22. *Business Week*, Oct. 6, 1945, 100, Oct. 13, 1945, 100; *New York Times*, Oct. 7, 1945, 3.

23. Lichtenstein, *Labor's War at Home*, 223.

24. *New York Times*, Oct. 2, 1945, 12.

25. Ibid.

26. Ibid., Oct. 4, 1945, 1.

27. Maurice Rosenblatt, "The Scandal of the Waterfront," *The Nation*, Nov. 17, 1945, 516; *New York Times*, Oct. 4, 1945, 1.

28. Rosenblatt, "Scandal of the Waterfront," 40, 45.

29. *New York Times*, Oct. 4, 1945, 1.

30. Ibid., Oct. 6, 1945, 1.

31. Ibid., Oct. 9, 1945, 1.

32. Ibid., Oct. 7, 1945, 1.

33. Howard Kimmeldorf, *Reds or Rackets: The Making of Radical and Conservative Unions on the Waterfront* (Berkeley: University of California Press, 1988), 152–53.

34. *New York Times*, Oct. 11, 1945, 1.

35. Ibid., Oct. 11, 1945, 14.

36. *Catholic Worker*, Oct. 1945, 3.

37. Vernon Jensen, *Strife on the Waterfront* (Ithaca: Cornell University Press, 1974).

38. Steve Rosswurm, "The Catholic Church and the Left-Led Unions: Labor Priests, Labor Schools, and the ACTU," in Steve Rosswurm, ed., *The CIO's Left-Led Unions* (New Brunswick: Rutgers University Press, 1992), 129.

39. *New York Times*, Oct. 18, 1945, 1.

40. Ibid., Oct. 19, 1945, 17.

41. Rosenblatt, "Scandal on the Waterfront," 45.

42. *New York Times*, Oct. 20, 1945, 1.

43. Ibid., Oct. 21, 1945, 35, Oct. 22, 1945, 9.

44. Ibid., Oct. 26, 1945, 1.

45. Ibid., Oct. 27, 1945, 16.

46. Jensen, *Strife on the Waterfront*.

47. *The Nation*, Jan. 12, 1946, 35.

48. Howell John Harris, *The Right to Manage: Industrial Relations Policies of American Business in the 1940s* (Madison: University of Wisconsin Press, 1982), 141.

49. GM workers at the South Gate plant remained on strike after the national agreement had been signed over precisely such local grievances. Local demands at South Gate concerned shift assignments, company "spying" on workers, disciplinary rules, line speed, transfers, pay for time spent preparing for work, safety rules, and involuntary overtime. See "1945–46 Strike Demands for Local Negotiations in UAW Local 216, South Gate, California," box 1, Louis Ciccone Collection, Labor History Archives, Wayne State University, Detroit, Mich.

50. Nelson Lichtenstein, "Defending the No-Strike Pledge," *Radical America* 9, nos. 4–5 (1975); *U.S. News and World Report*, Mar. 8, 1946, 38; *Daily Worker*, Dec. 11, 1945, 3.

51. Irving Howe and B. J. Widick, *The UAW and Walter Reuther* (New York: Random House, 1949), 135; quote on rank and file from *New York Times*, Sept. 18, 1945, 1.

52. *New York Times*, Oct. 21, 1945, 36.

53. Ibid., Oct. 6, 1945, 3.

54. *Business Week*, Dec. 22, 1945, 104.

55. Lichtenstein, *Labor's War at Home*, 226.

56. *Time*, Jan. 14, 1946, 16; *Daily Worker*, Feb. 8, 1946.

57. Lichtenstein, *Labor's War at Home*, 229.

58. Schatz, *The Electrical Workers*, 146.

59. Ibid.

60. *Monthly Labor Review* (Apr. 1946): 537.

61. *Labor Information Bulletin* (Washington, D.C.: Department of Labor, Aug. 1945), 3.

62. *New York Times*, Oct. 4, 1945, 1, Oct. 11, 1945, 1.

63. Art Preis, *Labor's Giant Step* (New York: Pathfinder Press, 1972), 267.

64. Ibid., 294–95; James F. Patterson, *Mr. Republican* (Boston: Houghton Mifflin, 1972), 306–7.

65. *Monthly Labor Review* (Jan. 1946): 427–28.

66. For different interpretations of the UE's role, see James Matles and James Higgins, *Them and Us* (Boston: Beacon Press, 1974), 144–49, and Preis, *Labor's Giant Step*, 279.

67. *U.S. News and World Report*, Dec. 20, 1946, 13.

68. William Shelton, "Of Meat and Men," *The Nation*, Feb. 9, 1946, 139.

69. *U.S. News and World Report*, Jan. 18, 1946, 13.

70. *UE Fights for a Better America*, 1946, 1, pamphlet in author's possession.

71. *Business Week*, Mar. 9, 1946, 81.

72. *Fortune*, Nov. 1946, 5.

CHAPTER FIVE

"We Will Not Go Back to the Old Days"

The General Strikes Begin

MORE THAN ten thousand workers streamed into Atlantic Square in Stamford, Connecticut, shortly after New Year's Day in 1946 as part of the first general strike in the United States in twelve years. One of the more prominently displayed placards in the crowd proclaimed "We Will Not Go Back to the Old Days." That sentiment found wide popular expression during a three-day general strike in Lancaster, Pennsylvania, six weeks later. Partially the result of a desire to reap the rewards deferred by wartime sacrifices, the insistence on not returning to the old days also stemmed from the "turn-back-the-clock" strategy by executives from small competitive corporations in those cities.

Government intervention in wartime labor-management relations provided stability, predictability, and security for large, monopolistic corporations. Because of their huge investments in machinery, their need to anticipate the amount of available capital, and the economy of scale that they derived from the size of their productive facilities, these firms could afford to pay higher wages and to recognize unions in pursuit of uninterrupted production. Smaller companies could not make those concessions as easily.

Plagued by competitive pressures, a reliance on hours worked as the only means of raising output, hampered by shortages of capital, and constantly vexed by uncertain markets, these businesses found themselves victimized by measures designed to help monopolistic industry. WLB decisions encouraged union recognition by corporations accustomed to paternalistic control over their employees. Government planners directed supplies and raw materials to large defense contractors while withholding them from smaller businesses. Even those competitive enterprises enjoying increased revenue from government spending soon discovered that their profits hardly kept pace with those of major contractors.

Business leaders from the competitive sector of the economy recognized the damaging effects of corporate liberalism on their kind of enterprise. Opposed to government regulations and unions as matters of principle and practice, they embarked on a postwar program designed to reverse encroachments upon their power over production, to lift government regulations, and, in some cases, to smash the unions that entered their plants during the war. In Stamford and Lancaster, two competitive firms attempted to gain the upper hand in postwar labor-management relations, but in the process provoked general strikes. Recognizing that their workers would strike and seek wage increases if conditions permitted, these companies attempted to return to the "old days" of no unions and unchallenged company control. In the battles that followed, the companies and the workers found themselves involved not only in a test of strength but in a competition for public opinion and popular sanction for their actions as well.

Located in Stamford's industrial south end, the Yale and Towne Manufacturing Company employed more than 3,000 of the city's 65,000 residents in 1945. A pioneer in the manufacture of pin-tumble locks, Yale and Towne had dominated Stamford's economy since the nineteenth century. Owned and operated by the descendants of corporation founder Henry Towne, the company enjoyed a paternalistic relationship with its employees, resisting unions and paying low wages but also loaning money at low interest rates to enable workers to pay bills or finance new homes. As one long-time employee recalled, "The company relations with employees was always bad in that Yale and Towne management thought employees should be grateful for having a job. Pay was always lower than other industries and any raises were always on an individual basis."[1]

In the thirties, Yale and Towne resisted unionization so bitterly that it closed down a plant in Detroit rather than deal with a union. At one point, a federal judge censured the company for its antilabor activity. Only after government military spending converted 93 percent of the plant's production to war needs, and after a WLB election enabled the International Association of Machinists to challenge (and defeat) the company union, did Yale and Towne reluctantly recognize a labor organization it did not control.[2]

Although the company tolerated a union during the war, even before the contract expired on March 21, 1945, its officers planned to negotiate for elimination of the maintenance of membership clause, which stipulated that once workers joined the union they had to remain in good standing with it to work in the plant. Yale and Towne wanted a new contract providing for an open shop with no mandatory union membership and no wage increase, while the union asked for union security in the form of maintenance of membership and a 30 percent wage increase.[3]

Both parties agreed to abide by the old contract as they negotiated for a new one, but Yale and Towne management consistently undermined the old agreement by failing to process grievances. When the company fired the union's chief steward on September 21, 1945, employees walked off their jobs in protest. Culminating many smaller work stoppages in isolated departments throughout the plant after the expiration of the contract, the September 21 disruption involved all three thousand production workers, and it took place without the approval of the local union. Although production resumed after several days of negotiations, the walkout alerted both the company and the union to the militancy of the rank and file. In an attempt to exert pressure in contract talks, the company announced that the illegal wildcat strike between September 21 and September 24 had terminated all contractual obligations between the company and the union.[4]

With the company unwilling to recognize the old contract, the machinists officially went on strike on November 7, 1945. Union picketers prevented company president W. Gibson Carey from entering the plant on November 8, and for the next two months the company and the union fought a verbal and sometimes physical battle as to which side had the power to determine entrance to the factory. Management complained about fire hazards in the plant and inadequate maintenance because of union limits on those allowed to enter the building, while the union made clear its determination to prevent supervisors from scabbing on the strike by doing work normally performed by hourly employees.[5]

Yale and Towne's refusal to bargain in good faith increased tensions on the picket line. As a war contractor, the company reaped the benefits of the excess profits tax, which subsidized losses by war industries in the reconversion period, so it could clearly afford to prolong the strike. When Stamford police refused to break up the picket lines forcefully, Yale and Towne officials appealed to Connecticut's governor to send in the state police. The state police assaulted strikers in late December, making numerous arrests. In protest against the company's bargaining tactics and against the repressive measures taken against picketers, the workers and their union decided to call for a massive show of support from their neighbors and fellow workers to pressure the company into a reasonable settlement.

On the cold, clear morning of January 3, 1946, workers all over Stamford reported to their jobs. But instead of going to work, they marched downtown to a mass rally. Many merchants closed their shops for the day. Others put signs in their windows announcing support for the strikers. Ten thousand people, accompanied by a band from the musicians' union, paraded in front of the town hall, shouting slogans of support for Yale and Towne workers.[6] A reporter described the atmosphere as "more like that of a carnival than of an industrial battle."[7]

Solidarity with the strikers—and contempt for Yale and Towne's president W. Gibson Carey, the husband of Henry Towne's granddaughter, united the crowd.[8] World War II veterans carried a banner that read "We licked the Axis and we can beat Carey." The crowd cheered when the union attorney Jerome Sturm told them, "Now the war is over and the company is seeking to break every union in this community." Sturm later told a reporter that Carey was "acting as the spearhead of a group here who think this is a propitious time to break unions."[9]

Downtown Stamford's theaters, stores, and streetcars closed down, while workers from industries in surrounding cities took the day off and sent contingents to the mass rally. The overwhelming display of public support elated the strikers, renewing their determination to win. As one striker enthused, "We knew that we had the support of 98 percent of the town when we went out but it does your heart good to see it out on the street, to know that there they are. People here in Stamford know each other. Why I could go through that crowd and pick out a bunch of my own friends and neighbors. Everybody could. We knew they were with us. But what a difference it makes just to see it."[10]

It made a difference to Yale and Towne executives, too. Just as the demonstration began, company negotiators made their first concession, offering a 14 percent wage increase while standing fast on the issue of union security.[11] Encouraged by this movement in negotiations, William Gatson, a conciliator from the U. S. Department of Labor, proposed a compromise settlement that would send most of the crucial areas in dispute to arbitration. "If the company doesn't follow along this suggestion," Gatson asserted, "it will be clear to my mind that they are trying to bust the union." Yale and Towne rejected the proposal.[12]

The turnout for the January 3 demonstration reflected deep support for the strike among many groups in Stamford. When company officials complained during that day's negotiations that the demonstration continued a pattern of illegal intimidation that city officials refused to stop, Mayor Charles Moore replied, "You haven't shown the spirit of the American way. You've put forth every argument as much as to say that you won't negotiate a contract. . . . I was slandered and the city of Stamford was slandered all over the country because I wouldn't send police to crack skulls."[13]

Labor groups clearly believed that Yale and Towne's negotiating posture threatened to initiate an era of union busting in Stamford. AFL and CIO locals pooled resources to support the strike and even voted to contribute one day's pay to the strike fund. "Why shouldn't we be united?" asked one striker. "You have AFL and CIO people in the same families, brothers and sisters. You wouldn't expect them not to go along with their own flesh and blood, would you?"[14] Shopkeepers also lent their support to the strikers. The Stamford Retail Merchants Association paid for a full-page advertisement in the January 11 *Stamford Advocate*, in which they urged Yale and Towne executives to negotiate a settlement in "keeping with the American Standard of Living." The ad went on to state, "We pledge our efforts on behalf of the families of the striking workers, and agree to make weekly contributions to the strike fund in order to maintain the health standard of the workers and their families."[15] One merchant who signed the advertisement later explained that he did so because he viewed the strikers' cause as just and because he thought he owed something to them, recalling, "Our store was three blocks from the plant. At the time Yale and Towne was the main industry. At least 60% of the workers passed the store every day. They were also, many of them, our customers. Without them we wouldn't have survived."[16]

Another motive for local small business support for the strike stemmed from long-standing suspicions about the greed of the company. It had long been rumored in Stamford that Ford Motor Company wanted to locate there, but that Yale and Towne kept them out for fear that their arrival would raise wages. Similarly, some wondered if the company wanted Stamford to get a reputation as a bad labor town in order to drive away industries that might force a rise in the cost of labor. A Westbrook Pegler column, syndicated nationally, intensified those suspicions when Pegler decried the violence in Stamford without ever having visited the city and without documenting any of his charges.[17]

The company's imperious attitude also helped build support for the workers. While Yale and Towne purchased newspaper advertisements that decried the illegal walkout on September 21 and condemned the "monopoly" held by the union, it never successfully established itself as the heroic party in the public mind. In a letter to the editor of the local daily newspaper, one resident asked, "When will Mr. Carey and others like him learn that workers aren't serfs to whom can be thrown a crust of bread in the form of a weekly paycheck?"[18] In a less-accusing tone, the paper's editorial column urged company officials to make concessions to the union, contending that Yale and Towne's past labor record called for a goodwill gesture. The editor warned the company that it might win the strike but wind up faced with a "sullen and dispirited" work force at a time when the nation needed high productivity.[19]

Despite broad popular support for the strike and despite threats of another one-day work stoppage, the company remained intransigent. Some workers who had witnessed the company's efforts to stall the processing of grievances, to harass shop stewards, and to provoke picket-line clashes as an excuse to use police power against the strikers responded with violence of their own. In late December, supervisory personnel who had been inside the plant found ignition wires torn out of their car engines. An unknown shooter destroyed an electric power insulator at the factory with a well-placed bullet. An epidemic of stone throwing shattered glass at the plant—and at supervisors' homes—early in January. James Callahan, a supervisor who had been reporting to the plant during the strike, left his home early on January 7, only to be confronted by two strangers who attacked him, inflicting injuries to his nose and upper lip. In the ensuing months police reported numerous incidents of supervisors' tires flattened, their car windshields smashed, and ignition wires torn from their engines.[20]

As the frustration of the long strike grew, workers explored more direct collective methods of advancing their cause. An office worker at Yale and Towne later related how white-collar workers and sales personnel hated to walk through the picket line because of the verbal abuse they received from strikers, recalling, "the women [on the picket line] were worse than the men."[21] On March 21, over six hundred strikers massed at the two entrances of the plant, kicking and jostling police officers who were attempting to shepherd supervisors into the building. "This is just a tip-off," exclaimed David Abrams of the combined AFL and CIO executive committee. "These people have got to get a decent legitimate contract," he warned.[22]

When company supervisors tried to charge through the picket lines the next day, eight hundred strikers stood fast and completely closed the factory. Police officers arrested twenty-one workers, and several days later the company secured a court order enforced by state police limiting the picket line to only twelve people at a time.[23]

On April 5, 1946, the company and the union negotiators reached an agreement with the aid of federal and state conciliators. The final settlement resembled the proposal rejected by the company in January in almost every detail, and consequently the strikers ratified it immediately by the surprisingly light vote of 563 to 251.[24]

Yale and Towne management had failed to break the union, agreed to wage increases they had previously rejected, and accepted the likelihood of arbitrators approving some form of maintenance of membership. On the other hand, they could look to the light vote on the final settlement and conclude that five months without pay had so demoralized the workers that they would be unlikely to strike again in the near future. In addition, if one accepts the argument that Yale and Towne wanted to establish an image of Stamford as a bad labor town, the bitter five-month strike with its mass demonstration and violence might very well have done so. From the strikers' perspective, the new contract raised wages and increased union security, but at a tremendous cost in lost wages and personal risk. The new agreement also provided no guarantee that the types of labor practices that provoked the September 21 walkout would be altered.

For both the company and the union, the strike involved a dimension beyond the terms of the final settlement. While management successfully utilized injunctions and state police power to protect its property, the strikers mobilized massive public support from people endorsing their demands as reasonable and just. The conscious attempt to transform the strike into a political struggle for public approval held the enduring significance of the conflict for both sides. For workers, the very act of articulating collectively their deeply held resentments against the company, and winning public recognition for them, constituted an essential part of the struggle. As one striker later affirmed, the presence of national news magazine reporters and the community solidarity "gave all a sense of participating in a great event." [25]

Whatever agreements the company and the union reached, workers enjoyed a sense of collective power and community support that would propel them in future shop-floor struggles with management. The one-day general strike had its own identity apart from the eventual resolution of the strike, and it provided a model strategy for workers in other cities, as evidenced by the general strike that gripped Lancaster, Pennsylvania, in February 1946.

Like Yale and Towne in Stamford, the Conestoga Transportation Company, operator of Lancaster's streetcar lines, traced its founding back to the nineteenth century. It was reorganized in 1931 while tottering on the edge of bankruptcy, and a new management team imposed 10 percent reductions in employee wages as one of its first acts. [26] Bitterly opposed to unions, the company reluctantly recognized the Amalgamated Association of Street, Electric Railway, and Motor Coach Employees as bargaining agent for its workers as a result of a WLB-sponsored election in 1942. Yet management took several years to negotiate its first contract and eagerly looked forward to the postwar period as a time to return to the "old days" of the open shop. [27]

Many of Lancaster's 60,000 residents found employment in defense industries during the war, and they feared massive unemployment once it ended. On August 21, 1945, the city's CIO council called for a forty-hour work week with forty-eight hours of pay to keep employment stable and compensate for lost overtime. In the two weeks after V-J Day, the local RCA plant laid off 1,200 workers with only one hour's notice, and citywide over 3,700 people lost their jobs. In the midst of these frightening developments, Conestoga Transportation Company announced that it would not renew its contract with the union.

The company asserted that it objected to the maintenance of membership clause in the old contract, as well as to a provision stipulating that the agreement would automatically be renewed at expiration unless either side gave advance notification. Conestoga officials claimed that maintenance of membership amounted to union dictatorship over employees and that the renewal clause constituted a perpetual contract. In response, trolley and bus drivers voted to strike at a midnight meeting as the old agreement expired on August 31. Perhaps aware of the divided 116–68 vote in favor of a strike, Lancaster's mayor, Dale E. Carey, confidently predicted a speedy resolution to the dispute, noting, "Lancaster people are not accustomed to strikes and public opinion will demand that transportation differences be quickly and amicably adjusted. I do not know anything about the current strike of transportation employees except what is reported in the newspapers but I do not feel their differences are great." [28]

Carey clearly underestimated the company's resolve to break the union, as well as the workers' determination to resist. The strike paralyzed transportation throughout the city, but efforts at mediation by prominent citizens proved fruitless. The company insisted that it could not accept a "perpetual contract," while the union countered that such claims obscured the company's real aim "to starve their employees and destroy the union." [29] Three weeks into the strike, the company sent letters to all strikers demanding that they report back to work or lose their jobs. Alleging that the walkout violated the old contract and the union's constitution—because the company had not received proper notification of a strike and because two-thirds of the drivers had not voted for the work stoppage as required by union bylaws—Conestoga announced its intention to resume trolley service. The union voted unanimously to continue the strike, but the company did lure a few drivers back to work. Although one strikebreaker received injuries from a woman picketer wielding a hat pin on September 21, city police officers pushed picketers off the tracks in front of the company's car barn on East Chestnut Street and trolley service resumed. [30]

To combat these reverses, the strikers turned to the community and called for a mass meeting on September 22 in Moose Hall. Over 1,200 people showed up. Even though AFL Central Labor Union vice-president Miles Messerman mentioned that some locals had talked of a "general sympathy strike in Lancaster County," the meeting adopted a more moderate course. After introductory speeches by union officials, speakers from the audience advanced various proposals for settlement of the dispute. Walter Mellinger, a local attorney and candy manufacturer, introduced a plan to send the strikers back to work without punishment, with all unresolved points to be sent to arbitration. Although different from the union's official position, the Mellinger proposal was endorsed by the union and workers in the name of community solidarity and the general welfare.

More important than the actual resolution was the process that produced it. Union representative A. H. Keeler told the crowd that the union
couldn't afford full-page advertisements to "bribe newspapers" and that
"we must depend on the people."[31] The people responded and expressed
their gratitude for being consulted. Dr. Charles Spotts of Franklin and Marshall College in Lancaster expressed dismay over the contingent of police in
the hall, asserting that "this is like an old town meeting." Rabbi Daniel L.
Davis told the crowd that he had approached Conestoga officials and volunteered his services as a mediator, but they refused. "Upon whomever
refuses to negotiate," he warned, "lies the burden of having a busless community."[32]

The Central Labor Union carried the Mellinger proposal (adopted at the
community meeting) to the company, after first empowering its officers to
call a "labor holiday" of all AFL unions in Lancaster County if management
turned it down. Conestoga officials announced that they might accept the
community proposal, but first they wanted union officers to admit in writing that the strike violated the law. Next they wanted a list of all demands
the union might make in future negotiations before they would consent
to arbitration. The company's intransigence torpedoed hopes for a settlement, and both sides redirected their efforts back to the picket lines.[33]

Four hundred picketers massed in front of the car barns to prevent the
trolleys from leaving on September 24. The crowd attacked drivers attempting to cross the picket line, injuring five, including one man stabbed in the
arm with a hat pin by a woman picketer.[34] Police officers arrested three
union officials on charges ranging from disorderly conduct to assault and
battery, while Conestoga representatives announced that they could not
meet with a citizen's mediation committee "in the midst of bloodshed
and riot."[35]

More violence accompanied the picketing on September 25, when a
strikebreaker attempted to drive his automobile through the picket line.
Angry picketers lifted one side of the vehicle off the ground and then
overturned it. Police officers arrested six strikers for rioting and unlawful
assembly, but several of the people on the picket line promptly brought
charges against the driver for assault and battery by automobile.[36] Incidents
of violence spread throughout the city. One man who crossed the union
picket line to return to work later recalled that the strike "made my life
miserable and in danger. They [strike supporters] burned down a chicken
house on my property one night and also upset my car when I was ordered
by the company to come to work or lose my job."[37]

By a vote of ninety-six to four, the transit workers decided to end their
work stoppage on September 26. They stipulated that the old contract
would remain in effect, that all drivers could return to work without pun-

ishment for their participation in the strike, and that negotiations continue. Paul A. Mueller, counsel for Conestoga, boasted that the settlement
represented "nothing but the company's original and unchanged position."[38] Yet the company's triumph was short-lived; workers drew upon
their picket-line experience, the solidarity formed during the walkout, and
the exhilaration of community support to continue to press their demands
in the ensuing months.

As Conestoga officers continued to drag out negotiations, the bus and
trolley drivers staged a one-day "work holiday" on Sunday, December 9,
to reaffirm the strike powers granted to their union officers in September. Charging that the new walkout voided the agreement that ended the
first strike, Conestoga terminated its contract with the union. As repeated
attempts at conciliation failed, the union launched another strike on February 6, 1946.[39]

As soon as picket lines appeared at the East Chestnut Street car barn,
Conestoga's management sent out letters warning strikers that they would
forfeit their jobs if they did not return to work immediately. In an effort
to rally popular opinion to its side, the company claimed that the real reason for the strike concerned the union's demand that management fire four
drivers for nonpayment of union dues. This attempted to place the onus for
putting people out of work on the union and to make the strike appear to
be nothing more than a power play by its officers. To help it win the strike,
the company called for "public spirited persons" to come forth and drive
its trolleys.[40]

The union also appealed to public opinion. Drivers decided to run a
free transportation service for the public by driving their own automobiles
along Conestoga's routes for the duration of the strike. On February 8, the
union began circulating petitions asking President Truman to seize Lancaster's trolley system and to put the strikers back to work under the terms
of the old WLB-approved contract. Two days later, the strikers announced
that their families would join them on the picket line to demonstrate family
solidarity in the face of the hardships imposed by the dispute.[41]

Conestoga used its political influence with the mayor's office to obtain
police protection for strikebreakers. When one hundred picketers clashed
with replacement drivers attempting to go to work on February 11, police
officers moved against the picket line, injuring six and arresting ten demonstrators (including the mother of one of the strikers). Believing that the
police presence provoked the clash, strike supporters rallied around local
CIO official Paul Shaub when he railed against "police using clubs on peaceful pickets, using them to hit the men over the head and poke them in the
eyes like animals. This kind of treatment is Gestapo rule and has no place
in Lancaster."[42]

As they did during the September strike, the AFL Central Labor Union called for a mass meeting to "enlighten the public as to the situation." This faith in the public produced extraordinary results, as a citywide mass meeting on February 14 formulated the decisive strategy of the strike.[43] Those present at the mass meeting voiced a clear interest in militant direct action, often to the dismay of union officials. When the crowd voted to go to the car barns en masse and enforce the picket line, Central Labor Union vice-president Miles Messerman admonished them that his organization could have no part in any mass uprising. When Messerman suggested that the meeting designate a committee to go see the mayor, a member of the audience suggested that they all go, but Messerman condemned that proposal as "mob violence." Finally a question from the floor demonstrated the sympathies of the crowd. Amid loud and sustained cheers, someone asked Messerman, "Why don't you call out all your AFL as they did in Connecticut?" Popular sentiment clearly favored a general strike patterned after Stamford's labor holiday.[44]

Within a week, almost all of Lancaster's workers went on strike in support of the trolley and bus drivers. Foundry workers from the Lancaster Malleable Castings Company instigated the walkout when 280 of them took a "labor holiday" to picket at the car barns on Saturday, February 16. After police arrested transit union official A. H. Keeler on charges of inciting to riot, the Central Labor Union voted on Sunday the seventeenth to declare a "no-work period" to begin immediately and "to continue until a settlement is effected."[45]

In the midst of an eight-inch snowfall, 14,000 workers from twenty-three AFL unions stayed away from work in Lancaster on February 19. Fifty picket lines appeared around the city, closing movie theaters, produce markets, factories, tap rooms, and chain stores. Women workers from the Ottenstein Garment Company turned out in large numbers to picket at the car barns.[46] Teamsters set up effective roadblocks on all access routes to the city to "remind" out-of-town drivers about the strike. More than 2,000 people showed up to enforce the picket line at Conestoga's car barns, and they easily turned away about 50 drivers attempting to work. A grocery store located a few blocks from the car barns served free coffee to the picketers, and AFL and CIO members mingled with their friends and neighbors in a triumphant atmosphere.[47]

By the second day of the general strike, the company felt compelled to resume negotiations. But it still complained that the crowd at its car barns constituted unfair intimidation and force. Not everyone agreed. When company and city officials asked County Sheriff John Pfeninger to call in state police to break up the crowd, he refused. Pfeninger insisted, "There is no trouble here, and we're not going to start any."[48] One striker later remembered the sheriff's role in the strike fondly: "The day before he [Pfeninger] called the CIO office and told us he was going to come out and check. John was an electrician and a union man. So we passed the word for everybody to hide. He came to the car barn and said everything is OK here. About fifteen minutes later the veterans the CTC hired tried to break the picket line [appeared] and the fight started again. Chief of Police Carlson was so mad he could bite nails."[49]

Slightly more than three days of a general strike produced what over seven months of negotiations could not—a signed contract between the company and the union. At 2:30 A.M. on Thursday, February 21, 1946, U.S. Conciliator John R. Murray announced an agreement that the union membership ratified that afternoon. By Friday, Lancaster went back to work. The two-year contract between the company and the union called for a small pay raise retroactive to September 1, 1945, increased retirement benefits, and contained a maintenance of membership clause without a union shop. As soon as the agreement went into effect, the city announced that all criminal charges stemming from the strike would be dropped.

Conestoga Transportation Company failed to break the union, had to grant higher wage increases than originally proposed, and wound up agreeing to a maintenance of membership clause. Yet the company held onto the open shop, secured employment for those who had crossed union picket lines, retained employees who had never joined the union, and paid a lower wage increase than the union originally requested. On the basis of contract provisions alone, neither side won a clear-cut victory.[50]

Yet in Lancaster, as had been true in Stamford, the strike experience itself produced important changes. The company had deployed its political and economic power in an effort to make the workers pay an extreme price for a small gain in wages and for limited union security. The workers and their allies relied on mass mobilization of their friends and neighbors to solidify wartime gains and to ensure their ability to fight for more in the future. The struggle made a lasting impression on those who took part in it. The strike was "all we heard about for a long time at home and work," one striker recalled, and another remembered the strike as "an inspiration."[51]

In both Stamford and Lancaster, medium-sized industrial cities with little history of labor conflict, old companies clashed with new unions as they struggled over the future. Militant actions by rank-and-file workers served as a pretext for employers to terminate contracts and force a strike. Aggressive behavior by state police in Stamford and by municipal law officers in Lancaster on behalf of company property motivated the machinists and trolley drivers to call upon their communities for demonstrations of support and expressions of defiance of management and its political allies. An undercurrent of violence underscored the failure of legitimate channels to end the disputes, and the emphasis on public support that developed during these strikes prefigured a politicized era of labor-management strife.

All parties to these strikes found themselves facing contradictions. The corporations wanted to break the power of unions, but instead unleashed mass disruptions and demonstrations. Resorting to government power to break the strikes ran the risk of counterintervention by federal judges and arbitrators, but local government—normally the tool of industries like Conestoga or Yale and Towne—proved unpredictable, as city officials occasionally favored the local residents on strike over the Yale and Towne executives with their offices in New York or over Conestoga's officers who took orders from the parent American Transit Company in Philadelphia.

Union leaders wanted to challenge the prerogatives of management and secure a role for themselves in managing production. Wildcat strikes and mass demonstrations offered them a bargaining tool with management, but, left uncontrolled, such activity threatened to undermine lasting contractual agreements. Union leaders encouraged and relied on rank-and-file militancy, but tried to control it at the same time.

Recognizing a temporary power vacuum necessitated by the uncertainty of the conversion era, workers wanted to overturn the wartime ban on strikes and wage increases and to secure steady employment with good working conditions. The purest expression of these desires came in the wildcat strike and mass demonstration, but company attacks made union survival the first priority. To strike for the survival of the union was to recognize a political reality, but it could also mean subordinating other goals for the time being. In addition, some of the forms capable of ensuring union survival, like arbitration, maintenance of membership, and work rules, often led to a situation that militated against expressions of other shop-floor needs.

In later years, competitive businesses would give in to corporate-liberal regulation as the surest means of obtaining labor peace, but in Stamford and Lancaster they stood fast in an attempt to protect their prerogatives from impingement by government, unions, and workers. In later years, unions would eye their own rank and file suspiciously as they clung to concessions granted by government or business, but in Stamford and Lancaster unions relied on the workers and their neighbors, merging their own institutional interests with those of the community at large. In later years, workers might find that militant struggles only brought their unions and their employers closer together into an alliance designed to ensure uninterrupted production, but in Stamford and Lancaster they transcended the barriers of institutional solutions and won victories by their own means.

In order to mount successful general strikes, workers in Stamford and Lancaster had to count on solidarity among their fellow workers and to expect widespread support from the general public. It is not easy to wage a sanctioned strike in even one workplace, and it is that much harder to pull other workers and members of the public at large into an unauthorized walkout that does not concern their own direct interests. As the sociologists T. Lane and K. Roberts explain, "To go on strike is to deny the existing distribution of power and authority. The striker ceases to respond to managerial command; he refuses to do his 'work.' "[52] But going on strike involves more than simply denying the existing power structure and its authority; it also entails the affirmation of oppositional power and the articulation of alternative sources of authority.

A general strike is especially significant, because it calls into being through collective struggle a community that has no legal standing or institutional status. Workers join a general strike because they see themselves as members of a class with fundamental interests in common. To give up wages and run the risk of being fired in order to help workers in another shop displays an extraordinarily intense class solidarity. Community members support general strikes when they view workers as representatives of a broad realignment of power that might benefit them as individuals and as a group. To defy legally constituted authorities as well as the interests of centralized wealth and power is not a step that most citizens take lightly. To see thousands of them doing so, as they did in the postwar general strikes, testifies to the potential for creating cross-class alliances emanating from within the incipient class formation of the postwar era.

Workers in the postwar era drew upon latent and active hostility to big business in building prolabor coalitions. Public opinion polls conducted for the National Opinion Research Center in 1945 found that almost 60 percent of respondents believed that most big businesses were making "more than a fair profit" at the time and that almost as many people felt that government should intervene and decide what constituted a "fair profit" for larger corporations.[53] During the 1945–46 strike in the electrical products industry, business executives found to their dismay that the unions enjoyed broad support both inside the factories and in the communities outside them. General Electric consultant Herbert R. Northrup later recalled that during that dispute "employees, including many new recruits of the war period, appeared vigorously to support the union's demands and to have little or no knowledge of the company side of the issues. Moreover, the community leaders, politicians, and merchants in areas where GE had plants, also seemed to support the union, to believe that General Electric employees were underpaid and to hold General Electric responsible for the strike."[54]

Like the General Electric strike, the general strikes in Lancaster and Stamford revolved around the usual disputes between labor and management, but they also entailed questions of the public interest and the general welfare. Those issues took on even more significance in the next wave of general strikes, as workers in industries serving the public took to the streets to provoke mass walkouts in Rochester, New York, in Pittsburgh, Pennsylvania, and in Oakland, California.

NOTES

1. While researching this book, I corresponded with more than fifty residents of Stamford and thirty residents of Lancaster with personal memories of the 1946 strikes. Many who provided information wished to have their identities protected, and I have respected their wishes. I have numbered all of the letters I have in my possession. I will identify letters by number in the notes. The quote is from Stamford letter 1, Apr. 14, 1978.

2. *New York Times*, Oct. 5, 1945, 24; *Time*, Mar. 4, 1946, 22.

3. *Stamford Advocate*, Jan. 2, 1946, 1, Jan. 7, 1946, 4.

4. Ibid., Sept. 22, 1945, 1, Sept. 25, 1945, 1, Jan. 7, 1946, 4, Jan. 12, 1946, 5.

5. Ibid., Nov. 7, 1945, 1, Nov. 8, 1945, 1.

6. Ibid., Jan. 2, 1946, 1, Jan. 3, 1946, 1–6; *Time*, Jan. 14, 1946, 17.

7. J. Mitchell Morse, "Stamford Sticks Together," *The Nation*, Jan. 12, 1946, 37.

8. Ibid.

9. *Stamford Advocate*, Jan. 3, 1946, 1–6; Morse, "Stamford Sticks Together," 37.

10. *Daily Worker*, Jan. 5, 1946, 2.

11. *Stamford Advocate*, Jan. 3, 1946, 1.

12. Ibid., Jan. 4, 1946, 1.

13. Ibid., Jan. 3, 1946, 1.

14. *Daily Worker*, Jan. 5, 1946, 2.

15. *Stamford Advocate*, Jan. 11, 1946, 9.

16. Stamford letter 4, Mar. 27, 1978.

17. Stamford letter 2, Mar. 10, 1978. In January, the *Stamford Advocate* dropped Pegler's column after it had printed numerous irate letters protesting against it.

18. *Stamford Advocate*, Jan. 29, 1946, 4.

19. Ibid., Jan. 3, 1946, 4.

20. Ibid., Feb. 8, 1946, 9.

21. Stamford letter 15.

22. *Stamford Advocate*, Mar. 21, 1946, 1.

23. Ibid., Mar. 22, 1946, 1, Mar. 25, 1946, 1.

24. Ibid., Apr. 6, 1946, 1.

25. Stamford letter 3, May 10, 1978.

26. Richard D. Shindle, "The Conestoga Transportation Company, 1889–1931," *Journal of the Lancaster County Historical Society* 80, no. 1 (1976): 49.

27. *Lancaster Daily Intelligencer Journal*, Sept. 8, 1945, 11.

28. Ibid., Aug. 22, 1945, 1, Sept. 3, 1945, 1.

29. Ibid., Sept. 15, 1945, 5.

30. Ibid., Sept. 20, 1945, 1, 6, Sept. 21, 1945, 1, 12; *New York Times*, Sept. 25, 1945, 16.

31. *Lancaster Daily Intelligencer Journal*, Sept. 22, 1945, 1, 4.

32. Ibid., 4.

33. Ibid., Sept. 24, 1945, 1.

34. *New York Times*, Sept. 25, 1945, 16.

35. *Lancaster Daily Intelligencer Journal*, Sept. 25, 1945, 1.

36. Ibid., Sept. 26, 1945, 1.

37. Lancaster letter 4, Aug. 4, 1978.

38. *Lancaster Daily Intelligencer Journal*, Sept. 27, 1945, 1.

39. Ibid., Jan. 16, 1946, 1, Feb. 5, 1946, 1.

40. Ibid., Feb. 7, 1946, 1.

41. Ibid., Feb. 7, 1946, 1, Feb. 9, 1946, 1, Feb. 11, 1946, 1.

42. Ibid., Feb. 12, 1946, 12.

43. Ibid., Feb. 13, 1946, 1; Lancaster letter 1, Aug. 4, 1978.

44. *Lancaster Daily Intelligencer Journal*, Feb. 15, 1946, 1, 6.

45. Ibid., Feb. 18, 1946, 1.

46. Ibid., Feb. 13, 1946, 1, Feb. 20, 1946, 1.

47. *Daily Worker*, Feb. 18, 1946, Feb. 19, 1946, Feb. 20, 1946; *Lancaster Daily Intelligencer Journal*, Feb. 20, 1946, 1, 5.

48. *Lancaster Daily Intelligencer Journal*, Feb. 20, 1946, 1, 5; *Daily Worker*, Feb. 20, 1946.

49. Lancaster letter 2, Aug. 3, 1978.

50. *Business Week*, Feb. 16, 1946, 90, Mar. 2, 1946, 99; *Lancaster Daily Intelligencer*, Feb. 22, 1946, 1.

51. Lancaster letter 2, Aug. 3, 1978; Lancaster letter 3, Aug. 4, 1978.

52. Quoted in Rick Fantasia, *Cultures of Solidarity: Consciousness, Action, and Contemporary American Workers* (Berkeley: University of California Press, 1988), 189.

53. *Business Week*, Dec. 24, 1945.

54. Ronald W. Schatz, *The Electrical Workers: A History of Labor at General Electric and Westinghouse, 1923–60* (Urbana: University of Illinois Press, 1983), 169.

CHAPTER SIX

"Everything Stops Today"

The General Strikes Spread

ORIGINATING as tactical responses to police violence and government intimidation, the general strikes in Stamford and Lancaster rapidly transformed themselves into expressions of a new kind of politics. When Connecticut's governor sent state police to break up picket lines at Yale and Towne, and when Lancaster's mayor unleashed the local police against strikers at Conestoga, workers in both cities counterposed their own mass activity to the power of legally constituted authority. By presuming to speak for the entire community, demonstrators in Stamford and Lancaster portrayed elected officials as not only unwise but also as illegitimate in their authority and no longer speaking for the people. This resort to participatory mass politics as an alternative to traditional legal rule spread to other cities in 1946, when repression of strikes provoked demonstrations and general work stoppages in cities across the country, including Houston, Rochester, Pittsburgh, and Oakland.

Houston's long history of moderate middle-class unionism made it an unlikely place for an insurrection, even a largely symbolic one, lasting only one day. But when municipal employees sought a 25 percent wage increase and the mayor and city manager responded with an offer of only 7 percent, they set in motion forces that evolved into a general work stoppage on February 26, 1946. The City-County Employees Union, Local 1347 of the International Hod Carriers, Building, and Common Laborers' Union of America, represented about 600 of Houston's city workers in 1946. Local president Oscar L. Duncan later recalled that his was a moderate union that began its meetings with the Lord's Prayer, a union that didn't have any radicals in it, "only just once in a while there'd be a drunk."[1] Yet the union voted to go on strike by a 179 to 41 vote, and their job action paralyzed city services, including street maintenance and garbage collection. The city manager declared that municipal employees had no right to strike and that he considered each of the strikers to have voluntarily resigned their positions with the city.[2] On the third day of the strike, the Houston Building Trades Council offered the strikers support from its 20,000 members. Less than a week later, the council, with approval from all AFL unions in the city, announced a one-day "labor holiday," asking all union members in "non-essential industries" to congregate at city hall to protest "the arrogance and utter lack of consideration from the mayor and city council for the welfare of the city employees and citizens of Houston.[3]

On Tuesday, February 26, Houston workers staged what the *Houston Chronicle* called "the greatest mass demonstration of organized labor's strength in Houston's history, or for that matter in Texas's history."[4] Somewhere between 5,000 and 10,000 workers demonstrated at city hall, with dockworkers, cab drivers, and construction workers particularly visible. City officials deployed nearly 90 percent of the police force to protect city hall, leaving only 35 officers to protect the city's 500,000 residents. Twelve hundred dockworkers walked off their jobs in the Houston Ship Channel, and 680 taxi cab drivers joined the march. The mass demonstration induced the city manager to meet with a "citizens' committee" (made up of labor representatives but called a citizens' committee so city leaders could insist that they had not engaged in collective bargaining with municipal employees) and he agreed to grant amnesty to the strikers and refer wage questions to the Civil Service Commission. Although the strikers did not win their desired wage increase, their public mobilization contributed to the defeat of Mayor Otis Massey and the election of labor-backed candidate Oscar Holcombe in November of that year.[5] Houston's general strike was a qualified success, but its greatest importance came from the unexpected militancy and mutuality it disclosed. Labor holidays in Rochester, Pittsburgh, and Oakland later in the year would reveal similar dispositions among previously moderate groups of workers.

Like Houston and most American cities, Rochester emerged from World War II with an increased demand for expensive city services but no corresponding increase in income. Wartime migrations sorely taxed the capacity of industrial cities to provide police and fire protection, welfare and health care, or educational and transportation facilities. As the federal government and large corporations passed these indirect costs of production on to municipalities, the cost of running local government in cities across the nation nearly doubled during the war years.[6] After the war, municipal employees attempting to keep pace with inflation and with wage gains granted to workers in private industry conducted strikes in more than forty cities in 1946 alone.[7]

In Rochester, municipal employees campaigned hard for postwar wage increases. On November 9, 1945, fire fighters, police officers, teachers, and other city workers "swarmed into City hall . . . to apply the heaviest collective pressure for salary boosts registered in recent years."[8] In December, the American Federation of State, County, and Municipal Employees announced plans to win recognition as bargaining agent for city workers in defiance of the wishes of the city manager and the "Committee of Twenty," an intensely anti-union civic group made up of the chief executive officers of local corporations.[9] Pressured by shortages of revenue, faced with increased demand for city services, and alarmed by the potential power of unionized public employees, Rochester's city administrators moved quickly to cut labor costs by eliminating jobs in the Department of Public Works so they could be contracted out to private firms.

With unconscious irony, city officials announced "sweeping changes" in street cleaning and garbage collection on April 8, 1946. The city instituted incentive pay and more rigid work standards for garbage collectors, street cleaners, and truck drivers. Intended as a means of transferring some of the city's financial burden on to its employees and to forestall the drive for union recognition, the measure backfired when angry workers announced that these moves had only strengthened their resolve to secure union representation for collective bargaining.

Opposed to unionization of city employees in theory and practice, City Manager Louis V. Cartwright took immediate steps to destroy the emerging organization. Contending that unionization would lead to exorbitant costs and would paralyze essential public services, he fired 489 maintenance, repair, and cleaning workers and abolished their jobs on May 15.[10]

More than class solidarity united the employees in the Department of Public Works. Many of them were Italian Americans who started working for the city because they felt they could not get higher-paying jobs in private industry because employment directors discriminated against Italian applicants. One later recalled, "When I was a kid when I got out of school you couldn't touch a job at Kodak because you were Italian. You would never get hired, believe me, that's the truth."[11] United by common cultural affinities as well as by their shared resentments about ethnic discrimination, the public works employees held firm. For them, their identities as workers could not be detached from their ancestry, from the neighborhoods in which they lived, from the churches they attended, or from the food they ate. In those respects, they were like many workers in the United States at the end of World War II. But like people in other cities, they also experienced the ways in which military service and shop-floor activism had broken down ethnic barriers during the war. They not only maintained solidarity within their own ranks but they found working-class allies from other ethnic groups as well.

Truck drivers in the Department of Public Works, belonging to no union themselves, became so outraged over the dismissals of their fellow employees that they refused to work the day after Cartwright made his announcement. Defying threats by supervisors that they too would be fired, all sixty-one of the department's truck drivers skipped work and joined a noon rally at city hall protesting the firings. Despite the anger of the five hundred workers and sympathizers at the demonstration, and despite assurances by organizers that the union constitution prohibited strikes by public workers and that the union had no intention of asking for more money, Cartwright reiterated his belief that to allow city workers to join a union would be countenancing the destruction of city government in Rochester.[12]

Continuing their defiance of their supervisors, truck drivers supporting the workers who had been fired reported to work on May 16, punched their time cards, and then refused to take trucks out of the garage. Enraged by this repeated truculence, Cartwright fired all sixty-one drivers immediately. The dismissed employees announced a strike against the city and its antilabor policies, setting the stage for public polarization between classes in Rochester. Labor groups condemned the city manager, while the daily newspapers inveighed against alleged attempts by union leaders to "run City Hall." For both sides, the main issue involved the use of government power. As the daily *Times Union* reminded its readers, whatever grievances existed over wages and working conditions paled in significance to the main problem, which was "that of control."[13]

On May 18, union workers and their supporters disrupted an appearance by New York State industrial commissioner Edwin Corsi at Rochester's annual "I Am an American Day" celebration at the Eastman Theater. As the ceremony began, a group of 150 union protesters elbowed their way into the auditorium and paraded through it chanting slogans and displaying signs protesting against the city's tactics in the labor dispute. They left the theater, but returned a short time later to demand that two of their representatives be allowed to speak. Vice-Mayor Frank Van Lare rejected that request, causing an outcry of protest from the audience that eventually led to a mass walkout joined by at least one hundred citizens from the audience. As the historian David Lee Hardesty notes, in this instance a celebration designed to obscure class differences in Rochester instead provided an opportunity for workers to present their demands for the right to speak and for the right to seek collective bargaining as consonant with the best traditions of the "American" past.[14]

City officials found other ways to try to exercise their control in the weeks that followed. On May 19 Republican party ward leaders telephoned several dismissed employees to offer them their old jobs back if they would only promise not to join the union. They refused. The next day over two hundred uniformed police officers and detectives attacked picketers at the

Department of Public Works garage "in a way which had not been seen in private industry since the passage of the National Labor Relations Act," according to an account in the *New York Times*.[15] Ultimately the police made 267 arrests as they tried to disperse the picketers and clear the way for trucks owned by private contractors hired by the city to collect refuse.

Once again repression made things worse for the city administration. A prominent Baptist minister complained that "it is undemocratic, unintelligent, and stupid to arrest people for disorderly conduct when no disorder exists."[16] Unionized private contractors feared being sucked into the city's labor strife at the expense of good relations with their own workers and refused to collect the garbage. A group of the local clergy defended the right of city workers to organize into unions, demanding that city officials initiate negotiations with union representatives. Representatives of the AFL and CIO unions announced plans for a mass rally on the steps of city hall, and three union leaders arrested for disorderly conduct on the picket line at the Department of Public Works garage warned of a strike by all workers in Rochester as a gesture of support for the city workers.[17]

On Wednesday May 22, Rochester workers added a new dimension to the strike. Mae Yost of the Waitresses' Union led a delegation of thirty women taking over the picket line at the Department of Public Works. At the same time, Baptist minister Antonio Perrata and Lutheran minister J. Norman Carlson led a delegation of seven members of the clergy serving picket duty.[18] The presence of women and clerics on the line made police officers less willing to arrest and beat demonstrators, keeping strikebreakers out of the shop, while it also emboldened workers who might be wavering out of fear of physical confrontations with the law. On Tuesday, the chief of police had ordered the arrest of more than fifty men for "hurling epithets" at police officers and scabs, but on Wednesday the police arrested no one despite "withering verbal assaults" from the waitresses.[19]

Over 5,000 workers from shops all over the city joined the AFL and CIO demonstration at city hall on May 23. Shaken by the overwhelming signs of public support mobilized by the city employees, City Manager Cartwright attempted to contain the upsurge before it got worse. He announced a three-day weekend "holiday" for public works employees and offered all dismissed workers the opportunity to resume their old jobs on Monday, May 27 under conditions as they existed before the firings. Despite these extraordinary concessions, Cartwright's gesture failed. The workers had come too far and risked too much to accept such a limited settlement. They demanded union recognition, back pay lost during the city's "lockout," and dismissal of all criminal charges arising from picket-line confrontations. When the city refused to comply with those terms, Rochester's municipal employees joined with approximately 35,000 AFL and CIO members to paralyze the city with a general strike.[20]

Early on Tuesday morning, May 28, Rochester bus and truck drivers halted their vehicles. Clothing workers walked away from their machines, and service workers in hotels and theaters stopped performing their jobs. Business establishments by the hundreds closed, but downtown Rochester filled up with curious and jubilant workers celebrating the expression of their collective power. Despite the crowded sidewalks, the difficulties of securing transportation, and the inconveniences of having stores closed, the mood on the streets remained festive. As one woman in the crowd exulted, "I would have come downtown today even if I had to crawl on my hands and knees. Just like V-J day, ain't it?"[21]

Another striker later recalled his amazement at the way the strike transformed the city: "It was a beautiful day, a beautiful sunlit day. As I walked I saw a spectacle I had never before seen in Rochester—a city proud of how clean it kept itself—the Flower City. But, on that day there was crap blowing all over the place. There was a nice breeze. Papers were blowing all over the place. That was a sight. No buses, and that was a sight never before seen in Rochester. No subways. Everything stopped."[22] The mess and the stunning silence both made evident the value of what workers did every day of the year; their importance and their power took on added significance when the strike made them inescapably clear. Rochester's consumption of electricity and gas fell by 25 percent on May 28, the percentage usually consumed by all business and industry combined.[23]

The successful and popular strike proved a huge embarrassment to New York's ambitious Republican governor, Thomas A. Dewey. Afraid of being labeled as a strikebreaker in an election year, Dewey intervened with members of his party in Rochester and urged them to use their influence to have the city recognize a union.[24] Dewey sent a state mediator to settle the dispute, but when he requested two rooms in city hall in which to conduct negotiations, he ran up against the obstinacy of City Manager Cartwright, who vowed that he would never let union officials set foot in the building. The mediator finally had to contact some of the city's leading industrialists, who recognized that Cartwright's attitude could hurt labor relations in all local shops and industries, and they prevailed upon him to settle the strike.[25]

In slightly less than twenty-four hours, Rochester's general strike brought labor a complete victory. The final settlement restored jobs to all the fired workers, promised dismissal of all disorderly conduct charges arising from picket-line incidents, and recognized the right of city workers to join a union. Although Cartwright emphasized that the agreement did not necessitate bargaining or official recognition of the union, no one could fail to see the gains made by city workers from the dispute.

As in all of the 1946 general strikes, worker solidarity held the key to victory in Rochester. The willingness of nonunion truck drivers to support the Department of Public Works employees, the cooperation extended between AFL and CIO unions, and the willingness of thousands of workers to mount a political and public response to city labor policies all helped shape the final settlement. The strike began with an attack on unorganized workers with little recognized capacity for resistance, yet worker solidarity turned a defensive struggle into a step forward. The ability to turn self-defense into victory exhibited in Rochester characterized strikes in other cities as well, most dramatically in the struggle between an independent unaffiliated local union and the Duquesne Power and Light Company in Pittsburgh.

Founded as a company-controlled union in 1937, the Independent Association of Employees of Duquesne Light Company (known as the IA) became truly independent during the war when it fought with management over arbitrary actions by supervisors. With no national union affiliation and extensive internal bickering, the IA found itself the frequent target of raids by AFL and CIO unions, but the IA always managed to close ranks when confronted with an outside threat, managing to maintain the allegiance of its membership.[26]

Composed of clerks, construction workers, meter readers, and repairers, the association found it difficult to formulate contract demands encompassing the interests of its diverse membership. Construction workers stressed fears of unemployment in response to company efforts to contract out its building projects to other AFL and CIO laborers. Repairers expressed concern over safety conditions, pointing out that they faced so many risks to life and limb that they were unable to obtain insurance. Older workers voiced complaints about inadequate pensions, while younger union members criticized their low pay and paucity of paid holidays.[27]

Duquesne Power and Light bitterly resisted all attempts by the union to challenge management decisions. Confident of their immunity from strikes because of the public's dependence on their services, Duquesne's management easily withstood a one-day walkout in February 1946, eventually agreeing to an arbitrator's ruling that pay be increased, but making no other concessions.[28]

At the time of the February walkout, the utility workers appeared timid, uncertain, and dispirited. But over the summer their mood changed. They notified the company that they would meet on September 3 to consider another strike. Whether the change in mood stemmed from the success of strikes in other cities, internal developments within the IA, or the company's intransigence remains unclear, but obviously there had been a change. As Pittsburgh's "labor priest" and radio commentator Charles Owen Rice reported from the September 3 meeting: "The atmosphere tonight is quite different from what it was last spring. Then the union members were tense, scared, and angry. Tonight there was no tension. Members of the union appeared very calm." [29]

Father Rice advised his listeners that the differences between the company and the union did not seem substantive enough to provoke a strike. But he warned that accumulated "bitterness, bad feeling, and frustrated pent-up anger" could prevent a peaceful settlement. They did. Infuriated by a last-minute letter from the company warning against a work stoppage, angry IA members voted by a two-to-one margin for a strike to begin on September 10 unless the company topped its last offer. [30]

Management personnel from Duquesne Power and Light made no official response to the union's strike declaration, but instead worked quietly to enlist the aid of city government to preclude a walkout. As workers began leaving their posts in anticipation of the strike deadline in the late evening of September 9, city officials requested and received a court order barring the strike because it threatened life, health, and property. The temporary restraining order prevented any strike activity until a hearing could be conducted ten days later. The specific wording of the complaint forced the IA to reconcile its own goals with the "public interest."

At the public hearing, IA president George Mueller denounced the injunction as unfair because it used the words "public interest" as an excuse to sanction antilabor practices by the company. Because the injunction took away the right to strike, Mueller charged that it mandated that "our souls belong to God . . . but our bodies belong to the Duquesne Light Company." Denying that public utility workers had any special responsibility to avoid strikes, he asked, "Who works for a living and in the long run does not serve the public?" Inverting the charges leveled at the union, Mueller presented the strike as a service to the public rather than an affront to it, reminding his fellow citizens, "We have shown the viciousness of this monopoly in existence in Pittsburgh today. We have shown how if they wish to change your rate, if the profits are in excess of what they should earn, if transportation is not as you desire . . . what can you do about it? What have you done about it?" [31]

Mueller did not offer to do anything about high rates, excess profits, or faulty transportation either, but he did argue that a strike could change working conditions at the $300 million corporation, which he characterized as "dominated by Wall Street interests." [32] When the court made the injunction permanent, Mueller exhibited further militance by lambasting the restraining order as a "scrap of paper."

Because of his flamboyant rhetoric and his public role as spokesperson for the IA, Mueller aroused suspicions among the populace that the strike might be a device to obtain personal power. David Lawrence, Pittsburgh's mayor, condemned the IA's "poor leadership," noting that "it has no international officers, no men like William Green or Phillip Murray to give it wise and competent counsel." Yet Mueller's militance seemed perfectly in step with the feelings and attitudes of the utility workers. Although he opposed the strike, Father Rice understood the logic of Mueller's behavior, telling his radio audience, "Mueller is not a power hungry megalomaniac. He is a tough union leader. He does not react in a way normal to the average union leader but he does not have a normal situation."[33] The situation that Mueller faced involved an angry and determined membership willing to defy their employer and a court injunction in pursuit of their goals. In the days after the court hearing, the company refused to negotiate and the union rejected any suggestions about arbitration. Amidst public apprehension about a complete power blackout, the IA stuck to its strike vote and began a new strike on September 24.

Outraged by this defiance of a legal court order, an incensed magistrate sentenced George Mueller to one year in the county jail for calling the injunction a "scrap of paper" and for allegedly fomenting the strike. As a hundred demonstrators massed outside the courthouse to protest his actions, the judge ordered an end to the walkout, threatening to jail all of the union's officers if the strike did not end immediately. The judge may have hoped that his stern actions would end the strike. In fact, they helped extend it into one of the most chaotic disruptions of the postwar era.[34]

At the very moment when the judge issued his orders, the IA voted to reject a new company offer by a vote of 1,771 to 402. When they heard of Mueller's imprisonment, the utility workers added a new threat, vowing to remain off the job at least until the judge lifted the injunction and freed Mueller.[35] Legal repression of the strike became an issue in itself, bolstering the militance of the IA and drawing thousands of previously uninvolved workers from other unions into the conflict. Sympathetic to the utility workers, angered by the partiality of the judge's ruling, and aware of the implications of a successful injunction for their own future struggles, rank-and-file workers throughout Pittsburgh surged into action by countering the power of the courts with the strength of their own collective direct action.

Sympathy strikes broke out all across Pittsburgh's vast industrial complex on September 25. Steelworkers from Jones and Laughlin's South Side and Second Avenue plants led the way, when 6,000 of them walked off the job and vowed to remain on strike until Mueller walked out of jail.[36] Streetcar operators and bus drivers withdrew their services, paralyzing the downtown area and forcing the closing of many offices and stores. Several

Westinghouse plants found themselves without a work force when electrical workers refused to use "scab power" provided by the struck utility.[37]

Not content with merely withholding their labor, the workers began to transform their protests into public political action aimed at settling the dispute on labor's terms. In response to a call by a local of the United Steel Workers union in nearby Homestead, 5,000 strikers and sympathizers marched on the city jail chanting slogans and demanding Mueller's release. Mounted police officers forcefully drove the crowd from the building, but by evening over 25,000 workers had joined the strike, portending even greater disruption and chaos in the future.[38]

Less carefully planned than the general strikes that preceded it, the Pittsburgh general strike nonetheless followed a familiar pattern. Responding to the use of repressive force, workers embraced mass disruption as the form of political action best suited to their needs. They also demonstrated their awareness of the effectiveness of general strikes elsewhere. Upon learning of Mueller's imprisonment, the United Electrical Workers District Council 6 issued a statement that warned, "What the workers of Rochester, New York, did recently, the workers of Pittsburgh can also do."[39] As a symbolic affirmation of power and self-worth, the strike also contained its own identity apart from the issues that provoked it. As one Pittsburgh striker exulted, "Boy, this is fun; we oughtta do this more often, but with pay!"[40]

The mass work stoppage sufficiently frightened the judge who put Mueller in jail that he asked for the prisoner to be brought from his cell after midnight to allow him to apologize to the court. The judge released Mueller on the condition that he attend a strike meeting and urge the IA to return to work. In a desperate effort to fulfill the intent of the original injunction, the judge recognized that he required Mueller's assistance to end the dispute, but he failed to understand the depth of commitment among the rank and file. Mueller and the strike committee counseled acceptance of the company's latest offer, but the rank and file still voted it down, refusing to accept any settlement as long as the injunction remained in force.[41]

Recognizing that the injunction had provoked the very disorder it attempted to contain, the Pittsburgh city administration executed a strategic retreat. Mayor Lawrence ordered the dissolution of the injunction after receiving promises from leaders of the CIO to support him against IA president Mueller. With Mueller free, and with no contempt citations pending, AFL and CIO leaders ordered a general return to work. But the utility workers refused to content themselves with a successful defense against an injunction; like the public works employees in Rochester, they intended to win their strike as well. Unhappy because the proposed new contract would eliminate too many construction jobs and offer too little in the way of improving pensions and vacations, the IA rejected management's offer by a secret ballot vote of 1,170 to 553 on September 27.[42]

The IA continued to ask for assistance from other workers—much to the dismay of most union leaders in Pittsburgh. When their own immediate self-interest appeared threatened by a punitive injunction, these officials sanctioned mass protest. Once the injunction ended, however, they resented having their members lose wages (and their own treasuries lose dues payments) because of a maverick local with no organizational affiliation and a proclivity for disrupting business as usual. The Pittsburgh Central Labor Union along with many AFL and CIO locals ordered their members to disregard IA picket lines. But they found it difficult to win rank-and-file cooperation to that end. Streetcar conductors and drivers from the Amalgamated Association of Street, Electric Railway, and Motor Coach Employees (Local 85) provided the bulwark of support for the striking utility workers. They refused to cross picket lines, shouted down representatives from the Central Labor Union, who told them not to recognize the legitimacy of the strike, and defied their own executive board to express militant solidarity with the strikers. Addressing a drivers' union meeting, AFL official Harry Travis demanded that they "get out and run those cars and destroy that union," but his audience responded with shouts of "no, no" and "not for me." John T. Morgan, business agent for the local, told the membership that "Mueller is not a competent or responsible labor leader and we do not recognize his union." Evidently the drivers disagreed. Father Rice noted that even the streetcar drivers who considered the IA to be wrong contended that it would be even worse to undermine their strike.[43]

Rank-and-file workers in other unions also pressured their leaders to back the strike. When CIO district director Anthony J. Federoff released a public attack on the strike, United Electrical Workers Local 610 repudiated his statement and issued a declaration of their own endorsing the walkout. Members of Teamsters Local 249 defied their own union executive board and honored IA picket lines. This support took on even greater significance when forces inside and outside of the union combined in an effort to end the strike once and for all and to break the union waging it.[44]

Once the utility workers went beyond their immediate goals of overturning the injunction and securing Mueller's release, they transformed the strike from a defensive struggle against repression into an aggressive challenge to the power and authority of labor leaders, business owners, and city officials. Because of their role in supplying electrical power, a crucial public resource, the strikers' threat was more than symbolic. Although they never shut off electrical power completely, the strikers did cause sporadic power shortages, and the possibility of a complete blackout permeated the entire dispute. In response to genuine ideological and political threats posed by the strike, leaders of business and labor joined forces against it, attempting to defeat the strikers with their own weapons by mounting a political and public campaign to discredit Mueller's leadership and to end the disruption.

Business leaders organized a public forum at Carnegie Music Hall at which the personnel manager of one of the city's major department stores urged citizens to contact strikers and urge them to revolt against their leadership.[45] Recommending arbitration already rejected by the union, Pittsburgh's daily newspapers praised an offer by the chamber of commerce to pay the costs of a mediated settlement. AFL and CIO officials continued to pressure local unions sympathetic to the strike, and on October 14 trolley conductors finally voted to return to work by a vote of 901 to 79. Union leaders hailed that decision as a sign of the strike's collapse and found further encouragement in the eruption of a factional fight within the IA itself.[46]

Early in October, a dissident group of utility workers claiming to represent 1,500 of the 2,000 strikers had condemned Mueller's leadership and pursued recognition from the company as a new union entitled to bargain for the striking workers. Supported by District 50 (the catch-all affiliate of the United Mine Workers) and enjoying the encouragement of Duquesne Power and Light executives, the dissidents secured an NLRB representation election for October 20 and announced plans for a referendum on accepting company offers of an arbitrated settlement.[47]

The dissidents lambasted Mueller as a dictator and presented themselves as defenders of democracy, a refrain calculated to appeal to the broader public finding itself at the mercy of the strike. Yet the charge evaded the deep rank-and-file commitment to the walkout, as well as Mueller's sensitivity to their wishes. As early as 1944 Mueller had incurred the wrath of the executive board of the IA by siding with wildcat strikers and refusing to order them back to work. During the 1946 strike, Father Rice attributed Mueller's actions to "his reading of the will and attitude of his members," and the priest actually cautioned Mueller that it was a mistake to be "so sensitive to the desires of his membership."[48]

Through a combination of physical force and political solidarity, IA members defended their association from all attacks. Acts of sabotage crippled Duquesne Power and Light's efforts to provide adequate delivery of electrical power; on October 9 two $50,000 transformers serving 30,000 people ceased to function for unknown reasons, and one week later a high-speed .22 rifle bullet shut off a 66,000-volt power plant.[49] Utility workers loyal to Mueller used physical force to break up a meeting called by dissidents to vote an end to the strike and negotiate a separate settlement with the company.[50] IA members established picket lines all over the city and defended them against police attacks when necessary.[51]

The violence undoubtedly intimidated the strike's opponents and fashioned a close bond among strikers based on participation in disciplined collective action, but it was political solidarity that ultimately proved decisive in the successful resolution of the dispute. In mid-October the IA won the NLRB election requested by the dissidents, garnering 958 votes to overwhelm three other unions who divided the remaining 457 votes. Having secured the survival of their organization, the IA agreed to arbitration by a narrow 1,197 to 797 vote and ended the strike on October 20.[52] Incidents of violence, internal dissension, and the inability of the strikers to fashion clear demands capable of retaining mass support all combined to retard efforts by the utility workers to extend the dispute's early triumphs into a satisfactory contract. Yet, in view of the forces arrayed against it, the IA's very survival must be considered a substantial victory in itself.

For twenty-seven days, this small union drew upon the support of fellow workers to withstand attacks from judges, city officials, labor leaders, prominent members of the business community, and the management of Duquesne Power and Light. Pittsburgh's working class walked off the job in defiance of monopoly power and state repression and attained their immediate objectives. When outside attacks and internal disputes transformed the strike into a battle for survival by the IA, it naturally spoke less directly to the needs and interests of other workers and commanded less enthusiastic support. Yet as a totality, the strike and mass demonstrations that accompanied it testified to the effectiveness of political action through public disruption. Within two months of the end of the Pittsburgh strike, workers in Oakland, California, provided a further demonstration of that power.

Shoppers in downtown Oakland became accustomed to the picket lines in front of two major department stores in November 1946. For better than a month, the Department Store and Specialty Clerks Union Local 1265 conducted picketing on behalf of the one thousand employees of Kahn's and Hasting's stores, in protest against their refusal to bargain in good faith with their employees. Although truck drivers from the AFL Teamsters Union respected the largely female picket line, the stores remained open for business as usual.

In the early morning hours of Monday, December 2, nonunion truckers from Los Angeles entered Oakland with shipments for the struck establishments. Somehow the strikers found out about the convoy, and 200 of them blocked the entrance to Hasting's store when the first truck drove up to it at 6 A.M. Anticipating trouble, the Oakland police force dispatched 250 foot patrol officers, 15 motorcycle riders, and 12 squad cars to shepherd the trucks through the picket lines at both stores. As word spread that city police were protecting strikebreaking truckers, demonstrators began to pour into the downtown area. Workers traveling to their jobs learned of the police action and took to the streets—stopping buses, streetcars, and cabs. The Alameda County AFL Labor Council announced a general strike to begin at 5 A.M. the next morning, but no announcement was necessary. The strike had already started in the spontaneous decisions by thousands of workers on Monday morning.[53]

In less than twenty-four hours, over 100,000 workers joined the Oakland general strike. By Monday evening, strikers had canvassed the city, ordering all stores to close except for pharmacies and groceries. The workers allowed bars to remain open on the conditions that they confine their sales to beer and that they place their jukeboxes out on the sidewalks and play them full blast. A carnival atmosphere prevailed as the jukeboxes played "Pistol Packin' Mama" and couples danced in the streets. Strikers directed traffic to allow anyone to leave but only permitting those with union cards to come downtown.[54]

On Tuesday night, 20,000 strikers crowded into Oakland Auditorium for a mass meeting while thousands of others stood outside in the rain, listening to loudspeakers broadcast speeches from inside. Representatives of 142 unions endorsed the strike and its demands, calling for an end to city interference in the strike and victory for the strikers at Kahn's and Hasting's.[55]

Throughout the city, strikers had to take direct action to enforce their control over work, traffic, and retail business. Bus drivers led the way in forming squads and conducting close-order drills. They kept order and prevented anyone from exploiting the strike for personal gain. Workers closed some grocery stores in order to extend diminishing food supplies, and they made sure that price gouging did not take place in those businesses allowed to remain open. Thousands of small and large decisions usually left to others had to be made openly and directly once the general strike went into effect. Out of desire and necessity, workers involved themselves in every facet of important choices that affected their lives.[56]

About 5,000 strikers picketed in front of Kahn's and Hasting's, yelling epithets at those inside the stores and preventing would-be shoppers from entering them. Workers stopped all traffic downtown, turning away trucks and buses at the city limits. "Everything stops today," said one picket captain, "and I mean everything."[57] As incidents of violence mounted and as the success of the strike became evident, condemnation of the strike rained down from several quarters.

The *San Francisco Chronicle* lambasted the work stoppage as an "emotional, unrestrained, juvenile reaction" to a police attempt to maintain order and protect property. Characterizing Oakland's labor leadership as "berserk," the paper editorialized against the labor holiday because it not only disrupted work but interfered with "the orderly processes of daily life" as well. Oakland's mayor, Herbert L. Beach, appealed for an end to the strike on the grounds that it exceeded the bounds of a legitimate labor dispute. It had become, Beach claimed, "an attempt to push aside the government created by all the people" and "an attempt to substitute the physical force of mobs for that government."[58]

Teamsters International president Dave Beck joined in the chorus of official disapproval of the strike, ordering members of his union back on the job. To Beck, the work holiday seemed "more like a revolution than an industrial dispute."[59] But rank-and-file Teamsters had other ideas. They continued to support the strike with such intensity that one local Teamster leader warned, "If Beck wants to enforce that order he'll have to come down here from Seattle himself and [even] then I doubt if he could do it."[60] Unable to end the dispute, Beck ordered the strikers to accept arbitration, but found that they had already rejected that possibility. "I say this damn general strike is nothing but a revolution," Beck fumed. "It isn't labor tactics," he added, "it's revolutionary tactics."[61]

Events on the streets seemed to confirm Beck's appraisal. Strikers battled with those they identified as "scabs" and forced the management of Kahn's to keep its employees in the store overnight when the Oakland police notified the store managers that they could provide no guarantee of safe passage for those challenging the strike.[62] Street disorders exceeded the capacity of the local police to control them, and suggestions to bring in outside force met with sharp resistance. One worker warned an impromptu rally in Lapham Square, "If the city fathers decide it is time to bring in the militia, we will decide it is time for us, not to lie down, but to dig in and fight."[63]

During the general strike, Oakland's workers took control over the city. They determined which businesses would open and what prices they would charge. Workers substituted their collective power for legally constituted authority, and they demonstrated a willingness to use any means necessary to enforce their control—including violence. The initial issues behind the strikes at Kahn's and Hasting's remained important, but city interference on behalf of management unleashed furious collective mass activity that added an important new dimension to the dispute. On a symbolic level, the strike became an affirmation of self-importance and self-assertion by workers, a warning to their enemies about the future. On a more immediate level, the strike itself brought into being a community, a social life, and a political process that gave those involved a glimpse of an appealing alternative to "business as usual." As strike participant Stan Weir recalled in his brilliant memoir of events, "Never before or since had Oakland been so alive and happy for the majority of the population. It was a town of law and order. In that city of over a quarter million, strangers passed each other on the street and did not have fear, but the opposite."[64]

Officials of organized labor could endorse the strike as long as it focused on censuring police strikebreaking, but the kinds of mass decision-making that accompanied the work stoppage threatened to undermine their authority and power. They took decisive action to regain the upper hand. After securing a promise from the city manager that police would no longer be used to escort strikebreakers across picket lines, the AFL Central Labor Council announced the end of the strike at 11 A.M. on Thursday, December 5. The workers, whose spontaneous actions initiated the walkout in the first place, played no role in ending it. They learned of their leaders' decision from a sound truck sent downtown by union officials. The settlement contained no victory for the striking clerks, and in fact, demobilized the strike at its peak. Almost immediately, angry workers attempted to defy their leaders and continue the general strike.[65]

On Thursday and Friday rank-and-file workers from various unions called for membership meetings to allow them to vote for a resumption of the work stoppage. Merchant sailors and truck drivers continued to picket downtown, and they asked others to join them. But without the official backing of their unions, workers found themselves subject to disciplinary action by employers for striking, and they failed to extend the walkout. After three days of merely reacting to the initiatives of the rank and file, union leaders finally took some action of their own; they used their power to end the strike and to dissolve the solidarity that had developed on behalf of the striking clerks.[66]

In the aftermath of the strike, a combined AFL and CIO political action committee successfully elected four prolabor representatives to the Oakland City Council. But with no ongoing movement behind them, they proved unable to translate elective office into any particular gains for labor. Yet despite its inability to win lasting gains, the Oakland general strike provided yet another example of the explosive possibilities of working-class mass action and of the new politics being forged in the streets of America's industrial cities.

In Rochester, Pittsburgh, and Oakland, defensive strikes with modest demands triggered mass uprisings among the entire working populations of those cities. Weak unions representing workers in jobs with histories of low pay and poor working conditions managed to win limited but real victories through mass disruptions that attracted substantial public support. In each case, employers used traditional methods of combating strikes: dismissals, injunctions, and physical force. But these conventional methods drew unconventional responses. By resorting to general strikes, workers expressed a collective understanding that their difficulties with management stemmed from public and political causes, that mass disruption could provide an effective tool for acquiring allies, and that their immediate needs as workers could and should be related to the needs of the community at large. Although their demonstrations were short-lived, and although they never found suitable mechanisms capable of securing gains in a continuing institutional way, working-class general strikes and disruptions in Rochester, Oakland, and Pittsburgh served notice—to friend and foe alike—of the potential power of direct action.

The wildcat strikes, mass demonstrations, and labor holidays of 1946 indicated the willingness of workers to defend themselves against attacks from management and government, as well as displaying the stirrings of independent political action. Labor's foes dismissed the strike wave at the immediate end of the war as "blowing off steam," a matter of releasing war-related angers and frustrations. But as they continued into 1947, these outbursts of working-class self-activity revealed themselves to be more than simple responses to wartime economic and social realignments. They displayed a revolt against work, against exploitation, and against hierarchies rooted in the experience of labor itself. As forceful repression produced only limited success, managers, sociologists, and industrial relations experts searched for ways to bring about industrial peace. To their dismay, they found that explosive and unresolvable contradictions lay imbedded within the very process of work under capitalism. Consequently, the pressure of rank-and-file labor unrest provided the definitive impetus for two major innovations in the American political economy in 1947—the Taft-Hartley Act and the Marshall Plan.

NOTES

1. Marilyn D. Rhinehart, "A Lesson in Unity: The Houston Municipal Workers' Strike of 1946," *Houston Review* 4, no. 3 (Fall 1982): 140.

2. Ibid., 141, 142.

3. Ibid., 145, 147, 148.

4. *Houston Chronicle*, Feb. 26, 1946, cited in Rhinehart, "A Lesson in Unity," 148.

5. Rhinehart, "A Lesson in Unity," 148, 149, 150. Rhinehart points out that the strike also contributed to the passage of repressive antilabor legislation including a state right-to-work law.

6. Sam Shulsky, "The Financial Plight of Our Cities," *American Mercury* (Jan. 1948): 17–19.

7. Sterling D. Spero, *Government as Employer* (New York: Remsen, 1948), 221–23.

8. *Rochester Democrat and Chronicle*, Nov. 9, 1945, 19, quoted in David Lee Hardesty, "The Rochester General Strike of 1946" (Ph.D. diss., University of Rochester, 1983), 11.

9. Hardesty, "The Rochester General Strike of 1946," 24.

10. *Monthly Labor Review* (July 1946): 87.

11. Hardesty, "The Rochester General Strike of 1946," 9.

12. *Rochester Times Union*, May 16, 1946, 1.

13. Ibid., May 17, 1946, 22.

14. Hardesty, "The Rochester General Strike of 1946," 52–56.

15. *New York Times*, May 30, 1946, 2.

16. Hardesty, "The Rochester General Strike of 1946," 147.

17. *The Nation*, June 8, 1946, 678; *Rochester Times Union*, May 21, 1946, 1, May 23, 1946, 1.

18. Hardesty, "The Rochester General Strike of 1946," 74–75.

19. Ibid., 74–76.

20. *Rochester Times Union*, May 24, 1946, 1, May 27, 1946, 1, May 29, 1946, 1.

21. Ibid., May 29, 1946, 1A.

22. Hardesty, "The Rochester General Strike of 1946," 31.

23. Ibid., 187.

24. *The Nation*, June 8, 1946, 678.

25. Spero, *Government as Employer*, 221–23.

26. File 10, box 76, Father Charles Owen Rice Papers, Archives of Industrial Society, University of Pittsburgh; *Business Week*, Feb. 5, 1944, 98.

27. *Monthly Labor Review* (Oct. 1946): 593; file 10, box 76, Father Charles Owen Rice Papers, Archives of Industrial Society, University of Pittsburgh; Charles Owen Rice Oral History, Pennsylvania State University Archives, 6.

28. Radio transcript for Sept. 9, 1946, file 10, box 76, Father Charles Owen Rice Papers.

29. Radio transcript for Sept. 3, 1946, file 10, box 76, Father Charles Owen Rice Papers.

30. Ibid.

31. Radio transcript for Sept. 22, 1946, file 10, box 76, Father Charles Owen Rice Papers.

32. Ibid.

33. The quote from Mayor Lawrence comes from Neil W. Chamberlain, *Social Responsibility and Strikes* (New York: Harper, 1953), 195. Rice's characterization of Mueller comes from the radio transcript for Sept. 3, 1946.

34. *Daily Worker*, Sept. 25, 1946; radio transcript for Sept. 24, 1946, file 10, box 76, Father Charles Owen Rice Papers.

35. *Daily Worker*, Sept. 27, 1946, 3.

36. Ibid.; *Monthly Labor Review* (Oct. 1946): 593.

37. *Daily Worker*, Sept. 27, 1946; *Monthly Labor Review* (Oct. 1946): 593.

38. *Pittsburgh Post-Gazette*, Sept. 25, 1946, 2, Sept. 26, 1946, 1.

39. *Daily Worker*, Sept. 27, 1946, 3.

40. *Pittsburgh Post-Gazette*, Sept. 27, 1946, 11.

41. Ibid., Sept. 26, 1946, 1, 3, 9.

42. Radio transcript for Sept. 28, 1946, file 10, box 76, Father Charles Owen Rice Papers; Chamberlain, *Social Responsibility and Strikes*, 205.

43. *Pittsburgh Sunday Sun and Telegraph*, Oct. 3, 1946, 2; *Daily Worker*, Sept. 30,

1946; radio broadcast, Oct. 1, 1946, file 10, box 76, Father Charles Owen Rice Papers.

44. *The Militant*, Oct. 12, 1946, 2.

45. *Daily Worker*, Oct. 8, 1946, Oct. 10, 1946, Oct. 13, 1946; *Pittsburgh Sun and Telegraph*, Oct. 3, 1946, 1.

46. *Pittsburgh Sun and Telegraph*, Oct. 14, 1946, 1.

47. *Daily Worker*, Oct. 13, 1946; *Pittsburgh Sun and Telegraph*, Oct. 13, 1946, 1, Oct. 16, 1946, 1.

48. *Business Week*, Feb. 5, 1944, 98; undated papers, file 10, box 76, Father Charles Owen Rice Papers.

49. *Pittsburgh Sun and Telegraph*, Oct. 9, 1946, 1, Oct. 15, 1946, 1.

50. Ibid., Oct. 15, 1946, 2.

51. Ibid.

52. Ibid., Oct. 21, 1946, 1.

53. *San Francisco Chronicle*, Dec. 3, 1936, 1, Dec. 5, 1946, 1.

54. Stan Weir, "American Labor on the Defensive: A 1940s Odyssey," *Radical America* 9, nos. 4–5 (July–Aug. 1975): 178. Weir's firsthand account of the strike constitutes an extraordinary document, which supplied most of the descriptive and interpretive concepts for this section.

55. *The Militant*, Dec. 14, 1946, 1–2; *San Francisco Chronicle*, Dec. 4, 1946, 1.

56. Weir, "American Labor on the Defensive," 178–79.

57. *San Francisco Chronicle*, Dec. 4, 1946, 8.

58. Ibid.

59. *Newsweek*, Dec. 16, 1946, 35.

60. *San Francisco Chronicle*, Dec. 5, 1946, 1.

61. Ibid.

62. Ibid., 2.

63. Ibid.

64. Weir, "American Labor on the Defensive," 181.

65. Ibid.

66. *San Francisco Chronicle*, Dec. 6, 1946, 1; Weir, "American Labor on the Defensive," 181.

PART THREE

Politics and Power,
1947–50

CHAPTER SEVEN

"More Radical Than Their Leaders"

The Taft-Hartley Act

FEW PIECES of legislation have evoked more emotion and less understanding than the Taft-Hartley Act. An enduring legacy of the confused state of labor-management relations in the postwar years, the bill remains cloaked in mythology for proponents and detractors alike. Neither a "guarantee of individual freedom" nor a "slave labor act," Taft-Hartley merely adapted existing labor legislation to the new challenges posed by rank-and-file militancy. Consistent with traditional corporate-liberal aims of stability, predictability, and security, the bill addressed itself primarily to restraining mass strikes, to ensuring management control over production, and to preventing rivalries within unions from leading to excessive demands on management.[1]

To be sure, some political conservatives and competitive-sector capitalists may have thought that passage of Taft-Hartley would break the power of "tyrannical" union leaders, secure freedom for individual workers, and, not so incidentally, improve the profits of business. Correctly diagnosing "monopoly" as the source of their declining economic and political power, they ignored monopoly capital and incorrectly assumed that union "monopolies" protected by the Wagner Act allowed unscrupulous leaders to foment strikes and make ruinous demands on management. Yet since most of the concrete measures capable of preventing labor unrest actually employed the powers of the state to help large corporations and big unions restrain the rank and file, many Taft-Hartley proponents unwittingly accelerated the very process they sought to reverse. Their failure demonstrated the ascendant power of corporate liberalism and prefigured the impending collapse of traditional conservative politics into a pale reflection of its liberal counterpart.

For both conservatives and liberals, the repeated strikes of the postwar era exposed fundamental inadequacies in existing labor legislation. Wartime frustration and the difficult adjustment to peacetime life could no longer explain labor unrest as it persisted into the winter of 1946–47. *Fortune* editorialized that American trade unionism "carried with it echoes of the class struggle and of Marxian dogma," and the independent activity of rank-and-file workers seemed to bear out the validity of that assessment.[2]

Teachers in St. Paul, Minnesota, went on strike in November 1946 when the board of education increased the budget for improvements on buildings, but not for teachers' salaries. Parents' groups and civic organizations supported the strike, successfully pressuring elected officials into changes in the city charter allowing for wage increases.[3] Public sentiment also proved decisive in Buffalo, New York, in February 1947, when 2,400 teachers walked off their jobs and secured wage increases consistent with rising living costs.[4] A work stoppage in the same month by coal miners in Pennsylvania's Panther Valley provided vivid illustration of the capacity of small disputes to explode into major conflicts. Thirteen miners who lost pay for refusing to work under unsafe conditions staged a sixty-hour sit-down strike, provoking a mass walkout in other mines. The protest paralyzed coal production in the area for weeks, until pressure from the federal government extracted a promise from employers to install better ventilation, remove stumbling hazards, place telephones in all active sections of the mines, provide hats and goggles for workers, and transport miners and explosives in separate cars.[5]

In addition to the continued spate of local strikes, John L. Lewis's recurrent battles with the coal industry combined with highly visible strikes by railroad workers to place labor-management relations squarely in the public eye. In a time of economic and political uncertainty, independent (and largely successful) action by the working class posed a major threat to business stability. Although both political parties wanted to limit the frequency of strikes, the Republican victory in the 1946 congressional elections ensured a major legislative effort in that direction.[6] Robert Taft, the leading Republican in Congress and a contender for his party's nomination for president in 1948, expressly sought the chair of the Senate Committee on Labor and Public Welfare to help write major revisions in the nation's labor law.

Testimony by business leaders before Senator Taft's committee revealed a belief that the Wagner Act of 1935 and subsequent NLRB activity favored labor, encouraged union leaders to exploit business operators as well as their own rank and file, and allowed practices inconsistent with traditional American freedoms. Yet when pressed for specifics, it was the general strikes and mass disruptions instigated by labor's rank and file in 1946 that often emerged as the "abuses" the business community wanted to be corrected.

General Motors president Charles Wilson told the committee that general strikes and nationwide work stoppages harmed the public interest and posed a direct threat to the legitimacy of government and its responsibility to maintain law and order.[7] Ira Mosher, chair of the Executive Committee of the National Association of Manufacturers, branded the general strikes in Rochester and Oakland as "the favorite tool of subversive forces to disrupt a stable government" and "coming as close as we can come to civil war without actual armed conflict." Mosher went on to link mass picketing with mob violence in a number of 1946 strikes, including the one at Yale and Towne, alleging that such tactics carried echoes of the sit-down strikes of the thirties.[8]

Calling the committee's attention to the "discomfort, violence, and grave public hazard" posed by the Oakland strike and its "mob violence resembling insurrection," Roland Rice of the American Trucking Association lavished praise on Teamsters president Dave Beck as a "responsible union head" who "much to his credit moved in rapidly and quelled the disturbance." Yet Rice added that with "effective federal law the outburst probably never would have started."[9] W. Homer Hartz, president of the memorably named Morden Frog and Crossing Works of Chicago and a director of the U.S. Chamber of Commerce, lambasted the Oakland strike as an unjustifiable attempt by unions to punish the public at large for the actions of a few employers and the city government.[10]

Although many business leaders could agree on their hostility to working-class strategies of independence, they disagreed sharply on its causes and on possible remedies. The battle over Taft-Hartley appeared to be a struggle between unions and management, but that surface conflict obscured an even more bitter struggle between the competitive and monopolistic spheres of American business. The growing power of monopolistic firms and the resulting pressure on competitive businesses shaped the contours of the debate over Taft-Hartley.

The experience of the steel industry provides graphic representation of the ascendancy of monopolistic firms at the expense of competitive ones. Despite government-approved monopolistic practices, steel factories in the depths of the depression operated at less than 20 percent of capacity. Wartime spending raised that figure to 98.1 percent of capacity by 1943, with larger companies securing particular advantages in obtaining materials and equipment. By September 1944, basic steel producers had almost completely absorbed the competitive steel-drum fabrication industry. The big mills controlled 87 percent of steel-drum fabrication amounting to 435,000 tons of steel per year, a form of "forward integration" that also removed large amounts of semifinished steel from the market, increasing pressures on nonintegrated small companies.[11]

After the war, close cooperation between the industry and government further advanced the concentration of power in the hands of the largest producers. United States Steel's purchase of the Geneva plant in Utah, built by the government for $202 million but sold for $47 million, increased the Pacific Coast capacity of that company from 17.3 percent of the total regional production to 39 percent. The government sold three other war plants to large producers and approved acquisitions consolidating regional near-monopolies for large firms, solidifying oligarchy within the industry at large.

Bolstered by these advantages, United States Steel raised prices on semi-finished steel in February 1948 by an average of $5 per ton, creating a greater expense for competitive firms. Three months later, the industry's giant led the way to reductions on finished steel products, concentrating on the products made by small competitors.[12] These practices, coupled with friendly assistance from monopoly corporations in other industries like the huge loans extended to Jones and Laughlin Steel and to Republic Steel by General Motors in 1951, helped secure the triumph of monopolistic steel companies over competitive ones.[13] While steel-drum fabricators went out of business, the profits of Republic Steel increased from $9 million in 1945 to $10.5 million in 1946, and those of United States Steel went from $58 million in 1945 to $88 million in 1946.[14]

In the face of an already-precarious economic situation, labor militancy in the postwar years presented a particularly grave threat to competitive enterprise. Monopolistic firms might be able to trade wage increases for the stability of long contracts, but smaller businesses could not. In fact, they sometimes wound up paying the price for concessions granted to workers in the monopoly sector.

Big businesses passed on to consumers the burden for higher wages by raising prices. Smaller firms had to pay these higher prices too, but then discovered that their workers also demanded higher pay in order to keep pace with price increases and to keep pace with monopoly-sector workers receiving the higher wages. In addition, as unions negotiated longer contracts covering wider areas, they established nationwide patterns that they expected to see reflected in all contracts regardless of the size of the employer. C. Dickerman Williams, the vice-president and general counsel of the American Locomotive Company, provided a graphic illustration of what that process could mean for competitive business in his testimony before the Taft Committee in January 1947. Williams charged that the 1946 steel strike produced a departure from decentralized bargaining by the United Steel Workers locals and that the union's international officers established "an absolute, flat rule" as to how wages should be negotiated. As the United States Steel wage increase became the pattern for the industry, American Locomotive felt compelled by union intransigence to pay the same raise—although unable to avail itself of the larger firm's profit structure, political influence, or price flexibility. President Truman allowed steel makers to increase their prices because of the wage increases, thereby increasing costs for steel buyers like American Locomotive. Unable to raise its own prices because of government price controls and existing contracts to deliver products at fixed prices, the company found itself subsidizing the wage increases of somebody else's workers and facing increased labor costs in its own plants, but denied the possibility of price relief.[15]

Williams directed his anger over this situation against the union rather than against U.S. Steel, but his description of the pressures on competitive enterprise accurately reflected the constraints facing companies like American Locomotive. Nor did Williams speak in isolation; numerous witnesses before the Taft Committee cited the plight of small firms as the most compelling reason for new labor legislation. Senator Taft himself stressed the point in a Senate speech in which he conceded that "large employers can well look after themselves," while he bemoaned the circumstances facing small businesses subject to the possibility of unions organizing their employees or "interfering with the conduct of their business."[16]

In their struggle to gain a new national labor policy, members of the competitive sector of the business community reacted to their declining status within the national economy. The campaign for Taft-Hartley embodied the last gasp of a declining group desperately trying to make national policy conform to their own interests. Unwilling or unable to identify the growth of the monopoly sector itself as the source of the problem, small business leaders aimed their political attacks at the increasing power of labor within the corporate-liberal elite and at the threat posed by rank-and-file activities. They identified real challenges to their own interests, but by making labor the scapegoat for all of their frustrations they attacked symptoms rather than causes, ultimately fashioning reforms that accelerated the very processes they sought to reverse.

The failure to present a comprehensive program capable of offering a viable alternative to corporate liberalism reduced competitive business leaders to the role of a subordinate pressure group—helping to determine the parameters of policies inimical to their own interests. Nothing more clearly illumines that process than the changing public posture after the war of the National Association of Manufacturers (NAM), the most important lobbying organization for competitive businesses and the self-appointed representative of all industry.

NAM clearly identified itself with the concerns of the competitive sector from the time of its founding at the turn of the century. The historic enemy of unions and the defender of the open shop, NAM bitterly resisted unions and opposed corporate-liberal innovations that granted short-term concessions to workers in the interests of long-range stability. Even when the Great Depression proved conclusively to millions of Americans that conventional economic wisdom had led the nation to the brink of ruin, NAM attributed public support for government intervention in the economy to false propaganda and popular ignorance of the accomplishments of free enterprise.

When NAM members spoke of free enterprise, they made no distinction between competitive and monopoly spheres, but their rhetoric focused on the concerns of small business. NAM's origins in the turn-of-the-century economy and its self-perpetuating executive board contributed to the kinds of conservative ideology associated with the competitive sector: hostility to government spending, opposition to federal regulation of private industry, and resistance to unions. These small-business interests remained relevant to NAM's membership in the postwar period, as over 70 percent of member firms employed fewer than five hundred workers and exhibited other qualities particular to the competitive sector.[17]

Of course, ideology cannot always be reduced to self-interest. B. E. Hutchinson played an important role in formulating and expressing NAM's policies, despite his role as a top executive of the huge Chrysler Corporation. General Electric—whose officers sometimes preached corporate-liberal principles while practicing paternalism with their own workers —held membership in the organization, although its top officers did not. Between 1933 and 1946, 125 large corporations comprising less than 1 percent of the total membership provided 63 percent of NAM's directors, 88 percent of its executive committee members, and 79 percent of the finance committee members.[18] Whether for reasons of personal experience, political conviction, or circumstantial self-interest, these executives from large firms provided leadership in articulating the problems and interests of smaller ones.

Consistent with its competitive-sphere outlook, NAM waged a relentless campaign to repeal the Wagner Act and the recognition that it gave to unions from the day of its adoption in 1935. Postwar labor-management strife provided new incentives for that effort, but changing conditions led to a drastic alteration in the organization's strategy. The failure of a million-dollar anti-union advertising campaign in 1945 and a growing recognition that NAM's negative image undermined its effectiveness motivated some members of the group to propose a more liberal labor policy.[19]

At the 1946 NAM convention, delegates expressly rejected a resolution to repeal the Wagner Act and opted instead for an appeal to make the law more amenable to the interests of business. *Newsweek* noted that, in the eyes of NAM's leadership, attempts to "turn the industrial time clock back to the early 1930s" had only provoked virulent opposition from labor and from the public at large. In order to create a climate of "stabilized prosperity," management had to get more power over its own affairs but also needed to "win the confidence of labor and hold the confidence of the buying public."[20] Newly elected NAM president Earl Bunting announced the organization's intention to pursue just such a program. Describing the group's shift as "an evolutionary thing, more than just an about face; it's an abandonment of prejudices which some of us have had in the past," Bunting resolved that "it's our aim now to go right down the middle of the road."[21]

That section of the road was already well traveled. NAM's support for Taft-Hartley grew logically out of its new commitments and placed it well along the path to corporate liberalism—in direct opposition to traditional conservative principles. At every turn Taft-Hartley conflicted with long-cherished principles of the competitive sector. It invoked the power of government to redress an alleged imbalance in the bargaining positions between labor and management—a principle that conservatives found repugnant when it worked in favor of unions in the Wagner Act, but evidently acceptable if state action favored business as it did in the Taft-Hartley bill. The proposed law's prohibition against the closed shop and restrictions on the union shop violated freedom of contract between employers and unions. Mandatory public financial statements by unions made a mockery of political rights and privacy rights, as did requirements that union leaders sign noncommunist affidavits to secure NLRB protection for their organizations. Juridical limits on the right to strike challenged the ideal of a job as a voluntary relationship between worker and employer and increased presidential authority to ask for antistrike injunctions gave the executive branch of government more power than ever before to regulate the affairs of private citizens. Attempts to ban mass picketing and sympathy strikes usurped the powers of local law-enforcement officials by superimposing federal law over existing municipal and state ordinances.

Why did competitive-sector conservatives lobby for and support a bill that conflicted with so many of their basic political beliefs? For some of them, conservatism simply masked self-interest and greed. They wanted to make as much money as possible without outside interference, and they would support any measure that facilitated that end. Others—with a more principled commitment—found that Taft-Hartley offered a way to explain and perhaps reverse their increasing powerlessness without having to question even more basic concepts about the capitalist system. Supporting the bill meant endorsing its tacit assumptions, especially the ideas that workers joined unions because of government regulations rather than their own wishes, that demagogic labor leaders provoked strikes against the will of contented workers, and that pressures on smaller businesses originated from actions by government and labor, rather than from the expanding power of monopoly corporations. In a rapidly changing world, Taft-Hartley offered the illusion that minor reforms could restore the validity of a world-view whose base had seriously eroded in the midst of economic changes brought on by the war.

Yet utilitarian self-delusion does not explain completely why principled conservatives like Senator Taft and his admirers could recommend policies inimical to all they held dear. Generalizing from their own experiences and personally comfortable economic circumstances, they projected a vision of America in which limited government allowed individuals to succeed on their own merits, where voluntary cooperation among citizens protected the general welfare. Proceeding from these goals, they identified serious flaws in the emerging corporate state: its regimentation, bureaucracy, and unresponsiveness to popular wishes. Yet the insights that made for such trenchant criticisms of the status quo also suffered from flaws of their own when conservatives tried to translate them into an affirmative policy around which the rest of society might be mobilized.

A genuine conservatism might have had enormous relevance for the postwar world. Policies designed to limit the reach and scope of government could have exposed the dangers of a garrison state and an economic expansionist foreign policy. Proposals for local autonomy and local control might have offered workers and employers mechanisms for negotiating contracts based on local realities rather than the needs for standardization of large business and government bureaucracies. In addition, a principled conservatism respecting the right of citizens to hold political opinions without persecution by the state might have posed a formidable obstacle to anticommunist hysteria. But the "conservatism" that emerged out of the postwar period favored big government, militaristic nationalism, and plutocracy. Conservatives in the thirties and forties had failed to explain what would prevent their cherished ideal of limited government from merely clearing the field for private exploitation or how their much-vaunted system of voluntary cooperation would not degenerate into elite collusion against the public at large. Economic policies that assumed a fundamental antipathy between all business and all government became obsolete when monopoly corporations and the state discovered ways to work together for their mutual advantage. Appeals to rugged individualism and the freedom to succeed on one's own merits understandably appealed more to the small minority that had already succeeded than to the vast majority that found limited opportunity blocking the way.

Conservatives had long charged that corporate-liberal policies would undermine old values and dangerously transform power relations in American society. Their predictions proved accurate, but those very changes made the conservative worldview increasingly irrelevant to large groups of people. Wartime economic changes strengthened the monopoly sector, decreased both the number and power of those in the competitive sector, and gave new initiative to workers. Under these circumstances, conservatives had difficulty formulating policies that could draw support from other groups, and increasingly they came to represent no interests but their own. Without a credible class consciousness capable of making their own interests synonymous with those of society at large, conservatives found themselves defending what was left of their immediate interests at the expense of fundamental principles.

Corporate liberals like Averill Harriman, Jesse Jones, Gardiner Means, and Paul Hoffman suffered no such handicaps. They knew that in order to maintain wartime prosperity, major adjustments in the economy would be necessary. They rapidly took the initiative to implement their vision of a harmonious, efficient, and productive society. Just as competitive-sector conservatives relied on NAM to advance their views, corporate liberals created lobbying associations of their own. From the turn of the century, corporate liberals had worked through groups like the National Civic Federation (1904), the Twentieth Century Fund (1919), the National Planning Association (1934), and the Committee for Economic Development (1942) to promote stability through labor-management-government cooperation.[22] As they faced the postwar world, corporate liberals committed themselves to drastically increased peacetime federal spending in pursuit of one main goal—full employment.

Elite research foundations and lobbyists did not originate the pressure for full employment. Through their votes, strikes, and demonstrations during and after the war, workers in the United States made clear the political dangers that depression-level unemployment might pose, but corporate liberals attempted to redirect popular desires for full employment for their own purposes. Under the right conditions, full employment could not only bring political stability and labor peace but it could also serve as a popular slogan capable of winning support for government programs to assist business in attaining full production, economic expansion, and high profits.

The Committee for Economic Development (CED) took the lead in articulating the interests of the monopolistic sphere in the postwar era. Founded in 1942 under the guidance of Secretary of Commerce Jesse Jones, CED attempted to advance business-oriented solutions to the problems of reconversion.[23] From the first, the committee's public statements stressed the importance of extending wartime employment and production levels into the postwar years. CED public reports argued that insecurity about unemployment undermined consumer confidence and lessened the demand for goods. Asserting that it would take a 30 or 40 percent increase in consumer spending to keep the economy at acceptable levels, the CED embraced Keynesian economics in its renunciation of a balanced federal budget and its encouragement of increased federal spending as a means of subsidizing consumer demand in times of recession. Fearful that another depression would seriously hurt the reputation of capitalism and cause it to lose legitimacy among the general public, the CED supported government action to keep up employment—even defying NAM and the U.S. Chamber of Commerce in its support for legislation in 1945 affirming the nation's commitment to full employment.[24]

That concern for full employment constituted a major preoccupation for Americans as they surveyed the postwar world. A study by the Federal Reserve System Board of Governors called "a rise of forty to fifty percent above pre-war levels in consumption goods . . . possible and necessary" to maintain wartime levels of production and employment.[25] Writing in the prestigious *Harvard Business Review* in 1945, Malcolm P. McNair noted a shift from popular acceptance of unemployment as the necessary price to be paid for a high standard of living to a public expectation that prosperity requires full employment. Yet, while acknowledging the overwhelming economic, political, and psychological pressures for high employment, McNair articulated a widely shared opinion that the United States would have enormous difficulties trying to implement such a policy.[26]

Full employment during the war had depended on enormous government expenditures and on the stability coincident to a market where one customer (the government) bought half of the goods. Despite the great wave of wildcat strikes, a spirit of sacrifice kept down labor disputes, while a steady flow of capital and guaranteed profits made it easier to maintain uninterrupted production. None of these conditions seemed likely to prevail in the postwar era. The return of more than ten million servicemen and women seemed certain to aggravate insecurities about unemployment. High peacetime government spending might lead to serious inflation and an increased national debt, but a return to prewar economics seemed certain to doom chances for even high and stable employment, much less chances of a job for everyone who wanted one.

As early as March 1945, a National Planning Association report argued that even enormous increases in government spending would not produce full employment. No reasonable projection of federal expenditures would be sufficient to guarantee wartime levels of production and employment. Even if public confidence in the economy reached unexpected levels and stimulated great increases in consumer purchases, the report found the economy structurally unable to support full employment without major reforms. One reform that the report said might help would be to raise the income and purchasing power of the poor without increasing prices. This suggestion asked business owners to subsidize consumer demand by lower-ing profits, essentially calling for narrowing the gap between rich and poor as the only path to a viable economy. Such short-term concessions might have actually led to long-term security for the system, but few business owners could accept a plan calling for lower profits, and fewer still could endorse the revolutionary effect such a scheme would have on American economic and political life.[27] Instead, they sought to persuade labor that it had more to gain from an expanding U.S. presence in the world economy than from a redistribution of resources at home.

The internal logic of their own position brought corporate liberals to the hard realization that the only way capitalism could guarantee full em-ployment would be by being something other than capitalism. Unwilling to make basic changes in the system, corporate liberals attempted to pacify popular demand for full employment by moderating the goal into keep-ing employment numbers as high as possible consistent with traditional notions of private property and profit.

In the winter of 1946–47, the Department of Labor's *Monthly Labor Review* presented a series of articles about the difficulties of implementing full employment. Contending that "there can be no basic difference of opinion" as to the desirability of universal employment, the articles went on to point out that achieving it required unprecedented increases in con-sumer and investment spending. The problem might be evaded for a few years in the early postwar period—as long as accumulated wartime savings and continued shortages of goods encouraged high spending—but in the long run only major economic adjustments could prevent large-scale un-employment.[28]

Corporate liberals did not want to go as far toward the goal of full employment as labor demanded, but neither could they endorse the hos-tility to full employment emanating from the competitive sector. To con-servatives, government efforts to increase employment could take three forms—all undesirable. Government could initiate public works programs that would take money away from "productive" investment to underwrite what they considered to be unnecessary and unproductive "make-work" programs. Government could raise taxes and increase spending, thereby provoking inflation and placing an intolerable tax burden on present and future generations. Or government could so closely control the economy in order to keep up employment that it would undermine traditional free-doms by collapsing the distinctions between economic and political power in a collectivist state.[29] Correctly assuming that corporate liberals wanted full employment largely for political reasons, competitive-sector conserva-tives exerted political pressure of their own against it.

Caught between the pressures from labor to ensure full employment and

from competitive-sector conservatives to limit government spending, corporate liberals faced a serious dilemma. To give in to labor's demands risked
moving toward socialism; to submit to the wishes of conservatives ran the
risk of an economic stagnation and renewed depression that might lead to
fascism. Public opinion reflected an awareness of this dilemma. Nearly 70
percent of the respondents to a January 1947 *Fortune* poll expected a widespread depression within the next ten years, with only 16 percent viewing
a depression as unlikely.[30] A postwar survey of labor leaders disclosed that
55 percent of AFL and 69 percent of CIO leaders viewed fascism as a serious immediate or potential threat to the United States.[31] Four separate polls
conducted between 1937 and 1946 demonstrated that anywhere from 12
percent to 21 percent of the general public perceived a drift to communism
as a real possibility in America.[32]

Through a mixture of sophisticated analysis, a clear sense of self-interest,
and shrewd manipulation of other groups, corporate liberals negotiated the
difficulties of the postwar era without capitulating to depression, socialism, or fascism. Ironically, the very complexity of the problem pointed to a
possible solution. The anger of competitive-sector conservatives provided
a means to restrain the aggressive demands of labor, while the specter
of labor uprisings led conservatives to accept government activity they
would otherwise oppose. Apprehensive about the anti-union sentiment
among conservatives, labor leaders embraced corporate policies with even
more zeal than before. Concerned about the apparently ascending power
of labor in national affairs, conservatives granted to the state powers that
they would have denied it under other circumstances.

Two of the nation's most brilliant social scientists identified the contours of this policy as it emerged. In a remarkably prophetic article in *The
Nation* in December 1946, Robert S. Lynd argued that capitalists could not
provide prosperity or full employment and that they would soon launch a
campaign to blame others for their failures. Lynd predicted that the business community would hedge on its promises of full employment, blame
labor unions for price increases, and ascribe their failure to find new markets overseas to Soviet subversion of world stability. Lynd further predicted
that capitalism's own failures would compel its leaders to drape free enterprise in the cloak of "democracy" as a way of avoiding concrete evaluation
of its real weaknesses, while simultaneously encroaching on democratic
processes themselves in the name of law and order. Finally, Lynd argued
that capitalists would try to extend wartime prosperity by tightening the
bonds between business and government, even to the extent of going to
war if that became economically necessary.[33]

In his 1948 *The New Men of Power*, C. Wright Mills advanced a similar argument. Mills contended that the corporate liberals (whom he called

sophisticated conservatives) made concessions to labor in prosperous times to keep production flowing smoothly. But they stepped back and allowed competitive-sector conservatives (practical conservatives in Mills's lexicon) to attack labor during economic slumps. Such policies restrained labor's demands and helped frighten union leaders into accepting "the lure offered by co-operative big business."[34] While these interpretations by Lynd and Mills may have imputed more self-awareness and cunning to individual capitalists than they actually possessed, their analyses nonetheless correctly identified the dynamics that led to the passage of the Taft-Hartley Act.

Despite his ringing veto message, President Truman had previously endorsed most of the main provisions of Taft-Hartley, as had other liberals in politics and business. Since assuming the presidency, Truman had himself proposed mandatory cooling-off periods to prevent strikes, bans against jurisdictional disputes and secondary boycotts, and increased federal arbitration and fact-finding. Truman had proposed even stronger antistrike measures during the May 1946 railroad work stoppage, when he called for selective use of military conscription as a way to break strikes. The president did not act in isolation; although genuine differences existed about what policies would be most effective, corporate liberals agreed on the need for some government action to restrain labor.

While the Taft Committee conducted hearings on the senator's proposed bill, CED released its own program for labor peace. CED advocated ten days of compulsory mediation before strikes and lockouts, asked that supervisors no longer receive NLRB protection in their efforts to unionize, and demanded punitive measures to prevent "minority" groups from staging sympathy and jurisdictional strikes.[35] In modified form, all three provisions eventually appeared in the Taft-Hartley law.

Corporate-liberal representatives took direct measures to influence the competitive sector's campaign against labor. Harold Stassen, formerly governor of Minnesota and now a corporate lawyer and spokesperson for the Republican party's eastern financial and industrial elite, addressed NAM's annual convention in 1945, urging legislation limiting strikes. "The right to strike must be maintained," Stassen claimed, but "rarely used," like "the right to shoot in self-defense."[36]

An even more important corporate liberal expressed similar sentiments at the group's 1946 gathering. Railroad and shipping magnate, secretary of commerce, and international diplomat Averill Harriman drew upon his years in business and government to alert NAM to the dangers of strikes. Pointing specifically to walkouts by the United Mine Workers and to speeches by their leader, John L. Lewis, Harriman charged, "Labor power has grown to the point where we find one man defying the government and recklessly tearing down the life of the nation."[37] Harriman and Stassen emphasized that NAM members had legitimate grievances against labor, but took pains to make sure that remedial action would be kept within the confines of the intentions of the Wagner Act—to encourage and stabilize collective bargaining.

Senator Taft accepted those limits. He told the Senate that labor peace hinged on "reasonable equality at the bargaining table" and reaffirmed in the law a national commitment to orderly and effective labor-management negotiations.[38] Taft encouraged participation in the drafting of his act by senators known to be sympathetic to organized labor and with characteristic fairness produced a bill truly representative of the committee's diverse opinions. Taft's moderation proved to be good politics; his Senate version contained the essence of the eventual law, while the more extreme House version drawn up in Representative Hartley's committee became buried under a barrage of objections. But Taft's commitment to collective bargaining represented more than a ploy to get legislation passed. It demonstrated the essentially moderate nature of the bill, its congruence with prior legislation, and the limited nature of the conservative critique. Attempting to accommodate traditional conservative theory to the new world shaped by corporate-liberal successes, Taft and his supporters found themselves co-opted by the assumptions and values submerged within existing government laws and practices.

One witness before the Taft Committee recognized the transformation in Taft's position and attempted to trap him in his own contradictions. Speaking out against the bill, attorney Louis Waldman proclaimed the desirability of limiting government's role in collective bargaining as much as possible. Taft recognized the argument and asked if the attorney would also favor repeal of the Wagner Act on that basis. When Waldman replied he would not, Taft scolded him with a revealing outburst indicative of the senator's reasons for accepting more regulation in the name of restraining labor. Taft replied, "Well, then, I think that your argument it seems to me, is perfectly foolish, because the whole field is so regulated by law that a few more additional laws, subjecting the field to a few more regulations than they have now would not make any difference whatsoever. I cannot see your point, where you say you want to leave everything alone, if you have the Wagner Act; there is hardly anything less [left?] to be left alone."[39]

Taft's contention that the Wagner Act's very existence contained an internal logic directing any reform measures to take the form of more laws and regulations articulated a very important truth. In fact, the Wagner Act was never the radical measure that competitive capitalists described it as. The bill's provision granting the "right" of collective bargaining to workers had only mattered in those shops where unions already had sufficient support and strength to demand representation elections. Wagner's law overturned the possibility that some courts might rule (as they had in the twenties) that both unions and corporations could enjoy rights as "legal persons." Instead, it defined unions as instruments of labor peace sanctioned by the state and bound within statutorily defined limits.[40]

Taft's belief that the law needed to be "balanced" to serve the interests of competitive-sector conservatives rested on the fiction that government regulation and trade-union coercion instigated rather than restrained rank-and-file militancy. Taft's efforts to write legislation consistent with his beliefs led him through trivial and tokenistic reforms until he came face to face with what corporate liberals already knew: that labor unrest originated with the rank and file and that effective restraints came from strong government and unions, not weaker.

Several provisions of the act challenged alleged government partisanship on behalf of unions. The new law replaced the U.S. Conciliation Service with the Federal Mediation Board. It divided the NLRB's investigative and judicial functions. It attempted to limit the Department of Labor's influence over the NLRB. In an effort to overturn specific NLRB decisions favorable to unions, Taft-Hartley limited the discretionary powers of the NLRB and strengthened the freedom for employers to counter union claims during organizing drives. These changes settled old scores and vented long-standing anger, but they addressed minor issues in minor ways, evading the major causes of labor disputes. But the sections of the bill designed to curtail "abuses" by labor unions spoke directly to those causes.

In contrast to the Wagner Act, Taft-Hartley proclaimed an intention to protect the interests of individual workers, as well as those of unions and companies. In truth, the desires of workers did often conflict with those of their leaders, but Taft-Hartley inverted reality by assuming that coercive leaders compelled contented workers to strike. To remedy that alleged condition, the bill demanded (1) that a majority of workers in a bargaining unit approve any provision calling for employees to join the union within a specified period of time after being hired, (2) that individual workers not risk losing their jobs by refusing to join a union, and (3) that employees be free to attempt to decertify unions if they no longer wished to be represented by them.

As subsequent experience under the law established, these "reforms" spoke to false issues. Workers joined unions by their own free will in most cases, and they went on strike because they wanted to, not out of fear of union retaliation. Attempts to secure labor peace had to move beyond reforms of union procedure and come to grips with the attitudes and opinions of the rank and file, as Senator Taft finally realized in an exchange with his Republican party rival, Harold Stassen. In an appearance before the Taft

Committee on February 7, 1947, Stassen advocated legislation allowing a secret ballot vote on management's last offer before any strike could take place. In an ironic reversal of roles, the liberal Stassen argued that union leaders must be prevented from forcing workers to strike, while the conservative Taft retorted that more often than not the leaders wanted to settle, but the rank and file wanted to strike. Taft claimed he had no objection to demanding such a vote, but argued that it offered a trivial remedy to a serious problem. The senator added, "I think he ought to have the right to vote, but I don't think it's going to solve the strike problem. I think the men are more radical than their leaders in most cases."[41]

More radical than their leaders? The implications of that statement did not escape the editors of Business Week, who made special note of Taft's observation. "If Taft is right," they argued, "we proceed best toward the goal of labor peace by strengthening the hands of those leaders of the unions by giving them a larger measure of control over their members than they now possess."[42] The editors did not view their conclusion as completely desirable at that time, but their formulation of the problem proved to be accurate. Ultimately, labor peace could be won only by restraining the rank and file and by strengthening the institutional power of trade unions. The Taft-Hartley law attempted to achieve both of those objectives.

Coming to grips with the problem of rank-and-file direct-action protests required more than just administrative changes in the NLRB or alterations in union procedures; it necessitated serious efforts to restrain mass strikes, to ensure management control over production, and to prevent union rivalries from leading to overtly militant demands on management. By increasing union powers to police their own members, the Taft-Hartley Act helped transform labor leaders into agents of labor peace, but also into agents of the state as well. Many practices proscribed by the new law already violated state and local statutes, but federalizing the offenses allowed for multiple penalties for the same act, while lessening the likelihood that popular local pressure could provide license for illegal measures. In addition, NLRB sanctions against unions for wildcat strikes, sympathy strikes, and secondary boycotts made the institutional survival of the unions dependent upon their control over the rank and file.

Consistent with Senator Taft's assertion that "the men are more radical than their leaders," the bill attempted to restrain that radicalism by specifying as unfair labor practices many of the tactics employed by workers in the 1946 general strikes. Threats, violence, and mass picketing violated local laws in every one of the general strikes, but they proved to be successful weapons when public support gave them sanction. The new law banned these tactics, not because of their violation of popular will, but because of their dramatic success in mobilizing and expressing it. Similarly, it was

the ways in which the 1946 strikes demonstrated labor's ability to go beyond its own immediate demands and unite the public behind issues with
broader implications that provided the impetus for Taft-Hartley's prohibitions against sympathy strikes and secondary boycotts.

As a potential political force, labor provided the only real obstacle to
corporate-liberal desires for export-oriented free-trade policies. But corporate liberals also worried about the possibility that labor might mobilize
political coalitions capable of extending the reforms of the New Deal era
into fundamental social change. Writing months before the introduction of
the Taft-Hartley Act, a vice-president of the St. Louis Union Trust Company advised an aide to President Truman, "I think there is no question
but that if labor is permitted to consolidate its power and to use that power
to elect more Claude Peppers and Henry Wallaces to positions of authority,
we shall find ourselves in a position in which labor is stronger than the
government of the United States and is able to dictate to it."[43]

Attempts to curb the rising political influence of labor coincided with the
parts of the law designed to ensure management control over production—
also an emerging goal of corporate liberals. In the early forties, decisions
by the NLRB and WLB—agencies dominated by corporate liberals—subor-
dinated workers' rights to measures designed to ensure stability and industrial peace. The Twentieth Century Fund's Committee on Labor issued a
report in 1944 advising unions that "to serve themselves best they must
serve the common prosperity most." A federal court of appeals in 1944
ruled that workers had no right to conduct a wildcat strike even though it
did not violate their union's contract with their employer, holding that the
purpose of the Wagner Act "was not to guarantee to employees the right to
do as they please but to guarantee to them the right of collective bargaining for the purpose of industrial peace."[44]

In order to help corporations secure control over production decisions,
the Taft-Hartley Act denied NLRB protection and procedures to foremen
and supervisors trying to unionize. In that way the bill's sponsors hoped to
curtail the growing strength of supervisory unions and preclude the possibility of an alliance between foremen and the rank and file. Opposition to
supervisory unions did not focus on any potential demands that supervisors
might make themselves or on their capacity to foment rebellion among the
workers. Instead, corporate hostility to organization of supervisory personnel stemmed from a largely correct perception that unionization indicated that foremen were willing to follow the strategic and philosophical
leadership of the rank and file in a struggle against management.

Collective bargaining for supervisors became a widespread demand in
mass-production industries in the early postwar years, as the strength of
production workers' unions stimulated interest in similar representation

for white-collar and supervisory personnel. Union contracts undercut the authority of supervisors, and gains made by the rank and file sometimes came at the expense of salaried personnel. Caught in between conflicting interests, supervisors had to bear the brunt of rank-and-file discontent with work, while serving as the focal point for management anger over inadequate production. Supervisors took on the responsibilities of management without the rewards, and they shared the hours and income of workers minus the security of union representation. Disillusioned with the promise of mobility associated with a management job, many foremen in mass-production industries cast their lot with labor and began to form unions of their own.

Witnesses before the Taft Committee stressed the threat posed by these unions to management control over production. Noting that supervisors did no essential work by themselves, labor relations specialist Theodore Iserman warned that foremen would have to court favor with the rank and file to win support for their demands and to assure respect for their picket lines. As an example, Iserman pointed to organizing efforts at Ford Motor Company by the Foreman's Association of America, where he alleged foremen threatened to strike when the company ordered them to discipline workers for leaving work early, punching each other's time cards, and loafing in washrooms. Whether out of fear or reprisal, as Iserman claimed, or out of an identification with the interests of the rank and file, such actions did support his contention that "an independent foremen's union lends itself to the purposes of the rank and file union."[45]

Those advocating restrictions on supervisory unions also worried about the effects of foremen's unions on productivity. "The foreman is responsible for efficiency," testified Clarence Bleicher, president and general manager of Chrysler's DeSoto division, "and when I speak of efficiency I am talking about turning out the stuff at the lowest possible cost." Bleicher went on to emphasize that management could control the speed of assembly lines, but that only the foremen could control the speed of the material handlers and other nonautomated workers. If management already experienced difficulty "turning out the stuff at the lowest possible cost," what would happen if foremen identified with rank-and-file workers, whom Bleicher referred to as "the other side?"[46] This determination to secure management control over production manifested itself in Senator Joseph Ball's opposition to supervisory unions. In testimony on behalf of the bill, the senator pointed to the "growing solidarity and discipline in unions" as reasons to suspect that foremen's associations would "divide the loyalties of management at the critical point where it is in direct contact with day-to-day production."[47]

Taft-Hartley's supporters recognized that even an unbroken chain of management command would not bring about labor peace. The most important sections of the bill attempted to enlist the aid of unions in disciplining the rank and file and securing labor peace by making unions responsible for damages stemming from wildcat strikes carried on or encouraged by "unions or their agents." These sections identified rank-and-file work stoppages as the real enemy of economic stability and wrote into law even greater incentives for unions to stop them than had previously existed.

Proponents of the Taft-Hartley Act often boasted of their intention to make the unions more democratic and to give the individual worker more power. Yet the new law respected individual rights only when their exercise helped prevent strikes. The bill steered clear of any attempt to regulate internal union politics to allow for more democracy, and by holding unions accountable for wildcat strikes it actually encouraged union bureaucrats to consolidate their power in the name of controlling the ranks. If forced to make a choice between unpredictable union democracy and labor peace, the authors of Taft-Hartley unhesitatingly cast their lot with labor peace. Philip Murray, who had already begun tightening the grip of the CIO on local affiliates, clearly understood the implications of this part of the bill when he told the Taft Committee, "If the financial responsibility of the union is to be expanded to include liability for actions of all these 'agents' even when the acts are not authorized or ratified, then this bill is actually encouraging and insisting that, in self-protection, the unions impose greater centralization so as to confine authority and agency only to the highest and most restricted levels of leadership."[48]

Perhaps that realization explains why Murray was able to make his peace with the law despite vocal (although largely tokenistic) initial opposition. When the bill became law, workers staged mass demonstrations in protest. More than 100,000 people marched against the law in New York City, and a mass work stoppage in Detroit drew an estimated 500,000 workers away from their jobs while 250,000 joined a mass protest march against the bill. The United Mine Workers and the United Electrical Workers both called for a general strike against the act, but the president of the CIO refused to support them.[49] In later years, Murray's godson Phil Curran recalled the CIO president telling a Republican member of Congress that he bore him no ill will for supporting Taft-Hartley and, had their positions been reversed, Murray claimed that he would have done the same thing. Curran added that Murray did not regard Taft-Hartley as "any sort of personal defeat" and that "he always remained fond and spoke well of Senator Robert A. Taft."[50]

By centralizing power in the hands of union leaders, Taft-Hartley assisted corporate liberals in overturning one aspect of the drift toward participatory mass democracy inaugurated by wartime activities. Between 1910 and 1941, over 80 percent of union officials in the United States ran for office unopposed, but in the postwar years rivalries and faction fights broke out in many large unions.[51] Although sometimes indicative of little more than the unrestrained ambition of leaders of both factions, these rivalries worked to the advantage of rank-and-file militants, as each side tried to gain supporters by winning victories for the workers. Recognizing the disruptive effects of this competition on uninterrupted production, corporate liberals had already begun to call for more stability in unions even before Congress enacted Taft-Hartley; the new law fit perfectly with their plans.

George Romney, director of the Automobile Manufacturers' Association and top officer at American Motors, asserted that his industry needed "responsible" rather than "democratic" unions, and UAW president Walter Reuther agreed that factional disputes in his union provoked needless strikes.[52] Officers of the United Steel Workers union defended the control and discipline that they exerted over local affiliates by citing factionalism in the UAW and National Maritime Union as proof of the dangers of "democracy too soon."[53]

These practical considerations became elevated into grand theory by labor relations specialist Philip Taft (no relation to the senator) in a 1946 article in the *Harvard Business Review*. Taft argued that bureaucracy in unions worked to the advantage of employers by encouraging stability and that too much union democracy made it harder for companies and unions to discipline and control the work force. Advising that a union should be a powerful economic organization and not a debating society, Taft applauded the efforts of union officers who "guide and sometimes even impose" their trained judgment on the rank and file in the cause of industrial peace.[54]

The provisions of Taft-Hartley that held unions liable for damages stemming from wildcat strikes supplied union leaders with an important weapon against rank-and-file militancy. They could now portray wildcat strikers as selfish individuals jeopardizing the entire organization, rather than as fellow workers with particularly acute problems. Union leaders could use the law as an excuse to crack down on dissidents, without having to take personal responsibility for it. By making it more difficult for workers to take direct action on the shop floor, the bill accelerated the trend toward solving grievances behind closed doors, where union representatives could temper their defense of the workers with their concern for the long-term security of the union.

For competitive-sector conservatives, Taft-Hartley appeared to be the opening wedge of a campaign to overturn the pernicious effects of the New Deal. Flattered by the way that corporate liberals courted their organization and requested its support in the battle to pass the Taft-Hartley Act, they scarcely noticed that most big business members of NAM withdrew from active membership once the law had been passed.[55] The Taft-Hartley

Act ultimately instigated the demise of meaningful conservative opposition to corporate liberalism. Unable to win the public over to more consistent conservative views, and convinced that indeed, the men were more radical than their leaders, conservatives advanced their immediate interests at the expense of their long-range philosophy. Their attempts to restrain mass strikes, secure management control over production, and prevent union rivalries from leading to excessive demands only strengthened the institutional power of government and unions at the expense of ordinary citizens and workers.

Taft-Hartley granted powers to unions that enabled labor leaders to subdue internal opposition and to join with business leaders from the monopoly sector to support corporate-liberal government expansion. Having reneged on their principles in the name of restraining labor, conservatives opened the door to future co-optations in which liberals would use the threat of communism to rationalize even greater government spending and power. Never again would conservatives articulate independent competitive-sector politics. Their principles collapsed into a feeble mixture of self-interest and anticommunism, and they became the shock troops of values they despised. When "conservatism" regained credibility as a political label during the Reagan presidency in the eighties, it presented itself as perfectly in tune with corporate-liberal principles—employing government spending to raise capital for private enterprise through heavy defense spending, pursuing free-trade policies oriented toward overseas economic expansion, and using state power to regulate and control labor-management relations.[56]

Senator Taft's legislation also created a new era for labor's rank and file. The general strikes of 1946 manifested the first stirrings of a new politics of incipient class formation, but they also represented the last expression of some traditional forms of struggle. The drift toward centralized union power, evident in the tensions between strikers and union leaders in 1946, accelerated decisively after the bill became law. Powerful international unions suppressed dissent and imposed longer contracts covering wider areas, while prohibitions on mass picketing, sympathy strikes, and secondary boycotts worked to isolate the rank and file from community support.

Yet the new law's repressive measures could not solve the causes of rank-and-file unrest; they merely channeled its expression into more covert forms. As the institutional power of trade unions increased so that they could better police the rank and file, workers shifted the focus of their strategies of independence toward more submerged, less easily controlled forms on the shop floor and all across the country.

In their zeal to end wildcat and general strikes, to break down local resistance to their authority and power, the new bureaucracies in labor unions only created new communities of interest and activism. Increases in standardization broke down old barriers and united diverse groups in communities of interest ranging from the primary work group on the shop floor to industrywide insurgencies. No longer dependent on face-to-face contact, these new communities could presume a unified experience with people they never met.

Taft-Hartley provided corporate liberals with a half solution to their problems. Centralization of power in unions and barriers against wild-cat strikes promised stability, while conservative acceptance of increased government power established a valuable precedent. Yet real problems remained. Centralizing power in the hands of union leaders could backfire if the wrong people led unions. Stability could be maintained only with high levels of employment and production. Competitive-sector conservatives still opposed the kinds of federal spending necessary to maintain wartime prosperity. One small section of the Taft-Hartley Act pointed the way toward a successful resolution of those problems, and, in conjunction with other policies, helped establish corporate-liberal hegemony. The section denied NLRB protection to unions whose leaders refused to sign affidavits swearing that they were not Communists. What they could not accomplish by other means, corporate liberals hoped to secure through anticommunism.

Although communism has been a relatively insignificant force within the history and culture of the United States, anticommunism has been tremendously important and influential. Conservatives in U.S. history have often attempted to build coalitions based on countersubversive principles; from anti-Catholic and anti-immigrant nativism in the nineteenth century to moral panics about the "behavior" of women, youth, or groups designated as different because of their race in the twentieth century, movements for egalitarian and democratic change invariably attract charges of subversion from their enemies.

In the late forties, anticommunism could be used on the home front to end union rivalries and to ensure that labor leaders sympathetic to corporate-liberal goals came to power, particularly in the auto, electrical, and maritime industries, where Communists held important leadership positions in unions. Striking at real and potential rivalries in unions, equating excessive militancy with treason, and employing legal restrictions to narrow the poles of acceptable political debate, anticommunism proved effective at home, but even more so in winning support for the one way to bring about full employment and production within the system—economic expansion overseas.

Loans and investment credits abroad might help corporations and financiers dispose of idle capital and surplus products while ensuring stable markets for the future. Government expenditures toward these ends could provide indirect subsidies to monopoly corporations involved in international trade and finance, stimulating production and employment without the risks inherent in increased domestic government spending or redistribution of wealth. Labor leaders raised to power on the strength of the anticommunist provisions of Taft-Hartley could play a particularly important role in winning support for overseas expansion.

By connecting labor's hopes for full employment to an expansionist foreign policy, anticommunist union leaders might channel rank-and-file discontent away from domestic solutions while delivering a solid block of support for government policy from a major interest group. They could also draw upon their own records of fighting communism at home to win conservatives over to anticommunist policies abroad by defining communism as the main obstacle to peaceful expansion. Their labor credentials could prove particularly useful in providing an example of anticommunist leadership to workers in other countries, particularly those old and new customers susceptible to leftist influence.

For labor leaders, anticommunism enabled them to gain admission to the corporate-liberal elite and to help make and administer policy to an unprecedented degree. In return, they provided a firm commitment to labor peace at home and economic expansion overseas. If this bargain had not actually been consummated in real-life events, only the most paranoid conspiratorial mind could have thought it up. But there was no conspiracy, only a sophisticated balancing of diverse interests into a coherent corporate-liberal program. The ramifications of that program soon became evident, as anticommunism fueled increased spending abroad, expulsions of dissidents from unions, and renewed attempts to suppress rank-and-file militancy and self-activity.

NOTES

1. For an excellent discussion of Taft-Hartley, see Christopher L. Tomlins, *The State and the Unions: Labor Relations, Law, and the Organized Labor Movement in America, 1880–1960* (Cambridge: Cambridge University Press, 1985).

2. *Fortune*, Nov. 1946, 2–3.

3. *Monthly Labor Review* (Jan. 1947): 79.

4. Ibid., (Mar. 1947): 494.

5. Ibid.; *Anthracite Tri-District News* (Hazleton, Penn.), Feb. 7, 1947.

6. One might assume that Taft-Hartley grew out of irresistible public pressure, but as Howell John Harris notes in his book about management ideology in the forties, lobbying and pressure by business interests had much to do with the introduction and passage of the bill. In addition, President Truman's strategy to appeal to both sides in the dispute by doing little to stop the bill's passage early on but publicly

vetoing it later on undermined political opposition to the bill. Finally, the refusal by labor leaders to mobilize the rank and file against the bill in direct-action protests left the business lobbyists virtually uncontested. See Howell John Harris, *The Right to Manage: Industrial Relations Policies of American Business in the 1940s* (Madison: University of Wisconsin Press, 1982), 125; Susan Hartmann, *Truman and the 80th Congress* (Columbia: University of Missouri Press, 1971), 87–90; Paul Romano, *Life in the Factory* (Boston: New England Free Press, n.d.), 22–23.

7. U.S. Senate, *Hearings before the Committee on Labor and Public Welfare*, 80th Cong., 1st sess., Feb. 5, 1947, 471.

8. Ibid., Feb. 15, 1947, 927.

9. Ibid., Feb. 4, 1947, 388–89.

10. Ibid., Feb. 8, 1947, 538.

11. Walter Adams, "The Steel Industry," in Walter Adams, ed., *The Structure of American Industry* (New York: Macmillan, 1961), 70–116.

12. Ibid.

13. Robert F. Lanzillotti, "The Automobile Industry," in Adams, ed., *The Structure of American Industry*, 256, 273. This also helped finalize consolidation in the auto industry as General Motors secured preferential access to steel supplies.

14. U.S. Senate, *Hearings*, Feb. 19, 1947, 1109.

15. Ibid., Jan. 29, 1947, 208.

16. *Congressional Record*, Apr. 23, 1947, 3834.

17. Alfred S. Cleveland, "NAM: Spokesman for Industry," *Harvard Business Review* (May 1948): 352.

18. *Fortune*, July 1948, 72; Cleveland, "NAM," 353.

19. *Fortune*, July 1948, 72.

20. *Newsweek*, Dec. 16, 1946, 78; *New York Times*, Dec. 5, 1946, 1.

21. *Time*, Dec. 16, 1946, 87; *New York Times*, Dec. 7, 1946, 5.

22. David Eakins, "Policy Planning for the Establishment," in Ronald Radosh and Murray Rothbard, eds., *A New History of Leviathan* (New York: Dutton, 1972), 188–205.

23. David Eakins, "Business Planners and America's Postwar Expansion," in David Horowitz, ed., *Corporations and the Cold War* (New York: Monthly Review Press, 1969), 143–71.

24. Keith Hutchison, "Heresy in High Places," *The Nation*, Oct. 27, 1945, 431; Karl Schriftgiesser, *Business Comes of Age* (New York: Harper, 1960).

25. *The Nation*, Oct. 12, 1946, 35.

26. Malcolm P. McNair, "The Full Employment Problem," *Harvard Business Review* 24, no. 1 (Autumn 1945): 1.

27. *The Nation*, Apr. 28, 1945; National Planning Association, *National Budgets for Full Employment*, Mar. 16, 1945, 432.

28. *Monthly Labor Review* (Feb. 1947): 163, (Mar. 1947): 41–42.

29. Lawrence Fertig, "The Fiction of Full Employment," *American Mercury* (Feb. 1944): 221.

30. *Fortune*, Jan. 1947, 12.

31. C. Wright Mills, *The New Men of Power* (New York: A. M. Kelley, 1948), 146.

32. Ibid., 187.

33. Robert S. Lynd, "Capitalism's Happy New Year," *The Nation*, Dec. 28, 1946, 750.

34. Mills, *The New Men of Power*, 27–30.

35. *Business Week*, Mar. 1, 1947, 80.

36. *Newsweek*, Dec. 17, 1945, 72; *New York Times*, Dec. 8, 1945, 11.

37. *Time*, Dec. 16, 1946, 87; *New York Times*, Dec. 5, 1946, 3.

38. *Congressional Record*, Apr. 23, 1947, 3835.

39. U.S. Senate, *Hearings*, Feb. 4, 1947, 407.

40. Tomlins, *The State and the Unions*, 101.

41. U.S. Senate, *Hearings*, Feb. 7, 1947, 574.

42. *Business Week*, Mar. 15, 1947, 98.

43. Tomlins, *The State and the Unions*, 248; Letter from Towner Phelan to A. B. Lansing, Clark Clifford Collection, Harry S Truman Library, Independence, Mo. Pepper and Wallace represented the progressive wing of the Democratic party, but neither should be considered a "labor" candidate.

44. Tomlins, *The State and the Unions*, 247, 318, 261.

45. U.S. Senate, *Hearings*, Feb. 7, 1947, 135–36.

46. Ibid., Jan. 31, 1947, 312–13.

47. Ibid., Jan. 23, 1947, 13.

48. Ibid., Feb. 19, 1947, 1157.

49. Rick Fantasia, *Cultures of Solidarity: Consciousness, Action, and Contemporary American Workers* (Berkeley: University of California Press, 1988), 57.

50. Phil Curran, Oral History Interview, Pennsylvania State University Library, State College, Penn., 21.

51. Mills, *The New Men of Power*, 64.

52. *New Republic*, Mar. 3, 1947, 31.

53. Ibid., 26.

54. Philip Taft, "Understanding Union Administration," *Harvard Business Review* (Winter 1946): 245, 253.

55. Harris, *The Right to Manage*, 125.

56. One need only compare Robert Taft's compassionate support for public housing (based on his conviction that the private market could not meet the needs of everyone) with the dogmatic free-market ideology of Ronald Reagan and George Bush, even when they were confronted with the colossal failure of private enterprise manifested in the rise of homelessness in the eighties and nineties. Of course, in fairness, it is important to understand that post-Fordist economics in deindustrialized countries in the eighties and nineties have encouraged the development of this free-market austerity.

CHAPTER EIGHT

"No Classes in This Country"

Labor and the Cold War

AS CONGRESS debated the Taft-Hartley Act in the spring of 1947, workers across the country continued to wage the kinds of strikes and demonstrations that the bill hoped to prevent. An explosion that killed 111 workers in a Centralia, Illinois, coal mine provoked a nationwide walkout by 400,000 miners. They eventually compelled the U. S. Bureau of Mine Safety to admit that only two coal mines in the entire country met government safety standards.[1] At the same time, 340,000 telephone workers, most of them women, staged the first national strike against AT&T despite enormous legal repression.[2] The proposed law itself sparked demonstrations by 20,000 Chicago packinghouse workers who engaged in a one-hour work stoppage to protest Taft-Hartley on April 16, by 100,000 Iowa workers who stayed home from work on April 22, and by 500,000 auto workers in the Midwest who walked off the job in protest on April 24.[3]

When the bill became law on June 23, two distinct strategies emerged. One, typified by the mine workers, relied on rank-and-file militancy to defy the law. On the heels of their massive strike in April, rank-and-file coal miners conducted unauthorized walkouts as soon as Taft-Hartley went into effect. Centered in Pennsylvania and Alabama, the walkouts paralyzed coal production right into the end of June when the miners' contractual ten-day vacation period started. These strikes forced the coal operators to sign a contract stipulating that miners furnished their services only "during such time as such persons are willing and able to work."[4] By making work voluntary, the contract defined wildcat strikes out of existence and gave the miners immunity from the provisions of the bill assigning damages for such strikes. A federal judge severely tested that immunity one year later, when he fined the union an exorbitant amount for its lack of zeal in keeping miners at work. But the refusal of the rank and file to knuckle under to the new law made it virtually inoperable in the coal industry.[5]

A walkout in July by seven thousand employees of Detroit's Murray Corporation provided the context for the other major strategy to cope with the new law. Instead of seeking a loophole similar to that won by the miners, the UAW simply tried to protect the union treasury from responsibility for damages arising from wildcats. The union negotiated a contract that banned all strikes and all picketing unless authorized by the international union hierarchy and conducted more than forty-five days after the filing of a grievance on the disputed point. Establishing that neither the union nor its officers or members could be held liable for damages caused by wildcats, the agreement authorized the company to discipline or discharge individual workers involved in unauthorized work stoppages. By shifting the burden for wildcat strike punishments onto individual workers and by carefully prescribing the limits of legitimate strikes, the union gained a significant tool for enforcing labor peace.[6]

Other unions accepted the auto workers' solution as a model, largely because it assured their institutional security and turned one of the presumed defects of the bill into an asset. Thus, the union leaders refused to mobilize a mass rank-and-file challenge to the law, concentrating instead on using it for their own advantage. The noncommunist affidavits mandated in the bill provided another opportunity for some labor leaders to win unprecedented power by lending aid to a crusade against communism supported by the most powerful individuals and corporations in the country.

Anticommunism in America existed long before the cold war, but the Truman administration's manipulation of diplomatic tensions between the United States and the Soviet Union transformed a relatively minor fear into a national obsession. Stung by Democratic party defeats in the 1946 congressional elections, apprehensive about the nation's ability to sustain wartime levels of production, and concerned with strategic and economic threats to U.S. interests posed by the Soviet presence in Eastern Europe, Truman turned to anticommunism as the main justification for expansion abroad and the primary tool for stifling criticism at home.[7] The president deliberately exaggerated the threat from overseas in order to "scare the hell out of the American people" and to produce in peacetime the kinds of unity, sacrifice, and acceptance of government spending that prevailed during the war.[8]

Asserting a crucial connection between foreign policy and domestic well-being, Truman identified American interests as contingent upon three connected principles: world stability, expanding markets, and the defense of freedom. In practice the three principles collapsed into one, as stability came to mean security for American business, and the measure of freedom became the extent of Western-style "free" enterprise in any given country. In highly visible public pronouncements and in crisis-shrouded

"emergency" actions, the Truman administration devoted its energies in
the spring of 1947 to convincing the American people that corporate-liberal
foreign policies constituted the only possible patriotic response to world
conditions.

In a major foreign policy address at Baylor University (certain to provide a sympathetic audience for a Southern Baptist Democratic president)
on March 6, 1947, the president alerted the nation to the increasing significance of foreign affairs. Stressing connections between America's economic and political interests overseas, Truman advised that cherished
American freedoms of speech and worship depended on freedom of enterprise, not just at home, but throughout the world. Only a healthy world
economy could absorb the necessary volume of U. S. exports, but Europe's
severe winter, slow recovery from the war, and susceptibility to imperial
or communist limits on free trade interfered with American hopes. The
nation's very supremacy in international trade proved to be a burden, since
other countries sold so little to the United States that they increasingly
lacked the dollars needed to purchase American products. Consequently,
the president proposed to increase European imports into the United States
as a means of making the region a better long-term customer for American
exports and investments. Although this policy might harm U. S. manufacturers and farmers in the short run, Truman argued that it held the key
to long-term stability by encouraging an expanded market. "Business is
good," he emphasized, "when markets are big."[9]

Six days later, the president announced the Truman Doctrine for Greece
and Turkey, requesting from Congress an emergency appropriation of $400
million to aid "free people who are resisting attempted subjugation by
armed minorities or by outside pressures."[10] In truth the Turks faced no
military threat, and the problems plaguing Greece stemmed from American
attempts to prop up a right-wing dictatorship. Anxious to supplant fading
British power in the Middle East with American control, intent on limiting
Soviet zones of influence, and determined to create stability for American
trade, Truman invoked a doctrine proclaiming the right to intervene in the
internal affairs of other nations in defense of American definitions of freedom and stability. Given corporate-liberal expansionist assumptions about
the national interest, communism in Europe did pose a real threat to the
United States in its potential to nationalize private industries and restrict
American economic penetration. Yet to Americans unconvinced about the
necessity for worldwide U. S. hegemony, those consequences hardly justified loans and military commitments overseas. Ever the skilled politician,
Truman appealed to anticommunism and economic self-interest as ways
of generating enthusiasm for programs that otherwise might have failed to
garner widespread support.

In his appeal for funds for Greece and Turkey, and in private meetings before and after the requests, the president chose to portray the situation in Europe as part of a worldwide battle between democracy and communism, allowing his listeners to equate Communist-led resistance fighters in Greece with the Soviet Army. When congressional leaders expressed reluctance to approve the expenditures at a White House meeting on March 17, Truman and his advisors won them over by harping on the threat of Soviet aggression. By linking political and economic objectives together, the administration used anticommunism and national security as devices to win approval for economic policies. Senator Vandenberg endorsed the Truman Doctrine because it appeared to be responding to a communist threat, while Senator Taft put aside his doubts about the wisdom of the plan because he feared undermining the president's credibility and freedom of action in dealing with other world leaders.

Equally convincing, but less publicly aired, were the ways in which American "aid" could be used to guarantee U.S. control over Greece's foreign exchange, budgets, taxes, credits, and currency.[11] In addition, Truman's aid plan to Greece and Turkey promised to make it easier for British customers to buy goods from the United States by relieving that nation of the financial burden of military expenditures in Greece. Ending the Greek revolution might serve as an important lesson to nationalist revolutionaries in other countries while at the same time granting greater security for U.S. access to oil reserves in the Middle East. "The loud talk was all of Greece and Turkey," *Time* magazine noted, "but the whispers were of the ocean of oil to the south."[12]

The Truman Doctrine served as the opening wedge for a general program of economic and political expansion. Undersecretary of State Dean Acheson launched a trial balloon for this program in a speech delivered at Cleveland, Mississippi, on May 8, 1947, where he tied "lasting peace and prosperity" to increased expenditures for relief and reconstruction in Europe. Citing the gap between American exports of $16 billion (four times prewar levels) and imports of less than $8 million, Acheson argued that the miseries of underconsumption abroad created a breeding ground for communism and robbed the United States of needed stability. Foreign nations needed more goods, yet could not afford to pay for more imports. The undersecretary called for a comprehensive program to increase American imports so that Europe would be better equipped to pay for American goods and to use loans to bolster "stability" and "democratic" institutions. Behind these declarations lay official hopes that such a program might keep American exports at wartime (meaning nondepression) levels, that dollars loaned abroad might indirectly subsidize domestic production, and that reconstruction aid in behalf of "democratic" institutions could extend

American economic and political control over potential markets and new areas for investment.[13]

Acheson's suggestions prefigured the arguments advanced in Secretary of State George Marshall's famous address at the Harvard University commencement on June 5, 1947. Pointing to the economic devastation of Europe, Marshall proposed that America play a leading role in that continent's recovery for both humanitarian and selfish reasons. Amid favorable worldwide response to Marshall's proposals, President Truman appointed the President's Committee on Foreign Aid to transform the secretary's ideas into a workable program and to win popular support for its implementation.

Sharing the president's political aversion to communism, committee members also overwhelmingly represented the economic interests and concerns of monopolistic corporations. Chaired by the millionaire secretary of commerce Averill Harriman and populated by representatives from major businesses and lobbying groups, the committee sustained a concentrated effort to use government loans abroad to create a favorable economic and political climate for American business. Nine of the sixteen members of the committee had direct ties to the CED, the corporate-liberal planning and lobbying group, including five of the nine business representatives and three out of the six academic members.[14] Auto industry executive and CED president Paul Hoffman played an important role on the committee and later served as chief American administrator of the program in Europe.

Corporate liberals not only dominated the membership of the Harriman Committee, they also determined its politics. Drawing on suggestions from earlier CED and Twentieth Century Fund reports, they proposed that Congress appropriate from $12 billion to $17 billion over a four-year period for European recovery.[15] Reasoning that the bulk of this money would ultimately be spent in the United States, corporate liberals on the committee understood foreign aid as a way to close the "dollar gap" between Europe and the United States, as well as a means of providing security for increased production at home and investment abroad.

Corporate liberals feared that both European and North American economies might have to resort to self-contained state-run economic policies if U.S. exports to Europe did not increase. Exports accounted for only 5 percent of the gross national product in 1947; they had been 10 percent in the pre-1929 era. Without an infusion of U.S. dollars into European countries, experts projected a 40 percent drop in U.S. exports to that continent in 1948.[16]

Secretary Marshall insisted that the plan intended no attack on the Soviet Union and that its benefits could be extended to all nations. Had that been the case, the United Nations or some other international agency could have administered it. The United States acted unilaterally precisely because it wished to limit Soviet influence and to reconstruct Europe on terms favorable to the U.S. economy. At best, the State Department hoped that American aid could restore Eastern Europe to its traditional role as a supplier of raw materials and a consumer of finished goods from the West. At worst, the plan could still strengthen the American zone of influence in the West. The Soviets had to choose between two unpalatable alternatives if the Marshall Plan succeeded: they could have a unified Europe under American control or a divided Europe that isolated them and their allies. The Marshall Plan could succeed only at the expense of the Soviet Union and could be justified to the American people only in terms of anticommunism.

Undersecretary of State Will Clayton grasped the clear relationship between fighting communism and economic self-interest when he told supporters of the Marshall Plan in December 1947 that communist governments on the continent of Europe threatened American access to needed markets. Exclusion from European markets, Clayton warned, could only be overcome by radical changes in the domestic economy—changes that "could hardly be made under our democratic free enterprise system."[17] The survival of capitalism at home thus hinged upon control over actual and potential overseas markets, necessitating an expanded international role for the United States. American economics and politics became world politics and economics, as corporate liberals tried to convince their fellow Americans to follow the advice of a *Fortune* editorial in June 1947, which urged them to "go over the earth, as investors and managers and engineers, as makers of mutual prosperity, as missionaries of capitalism and democracy."[18]

Yet for all the compelling economic self-interest behind the Marshall Plan, the administration also found it necessary to create a crisis atmosphere—replete with claims of a direct threat to American security from communist aggression—in order to make the American people accept its foreign policy. Disclaiming any responsibility for the polarization of Europe, the United States hypocritically pointed an accusing finger at the Soviets for trying to protect their own zone of influence and for resisting the expansion of American power, while asserting American license to intervene against revolutions that might have communist leadership, to control the economies of states that might adopt communism, and to view threats to American expansion as evidence of a monopolistic international communist conspiracy.

In their own way, policy planners genuinely felt that communism presented a threat to long-range American plans for economic stability, but they deliberately misrepresented the nature of that threat because it served so many of their purposes to do so. The Soviet "menace" overseas enabled the State Department to portray U.S. control of Europe's economy as a defense of freedom-loving peoples against communist aggression, while providing a ready scapegoat for any failures by the capitalist economies.

Despite a surface prosperity that confounded predictions of a postwar depression, the U.S. economy faced serious problems by 1949. Accumulated wartime personal savings and unusually high demand for previously unattainable consumer goods began to decline. Government spending proved too low to maintain full production, even though the federal budget remained four times greater than it had been in 1940.[19] The Dodge Plan to reindustrialize Japan produced a severe trade imbalance, which left that nation on the brink of financial disaster, while the more successful Marshall Plan still left Europeans dangerously short of dollars for the purchase of U.S. goods.[20]

Militarization of the economy once again provided the solution for corporate liberalism. Early in 1950, the National Security Council circulated a proposal known as NSC-68 (National Security Council resolution 68) for massive hikes in military expenditures, reductions in social welfare programs, a more public policy of anticommunism to rally support for economic expansion, and significant increases in taxes designed to sustain the new powers such policies would give the federal government. President Truman approved this policy in April 1950 and began to prepare a budget that would triple the amount that the Pentagon had requested for defense spending. Any doubt that this policy could be sold to the public disappeared in June with the outbreak of war in Korea; as Secretary of State Dean Acheson would observe later, "Korea came along and saved us." Military spending grew from $14 billion per year in 1950 to $53 billion by 1953, and it remained between $34 and $40 billion for the rest of the decade. NSC-68 placed the U.S. economy on a permanent war footing, and it institutionalized the role of government as the prime agent of capital accumulation for big business.[21] This spending helped launch an age of U.S. supremacy in the world economy and led to one of the greatest growth periods in the history of world capitalism. Yet it also sowed the seeds for social and economic crises to come.

As it had done during World War II, military spending provided large corporations with a steady flow of capital and a predictable and almost insatiable market, but it also exacted terrible costs on the nation's economy, politics, and culture. Reliance on defense spending left U.S. corporations with little incentive to develop new or better consumer products, it encouraged an outflow of dollars, capital, and technology overseas, and the huge tax expenditures required to pay for defense production diverted money away from education, housing, health, and transportation projects that could have greatly improved the nation's economic and social infrastructure. By the seventies, the United States faced a dollar drain, competition from manufacturers overseas with superior products and technology, and enormous accumulated social costs emanating from the maldistribution of wealth and resources. In addition, two decades of demanding absolute obedience to anticommunist efforts overseas left the nation with little opportunity to debate the causes and consequences of its bloody intervention in Vietnam until it was too late.

The anticommunist mobilization required for selling the level of government intervention in the economy mandated by NSC-68 to the public left a disastrous legacy of its own. Only an anticommunist cold war could make the right wing support the growth of big government, while at the same time marginalizing the left opposition by tarring it with the brush of disloyalty. NSC-68 and policies attendant to it institutionalized into law what Michael P. Rogin has termed the countersubversive tradition of U. S. politics. Rogin argues that conservative agendas in the United States have long been served by the demonization of internal enemies as agents of alien power. "The countersubversive needs monsters to give shape to his anxieties and to permit him to indulge his forbidden desires. Demonization allows the countersubversive, in the name of battling the subversive, to imitate his enemy." Operating by these countersubversive principles in the postwar period allowed the government to channel massive amounts of money to a few corporations in the name of "free enterprise," to trample on the civil liberties of citizens accused of disloyalty in the name of defending the American way, and to use the power of the state to further regiment public opinion in the name of democracy. Rogin argues that "the countersubversive interprets local initiatives as signs of alien power," and it was precisely that interpretation that made the government such an enthusiastic participant in efforts to turn back working-class strategies of independence in the postwar era.[22]

The threatening presence of communism overseas had important domestic uses. Anticommunism could make economic expansion a matter of patriotic obligation. It enabled the government to equate opposition to its foreign policy with disloyalty to the country. Members of Congress hostile to government spending could be persuaded to support expenditures overseas in the name of fighting communism, while advocates of cooperation with the Soviet Union could be branded as disloyal. In one package, expansion overseas and anticommunism at home provided the president with a way to simultaneously rescue the economy and disarm potential critics.

The Truman administration employed a vigorous anticommunist program at home as a means of sustaining the crisis atmosphere so necessary for public approval of its foreign policy. Within ten days of the announcement of the Truman Doctrine, the president issued an executive order initiating the Federal Employee Loyalty Program designed to remove alleged subversives from the government payroll. In ensuing months, Attorney General Tom Clark cooperated with the House Un-American Activities Committee to conduct highly publicized "investigations" intended to focus public anxiety on the threat of domestic communism. The State Department dismissed ten employees as security risks, and the Justice Department engaged in a vigorous program of deporting resident aliens.

Long on accusations but short on proof, the administration's hysteria about Communists accomplished more in the way of propaganda benefits than it did in discovering any actual subversives. The attorney general had to compel J. Edgar Hoover to testify before HUAC, even though the FBI director protested that his appearance would make it more difficult for his agency to police communism. The State Department rescinded its dismissal of employees as security risks when a court challenge raised the possibility of having to provide actual evidence of their disloyalty. The Justice Department's deportations focused on resident aliens critical of the administration's foreign policy, and seemed more designed to protect that policy from criticism than to protect the nation from agents of a foreign power. Pointing to the deportation of Gerhart Eisler, arrested in the middle of a speaking tour against American policy in Germany, the attorney general freely admitted that he "ordered Mr. Eisler picked up because he had been making speeches around the country that were derogatory to our way of life."[23]

Labor provided a special target for the Truman administration's anticommunism. As a large and politically active interest group with the power to disrupt production, labor's opposition to foreign loans might have doomed the program. In addition, the strikes and mass demonstrations of the early postwar years raised the possibility that workers might find their own solutions to the problems of full employment. Finally, unions constituted one of the few institutions in U.S. society where Communists, although few in number, actually maintained a visible presence and provided a potential threat to stability. Anticommunism offered a convenient way of drumming up labor support for Truman's foreign policy, of isolating and discrediting militants within the working class, of further consolidating the power of union bureaucrats, and, just in case any of those failed, of identifying real Communists as scapegoats.

Secretary of State Marshall stressed the role that labor could play in support of American foreign policy in an address to the CIO convention in Boston in October 1947. Making the first appearance in history by a secretary of state at a major labor conclave, Marshall described American loans to Europe as essential for stability and peace. He urged labor to fulfill its proper role by supporting the interests of "the community of which it is a part," by supporting the government, and by opposing the "enemies of democracy" who tried to "undermine the confidence of the labor element in the stability of our institutions and the soundness of our traditions."[24] Few could have missed the secretary's meaning: to oppose the proper "functioning of the modern state" would be to be aligned with the "enemies of democracy," but support of the state could bring handsome rewards.

The Harriman Committee, set up to design and win support for the Marshall Plan, provided an excellent model of the rewards available for compliant labor leaders in the emerging corporate-liberal state. Reproducing the tripartite power-sharing of wartime production boards, the committee offered anticommunist labor leaders like James Carey of the CIO and George Meany of the AFL important roles on an equal basis with representatives from corporations and government.[25] Labor leaders had long envisioned such a role, but they previously lacked sufficient bargaining power to achieve it. In 1947, foreign policy imperatives and fear of the rank and file made the state receptive to the needs of anticommunist labor leaders, many of whom had already been making major efforts to consolidate their own power in the name of fighting communism.

Although almost all of the AFL, and important factions within the CIO, had long histories of anticommunism, major purges did not begin until 1946. The overwhelming majority of Communists in the labor movement belonged to CIO unions whose members, for the most part, viewed anticommunism as a false issue raised by companies or rival unions as a device to hamper organizing. Communists played important roles in taking the risks necessary to organize the CIO, and they enjoyed the protection of the organization's leaders who understood their great contribution. Only with the end of the war (and the end of the Communist-supported no-strike pledge) did important noncommunist union leaders begin to join ranks with traditional anticommunists to crack down on Communists within the unions.

In the postwar situation, Communists within their ranks became a liability to union leaders, because their presence tarnished labor's image at the very moment that union bureaucrats wanted to appear respectable enough to share in the administration of the corporate-liberal state. Communists also became vulnerable to attack because their support for the Soviet Union often motivated their vigorous opposition to the Truman Doctrine and Marshall Plan, the most likely vehicles for labor's new power. Finally, union rivalries between Communists and anticommunists augured perpetual militancy at a time when labor leaders increasingly viewed their own best interests to lie with labor peace.

A Gallup poll in the summer of 1946 showed that 38 percent of the American people believed that Communists wielded a "great deal" of influence in unions. *Newsweek* noted that "from the standpoint of public opinion,

the job of whitewashing the red taint was more vital than the actual re-
moval of Communists from labor leadership."[26] Later that year, at the CIO
convention, Philip Murray coupled pledges of labor-management cooperation with a warning to CIO city councils that they must follow national
CIO policies, particularly on foreign affairs. Delegates to the convention
later gave President Murray the power to expel known Communists from
the organization.[27]

As labor leaders gained power within the corporate-liberal elite and
strengthened control over their own organizations, they rationalized their
behavior by expressly denying the class character of American society.
Writing in the *American Magazine*, Philip Murray argued, "We have no
classes in this country; that's why the Marxist theory of the class struggle
has gained so few adherents. We're all workers here. And in the final analysis the interests of farmers, factory hands, business and professional people,
and white collar toilers prove to be the same."[28]

In the context of the postwar strike experience, Murray's observations
left a great deal unexplained. If classes did not exist, what caused the
industrial warfare of the preceding years? If all groups had the same interests, why did they behave so differently? To answer those questions, corporate liberals allowed their anticommunism to expand into xenophobia.
Presuming social harmony to be an organic part of American society, they
attributed disruption to "unnatural" forces attacking from without or subverting from within. They sanctioned extreme measures to rid the body
politic of this infection. The distinguished liberal Supreme Court Justice
(and former Securities and Exchange Commission attorney) William O.
Douglas carried this argument to its logical—and chilling—conclusion,
when he told the 1948 CIO convention: "While the aim of European political parties has been to draw men of different ideologies into separate disciplined groups, the aim of our parties has been to unite divergent groups into
one. That means compromise of various ideas and ideologies and the doc-
trinaire acceptance of none. It means the elimination of extremists both
Right and Left, and the development of middle of the road policies."[29]

Under such conditions it is not difficult to pursue middle-of-the-road
policies. Once the Right and the Left have been eliminated, they are all
that remain. Douglas's speech crystallized an emerging liberal totalitari-
anism that viewed government policies as the expression of a fundamental
consensus in American society—a consensus that neither required, nor
could it tolerate, extensive public debate on foreign policy. One year later,
the CIO implemented his suggestions by expelling twelve unions because
alleged Communists hostile to Truman's programs held leadership positions in them.

Demanding the power to bar individuals from the federation's executive board and to expel member unions without a vote, Philip Murray told the 1949 CIO convention that Communist union leaders had attended secret meetings at which "there evoked plans and policies to corrupt and destroy if possible the trade union movement in America."[30] The well-disciplined and carefully selected delegates roared their approval as the CIO president rid the organization of the "red menace" and set the stage for raids on the expelled unions by those remaining.

Faction fights between anticommunist unions and those allegedly under Communist party domination had a detrimental effect on the labor movement. New organizing all but stopped as established unions battled each other for the same workers. The newly found closeness between leaders of the big labor federations and the Democratic party meant that unions pulled back from efforts to organize in the South or to push a stronger civil rights agenda in order to protect the political power of the segregationist and anti-union Democratic members of Congress from that region. As Barbara Griffith shows in her excellent study of the CIO's "Operation Dixie," ideological fights divided the labor movement at the very moment when unity was most needed to organize southern industries, to challenge racial segregation inside and outside of the plants, and to challenge the political power of the "race-baiting 'Dixiecrat' conservatives."[31]

Ideological splits over the "communist" issues handed employers an opportunity to attack progressive and integrated southern unions including the Food and Tobacco Workers Union of America (FTA) and the International Union of Mine, Mill, and Smelter Workers (IUMMSW). Instead of organizing new members, these locals had to fight to hang onto the right to represent their members in the face of attacks by employers and raids by conservative AFL and CIO unions. For example, when the R. J. Reynolds Tobacco Company tried to use contract negotiations in 1947 as an opportunity to break Local 22 of the FTA at their Winston Salem plant, management stressed the presence of Communists in the union as a rationale for their actions. When the union called a strike, the House Un-American Activities Committee conducted widely publicized hearings on alleged Communist influence in the FTA. The 1947 strike ended inconclusively, but in 1950 CIO officials sent representatives from the United Transport Service Employees union to raid Local 22. After two disputed elections, the CIO succeeded in defeating Local 22 by sixty-six votes.[32] The combination of bad publicity, government investigations, raiding, and expulsions of "communist" unions from the CIO combined to thwart any chance of success for "Operation Dixie." Even when conservative CIO and AFL unions succeeded in the South, they often did so by organizing management rather than the workers, offering compliancy and labor peace to employers interested in alternatives to facing militant and aggressive unions.

Had labor unions been able to organize southern textile mills successfully in the postwar period they might have laid the groundwork for a
progressive future for the entire nation. A unionized southern work force
would have denied industrialists the threat or actuality of moving plants to
low-wage, nonunion areas. It would have transformed the social life and
political culture of the South, bringing new energy into the labor movement and new possibilities for national politics. But the organizing drive
failed miserably.

In addition, many of the unions expelled from the CIO during the anticommunist purges had large numbers of women, "minority," and white-
collar workers in them. By removing them from the labor movement, the
CIO positioned itself poorly for the future when increasing numbers of
workers would be from those categories.[33] In his later years, even Murray's
fellow anticommunist, Monsignor Charles Owen Rice, would admit that
"the American trade union movement would be healthier today if Phil
Murray had not purged the CIO and if a strong broad-based Communist
minority had been able to survive in the trade unions."[34]

Had Communists in the labor movement actually done the things that
Murray charged them with, they might have been better off. They found
themselves vulnerable to attack not because they behaved so differently
from other union leaders, but because they were so much like them. For
years, Communist union leaders had favored labor-management cooperation and had been prominent advocates of more power for the labor federations and their officers. Unfortunately for them, the final consolidation
of that power came only with the stimulus of anticommunism. Far from
being the saboteurs, traitors, and fomenters of disruption that their enemies feared, Communists in labor unions were the unwitting and uncomprehending architects of the system that ultimately destroyed them.

Communists threw themselves into the CIO organizing campaigns of the
thirties out of a sincere commitment to trade unions, as well as out of a
recognition that the CIO offered a chance for them to end their isolation
from the masses of workers. In their pursuit of union recognition, higher
wages, and better working conditions, they held to their belief in an essentially nonpolitical role for the trade union. Thus, Communists in the CIO
functioned as enthusiastic, but largely conventional, trade unionists.[35]

The foreign policy needs of the Soviet Union also shaped the behavior
of Communists in trade unions. Acting on Stalin's belief in the midthirties
that the Soviet Union would soon be at war with Nazi Germany, Communists throughout the world attempted to build a "united front" of liberal and left forces against fascism. In the United States, the united front
revolved around support for the New Deal and defense of the Roosevelt
administration against rightist attacks. From the mid- to late thirties, the

American Communist party stood for liberalism at home and intervention abroad to fight fascism. When Hitler and Stalin signed a nonaggression pact in 1939, Communists in the labor movement called for a period of renewed class struggle and labor militancy—while decrying war hysteria. But when Germany invaded the Soviet Union two years later, they demanded mobilization for war and an end to strikes. During World War II, Communists and their sympathizers remained firm defenders of the no-strike pledge, and they committed themselves to increasing production.[36] They spared no excess in condemning strikes, regardless of the provocation. When John L. Lewis's United Mine Workers conducted a work stoppage in protest against war profiteering and unsafe working conditions in 1943, Communist leader Earl Browder charged, "There is not the slightest doubt that Lewis is working and has worked during the last two years at least, as an integral part of the pro-Nazi fifth column, aiming at a negotiated peace with Hitler and at the Nazi subjugation of the U. S. itself."[37]

A 1944 article in *The Communist* applauded Philip Murray and R. J. Thomas for disciplining striking locals in the steel workers' and auto workers' unions. It singled out for special praise the Teamsters' leadership for their crackdown on a Minneapolis local with a long history of militant (and Trotskyist) action. The article even supported government prosecution of Trotskyists in the Minneapolis local for alleged violations of the repressive Smith Act, which made it a crime to advocate the overthrow of the government. According to the journal, these prosecutions attempted to protect the war effort from sabotage and therefore constituted no violation of civil liberties.[38]

The communist commitment to wartime labor peace assumed concrete form in the everyday affairs of unions, much to the delight of employers and much to the dismay of the rank and file. Leaders of the National Maritime Union known for their communist views taught classes in labor-management cooperation aboard ships and even helped the Coast Guard weed out "undesirables" from employment in the industry.[39] William Sentner, an avowed Communist in the United Electrical Workers union, enforced labor peace in St. Louis defense plants—volunteering his union for wage cuts when an employer threatened to move operations to another city.[40] Small wonder that in 1944 *Business Week* observed that "unions identified as communist-dominated have the best no-strike record, are the most vigorous proponents of labor-management cooperation, the only serious advocates of incentive wages, and the only unions which support the president's call for a national service act."[41]

These Communist party policies won gratitude from management, but earned the enmity of workers. In the 1942 election for president of the California state CIO, an anticommunist challenger lost by a five-to-one margin. The next year the margin diminished to two to one, and by 1944, two years of the no-strike pledge had so discredited the candidates identified with the communist position that they withdrew from the race rather than suffer repudiation at the ballot box.[42] In the United Electrical Workers (UE) and the IUMMSW, anticommunist groups used rank-and-file discontent with the no-strike pledge as a basis for challenges to union leaders. Communist identification with the pledge in the UAW helped anticommunist Walter Reuther gain the support of shop-floor militants in his rise to the union presidency, even though Reuther had supported the no-strike pledge as well.[43]

Instead of addressing the concerns of workers on the shop floor, Communists in labor busied themselves with grand schemes to expand the role of labor in the corporate state. Harry Bridges of the ILWU put the California CIO on record in favor of a state reconstruction finance corporation, capitalized at $500 million, to directly aid businesses.[44] Party theoretician Gilbert Green devoted an article in *The Communist* to plans for bridging "class, sectional, and partisan rifts" in the United States by finding sufficient domestic and foreign markets to support wartime levels of production. Lauding the efforts of the Committee for Economic Development, Green predicted that in order to survive in the future, capitalism would meet people's needs.[45]

Eugene Dennis offered even more elaborate predictions in a 1945 article in the same journal (now renamed *Political Affairs* as further demonstration of the party's reluctance to proclaim a class struggle).[46] Dennis praised the efforts by industrial and labor leaders to extend the no-strike agreement into the postwar years, noting their mutual concerns for high levels of production, respect for capital's property rights, and more productivity. Differentiating the new program from past efforts at labor-management cooperation, Dennis contended that this time the plans called for no subordination of the "interests of the worker."[47] The only cloud on the horizon stemmed from the specter of strikes, which Dennis attributed to conspiracies by some union leaders to "create renewed divisions in labor's ranks" and "to disrupt essential war production and the post-war unity of the nation."[48]

In their support for the no-strike pledge, their zeal to punish wildcat strikers, and their projections of labor peace in the postwar world, Communists in labor could not have been more poorly prepared for the postwar strike wave. When the party ultimately changed its positions, it did so not out of any serious self-criticism of its disastrous wartime practices but because of pressure from Stalin, who correctly recognized that corporate-liberal postwar policies could succeed only at the expense of the Soviet Union. Refusing to admit their past mistakes and reluctant to identify themselves directly with Soviet foreign policy, U.S. Communists attributed their rediscovery of the class struggle after the war to the fiction that Truman's policies constituted a decisive break with the New Deal past.[49] This posture prevented the party and its adherents from seeing the organic link between government policies and the maintenance of wartime production levels, causing them instead to speak of a conspiracy of powerful forces pushing the nation toward fascism. Communists correctly identified the totalitarian implications of the corporate-liberal state (especially when it directed its repression at them), but they wrongly identified them as a betrayal of New Deal liberalism—rather than its fulfillment.

A poor record on shop-floor activism, miscalculations about the postwar world, and an awkward political dependence on the foreign policy needs of the Soviet Union did not exhaust the Communist party's liabilities. Even had they opposed the no-strike pledge, had they fully realized the implications of wartime class collaboration, and had they been completely independent from the Soviet Union, U.S. Communists would still have been tied to forms of organization that inevitably placed them in direct opposition to the strategies of independence behind the postwar strike wave. In keeping with their Leninist tradition, Communists in the labor movement believed in disciplined organizations as the vanguard of the workers' movement. A radical party could exercise leadership in the trade unions; progressive unions could lead the working class; and eventually a strong base of institutional power would lead to state power. They assumed that unions represented the interests of workers, that union successes would be victories for the working class as a whole, and that leadership of the unions would eventually mean leadership of the working class. Seriously misreading the function of trade unions in capitalist society, their analysis wedded the Communists to bureaucratic and hierarchical forms, isolating them from the very constituency most likely to bring about radical change.

Trade unions play a dual role under capitalism. Important in winning material advances, unions also represent the institutional expression of all the shared experiences that bind workers together in everyday life. They provide an important frame of reference for their members as a legitimate forum for the expression of work-related concerns. On the other hand, unions also take on an institutional life of their own. To survive they must protect the competitive position of the employer, guarantee stability at the workplace, and legitimate the capitalist division of labor through job classifications and unequal rewards. Both roles co-exist uneasily within the same institution, constantly vying with each other for supremacy. In the forties, Communists cast their lot more with the institutional form and viewed the unpredictable class consciousness of everyday life with suspicion, fearing that it might lead to syndicalism or anarchism. Thus they aligned themselves with bureaucracy, trusting the ends to which they wanted to apply their power to overcome the limits of the form. But in the subjective experience of workers, the form itself had a political content. A Communist bureaucrat was still a bureaucrat, and if they were no worse than other union leaders, they were also no better.

Many Communists entered the labor movement as organizers at a time when few people wanted to endure the dangers and hardships of the job. Like other organizers, they assumed executive board positions when unions became more secure. Holding leadership posts disproportionate to their numbers among the rank and file, Communists owed their offices to their work as trade unionists, not to their political beliefs. Few surfaced as open Communists; most tried to lobby for their political views within the higher circles of unions without involving the rank and file. Partly out of a principled commitment to their unions, and partly out of a desire to retain power, they offered no autonomous communist trade-union program. They loaned their names and the prestige of their organizations to "progressive" causes, but relied on a few highly placed individuals to make their influence felt. Rather than trying openly to mobilize their own rank and file for political action, Communists in unions relied on the ability of party members and sympathizers like Harry Bridges of the ILWU, Lee Pressman of the CIO legal staff, and James Matles of the UE to use their positions to quietly create an advantageous political climate.

The same skill at organization that enabled a few Communist labor leaders to exercise political power on a national scale greater than their true support among workers also made them incapable of defending themselves once the anticommunist hysteria broke. Isolated in leadership positions, they incurred rank-and-file hostility to bureaucracy. Even when directly attacked for being Communists, they did not defend their views to the rank and file, arguing instead for the privacy of political opinions and the autonomy of unions from political considerations. They could not defend communism in unions, because they had no concept of what that might mean, apart from gaining more power for themselves and their associates. They never articulated or built a base for distinctly communist politics. Yet, because they were in fact Communists, their silence made them look like conspirators with something to hide.

As opportunistic anticommunists exploited rank-and-file resentments of bureaucracy as a preface to setting up bureaucracies of their own, Communists used their institutional power to stifle debate in the unions they dominated, and they shied away from open defenses of their record in others. When it appeared that they might lose elections or crucial tests of strength, they frequently withdrew rather than suffer public repudiation, a process that deprived their own supporters of an open airing of the issues.[50]

Emphasis on leadership and institutional power also backfired when former Communist sympathizers became anticommunists. Union leaders like Joe Curran of the maritime union and Mike Quill of the transit workers employed the same ruthless methods against Communists that they had previously used to support them. After years of Communist lobbying to have all members of the CIO back Philip Murray's policies, the organization's president used his power to expel Communists and to demand unqualified support for the Marshall Plan. Long after Communists had accused their opponents of conspiracy and subversion for disagreeing with the government, they found themselves subjected to the same charges.

Ugly uses of power by Communists hardly justify the vicious repression directed against them, but they underscore the dangers of relying on institutional power rather than on popular support. Neither side came to the union rivalries of the postwar period with clean hands, but the anticommunists did not need to. Backed by government repression, big business approval, and a sympathetic press, anticommunists could only profit from exercises of institutional power. Enjoying none of those advantages, Communists needed the kinds of counterpressures an open, democratic, mass movement could provide. They cannot be faulted for failing to create that kind of movement under such difficult conditions, but they can legitimately be criticized for not making the attempt.

The communist faith in disciplined hierarchical organizations provided one additional disadvantage. Communists in the labor movement belonged to a party that proclaimed the interests of workers and that gained some of its greatest prestige through labor militancy. But it was not a working-class party. Out of party discipline and loyalty, Communists in labor implemented policies originating in the highest levels of the party whether they met the immediate needs of workers or not. One tragic example of this came in the participation of the party's best labor representatives in the Wallace for President campaign in 1948. Whatever honor is due Henry Wallace for his courageous opposition to the early cold war, neither his politics nor his campaign served working-class interests. At the very moment when they most needed to rouse the rank and file in defense of their class interests, Communist labor leaders devoted their efforts to the presidential campaign of a disillusioned member of the ruling elite, whose main argument seemed to be that American capitalism could dominate the world without having to resort to encirclement of the Soviet Union. The Wallace response to corporate liberalism did not present an alternative based on worker control of the means of production; in fact, Wallace and his allies may have been the last believers in old-fashioned laissez-faire capitalism.[51]

The real question that arises from the expulsions of Communists from American trade unions is not how they were driven out, but why they lasted as long as they did. In every respect, the Communist party and its supporters in the labor movement comprised a perfect foil for the anticommunist hysteria around them. Steeped in bureaucracy, isolated from a rank-and-file base, faithful to Soviet foreign policy, and unwilling or unable to articulate a political position all their own, Communists provided an ideal target for the repression directed against them.

Considered in the light of the crisis atmosphere surrounding Truman's foreign policy, the sense of fear and betrayal emanating from the collapse of hopes for security in the postwar world, and the blatant repression by the government, the Communists in unions should have been quickly and easily driven out. But they were not.

In local unions throughout the country, workers remained loyal to leaders identified with communism. Rank-and-file Communists participated in the 1945 ILA strike in New York, and they publicly backed George Mueller and the IA in Pittsburgh in September and October 1946. In the Oakland general strike, leaders sympathetic to communism—like Harry Bridges—undermined the efforts of the rank and file, but many individual Communists recognized the necessity of involvement and support for the strike. At the highest levels, Communists could not escape their identification with bureaucracy, but on the local level in many instances they represented the best in shop-floor politics. One reason for the extraordinary pressures brought to bear against them from "official" sources (deportations, raids, congressional hearings, union discipline) grew out of the bitter and inconclusive nature of struggles to oust them from the bottom up. Anticommunists expecting to attain power merely by crying "Communist" generally failed, while even open Communists retained considerable support when they had good reputations on local issues.

Confronted with competing groups of bureaucrats, the rank and file forced both of them to assume militant positions against bureaucracy. Where Communists had been effective organizers, where they had helped improve working conditions, and where they had established reputations as part of the community of workers, they proved extremely difficult to dislodge despite intense outside pressures. Anticommunists assumed that rank-and-file loyalty to Communists manifested working-class conservatism: a reluctance to accept any change. They argued that workers did not understand or relate to ideologies and shortsightedly acted on the basis of their own interests. In truth, loyalty to union leaders or activists associated with past struggles constituted an endorsement of previous militancy and affirmation of that militancy as part of working-class identity. Coupled with an enduring faith in direct action, rank-and-file defense of Communist leaders represented a clear ideology, although it did not involve a choice between abstractions of capitalism or communism. That ideology contradicted Philip Murray's assertion that America had no classes. Even in the face of concentrated repression, workers chose to advance their class interests. The struggles of factory workers in 1948 in Evansville, Indiana, and Fairmont City, Illinois, in support of unions charged with Communist domination graphically illustrate both the nature and depth of that class feeling.

NOTES

1. *New York Times*, Mar. 26, 1947, 1, Apr. 2, 1947, 20.

2. *New York Times*, Apr. 7, 1947, 1.

3. Art Preis, *Labor's Giant Step* (New York: Pathfinder Press, 1972), 313; *Newsweek*, May 5, 1947, 26.

4. *Monthly Labor Review* (May 1947): 71.

5. Preis, *Labor's Giant Step*, 317; *Monthly Labor Review* (May 1947): 71.

6. *Business Week*, Aug. 2, 1947, 63; *Newsweek*, Aug. 4, 1947, 70; *Monthly Labor Review* (Aug. 1947): 203.

7. Historians sometimes use these election results to argue that Truman and the Democrats had no choice but to cater to an increasingly conservative electorate. But their showing in 1946 owed less to increased votes for Republicans than to decreased votes for Democrats. In the election, the Democratic vote fell from 25 million to 15 million, while less than 40 percent of eligible voters actually voted. See Barbara S. Griffith, *The Crisis of American Labor: Operation Dixie and the Defeat of the CIO* (Philadelphia: Temple University Press, 1988), 145.

8. The phrase is Senator Arthur Vandenberg's. He advised Truman that it would be necessary to scare the hell out of the American people to convince them of the necessity for the Truman Doctrine. See Richard Freeland, *The Truman Doctrine and the Origins of McCarthyism* (New York: Knopf, 1972), 372; Stephen Ambrose, *Rise to Globalism* (London: Penguin Press, 1971), 151.

9. *New York Times*, Mar. 7, 1947, 3.

10. Ibid., Mar. 13, 1947, 2.

11. Walter Lafeber, *America, Russia, and the Cold War* (New York: Wiley, 1972), 44–45.

12. Quoted in Thomas J. McCormick, *America's Half-Century: United States Foreign Policy in the Cold War* (Baltimore: Johns Hopkins University Press, 1989), 76.

13. Dean Acheson, *Present at the Creation* (New York: Norton, 1969), 229; David Eakins, "Business Planners and America's Postwar Expansion," in David Horowitz, ed., *Corporations and the Cold War* (New York: Monthly Review Press, 1969), 143–71.

14. Ibid., 164–65.

15. Ibid., 165.

16. McCormick, *America's Half-Century*, 74.

17. Eakins, "Business Planners and America's Postwar Expansion," 164.

18. *Fortune*, June 1947, 83.

19. Gabriel Kolko, *Main Currents in Modern American History* (New York: Harper and Row, 1976), 317.

20. McCormick, *America's Half-Century*, 95–96.

21. Ibid., 105. Ernest R. May identifies Truman's military budget as under $13 billion in 1950, less than 5 percent of the gross national product. After adopting NSC-68, Truman's budget climbed to $60 billion, 18.5 percent of the GNP. Ernest R. May, *American Cold War Strategy: Interpreting NSC 68* (Boston: Bedford Books, 1993), vii. See also Gore Vidal, *At Home* (New York: Vintage, 1988), 126–27.

22. Michael P. Rogin, *Ronald Reagan, the Movie: And Other Episodes in Political Demonology* (Berkeley: University of California Press, 1987), xiii.

23. Richard M. Freeland, *The Truman Doctrine and the Origins of McCarthyism* (New York: Knopf, 1974), 219.

24. *New York Times*, Oct. 16, 1947, 3; *St. Louis Post-Dispatch*, Nov. 30, 1947, 1B.

25. *St. Louis Post-Dispatch*, Nov. 30, 1947, 1B.

26. *Newsweek*, July 20, 1946, 27–28.

27. *U.S. News*, Nov. 22, 1946, 20–22.

28. *American Magazine*, June 1948, 136.

29. *Monthly Labor Review* (Jan. 1949): 14.

30. *Time*, Nov. 14, 1949, 22–23.

31. Griffith, *The Crisis of American Labor*, 150.

32. Ibid., 153–54.

33. Steve Rosswurm, ed., *The CIO's Left-Led Unions* (New Brunswick: Rutgers University Press, 1992), 4, 5, 14.

34. James C. Foster, ed., *American Labor in the Southwest* (Tucson: University of Arizona Press, 1982), 232.

35. Bert Cochran, *Labor and Communism* (Princeton: Princeton University Press, 1977), provides a balanced account of the Communist party and the labor movement.

36. Nelson Lichtenstein, "Defending the No-Strike Pledge: CIO Politics during World War II," *Radical America* 9 nos. 4–5 (1975); Preis, *Labor's Giant Step*; and Richard Boyer and Herbert Morais, *Labor's Untold Story* (New York: UE, 1955), provide different interpretations of Communists and the no-strike pledge.

37. *The Communist* (July 1943): 582, (May 1943): 483.

38. George Morris, "The Trotskyite Fifth Column in the Labor Movement," *The Communist* (Aug. 1944): 713.

39. M. A. Verick, "The Unambiguity of Labor History," *New Politics* (Winter 1968): 60; *Collier's*, Apr. 21, 1945, 22–23.

40. *Fortune*, Nov. 1943, 212.

41. *Business Week*, Mar. 18, 1944, 83–84.

42. *Business Week*, Mar. 18, 1944, 80.

43. Preis, *Labor's Giant Step*, 228, 230.

44. *Business Week*, Dec. 12, 1945, 93.

45. Gilbert Green, "Postwar Economic Perspectives," *The Communist* (Apr. 1944): 306.

46. The new name for the journal came as part of the strategy by party leaders to dissolve the party and become a "political association" instead.

47. Eugene Dennis, "Postwar Labor Capital Cooperation," *Political Affairs* (May 1945): 415.

48. Ibid., 416.

49. The party also made a public display of blaming all that had gone wrong on Earl Browder, who soon found himself replaced by his old foe, William Z. Foster.

50. The UE walked out of the 1949 CIO convention before it could be expelled. District organizer William Sentner resigned to take a higher position in the union when it appeared as if an electoral challenge to his power might succeed. Sentner supporters walked out of a December 1949 meeting at Wagner Electric in St. Louis before the membership could vote on remaining in the UE. Earlier, Sentner and his faction initiated expulsion proceedings against anticommunist challengers. Communists and their supporters in the California state CIO elections withdrew as candidates rather than suffer public defeats in 1944. In August 1946, Communist sympathizers at the Philadelphia CIO Council surrendered before an anticommunist resolution could come to a vote.

51. Wallace's belief that the Soviet Union provided a good market for U.S. goods and that its economic needs would inevitably drive it closer to capitalism were not exactly incorrect, but they hardly challenged the rationale for the cold war. Wallace believed that capitalism could win out in free and fair competition; corporate liberals did not agree. Understandably, business sided with the corporate liberals. Wallace's subsequent uncritical support for the U.S. role in the Korean War demonstrated the limits of his critique of U.S. foreign policy.

CHAPTER NINE

"Red Baiting at the Grass Roots"

Evansville and Fairmont City

WHEN THE BILL became law, both Communists and noncommunists attacked the Taft-Hartley provisions mandating noncommunist oaths from union leaders as a prerequisite for NLRB coverage. Some refused to comply, charging that the requirement discriminated against unions by singling them out for affirmations of loyalty. Others claimed that the provisions subjected union leaders to possible perjury charges since it did not define what it meant to be a Communist. Still others felt that the affidavits violated the political autonomy of unions by imposing political qualifications for leadership. Yet once the United Auto Workers strike at the Murray Corporation established the principle of penalizing individual workers for wildcat strikes, once union leaders saw the ways in which Taft-Hartley actually strengthened contractual relations with management, and once anticommunist union leaders saw the rewards awaiting them if they cooperated with government and business, most union leaders signed the affidavits.

Recognizing an opportunity to replace militant unions with cooperative ones, some employers exploited the anticommunist affidavits. They refused to sign contracts with locals of the UE and the IUMMSW because the national officers of those organizations persisted in refusing to pledge that they were not Communists. In Evansville, Indiana, and Fairmont City, Illinois, companies used the issue of communism to provoke bitter and violent strikes in the hopes of gaining the upper hand against conscientious and militant unions. The Taft-Hartley law and anticommunist hysteria provided these companies with powerful weapons, but rank-and-file solidarity fueled by the shared alienations and indignities of work enabled the unions to muster determined and effective resistance.

Like so many other American cities, Evansville experienced enormous changes as a result of wartime production. Located on the Ohio River at the Kentucky border, this city of 125,000 witnessed an influx of workers from rural areas during the war. Appliance, auto parts, farm implement, and construction equipment manufacturers shifted to military production, and the resulting steady work and high wages drew new workers into the city as rapidly as the draft and enlistments drew old ones out.

Demographic changes altered social relations in Evansville. One resident later recalled his father's alarm over the changes occasioned by the war, specifically mentioning some murders which he blamed on "those Kentuckians that come up across the river to work in our war plants here." When his son protested that there had always been a few murders a year in town, the father conceded that there had been murders in the past, "but not until these Kentuckians came up across the river in such numbers to work in our war plants, has anybody been killed in this town by anybody he didn't know." [1]

Murders by strangers probably loomed quite small among all the changes brought by the war to executives at Bucyrus-Erie Company, makers of digging and construction equipment and one of Evansville's largest employers. Although it had weathered the depression in reasonably good shape, Bucyrus-Erie's financial picture improved considerably with mobilization for war. Orders on hand in 1940 exceeded those of any year since 1929, and shipments in 1940 increased 40 percent over 1939.[2] Between 1942 and 1945, the company's entire output went for war production, assuring an unlimited, stable market and a steady flow of capital. Yet along with this financial bonanza, the war also brought collective bargaining to the Evansville plant.[3]

Like most of the city's employers, Bucyrus-Erie successfully resisted union organization in the thirties. War production doubled the size of the work force, but also disrupted primary work groups—replacing longtime workers with newcomers from rural areas traditionally hostile to unions. Yet in November 1942, the International Association of Machinists (IAM) won bargaining rights by polling more than 70 percent of the vote in a WLB election. Company officials refused to negotiate with the union for months, and they signed a contract including union dues checkoff and maintenance of membership only after the WLB ordered those practices at a Bucyrus-Erie plant in Pennsylvania. From the signing of the contract in May 1943 until the end of the war, resentments and grievances accumulated at the Evansville plant over the company's piecework and wage systems, but the union won no appreciable improvements.[4]

Bucyrus-Erie's refusal to pay a wage increase awarded to its workers by the WLB provoked a wildcat strike in October 1945, involving over two-thirds of the firm's 670 production workers. Union members then voted to transform the wildcat into an authorized strike, and in the next few months worked aggressive picket lines to defeat company-instigated back-

to-work movements. Despite their determination, the strike ended after
fifteen weeks on the company's terms. A contract between the IAM and
Bucyrus-Erie in April 1946 overturned union security provisions—like
maintenance of membership and dues checkoff—established during the
war. The strike and resulting contract so damaged the union's reputation
that by July 1946, it could not attract enough volunteers to maintain a
grievance committee, while the company operated the plant "as if we had
no union."[5]

Both the UAW and the UE tried to fill the void created by the demise of
the IAM at Bucyrus-Erie. After a four-month campaign, the UE emerged
victorious, winning 581 out of 825 votes in a May 1947 bargaining election.
The new union immediately demanded restoration of maintenance of membership and establishment of super seniority for shop stewards and union
officers, but the company felt no obligation to sign a contract with the UE
simply because it had been designated as the bargaining agent. Piecemeal
negotiations collapsed in 1947 and did not resume until 1948.[6]

Shortly after the resumption of talks with the union, Bucyrus-Erie announced that it would not sign a contract with the UE because the organization's international officers refused to sign the noncommunist affidavits
requested by Taft-Hartley. The company management knew perfectly well
that the law did not demand that union leaders sign the oaths and that
other unions at that time, including Philip Murray's United Steel Workers,
preferred to forego the services of the NLRB rather than have their leaders
sign. Yet Bucyrus-Erie's spokespersons concocted an elaborate chain of supposition, starting with the affidavits and ending with the control of their
workers by the Kremlin. For all the hysterical and superpatriotic rhetoric
accompanying it, the real sources of the company's enmity to the union
stemmed from nothing more dramatic than the record of UE Local 813 in
representing Evansville workers in the preceding year.

In a letter to UE district president William Sentner (who proclaimed
openly that he was a Communist), Bucyrus-Erie complained about the
union's "bad faith bargaining." Company officials charged that Sentner
wanted complete domination over the workers and that he intended to "deprive us of the right to manage our business."[7] Curiously, the only concrete
example that management could cite to justify its accusations concerned
a proposed change in the union constitution to elect the district president
by delegates, rather than by the membership at large. Whatever the merits
of that change, it hardly constituted bad-faith bargaining (having no relation to bargaining at all) or a slap at management rights. The power of the
union frightened the company because of the UE's aggressive defense of
rank-and-file interests in the plant and management's reluctance to grant
contract recognition to such an aggressive opponent.

Accustomed to cooperative relationships with United Steel Workers locals at its other installations, Bucyrus-Erie viewed the UE performance in Evansville with trepidation. Company attorney John Kamps later told a congressional investigating committee that the firm opposed the union because of its propensity "to insist on a control of the plant and an interference with the actual operation of the plant that was beyond that ordinarily demanded or requested by unions."[8] Specifically, Kamps complained about union efforts to control the hours of work and provisions for overtime and its practice of "policing a plant, and by that I mean going out and seeking grievances." Such practices seem well within the pale of legitimate trade-union activity, but in the midst of a national anticommunist hysteria they provided the basis for a concentrated campaign to drive UE Local 813 out of Evansville.

Bucyrus-Erie's allegations helped mobilize an anticommunist opposition group within the local. Encouraged by the city's newspapers, the dissidents challenged union officers to prove that they were not Communists and demanded resignations from those who were.[9] Fistfights erupted between members of opposing factions at one union meeting, and another session had to be adjourned prematurely when tempers reached the boiling point. Yet this factionalism never blinded union members to the company's intentions. Union leadership denounced Bucyrus-Erie for trying to weaken the union by provoking a strike, and even the opposition faction supported the drive to win a contract. "Although we oppose our leadership," they maintained, "we do not believe Bucyrus-Erie is on honest ground. We think the company is trying to use the communist issue to avoid bargaining."[10]

Workers finally did vote to strike on July 30, 1948, after fourteen months of unsuccessful negotiations and after company threats never to sign a contract with the duly-elected bargaining agent. The strike vote took place while the district president and local leadership attended a union meeting out of town, causing some supporters of the local to speculate that dissidents may have promoted the walkout to discredit the leadership. Whatever the motivation, the strike vote carried by a margin of 479 to 8, and the union faithfully carried out that mandate and proceeded to organize a militant strike.[11]

The union presented its case to the people of Evansville in a series of radio broadcasts over station WGBF. On these programs, UE members stressed their need for better working conditions and pay, while condemning the company's accusations about communism as a ploy designed to obscure real economic issues. As rank and filer Ralph Finan explained on an August 8 broadcast, "The company thinks it is going to fool a lot of us people with all its yapping about reds and red plots, but I'll tell you, this company doesn't fool me one minute with its propaganda." On the same show, union member Lawrence Robinson complained about Bucyrus-Erie's refusal to implement adequate grievance procedures, its arbitrary rate schedules, unfair discharges, and its insurance plan that forced workers to pay premiums while the company collected the dividends. Assembly-line worker Ed Ritter chimed in with an allegation that workers in the plant once had twelve hours in which to complete a job, but that the company unilaterally cut the time to ten, and then to eight hours.[12]

Despite deep divisions on other issues, Local 813 maintained effective solidarity when it came to the strike. With the assistance of the Evansville Labor Union Council (representing unions in the auto, clothing, and machine industries), and with the solid backing of the local's members in other Evansville plants (Servel, Seeger, Faultless Caster), the Bucyrus-Erie strikers presented their fight as a contest between a responsible union and an antilabor employer. Recalling the bitter struggle to establish unions in the city and aware of the close cooperation among Evansville's leading manufacturers, workers throughout the area supported the strike despite the company charges of Communist influence in the union. Mass picketing stopped production at the plant, and union picket captains determined whether supervisory personnel could go to work. A company strategy intended to secure management control over production in May led to a strike that paralyzed it by August.[13]

Management resorted to a variety of tactics to gain the upper hand. On August 19, supervisors attempted to break the picket line by sending out a shipment of construction equipment ordered from the plant by the Atomic Energy Commission. Company strategists knew that this would provoke an incident, but they hoped that the destination of the shipment would cast additional doubt on the union's patriotism. As the truck started toward the gates, picketers passed in front of it and stood shoulder to shoulder, preventing it from leaving the lot. Strikers stopped the shipment, not out of a diabolical scheme to deprive the Atomic Energy Commission of a needed machine, but to enforce the union picket line.[14]

On the same day that the AEC ploy failed, the company sent letters to all striking employees in an effort to trigger a back-to-work movement. Reiterating its opposition to communism, the company enclosed cards for workers to return which read, "I want to return to work immediately under conditions stated in your letter." The UE official strike bulletin pointed out that the letter failed to state any conditions and that returning workers could look forward to low wages, rate cutting, and an open shop. Reminding its members of the disastrous 1945–46 IAM strike, the union bulletin contended that charges of Communist domination constituted only the latest in a long list of lies by the company about "unions that sought to get decent wages and conditions for Bucyrus workers."[15]

Supplied with movies and photographs of the AEC picket-line incident that management provoked on August 19, Bucyrus-Erie lawyers asked for and received civil contempt charges against eleven picketers for violating a restraining order against obstructive picketing. As the courts were complying with that request, AFL representatives applied to the NLRB for a representation election at the plant, knowing full well that the UE could not appear on the ballot because its officers refused to sign the noncommunist oaths. CIO members picketed AFL headquarters in protest against the federation's raiding and strikebreaking, but the NLRB quickly scheduled an election for September 22.[16]

Bucyrus-Erie secured another restraining order on August 27 prohibiting mass picketing. The next day, forty supervisors crashed the picket line, provoking a near riot that led to twenty-seven arrests and—as it was designed to do—more contempt-of-court charges. Workers waged a pitched battle with supervisors and police. The violence was intensified by increased despair about ever obtaining a peaceful settlement. One supervisor, attempting to drive his car through the picket line, reported that a striker shouted: "I lost my job; I am going to jail anyway and I am going to kill you, you s.o.b." and then smashed the side window of the car with a two-by-four.[17]

An advertisement in the *Evansville Press* the day after the picket-line violence promised that the plant would reopen on Tuesday, August 31. When it did, 140 Indiana state police officers showed up on orders from the governor to escort strikebreakers past the picket line, now composed of seven women strikers. Yet even with that "protection" only 420 of the plant's 1,100 employees reported for work. In retaliation, the Evansville Union Labor Council called for a labor holiday to protest against strikebreaking at Bucyrus-Erie.[18]

Unlike the general strikes of 1946, this one failed. Almost half the work force at Faultless Caster stayed home, and other plants reported "some" absenteeism, but not enough to significantly reduce production. For a time it appeared as though a general strike might take place—when AFL Motor Coach Operators struck the city bus line in what management termed an illegal strike in defiance of state law—but the walkout had only a coincidental relationship to the Bucyrus-Erie strike. The bus drivers walked out because their own contract negotiations faltered, not out of sympathy with Local 813. Although the general strike failed to materialize, Bucyrus-Erie strikers retained sufficient support and solidarity to drive the company to even greater repression.[19]

State police returned to the plant on September 7 to enforce a restraining order barring all picketing, but the most unusual assault on the strike came two days later. A special subcommittee of the U.S. House of Representatives Committee on Education and Labor announced that it would conduct hearings in Evansville on Communist influence in the Bucyrus-Erie strike, and it subpoenaed 30 strikers and strike sympathizers. In making this intervention, the committee followed what had by now become a familiar pattern. Ever since the summer of 1947, when the House Committee on Un-American Activities held hearings designed to publicize the presence of Communists with the UE on the East Coast, congressional committees and subcommittees routinely tried to bring the weight of public opinion against the left-wing factions in the union.[20] In the wake of highly publicized House Un-American Activities Committee hearings—in which congressional immunity allowed sensational accusations of disloyalty without recourse to cross-examination or legal standards of evidence—the Evansville hearings had a chilling effect on the union's exercise of its right to strike. Almost as soon as subpoenas went out, the UE abandoned the strike.[21]

Clearly devoid of any legislative intent, the hearings drew largely upon the testimony of one witness for most of its accusations. Kathryn Bell, who claimed to have been a member of a Communist party cell in Evansville, provided names of people she alleged to be Communists. Investigators then called forth the accused to confirm or deny the charges. Those who refused to testify on the basis of their constitutional rights or who claimed that they had insufficient time to obtain counsel found themselves ridiculed by the members of Congress and spotlighted in the newspapers as noncooperators suspected of communism. In some cases, the committee produced what it described as (and which very well may have been) Communist party membership cards signed by the accused. On the other hand, some of those accused asserted that their signatures had been forged. In either case, the committee's interests lay with accusations more than they did with proof.[22]

After two days of these proceedings, the committee left town and allowed others to follow up on its work. Some employers demanded that those accused renounce communism and affirm their belief in God as a precondition for continued employment. Others acted in more subtle ways. Bucyrus-Erie fired forty-one of the returning strikers for their alleged participation in picket-line violence, and other companies used the strike's end as a stimulus to crack down on working conditions in their factories. Faultless Caster stalled on processing grievances, Servel laid off a shop steward and fired two members of the union grievance committee, and the Seeger Company cut incentive pay rates for its workers.[23]

Following the hearings, Evansville's newspapers reported a new kind of "spontaneous" shop-floor action—angry workers running accused Communists out of the plants. According to these accounts, two hundred outraged auto workers at Briggs Indiana refused to work until a man named as a Communist at the hearings left the building; electrical workers at Faultless Caster circulated petitions demanding that the company fire five of the accused; parallel incidents took place at Seeger, Servel, and International Harvester.

In truth, the "shop-floor purges" represented carefully orchestrated plans by outsiders, not the spontaneous actions of the rank and file.[24] Attacks on accused Communists in three separate plants occurred at exactly the same time. At Servel and Faultless Caster, supervisors and foremen made the threats and instigated the intimidation. Workers associated with the Ku Klux Klan and the anticommunist Association of Catholic Trade Unionists played prominent roles in physically intimidating victims at Briggs Indiana and Seeger. During most of the assaults, company supervisors calmly watched one group of workers stop production and physically threaten individuals whose work had been satisfactory. Incredibly, management took no disciplinary action against those perpetrating this disruption of production.[25]

One worker at International Harvester, who had refused to answer the committee's questions on September 10, went to work that night and received only good-natured teasing from fellow workers. Six nights later, four men accosted him in the parking lot and threatened to knock his head off unless he stayed away from the job. After a few days at home, he returned to work without incident, despite the refusal of the company or the union (UAW) to help him. The individual chased out of Briggs Indiana found everyone in his section friendly and willing to talk to him when he arrived at work after the hearings, but when the production line started, about forty-five workers shook hammers in his face, made threats, and forced him to leave.[26]

Although hardly spontaneous, the shop-floor attacks did manifest real and understandable anger. Whether orchestrated for the upcoming September 22 NLRB representation election at Bucyrus-Erie or merely as part of a general anticommunist campaign, the shop-floor attacks doubtlessly picked up support from ordinary rank and filers frightened or angered by the "discovery" of actual Communists operating secretly at Evansville. These individuals kept their political affiliations with a legal political party secret as they had every right to do, but their secrecy contributed to the appearance of a real conspiracy consonant with the company's charges. They paid dearly for their tactical errors when a congressional committee recklessly directed sensational charges against private citizens in order to break a strike and destroy a union.

For all the harm coming out of the hearings, UE members and supporters might have weathered the storm had it not been for another instrument of repression: the specter of a blacklist. Many of the workers fired at Bucyrus-Erie or named in the congressional hearings found it impossible to get work in Evansville's factories, despite an acute labor shortage. Some reported favorable receptions from personnel interviewers until their past employment became known, at which point they were told that the company was not hiring new workers.[27] When the congressional committee returned to Evansville on September 19 to allow those accused previously to beg public forgiveness, the rumored blacklist provided an unspoken threat to noncooperators. Eleven witnesses from the first hearings asked to clear their names by testifying, either admitting to having once been a Communist, or explaining that they had been lured to Communist meetings under false pretenses. As one finished his testimony, he asked the committee to make sure he could now be hired in Evansville since he had cooperated with them.[28]

Injunctions, state police patrols, congressional hearings, threats, and reports of a blacklist achieved their intended purpose. Two weeks after the end of the strike, an AFL federal local won bargaining rights at Bucyrus-Erie by a vote of 549 to 288 in an NLRB election that barred the UE from the ballot. The no-union votes were essentially pro-UE votes, protesting against the union's omission from the ballot.[29] Bucyrus-Erie signed its first contract in nearly five years on November 1, 1948, having secured at last the kind of union it wanted. Those fired for their participation in the strike found industrial employment closed to them in Evansville, and most eventually left the city.[30]

Other employers also reaped benefits from Bucyrus-Erie's victory. In a letter to its workers on October 8, 1948, Faultless Caster management announced layoffs due to high production costs aggravated by alleged work stoppages, slowdowns, and idleness during work. Noting that some workers had been charging management with running a "sweatshop," the company indignantly denied the charge and then threatened more layoffs if productivity did not increase. Taking a page from Bucyrus-Erie's book, the letter reminded workers that "recently the employees demonstrated their dislike for the radicals in our employ and who were fostering this havoc in our company" and went on to pledge that the company would not hire or rehire "any person who is a member of, or supports any organization which advocates or endeavors to overthrow the Government of the United States through force." Having connected shop-floor militancy to selected radicals, the letter did not explain why militancy persisted after these same radicals had been driven from their jobs, but it clearly indicated the firm's predilection for viewing shop-floor activism as evidence of subversion and its willingness to use anticommunism as a cover for crackdowns against strategies of independence in the plant.[31]

Anticommunism among rank-and-file workers contributed very little to the UE defeat in Evansville. At every turn, the company relied on "official" sources of power: legal repression, economic and political influence, and physical force. The Taft-Hartley law gave management an excuse to delay bargaining, NLRB rulings facilitated raids by the AFL, court injunctions and police power restrained the strikers while allowing the company a free hand, and cooperative members of Congress provided the pretext for a blacklist. Bucyrus-Erie resorted to these extreme measures precisely because charges of Communist influence alone could not produce the desired results. Not that workers favored communism. They favored shop-floor militancy and aggressive trade unionism and would support those principles even if it meant incurring accusations of Communist domination.

Considering the forces arrayed against it, Local 813 retained impressive popular support. Even the anticommunist faction conceded that union leaders derived their strength from their record of winning gains for the rank and file. "Maybe they do have more to offer in that way than we do," admitted opposition leader Ernest Rutherford.[32] When Al Eberhard won re-election as Local 813's president at the start of the 1948 strike, both sides felt that the election honestly represented the wishes of the membership.[33] Pressed for details as to exactly how Communist leadership hurt the local, anticommunist William Debes admitted, "It's hard to put your finger on things you can prove" and lamely charged the other side with "running things with a high hand," particularly resolutions on national politics.[34]

Loyal to the record of their union, noncommunists in Local 813 resented the implication that Communists among their number made them dupes. As the local's president told a reporter, "Nobody could accuse me of being a Communist. I'm a Catholic and a good one. I go to church and send my children to parochial school. But just because I won't go along with this bunch in their efforts to take over I'm accused of being a stooge."[35]

Workers in Evansville knew that district president Sentner and some others in their union held communist views, but they refused to allow that single consideration to determine their positions on union politics. Many admired the UE because of its militancy on shop-floor issues. Wilder "Hoop" Allen, a Sentner supporter who worked at Servel, remembered that before the UE won bargaining rights at his shop he had to give the boss a pint of whiskey to avoid being laid off and that he would often have to be at work for ten or twelve hours to get eight hours of pay. But after the union came in, Allen received seniority rights that protected him from layoffs and he worked according to a contract that guaranteed his pay for all hours worked.[36] Allen admired Sentner despite the "red taint" on the union leader, feeling that "he never tried to ask me to join the party. I don't know whether he belonged or not. If he did, that's his business, that's none of mine."[37]

Similarly, Faultless Caster employee Esther Zieman recalled how she had to depend upon the whims of supervisors for permission to use the restroom at work before the UE won bargaining rights at her shop, but that after winning a contract the union protected her rights and doubled her wages.[38] "They tried to say we was communist," she later recalled. "We knew we wasn't."[39]

Residents of Evansville with no direct stake in the controversy exhibited a similar sense of fair play. On June 30, 1949, a superior court jury found eleven defendants guilty of violating a judicial restraining order by their actions on the Bucyrus-Erie picket line a year before, but the union members received light punishments because the jury didn't believe that they did very much wrong. Bucyrus-Erie asked for fines amounting to $33,000, but the jury assessed the strikers only $445—$200 apiece for union officers William Sentner and Charles Wright and only $5 apiece for the other defendants.[40] Some of those arrested even sued the city for malicious prosecution and won small damages.[41] And less than two months after the union's defeat, Evansville voters turned out of office the member of Congress who presided over the "investigation" of Local 813's Communists.[42]

One reason for the UE's resilience in Evansville stemmed from its involvement in every facet of workers' lives. Esther Zieman remembers that every Christmas she would go shopping at Fischer's novelty store with union spokesperson Sadelle Berger to buy presents for children attending the UE Christmas party.[43] On Saturday nights the union brought in nationally known orchestras like Erskine Hawkins and his fourteen-piece band to play at union dances.[44] In addition, daily radio broadcasts of "UE on the Air" on local station WGBF (and later on WJPS) presented the union's position on national and international issues ranging from labor issues like unemployment and antistrike legislation to broader concerns including the postwar housing shortage and foreign aid.[45]

During the Bucyrus-Erie strike, power exercised beyond the reach of popular local pressure proved decisive to the success of anticommunists in Evansville. The NLRB, the courts, the Taft-Hartley Act, and the state police all rendered concrete assistance to the company during the strike, while bureaucratic mechanisms encouraged resolution of differences on management's terms. Regardless of their decisions in any specific case, the courts and government administrative bodies always favored the company, because their very processes denied to workers the power to directly solve their own problems in time to do some good. For example, the NLRB eventually ruled against company complaints that picketing at the plant constituted an illegal secondary boycott under the terms of the Taft-Hartley Act, but did so almost a year after the strike had ended. The union gained nothing for its "victory" and lost the use of a legitimate pressure tactic during the strike. Relying on its own resources, Local 813 could put up a good fight, but when outside forces intervened, even triumphs became defeats.[46]

Bucyrus-Erie officials used the noncommunist affidavits as a pretext for a union-busting campaign aimed at giving the company unchallenged control over production. When simple red-baiting proved ill-suited to that end, the employer provoked a strike, secured court injunctions, encouraged raids by rival unions, instigated violence at the picket line, enlisted the aid of a congressional committee, fired strikers, condoned shop-floor attacks on individuals, and gave credibility to fears of a blacklist. Workers resisted those tactics because they wanted to make their own decisions and because they wanted to control the conditions and rewards of work. Similar motives lay behind the resistance of workers in Fairmont City, Illinois, that same year, as they conducted a bitter struggle against another employer trying to use anticommunism as a means of securing greater control over production.

A small industrial community on the outskirts of East St. Louis, Fairmont City experienced less sensational changes during the war than larger and more diversified manufacturing cities. Local unions already held bargaining rights, which they won in the thirties, and earlier migrations accounted for the bulk of the town's Polish, Italian, and Mexican residents. Yet the war did bring one crucial change. Military spending completely reversed the dismal economic situation of American Zinc, the town's largest employer, creating new possibilities for both the company and its workers. As American Zinc president Howard I. Young later claimed, World War II established the metals industry just as World War I solidified the profit-making potential of chemical companies. His own firm lost $50,000 in 1938, but reported profits exceeding $900,000 in 1944. Despite expenditures for improved facilities, the company paid dividends to stockholders for the first time in history in 1945. Government spending accounted for almost all of this improvement, generating 67 percent of the firm's net profits in 1944 and 96 percent the next year.[47]

Even when government subsidies diminished at the end of the war, American Zinc's financial position remained strong. Increased integration of producers in the United States ended wide fluctuations in zinc prices, and increased world demand—aggravated by wartime damage to foreign zinc producers—offered companies like American Zinc an opportunity to sell overseas for the first time. The firm's improved financial status, its opportunity to sell more zinc, and a shortage of skilled labor impelled workers in the Fairmont City plant to view the postwar era as an opportunity to compensate for past deprivations.

Like many companies with low capitalization, a poor competitive position, and uncertain markets, American Zinc treated its employees with paternalism. Management opposed unions because their existence seemed to presume a fundamental antagonism between employees and employer. Company officials contended that dissatisfied workers could always bring complaints directly to them, but often the workers preferred the protection of a union. In 1933, they voted bargaining recognition for Local 82 of the IUMMSW. Conscious of the company's precarious financial position, the union accepted wage cuts during periods of recession and at all times refrained from making demands about wages or working conditions that might threaten future employment.[48]

After the war, the union campaigned for wage increases and better grievance procedures, while management complained about slowdowns, wildcats, and alleged union intrusion on management prerogatives. The steadily deteriorating labor situation at the plant produced an impasse in April 1948, when the union asked for a wage increase that the company insisted it could not afford. A strike seemed inevitable as the July 1 contract expiration date neared.

Expecting a strike, American Zinc's management wanted it to take place on the best possible terms for the company. Fearful that rank-and-file pressure would compel the union to demand expensive wage, pension, or welfare benefits without assurances of increased productivity, the firm explored ways of forcing a strike on other issues. The Taft-Hartley Act and Local 82's national affiliation provided just that opportunity.

The IUMMSW's national officers refused to sign the noncommunist affidavits prescribed in Taft-Hartley. Anticommunists in the union charged executive board members with being Communists, and a large bloc of locals seceded from the international in 1946 in protest against an election that they charged Communists had stolen from them. Industry officials took careful notice of these developments. An article in the *Engineering and Mining Journal* in June 1947 stressed the similarity between IUMMSW political positions and those of the Communist party, while a series of editorials in *American Metal Market* in October of the same year condemned Communist influence in the union. A number of employers in the industry—including American Zinc—decided to refuse to sign contracts with the union unless its officers signed the noncommunist affidavits.[49]

Knowing that a strike would probably occur anyway, American Zinc's management decided to fight the union over the issue of communism. An aide to the company president counseled in a May 7 confidential memorandum that "there is little hope of increasing efficiency in a plant where the union teaches that the company is the 'common enemy' of its employees." He advised management to make communism the core issue of the strike, reasoning that "more support could be mustered for, or at any rate, less active opposition raised against, an economic strike than would be the case when the issue was understood to be compliance with the law and communism."[50] A strike on economic grounds might attract considerable worker and community support, but a strike where communism provided the main issue might divide the union, win support from the community, encourage raids by unions likely to be more cooperative than Local 82, and demoralize the strikers. The opportunity appeared too good to pass up.

Early in June, company president Young notified workers in the Fairmont City plant that American Zinc would no longer negotiate with the IUMMSW because it had Communist leaders. Young proclaimed, "At this time of danger to our country, we will not deal with men who take orders from, and who are loyal to, the government of communist Russia. Ours is a critical industry for America's defense. We will not endanger it."[51]

Company officials knew that Local 82 offered no real threat to the national defense, but raising the charge enabled them to face the strike on their own terms. American Zinc's executives sincerely opposed communism and honestly believed that Communists dominated the union, but the issues separating labor and management at Fairmont City had more to do with wages and working conditions than with differing opinions about the Soviet Union.[52]

After working without a contract for six weeks, Local 82 finally called a strike against American Zinc on August 13, 1948. Flatly denying the charge of Communist domination, the union's officers noted that the company announced its stand only after learning of the local's 1948 wage demands. The zinc workers stood behind their union because of the way it had represented them in the past. As a reporter for a local newspaper surmised, "individual members of Local 82 do not want to believe that the officers of the union which has done so much for them within the last 15 years are communists."[53]

American Zinc's exploitation of the communist issue brought immediate results. It stimulated community opposition to the union, increased factionalism in the local, and encouraged other labor leaders to raid Local 82's membership. In September, company attorneys secured a circuit court injunction against obstructive picketing at the plant. In October, a local priest sent letters to his parishioners under the heading "With Christ at Our Side We Can Lick Communism and the Strikers." In December, an opposition candidate narrowly defeated Local 82's president in his bid for reelection, and in January the International Chemical Workers Union of the AFL announced plans to seek representation rights at the plant. But the strike continued because of rank-and-file solidarity.[54]

Despite many setbacks, Local 82 kept the plant closed without mass picketing. Catholic workers remained loyal to the union even when they had to defy their parish priest. Factionalism in the local did not interfere with the strike, and most area labor leaders condemned the Chemical Workers for raiding during a work stoppage.[55] Most important for the union, many residents of Fairmont City sided with the workers rather than with the town's big employer.

Grocers, tavern owners, and service station operators complained about damage done to their businesses because of the strike, and they urged American Zinc to settle on the union's terms. Even some representatives of American Legion Post 961 cast their lot with the strikers, dismissing out of hand the company's charges about communism. Management personnel generally lived outside the town, but strikers did their shopping and living in Fairmont City, helping them to retain the allegiance of their neighbors. Several hundred people turned out for a community rally on January 23, 1949, to hear IUMMSW International president Reid Robinson denounce American Zinc's efforts to use communism as a smokescreen for an attack on worker security.[56]

American Zinc wanted a long strike to demoralize the union, but the company's refusal to bargain brought unexpectedly stubborn resistance from the strikers and their supporters in the community. By May the strike had been going on for 260 days at a cost in lost wages of $2,200 per worker, in lost payroll of $2 million, and in lost production of 190 work days. In order to break the strike, the company announced on May 7, 1949, that it would close its furnaces and leave Fairmont City for good if the workers did not join another union by June 10.[57] Even if that threat failed by itself, management hoped that it would influence the outcome of an NLRB representation election at American Zinc scheduled for the middle of June.

From the earliest days of the strike, the Progressive Metalworkers Council (PMC) of the CIO tried to wrest bargaining rights at American Zinc from the IUMMSW. Angelo Verdu, a former IUMMSW executive board member and longtime opponent of the national officers, led the raiding by the PMC at Fairmont City with the backing of anticommunists within the local and national CIO. The PMC not only secured a representation election but the NLRB barred the IUMMSW from the ballot because its leaders refused to sign the noncommunist affidavits. Those who favored Local 82 would have to vote for "no union" to keep representation as before.

In the emotion-charged atmosphere of the ten-month-old strike, intense rivalry between the two unions erupted into violence. A group of men associated with the PMC, including Angelo Verdu's brother, fired shots at the IUMMSW education director on May 26. Another IUMMSW staff member who witnessed the shooting identified the attackers to the police, only to have two men accost him a short time later and beat him with brass knuckles.[58] Two days before the election, the Illinois Highway Patrol had to break up a fight that started when PMC adherents drove past IUMMSW headquarters shouting threats and brandishing a revolver.[59] Local police nervously patrolled a tense community on the eve of the election.

Despite endorsements from regional officials of the CIO and the exclusion of the IUMMSW from the ballot, the PMC lost the NLRB election when only 339 workers voted for them, while 373 opted for "no union." Threats of a plant shutdown, NLRB bias, physical attacks, and ten months without work failed to shake the commitment of a majority of strikers to their union and dealt a stunning rebuff to company strategy. But management remained obstinate. Howard I. Young insisted that the vote did not change his position. "We will not deal with representatives of unions whose officials defy the laws of the country respecting the filing of non-communist affidavits," he maintained.[60] With that declaration, hostilities resumed.

Three days after the election, Fairmont City police required the assistance of sheriff's deputies and state troopers to break up a melee between rival factions outside the city hall. Police charged an official of the CIO Gas, Coke, and Chemical Workers Union with shooting two strikers, and they arrested thirty-seven people in all, including the two men who were shot.[61] Amid reports of the impending shutdown of the furnaces forever, two strikers committed suicide on June 24. The next day, the company put out the furnaces and announced the elimination of 450 jobs.[62]

The IUMMSW position continued to deteriorate in July. The NLRB ruled that attempts by Local 82 representatives to see who was voting during the June 15 election constituted intimidation. The board voided the election and ordered a new one to be held on August 20, again barring the IUMMSW from the ballot. The NLRB also turned down all complaints of unfair labor practices against the company filed by IUMMSW members as individuals.[63]

Help for the local arrived in late July from an unexpected source. Local 82's vulnerability stemmed from the refusal of the IUMMSW officers to sign the noncommunist affidavits. Aware of the consequences of this decision on representation election results and preparing for the impending attack on left-wing labor leaders at the CIO fall convention, the IUMMSW reversed itself and instructed its officers to sign the affidavits. To do so, the union's national secretary, Maurice Travis, resigned from the Communist party to avoid perjuring himself, thereby confirming all the charges leveled against him in the past, but at the same time depriving anticommunists of their main complaint. With Travis's signature on the affidavits, American Zinc now faced a union that had complied with its ultimatum.[64]

The union also won a place on the NLRB ballot once its officers signed the oaths. When American Zinc workers voted on August 20, the IUMMSW received 398 votes as opposed to 260 for the PMC. Two days later, negotiations between the company and Local 82 resumed. Within a month they settled on a contract. The union won a thirteen-cent wage increase in exchange for a pledge not to strike for two years. The dispute cost management more than $1,350,000 and a year of lost production, only to wind up with the same union at the strike's end that it had tried to eliminate at the beginning.[65] Despite its threats to leave Fairmont City, and despite help from the NLRB, the local Catholic church, cooperative CIO union leaders, and the courts, American Zinc failed to dislodge Local 82.

Fear of losing control over production motivated American Zinc's resort to anticommunism, just as it did for Bucyrus-Erie executives in Evansville. An admirer of Senator Taft and an executive steeped in the ideology of the competitive sector, company president Young never begrudged unions their wage demands, but he vehemently resisted union encroachment on management prerogatives. Near the end of the strike, Young admitted to an associate that the dispute had been extremely costly, but he defended it as necessary "to regain control" of production.[66]

Employers in the electronics and metals industries in other cities used the Taft-Hartley noncommunist oaths as a means of attacking IUMMSW and UE locals in their plants, just like Bucyrus-Erie in Evansville and American Zinc in Fairmont City. At the Colt Manufacturing Company in Hartford, Connecticut, management's refusal to deal with the union consolidated a number of opposition factions into one group that succeeded in throwing out the UE. The Precision Castings Company used the same tactics at its many plants and succeeded in enticing the United Auto Workers to conduct successful raids on the IUMMSW—aided by the NLRB ballots that excluded the old union. Celebrating its triumph, Precision Castings sent a letter to its employees reiterating that communism had been the real issue and that UAW support for the company position proved that "our cause was a common cause and that it was just and worthy."[67]

Once the CIO expelled communist-identified unions in November 1949, raiding became easier. Management officials moved quickly to encourage representation by unions more to their liking. Yet workers in many cities proved no more responsive to anticommunism than those in Evansville and Fairmont City, often taking sides with the faction most identified with shop-floor activism.[68] Anticommunists enjoyed their greatest success in unions where the rank and file had no real control over union politics or where Communists had been associated with bureaucratic leadership.

In Evansville, the UE's William Sentner appeared as a militant defender of rank-and-file interests, and the workers took great risks to support him. But at Emerson Electric in St. Louis, Sentner symbolized the wartime no-strike pledge, efforts to protect the company's position, and a union administration that gave its friends jobs as organizers and passed resolutions on national issues without consulting the rank and file. Consequently, Emerson workers consistently battled against Sentner's rule in the UE, while those in Evansville took great risks to support him. Similarly, the IUMMSW's Reid Robinson commanded great loyalty in Fairmont City, where he appeared as someone the company despised. But he attracted virulent opposition in Connecticut's Brass Valley, where he seemed to be a man who dragged his feet on local issues and packed the union staff with outsiders in order to win power struggles with local leaders.

Even after the CIO expelled the IUMMSW, its members often remained passionately loyal to the union in those places where its record corresponded to rank-and-file needs. Black workers in the Southeast remembered the union's struggle to end pay differentials between whites and blacks, and they stood by the IUMMSW during raiding campaigns by the United Steel Workers.[69] In the Southwest, other unions found it very difficult to compete with the IUMMSW because of its record on local issues and its role as the center of working-class social life.[70] For the rank and file, weak or collaborationist unions held more terror than Communist ones. As an IUMMSW staff member later explained when asked about Maurice Travis's membership in the Communist party, "I didn't care what anybody else was, as long as they didn't try to force their beliefs on me—as for what he had done for the workers, I could back him."[71]

UE members expressed similar priorities in their union, often resisting anticommunism in cases where it offended their sense of justice and self-interest. When Westinghouse Corporation and U.S. Navy officials discharged two Philadelphia shipbuilders as security risks in July 1948, the entire day shift walked off the job in protest and got the two workers reassigned to other jobs. As members of the Trotskyist Socialist Workers party, the two "security risks" could not have been very popular with Stalinist Communist party members in the union or with anticommunist workers, but the issue of their discharges for political reasons offended the sensibilities of all camps.[72]

Anticommunists in the UE received enormous assistance from the government, corporations, labor federations, and the press, yet found little enthusiasm among the rank and file for their red-baiting. Victories came from outside pressures or from those cases where anticommunism could be identified with resistance to bureaucracy. As Harry Block, a leader of the anticommunists within the UE, later admitted, communism was never much of an issue with the average rank-and-file worker.[73]

Yet the communist issue had an enduring effect on the average rank-and-file worker. The Taft-Hartley oaths, expulsions of left-led unions from the CIO, and the myriad of other forms of repression against communism left a lasting impact on the structure of the labor movement.[74] Once power became centralized in the hands of labor leaders in the name of fighting "communism," it remained in their hands long after the Communists had been driven out. Collaboration between unions and employers in the name of industrial peace flourished with the demise of competitive rivalries between union factions. Union leaders increasingly played important political roles in making foreign and domestic policy as a result of their anticommunist credentials. Never before had unions, companies, and the government experienced such a harmony of interests.

As a result of these changes, workers increasingly came to see their unions as obstacles to independence rather than as vehicles for obtaining it. Union dues began to seem like just another tax on wages, and union officials began to look like just another group of managers. Workers still used the mechanisms of trade unionism when it suited their purposes, but they never believed in them or worked for them quite as passionately as they had before. Organizing new workers all but stopped, attendance at union meetings plummeted, and the union lost its central place as a focal point of working-class identity. In the future, that identity would have to come from other sources.

Having lost the battle on the institutional front, the struggle for a better life sometimes assumed more covert forms. Utopian aspirations for the future that propelled the mass strikes and demonstrations of the early postwar period did not perish with the consolidation of bureaucratic power in unions and the state. Instead, feelings and aspirations denied political and institutional expression surfaced within the politics of everyday life, on the shop floor to be sure, but also in the community, in the home, and in new kinds of commercialized leisure. New forms of popular culture carried on traditional working-class strategies of independence, but in an increasingly homogeneous society they enabled working-class music, art, and sports to express the aspirations of many other groups. Working-class culture became mass culture, and working-class ideas dominated the paradoxical search for freedom and community that increasingly pervaded American society in the postwar years.

NOTES

1. B. A. Botkin, *Sidewalks of America* (Indianapolis: Bobbs-Merrill, 1954), 64.

2. Harold Williamson and Kenneth Myers, *Designed for Digging* (Evanston: Northwestern University Press, 1955), 268.

3. Ibid., 268–69.

4. Ibid., 281.

5. Ibid., 295.

6. Ibid., 297.

7. *Evansville Press*, May 5, 1948, 1; *Evansville Courier*, May 5, 1948, 1.

8. U.S. House of Representatives, *Hearings before a Special Subcommittee of the Committee on Education and Labor*, 80th Cong., 2d sess., Sept. 10, 1948, 1.

9. *Evansville Press*, May 11, 1948, 1; *Evansville Courier*, May 11, 1948, 1.

10. *Evansville Press*, May 17, 1948, 1.

11. *Evansville Courier*, July 29, 1948, 1, July 31, 1948, 1.

12. Script of WGBF broadcast, Aug. 8, 1948, Bucyrus-Erie Clippings File, Evansville Public Library, Evansville, Ind.

13. U.S. House, *Hearings*, Sept. 10, 1948, 13; script of WGBF broadcast, Aug. 15, 1948, Bucyrus-Erie Clippings File.

14. U.S. House, *Hearings*, Sept. 10, 1948, 14.

15. *UE Strike News*, Local 813, Evansville, Ind., Aug. 27, 1948, 1.

16. *Evansville Press*, Aug. 21, 1948, 1, Aug. 27, 1948, 14.

17. U.S. House, *Hearings*, Sept. 10, 1948, 18; *Evansville Press*, Aug. 28, 1948, 1, Aug. 29, 1948, 1.

18. *Evansville Press*, Aug. 29, 1948, 1, Aug. 31, 1948, 1.

19. Ibid., Aug. 31, 1948, 1.

20. See Ronald W. Schatz, *The Electrical Workers: A History of Labor at General Electric and Westinghouse, 1923–60* (Urbana: University of Illinois Press, 1987), 176–78; Ellen Schrecker, "McCarthyism and the Labor Movement: The Role of the State," in Steve Rosswurm, ed., *The CIO's Left-Led Unions* (New Brunswick: Rutgers University Press, 1992), 139–57.

21. *Evansville Press*, Sept. 9, 1948, 1.

22. Ibid., Sept. 10, 1948, 1; U.S. House, *Hearings*, Sept. 10, 1948, Sept. 11, 1948, Sept. 18, 1948.

23. UE Local 813 leaflet, Sept. 14, 1948, Bucyrus-Erie Clippings File; *UE News*, Sept. 25, 1948, 2, Bucyrus-Erie Clippings File.

24. *Evansville Press*, Sept. 13, 1948, 1, Sept. 14, 1948, 1.

25. *UE News*, Sept. 25, 1948; "What Is the Evansville Formula?" UE leaflet, 1948.

26. Information about these and other incidents came from Evansville residents who asked that their names not be used. Corroborating evidence can be found in the William Sentner Collection, Washington University Libraries, St. Louis, Mo.

27. "UE on the Air," radio broadcast 76 by Arthur Gaeth, Sept. 27, 1948, transcript in the author's possession.

28. *Evansville Press*, Sept. 19, 1948, 2.

29. Ibid., Sept. 23, 1948, 1. One needs to understand the contours of U.S. labor law to understand why a "no union" vote was a UE vote. The union had to campaign for this position among its supporters to keep itself from losing designation as bargaining agent.

30. Radio broadcasts, Aug. 10, 1949, Mar. 13, 1950, Mar. 14, 1950, Mar. 16, 1950, Mar. 17, 1950, box 1, Sadelle Berger Collection, University of Southern Indiana Archives, Evansville, Ind. This collection consists of local radio broadcasts by UE Local 813. My examination of Evansville city directories and telephone directories confirmed the information supplied by correspondents that most of the forty-one workers fired at Bucyrus-Erie found nonindustrial jobs or left town.

31. Letter to employees from Faultless Caster Corporation, Oct. 8, 1948, author's possession.

32. *Evansville Press*, Sept. 11, 1948, 2.

33. Ibid., Aug. 6, 1948, 1.

34. *St. Louis Post-Dispatch*, Oct. 3, 1948, 2.

35. Ibid.

36. Wilder "Hoop" Allen, oral history 112, interview by Glenda Morrison, Oct. 22, 1981, University of Southern Indiana Archives, Evansville, Ind., 5, 8.

37. Ibid., 14.

38. Esther Zieman, oral history 113, interview by Glenda Morrison, Aug. 6 and 12, 1981, University of Southern Indiana Archives, 4–5.

39. Ibid., 5.

40. "UE on the Air," box 1, Sadelle Berger Collection, University of Southern Indiana Archives.

41. *St. Louis Post-Dispatch*, Oct. 3, 1948, 2; Evansville letter 4, Apr. 21, 1950, box 1, Sadelle Berger Collection, tells of the out-of-court settlement of a suit brought against the UE by Bucyrus-Erie in which the company sought $100,000 and settled for $1. See also *Evansville Press*, Apr. 22, 1950, 2.

42. *Evansville Press*, Nov. 3, 1948, 1.

43. Zieman oral history, 11.

44. Circular, May 21, 1952, box 3, Sadelle Berger Collection.

45. "UE on the Air," Sadelle Berger Collection.

46. *Evansville Courier*, Aug. 2, 1949, 3.

47. James D. Norris, *AZn: A History of the American Zinc Company* (Madison: State Historical Society of Wisconsin, 1968). Norris's book is an excellent company history and provides a rare look at the inner workings of a competitive sphere company.

48. Ibid., 175–92.

49. Vernon H. Jensen, *Nonferrous Metals Industry Unionism, 1932–1954: A Story of Leadership Controversy* (Ithaca: Cornell University Press, 1954), 173–74.

50. R. C. Perkins to H. I. Young, Inter-Office Correspondence, May 7, 1948, American Zinc Collection, Western Historical Manuscripts Collection, University of Missouri–St. Louis, St. Louis, Mo.

51. Letter to American Zinc employees from Howard Young, June 16, 1948, American Zinc Collection.

52. Norris, *AZn*, 189–90.

53. *East St. Louis Journal*, Aug. 29, 1948, 8A.

54. Ibid., Sept. 9, 1948, 1, Oct. 8, 1948, 2, Dec. 30, 1948, 1, Jan. 6, 1949, 1.

55. Ibid., Jan. 21, 1949.

56. Ibid., Jan. 23, 1949.

57. *St. Louis Post-Dispatch*, May 9, 1949, 2A.

58. *East St. Louis Journal*, May 26, 1949, 1; *St. Louis Post-Dispatch*, May 26, 1949, 3A.

59. *St. Louis Post-Dispatch*, June 13, 1949, 3A.

60. *East St. Louis Journal*, June 15, 1949, 1; *St. Louis Post-Dispatch*, June 15, 1949, 1. Of course, failing to sign the affidavits violated no federal law, as Young knew perfectly well.

61. *East St. Louis Journal*, June 18, 1949, 1.

62. Ibid., June 24, 1949, 1, June 25, 1949, 1.

63. *St. Louis Post-Dispatch*, July 2, 1949, 3A; *East St. Louis Journal*, July 1, 1949, 1, Aug. 11, 1949, 1.

64. *East St. Louis Journal*, July 21, 1949, 1; Jensen, *Nonferrous Metals Industry Unionism*, 248; *St. Louis Post-Dispatch*, July 21, 1949, 1.

65. *East St. Louis Journal*, Sept. 7, 1949, 1; Norris, *AZn*, 190.

66. Norris, *AZn*, 190.

67. *Business Week*, May 15, 1948, 116–20.

68. Jensen, *Nonferrous Metals Industry Unionism*, 139–52; Len De Caux, *Labor Radical* (Boston: Beacon, 1970), 496.

69. Asbury Howard, oral history, Pennsylvania State University Archives, State College, Penn.

70. Maclovio Barraza, oral history, Pennsylvania State University Archives.

71. Howard oral history.

72. *Business Week*, July 24, 1948, 90; James Matles and James Higgins, *Them and Us* (Boston: Beacon Press, 1974), 174–76; Schatz, *The Electrical Workers*, 115.

73. Harry Block, oral history, Pennsylvania State University Archives.

74. For an interesting assessment of the void left in American labor by the expulsions see Rosswurm, *The CIO's Left-Led Unions*.

PART FOUR

Class and Culture, 1945–53

CHAPTER TEN

"Damn Foolishness"

The Fight for Control
at the Point of Production

WILDCAT STRIKES, mass mobilizations, and general strikes in the forties posed a profound threat to the institutionalized hierarchies and power imbalances within U.S. capitalism. Workers and their allies challenged the prerogatives of supervisors on short-term issues on the shop floor and on matters of long-term investment and planning at the highest levels of management. In politics, they initiated political demands on the government for full employment, universal access to housing, medical care, and education.[1] But they also articulated the inner logic of incipient class formation in their view of economic problems as social rather than personal, as well as in their conceptualization of politics as direct action and mass mobilization rather than as delegation of power to representative individuals and institutions. Perhaps most important, they expressed complicated and sometimes contradictory desires for dignity and pleasure, for autonomy and social connection, for material gain and moral reward, that any capitalist system would have difficulty accommodating.

In his important study of management strategies for control during the war and postwar periods, Howell John Harris notes that "businessmen in the 1940s might not score very high as prophets or thinkers, but they knew how to look after themselves in a fight."[2] In this fight, business executives had to contend with employees demanding higher wages, increased control over work on the shop floor, and greater influence on the political and economic decisions that affected their lives. The material advantages they had gained from government spending during and after the war made it possible for business leaders to make some economic concessions on wages and fringe benefits, but they insisted on retaining management control over production and investment decisions in their own enterprises. Even more

important, they struggled to divert, deflect, and, if possible, destroy the
threat to their power emanating from working-class self-activity. As Harris observes, "Public acquiescence in the continuation of a social system
which distributed authority and other rewards unequally could be neither
guaranteed nor simply enforced."[3] Business leaders needed to pursue their
own short-term interests, but they also had to struggle for moral authority
and political leadership in society.

Many contemporaneous journalistic accounts and some subsequent historical studies have emphasized the centrality of worker demands for higher
wages in the upheavals of the forties. "During the 1940s more money was
the number one item on the shopping list of every trade unionist," explains
one historian.[4] One can certainly understand how this might have been
the case. After the settlement of the 1945–46 General Motors strike provided President Truman with an excuse to lift ceilings on price controls,
a 22.5 percent increase in the cost of living wiped out most of the gains
that workers made during the first round of postwar strikes.[5] Between 1944
and 1946 alone, prices increased by 11 percent while average weekly earnings fell by 10 percent. For the entire decade of the forties, the consumer
price index rose 71.6 percent—in sharp contrast to the thirties, when it
declined by 16 percent.[6] Workers certainly wanted to maintain and extend
the standard of living they had secured during the war, and they pursued
wage demands aggressively.

Yet managers and union leaders knew that wage demands ultimately
held less importance for both workers and managers than did questions
of control. In fact, however distasteful it might have been for executives
and stockholders, making concessions on wages emerged as an important
strategy for the preservation of management prerogatives and initiatives in
other areas. As one General Motors executive opined, "Give the union the
money, the least possible, but give them what it takes. But don't let them
take the business away from us."[7] During negotiations in 1946, 1948, and
1950, General Motors expressly followed that policy, softening union resistance to the company's refusal to bargain about working conditions by
making generous concessions on wages and benefits.[8]

Social science surveys of attitudes among workers in the war and postwar periods reveal the relative unimportance of wage demands compared
to issues of control over the job. Desires for pleasant working conditions,
independence from supervision, and fellowship with other people consistently overshadowed concerns for higher wages in these studies. To be sure,
workers certainly wanted more money, but they often seemed to value
wages as much for their significance as reparations due for the indignities
of labor as for their intrinsic utility.

A survey conducted for the American Vocational Association contended that business leaders tended to overestimate the importance of wages to workers and correspondingly underestimate the value of communication and satisfaction derived from the job itself.[9] In his motivation studies, Eugene J. Benge found that financial interest alone held little significance for most people compared to emotional and moral incentives. Similarly, Benjamin Selekman depicted wage demands by workers as largely symbolic because wages constitute "the social measure by which a place among his fellows is accorded each man for his particular contribution to the work needed by his society."[10]

In a brilliant study of workers in the gypsum industry, Alvin Gouldner explained how concerns for the quality of life become translated into wage demands. Because collective bargaining in the United States has historically involved wage increases only as an incentive to higher productivity, workers with qualitative nonwage demands recognize that their goals will appear illegitimate and unsuited to resolution in contracts. But money demands always seem legitimate. In addition, wage-related demands affect all workers in the same way—everyone knows what it will mean to receive three cents more an hour. But "quality of life" concerns involving power over the job, the solidarity of primary work groups, or issues of dignity and autonomy affect different workers in different ways, making them less likely to serve as a focal point for plantwide or industrywide unity during collective bargaining. Trade unions can unite diverse groups of workers around wage issues, and working-class families find it easier to understand the impact of wages on their lives than struggles for autonomy and power in the workplace. Community members outside the factory stand to gain directly from wage increases due to increased purchasing power among workers. As a result, strikes and other forms of labor negotiation lend themselves to wage adjustments while obscuring complex issues of power and autonomy, which often initiate industrial conflict in the first place.[11]

Ross Stagner's research offered a perceptive critique of studies sponsored by the Department of Labor that claimed that wage issues caused 73.9 percent of strikes in the early postwar period. Stagner noted that dollar demands lent themselves easily to concise formulation, but that they routinely followed anger over other issues involving considerations of power and recognition. As a union organizer from Illinois told Stagner, "The real issue wasn't the 15 cents an hour we asked for or the 5 cents we got. The real cause of the strike was that we had to convince that guy he couldn't be a little dictator any longer."[12] An auto assembly-line worker interviewed by Robert Guest gave a similar account of a wildcat strike that could just as easily have been settled by using the regular grievance procedure—if it had not had an important symbolic meaning for those involved. As the worker recalled,

It was one of those things it's hard to explain. When word got around that the guy was bounced—we all sort of looked at each other, dropped our tools and walked. Somehow that guy was every one of us. The tension on the line had been building up for a long time. We had to blow our top—so we did. We were wrong—the union knew it and so did the company. We stayed out a few hours and back we came. We all felt better like we got something off our chests.

Some of these strikes you read about may be over wages. Or they may just be unions trying to play politics. But I sometimes think that the thing that will drive a man to lose all that pay is deeper than wages. Maybe other guys feel like we did the day we walked out.[13]

Many other studies claimed a limited role for wages in industrial conflict. H. Meltzer's examination of wage disputes identified prestige, recognition, and other personal considerations as the root causes of most disputes that appeared on the surface to concern remuneration.[14] P. F. Hurst's description of a morale survey in a small plant related that workers listed a desire for more knowledge as their most important expectation from their jobs, more important than higher wages, shorter hours, or better working conditions.[15] Surveying the most important needs felt by workers, Glen Cleeton found that desires to share thoughts and feelings with others and to engage in realistic, artistic, and projective thinking rated higher than wage increases, as did aspirations for self-determination, achievement, dominance, and outside approval.[16]

Of course, wages do have real as well as symbolic meaning, and workers usually try to get as much money as possible. But job-attitude research shows how the qualitative aspirations of workers on the shop floor threaten labor peace even when compensation for their labor is high. Big business can often afford to pay higher wages, especially if they lead to increased productivity that lowers aggregate labor costs. Union leaders have generally been willing to trade control over shop-floor conditions in return for wage gains, because higher wages mean more dues and benefits for the union and may appear to secure a share of the profits for the worker. Consequently, management and labor both pin much of their hopes for labor peace on the importance of wage gains to the worker. But the persistence of nonmaterial values at the point of production, the symbolic nature of many struggles over wages, and the willingness of workers to actually lose money rather than surrender dignity or happiness continuously threaten to undermine the foundation of labor peace in a capitalist society.

Management concessions on wages often satisfied union leaders, and the gains they received in return on control issues often enabled supervisors to automate plants or reorganize production to the detriment of rank-and-file workers. But while winning the appearance of labor peace, these arrangements failed to address the broader qualitative concerns motivating working-class resistance to the imperatives of capitalism. When the Teamsters International president condemned the Oakland general strike as "a lot of damn foolishness with no rhyme, reason, or sense" he failed to distinguish between the short-term institutional interests of the union and the long-term qualitative aspirations of the workers. If the strikers had been willing to surrender control over their work to management in the pursuit of higher productivity and higher wages, then the work stoppages of the postwar era would indeed have been "damn foolishness." But in fact, they were damn seriousness. Deeply dissatisfied with the nature, pace, and conditions of work, resentful over the lack of individual autonomy, and desirous of better relations with other human beings, workers utilized informal relations at work to communicate strategies of producing less, of helping each other, and of resisting the desires of employers.[17]

Business executives often understood the rational and coherent motives behind small walkouts and large demonstrations. An "employee cooperation expert" from General Motors informed a 1945 gathering of 450 leading industrialists that the compilation of "unbiased and accurate" facts about worker attitudes held the key to labor peace.[18] A former president of the National Association of Manufacturers addressing the group's 1945 convention admitted that management often deserved the blame for strikes because of its inability to listen to the problems of its employees.[19] The top executive of the Warner-Swasey Corporation elaborated on the same theme at the 1947 NAM convention, when he proclaimed, "We haven't had time to be human in our relations with our employee partners. We are going to have to make up for a point in which we have failed—failed to give our men the sense of importance which is the greatest driving force in the world. Because of our failure they have looked for it and found it elsewhere—on union committees, in anti-business lecture halls, yes on picket lines."[20]

Such sentiments compelled managers to commission sociologists, psychologists, and industrial relations experts to study job attitudes systematically. Employing the most sophisticated social science techniques of their day, and widely disseminating their findings in management journals, the resulting surveys, experiments, and participant observation studies clearly identified aspirations for freedom and community as the key determinants of working-class action. Although deficient by current social science standards, these studies retain historical importance as descriptions of working-class attitudes by trained observers, as part of the shared understanding of the world by managers in the postwar years, and as part of a long history of attempts by managers and social scientists to understand (and control) the motivations and opinions of workers.

Government-sponsored compilation of statistical information in various phases of the war effort stimulated greater use of such information in diverse aspects of American life. Business's acceptance of attitude surveys increased markedly during and immediately after the war, but employer attempts to fathom the consciousness of workers were as old as industrialization itself.[21] Students of working-class behavior and attitudes in the forties and fifties inherited a tradition of factory counterinsurgency in the United States that went back to the nineteenth century.

The ability of American capitalists to impose time and work discipline and its corresponding political, religious, and cultural ideologies on an ethnically diverse working class provided the basis for industrialization in the nineteenth and early twentieth centuries. Time and work discipline substituted factory time for the biological clock—factory workers slept, ate, and worked on a schedule determined by the sale of their labor power. They produced parts of commodities they would never see as finished products to be sold to strangers they would never meet for the benefit of capitalists they would never know. Capitalist enterprise introduced a division of labor in the workshop, breaking up purposeful work into tasks that appeared to exist for their own sake.

Imposing capitalist work habits on people accustomed to agricultural or artisan labor presented enormous difficulties. European immigrants and displaced American farmers entered factories out of financial need, but even relatively high wages failed to reconcile them to the demands of industrial labor. Managers complained about irregular work habits, absenteeism, and damage to equipment, while workers used informal and formal means to limit production and try to control their own labor.[22]

Preindustrial experiences helped shape resistance to time-work discipline. Traditional feast days celebrating seasonal changes provided excuses for absenteeism, while desires for social contact with others led to interrupted production and spontaneous breaks in factory routine.[23] In some cases, workers preferred inefficient methods of labor when they preserved traditional family ties and recalled satisfying preindustrial social relations.[24] Exaggerating their ties to the past in order to ameliorate current conditions, workers sometimes told their bosses that proposed changes in production could not possibly be implemented, when they knew that they could. Immigrants occasionally used language differences as excuses for slowdowns, feigning misunderstanding of orders they did not want to carry out.[25]

Preindustrial values provided one model of behavior contrary to the dictates of the factory system, but new sources of opposition also emerged. Skilled workers steeped in an industrial tradition also opposed time and work discipline when it threatened cherished privileges and methods of work. Skilled workers led the fight for control over production between 1890 and 1920, as managers developed technological innovations as much to combat the militancy and power of the workers as to improve production.[26] Opposition to time and work discipline drew upon memories of the past and hopes for the future. But it also emerged as a logical response to current conditions of labor, as Frederick Winslow Taylor—the first great scientific American student of worker attitudes—so clearly demonstrated. Popularly associated with changes in technology and drives for efficiency, Taylorism developed primarily as a strategy for counterinsurgency in the factory. Taylor, whose work began in the 1890s and continued to influence industry throughout the twentieth century, observed that workers in industrial situations always impose their own direction on production. He complained that "hardly a competent workman can be found in a large establishment . . . who does not devote a considerable part of his time to studying just how slowly he can work and still convince his employer that he is going at a good pace."[27]

Taylor extracted pledges of complete effort from workers as a condition for learning new skills. All pledged to work hard before being trained; all refused once they had acquired skills. Taylor did not blame the workers for their attitude; he recognized that they were acting in their own interests. Yet as a manager he recommended changes in the industrial system to break down each job to its component parts and prescribe the most efficient method of performing each task. Taylor understood that paying high wages offered another form of self-interest to workers and actually could cut costs by increasing productivity—and decreasing the worker's control over the job.

Elton Mayo's industrial relations research in the twenties and thirties attempted to build on Taylor's insights, but give them a more human face. He stressed the efficiency of happy employees and the importance of group cooperation on the job. Owing much to Taylor and Mayo, job-attitude research of the forties and fifties continued their inquiries in the context of the enormous changes in production and the work force necessitated by World War II.

Either directly commissioned by or expressly designed for management, job-attitude research contained a bias toward the interests and needs of industry. Opinion surveys especially lent themselves to distortion. By using general questions, by limiting possible responses to a few prearranged alternatives, and by ignoring the circumstances in which interviews took place, these studies sometimes betrayed the standards of social science and imposed predetermined conclusions on their research. Even under the best of circumstances, such studies tended to assume that answers given at one historical moment remained valid for others, that abstract statements of opinion meaningfully related to subsequent actions, and that interviewers and workers meant the same things when they used the same words.

These assumptions may have been correct in particular cases, but one episode among auto workers during World War II underscores the caution with which such statements must be approached. In February 1945, members of the United Auto Workers endorsed that union's no-strike pledge by a better than two-to-one majority of the thirty thousand votes cast. Yet the same workers who endorsed the no-strike pledge as patriotic citizens and responsible union members also conducted repeated wildcat strikes when conditions on their jobs warranted it. They no doubt still believed that strikes should be avoided in general, but their own circumstances dictated actions at variance with their abstract opinions.[28] Opinions do shape actions, but actions do not always follow previously articulated opinions.

Job-attitude research during the forties reflected the concerns of capital, employed language that distorted the complexity of human activity, and demonstrated imperfect application or the intrinsic limits of social science research. Yet any attempts to explore the relationship between ideas and action necessarily depend upon reasoned speculation from ambiguous evidence. The dangers of such explorations should not obviate their importance, since human subjectivity constitutes a crucial part of historical action. Inadequate as social science, job-attitude research of the forties and fifties offers important descriptions of everyday attitudes of people who left few other written records of their feelings. At the very least, they reveal a body of knowledge crucial to management attitudes and decisions; at the most, they offer a penetrating insight into the attitudes and opinions of the American working class. When viewed in the light of microsocial organization and macrosocial disruption, they lend strong support to an argument that sees the desire for independence from supervision and for closeness with other workers as crucial motivations for American workers in the post-war era.

Some of those conducting job-attitude surveys hoped that their work could help to reform industry by showing its oppressiveness to be inefficient. Allison Davis contended that the "habits of 'shiftlessness,' 'irresponsibility,' 'lack of ambition,' absenteeism and quitting the job . . . are in fact normal responses that the worker has learned from his physical and social environment."[29] Yet by accepting the basic premises of industrial organization and only asking how to make them work better, most of these studies ultimately committed themselves to breaking down worker resistance to higher productivity.

For example, E. William Noland's study of wartime absenteeism attempted to construct a profile of workers prone to frequent absences, so that personnel directors could avoid hiring that type of individual.[30] H. G.

Martin devised a factor-analysis study to identify "co-operative, objective, and agreeable" people to help employers spot potential "troublemakers."[31] Worker resistance to changes in production posed particular problems during the conversion to and from war industry, and consequently studies by Lester Coch and John French, by Paul Lawrence, and by Benjamin Selekman offered advice to management on means of overcoming that resistance.[32]

Yet their very zeal in supplying corporations with useful information often led job-attitude researchers into disclosing the breadth and depth of working-class dissatisfaction with the alienations and indignities of waged work. Absolute and general questions about job satisfaction often brought positive responses, but the more specific the question the greater the dissatisfaction expressed. A survey of Illinois coal miners found 70 percent characterizing management as fair, 60 percent claiming satisfaction with safety conditions, and 88 percent expressing qualified or strong support for their union leader. Yet when asked if they would be miners if they had it all to do over, an overwhelming 90 percent said they would not want their present jobs because mining was dangerous, unpleasant, too hard, dirty, and had no future.[33] A summary of job-attitude surveys found similar results: asking if workers were satisfied usually drew a positive response; asking if the worker would want the same job again if starting over usually brought a negative one.[34] Similarly, Walter H. Eaton's study of worker frustrations identified significant sources of unhappiness on the job: (1) a feeling that work is insignificant; (2) a resentment over not controlling the product of one's labor; (3) unhappiness over unfulfilled expectations of upward mobility; (4) anxiety stemming from an undefined role at work; (5) hostility to changing techniques and conditions on the job; (6) a perception of performing work in isolation from the rest of the community; and (7) economic insecurity.[35]

Not surprisingly, the nature of the job often helped determine responses to questions about employee satisfaction. Workers with more status and better pay expressed higher opinions of their work than others, while unskilled and assembly-line workers indicated less interest in their jobs.[36] A survey of one thousand males constituting a cross-section of the population revealed that over 25 percent of unskilled and a slightly smaller percentage of skilled workers disliked their jobs, but none of the big business executives surveyed expressed unhappiness with their work. The same study found that 25 percent of manual workers interviewed did not believe they had as good a chance to enjoy life as they should have because of their jobs.[37]

Auto assembly-line workers expressed similar pessimism about their future in another survey. Sixty percent of the younger and 80 percent of the older workers stated they did not believe they would get the chance for a better job.[38] "We don't have anything to look forward to except working the rest of our lives," one worker told an interviewer.[39] In another study, meat-packers in Minnesota related that they spent their days hoping for a fight or a mechanical breakdown at work—anything to break the monotony.[40] One worker in an auto plant summed up these attitudes toward waged work: "All I want is to get out of there."[41]

Just as shop-floor conditions played a powerful role in shaping worker dissatisfaction, those workers expressing satisfaction with their jobs tended to identify good conditions at work and pleasant relations with fellow employees as significant sources of satisfaction. Nancy Morse and Robert Weiss found that workers viewed their jobs primarily as a way of leading a purposeful life, of being tied to society at large. The people they interviewed valued the social aspects of their jobs, describing work as a way of warding off loneliness and isolation. When asked what they would miss most by not working, 31 percent of the workers questioned mentioned people they knew at work, 25 percent indicated they would miss having something to do with their time, 12 percent cited the work that they did, 9 percent said they would miss the sense of self-respect they got from doing important labor, 6 percent pointed to the loss of a regular routine, another 6 percent said they would miss nothing at all, 5 percent expressed anxiety about not having interesting lives, and only 2 percent indicated that they would miss the money they earned.[42]

Coal miners in one study mentioned freedom from supervision, the ability to stop working once tasks have been completed, and high pay as the most desirable features of their work.[43] A study of adult male workers in San Francisco found them privileging interesting work, the ability to do useful work well, the opportunity to make a living, working with congenial people, a chance for advancement and job security, and having a fair and understanding supervisor over other components of the job.[44] An overview of sixteen surveys of eleven thousand workers ranked the most important sources of job satisfaction as security, intrinsic interest of the job, opportunity for advancement, appreciation from supervisors, attitude of supervisors, ease of the job, and wages.[45]

Expressions of job satisfaction sometimes contained a mixed message. A survey of auto assembly-line workers by Robert Guest disclosed that over half the workers said they would leave if they had a chance to get a better job. They complained about working conditions, the nature of assembly-line labor, the amount of work they were expected to do, the monotony of their jobs, bad relations with supervisors, and the fear of not being able to keep up with the pace of the work. Yet workers who expressed satisfaction with their jobs had exactly the same complaints, but feared that their new jobs might be even worse. They feared losing security and seniority in addition to facing the uncertainty of new and possibly worse working conditions, and so expressed "satisfaction" with their current employment.[46]

Although studies of job attitudes originated in the assumption that social attitudes at work stemmed from the personality and character of individuals, perceptive observers had long noted the importance of the small group as a central force in the workplace. As a consolation for the indignities of labor, as a source of sociability and pleasure, and as the focal point of strategies of resistance against management, informal relations among workers played a major role in shaping the job attitudes recorded in social science surveys.

W. Lloyd Warner concluded that differences among individuals had little effect on job attitudes, because those attitudes were part of a commonly held value system of workers as a class.[47] Fred Blum's study of meat-packers in a small Minnesota town revealed that responsibility to other workers brought more satisfaction than high wages.[48] F. J. Roethlisberger and W. J. Dickson's studies of electrical workers demonstrated that group morale depended primarily upon pride in the work group. Workers perpetuated practices designed to preserve primary work groups like trading jobs, helping each other, talking, teasing, and horseplay even when supervisory personnel expressly ordered them to cease and desist.[49] Raymond E. Bernberg's research on job attitudes found that job happiness generally depended upon satisfaction in working with others, increases in production due to group effort, and intimacy with other workers in and out of the workplace.[50] Interviews conducted by Richard Centers disclosed that unskilled workers mentioned their associates at work as the main source of satisfaction from their jobs, while white-collar workers valued equally the varied nature of their jobs and their fellow workers.[51]

Experiments and participant observation studies also found that primary work groups established norms of behavior that presented significant challenges to the prerogatives of management. Adam Curle's study of work incentives showed that real attachments to other people at work could become powerful incentives to live up to group expectations in an age of increasing individual isolation.[52] Experiments in a Virginia sewing plant found that workers in groups produced only half as much as those who worked in isolation, largely because the groups set collective production standards.[53] Similarly, Benjamin Selekman observed that when workers became angry and fearful over disruptions of their routine, they retaliated through group strategies, such as unauthorized work stoppages or pooling of pay envelopes under piecework as a means of refusing to compete with one another.[54] Charles Walker's examination of life in a town dominated by steel production placed heavy emphasis on the importance of team spirit in production, contending that "the group, not the supervisors, was the most powerful disciplining force in the mill."[55]

The affinity and pleasure derived from group associations at work did not stop workers from expressing a desire for individual freedom and independence from supervision. Forty-one percent of the respondents to Gladys Palmer's study of work attitudes in an industrial community expressed an interest in getting another job, and 80 percent of those indicated that they would like to try professional or white-collar work because of the autonomy they believed it offered. In the same survey, housewives cited their independence from supervision and their control over their own time as the main reason for not wanting to work for wages, while workers with outdoor jobs listed the ability to work at their own pace and the absence of direct supervision as the main source of satisfaction in their jobs.[56] Blum's investigation of meat-packers concluded that the "theme of independence and ability to control one's own work rear again and again as the crucial factor determining his attitude toward the company and the union," while Centers found that freedom from supervision played an important role in providing satisfaction to unskilled workers.[57] Lloyd G. Reynolds and Joseph Shister concluded from their studies that excessive supervision often provided the main cause of dissatisfaction on the job.[58]

Desires for independence and autonomy among workers often appeared in statements extolling the virtues of small business ownership. Over one-fourth of white- and blue-collar workers surveyed in Greenbelt, Maryland, indicated that they wanted to go into business for themselves.[59] Morse and Weiss found that small-business ownership appeared as the most frequently cited alternative to present employment, although respondents rarely indicated a particular business they wished to enter.[60] More than a third of the unskilled workers questioned by Centers expressed a desire to own their own business, and Robert Blauner, Reynolds and Shister, and Eli Chinoy observed similar aspirations.[61]

Strategies for independence often took spontaneous and explosive forms because legitimate channels were ill-suited for implementing them. Job-attitude research noticed increasing tensions between workers and unions as contracts increasingly began to rationalize production and conflict with the personal wishes of workers. Selekman noticed that workers resisted changes in shop procedures even when their union endorsed these changes.[62] Clifford E. Jurgensen observed that job applicants tended to express hopes for security, good supervisors, communication, and enjoyable work, while their unions stressed wages, hours, and working conditions.[63] Arthur Kornhauser's survey of attitudes in Detroit claimed very little correlation between union membership and job satisfaction, while other studies of unionized workers indicated that they selectively participated in union activities only when they felt they had a direct stake and voice in them.[64] Blum observed that not more than one hundred out of four thousand packinghouse workers attended general union meetings, but that department meetings drew large numbers, while Eugene H. Jacobsen contended that workers directed their loyalties to the company or to the union by choosing the institution whose first-line contact with them gave the greatest feeling of participation in decision-making. In a clash between formal and informal allegiances, the informal grass-roots ties held first claim.[65]

Despite their biases and limitations, job-attitude surveys illumined much about the consciousness of American workers in the forties and fifties. They portrayed workers as dissatisfied with their jobs, angry at the limits imposed on their talents, and deeply committed to collective social tactics as a means of making life more enjoyable. Researchers learned in a systematic way what workers had long known about each other through informal means. Yet the compilation of "unbiased and accurate facts" did little to alleviate the human suffering and repressed longings they described. If worker unhappiness stemmed from trivial irritations or breakdowns in communication, job-attitude research might have led to meaningful reforms. But grievances arising from the very process of production for profit could be remedied only by a radical change in the system itself. Because of their commitment to the logic of capitalist production, managers and social scientists could offer only trivial solutions to the serious problems identified by job-attitude research. As Harry Braverman points out in *Labor and Monopoly Capital*, job enrichment schemes have generally been little more than public relations efforts by personnel departments, not fundamental changes in the production process.[66]

Unencumbered by that unswerving commitment to capitalist production, workers knew what the social scientists did not. In their collective actions, if not in their perceptions as individuals, workers realized that the increasing centralization of power in the factory, the unions, and the state left little or no room for individual aspirations for freedom and community. Through informal relations in small groups and through mass disruptions of business as usual, workers united their critique of everyday life with a strategy that went outside legitimate channels to carve away limited areas of power, recognition, and mutual support in the present—and to create the possibility of a society based on those principles in the future. Business leaders did not always understand the qualitative aspirations of American workers, and they rarely offered ways to fulfill those desires. Yet they understood that real interests and fundamental principles were at stake in labor-management disputes, and they acted with determination and resolution to struggle for moral and political authority over production inside factories and over social relations outside them. They wanted to solve immediate economic problems, but they also aimed at solutions that might guarantee long-range security, stability, and predictability.

Despite a surface prosperity that confounded predictions of a postwar depression, the U.S. economy faced serious problems by 1949. Accumulated wartime personal savings and unusually high demand for previously unattainable consumer goods had begun to decline. War-related tax breaks to large corporations to finance reconversion to peacetime production could no longer finance industrial expansion. Federal government spending proved inadequate to the task of maintaining full production, even though government expenditures remained four times greater than they had been in 1940.[67] Worse yet, unemployment began to climb from an average of 4 percent of the work force between 1946 and 1948 to 6.6 percent by the third quarter of 1949. By February 1950, unemployment reached 7.9 percent with 4.7 million workers out of a job.[68]

Unwilling to face the political consequences of high unemployment, leaders of government and monopolistic industries reasoned that one way to solve the economy's problems would be to finance increased employment and consumer spending with increases in productivity. If the existing work force produced more, wages could rise, leading to more consumer demand and, consequently, more employment. But raising productivity entailed either automation (which would decrease rather than increase jobs) or speeding up the pace of production for the present work force, a strategy that necessitated undercutting workers' control over the job—one of the strongest sources of employee satisfaction and one of the main goals of working-class strategies of independence.

Managers felt that they had to reorganize the process of work by increasing their control over production. Given the amount of working-class resistance to such changes in the preceding period of relative prosperity, accomplishing those aims in the midst of rising unemployment would not be easy. Although the Taft-Hartley Act and subsequent labor-management agreements gave employers the power to dismiss instigators of wildcat strikes, the strikes continued to occur. Throughout 1948, Detroit auto manufacturers complained about unauthorized walkouts stemming from worker resistance to company discipline and production schedules.[69] Citing wildcat strikes in the rubber, brewing, and automobile industries, Business Week expressed concern for the stability of unions in November 1948, noting with alarm, "rank and filers can be swayed by an argument that leaders aren't doing enough for them on work standards."[70] Most union officials already knew that, although few had the resourcefulness of Joseph "King" Ryan of the International Longshoreman's Association, who denounced a New York wildcat as a Communist plot and then assumed leadership of the walkout when he saw it gaining popularity in other ports.[71] More commonly, union leaders fought ferociously with recalcitrant members to help employers increase productivity. That kind of collaboration lent a particularly volatile tone to many of the 3,606 strikes that erupted in 1949—the most since 1946 and almost as many as in 1919—the previous high year for strikes.[72]

Rank-and-file dissatisfaction with working conditions provoked political threats to union leaders and strikes throughout 1949 and 1950. Complaints about speedup and outrage over a union-conducted study to set work standards at the Ford River Rouge plant in Detroit in May 1949 led to a major quarrel between the local and the international. Some sixty thousand employees stopped work at Ford and Lincoln plants in Detroit to protest against management's speeding up production schedules.[73] Walter Reuther and the union's other international officers favored a strike to gain wage increases, pensions, and a health plan, but by a vote of thirty thousand to four thousand the local forced a strike on the issue of speedups.[74]

Wildcat strikes over working conditions so convulsed operations at the Hudson Company in Detroit that the local union threatened to use "flying squadrons" of enforcers against its own members to keep production running after a year of frequent disruptions.[75] Coal miners in Pennsylvania became so angry with union attempts to end one of their strikes that they ran one organizer out of town and threatened to dump another in the river.[76] After the war, wage increases generally kept pace with rising prices, but workers remained as willing to strike in 1949 as they had been in 1946. The capacity of labor to mobilize communitywide support had clearly diminished since 1946, but rank-and-file workers still interrupted production, resisted increased productivity, and undermined the stability of labor-management contracts.

If the problems of the economy were to be solved without reverting back to the depression or lurching ahead to revolutionary changes, labor and management had to devise a system of punishments and rewards to contain labor's rank and file and win their acquiescence to plans linking economic growth to increased productivity. C. E. Wilson of General Motors took a major step toward this end in his 1950 contract negotiations with the United Auto Workers when he offered bold proposals aimed at implementing a system of welfare capitalism for GM workers. As Howell John Harris observes, proposals like these intended "to attach individual workers to the corporate system by ties of self-interested 'loyalty' and frank dependence."[77]

Wilson's plan called for longer contracts (five years in this case) with stricter enforcement powers over technological improvements and worker behavior, tempered by "concessions" to the workers in the form of pensions and other welfare benefits. "For our part," Wilson explained, "we have always kept in mind not what might be expedient from a short-range viewpoint, but what is right and fair for our employees and the corporation in the years ahead."[78] True to Wilson's word, the 1950 contract not only solved some immediate problems but it also took steps to secure the long-range future of the entire capitalist system by putting in place a system based on high productivity, increased capital for investment, and carefully nurtured divisions among the working class. The specifics of Wilson's pension proposal provide a revealing demonstration of his hopes and intentions.

Pension plans enable companies to encourage older and presumably less efficient workers to retire so they can be replaced by younger ones. They also attract young workers to the job by promising future security. They help limit voluntary quitting among workers by providing a financial stake in long and continuous employment. Seemingly guided by the sociological studies and firsthand observations that found that worker insecurity caused strikes, Wilson tried to use pensions as an assurance of future security. In addition, company contributions to pension funds provided important tax advantages for General Motors as a deductible business expense. Those reasons alone justified the plan as far as the self-interest of General Motors was concerned, but Wilson was after even bigger game.

The General Motors president insisted that pension funds be invested in the capital market in those firms paying the highest returns—generally the monopoly sector of American business. By connecting the retirement income of GM workers to the dividend-paying capacity of monopoly industries, Wilson wanted to give workers a stake in higher productivity and in the profitability of American industry. He reproduced in more sophisticated form and on a broader scale the schemes of United Mine Workers president John L. Lewis, who tied retirement benefits to current coal production—giving retirees a stake in higher productivity and forcing workers to choose between their working selves and retired selves whenever they contemplated a strike.

The pension plan also supplied capital for monopoly industries at the expense of workers, small businesses, and the public at large. Consider the alternatives to Wilson's plan. Had there been no pension fund at all, General Motors would have probably had to pay higher wages to workers trying to save for their old age. With the pension fund, that money became invested in industry, increasing its supply of capital and releasing the purchasing power of workers that would have been tied up in savings.

Had pension funds been invested in the employing company, many smaller firms would have shared in the capital provided by their workers' payments to the pension fund. Instead, it all went into the coffers of the best investments—the monopolistic firms. Wilson could have taken all of the General Motors pension fund for his own company, but he realized that would encourage other companies to do the same. By emphasizing the rewards of investing in the capital market, General Motors and the rest of the monopoly sector would eventually share in the pension money of many more workers whose own firms would be contributing to the investment capital available to monopolies. Had there been a pension fund investing in government securities, the country as a whole might have enjoyed lower taxes or the benefits of public spending subject to the political control of private citizens. Instead, the money went to increase the profits of concentrated monopolistic firms.

The General Motors plan also encouraged sharp divisions within the working class by rewarding some workers at the expense of others. Rank-and-file workers often favored pensions because they understood clearly the inadequacies of the Social Security system. But by paying private pensions to those workers most capable of effective political action, large corporations diffused the pressure for increased Social Security benefits for all workers. Unionized laborers with pension plans in their contracts paid for their own retirement programs and consequently tended to view state-administered pension programs like Social Security and other welfare expenses as an additional "tax" that brought them no direct benefits as individuals. Those workers with no pension protection had to build up their personal savings in anticipation of retirement, but they had to pay the same prices for products as workers with pension protection who did not have to save. Even within firms that had pension plans, young workers interested in higher wages found themselves at odds with older workers who had a higher stake in large pensions.

These pension plans and other state-sponsored systems of welfare capitalism also exacerbated divisions within the working class by gender and race. They rewarded white male workers for past discrimination by channeling important benefits to companies and unions that had kept women and aggrieved racial "minorities" out of production jobs and that had negotiated contracts with discriminatory clauses in them. Conversely, welfare capitalism denied benefits precisely to jobs where women and people of color tended to be overrepresented—farm workers, domestics, and employees in small shops owned by competitive-sector capitalists. On issues of pensions, unemployment insurance, educational benefits, and health care, welfare capitalism helped set up a two-tiered system that used the power of capital and the state to drive a wedge between organized and unorganized women, between men and women, and between white workers and African Americans, Mexican Americans, Native Americans, and Asian Americans.[79]

Pension plan provisions in contracts also brought companies and unions closer together. GM's Wilson stated that he could only offer such "generous" benefits to workers because of the UAW's "sincerity and responsibility in carrying out agreements," and he made it clear he expected more of the same. For their part, union leaders proved more than willing to play the role of industrial police officers in return for a role in administering pension fund investments. Having already demonstrated their commitment to labor peace in return for high wages, union leaders saw pension plans as a wedge holding open the possibility that later they might assume the power of co-management with capital.

Representatives of business applauded the new "responsibility" displayed by union leaders. Citing a reported decline in the frequency of wildcat strikes in 1948, *Business Week* credited Walter Reuther and the discipline he exerted over the rank and file in the UAW as the main reason for uninterrupted production. In actuality, neither Reuther's discipline nor any subsequent reorganization of production measurably reduced strike activity among the rank and file, but Reuther's policies did provide important services to management.[80] The union had negotiated contract provisions mandating penalties for wildcat strikers, and it assisted companies in speeding up work. One example of UAW efforts on behalf of increased production came in the crank shaft department at Chevrolet in Flint, Michigan, in April 1948. Workers there had refused to work at the pace demanded by management, while numerous time studies by the company "only put on record the delays that were being injected deliberately" by the workers who refused to vary the speed of their work while being tested. Chevrolet's management then secured the assistance of UAW International officers. They came to the plant and confirmed the company's charges that the workers were not putting forth "normal effort." General Motors proudly cited that incident in a letter to workers throughout its system, boasting triumphantly that "when the employees became aware that the Union would no longer support them in their deliberate restriction of out-put they produced the standards."[81]

The new pension plans gave union leaders added incentive to cooperate with management. The fund functioned as an indirect kind of union shop, tying workers to the union as well as the company. The rank and file would be more amenable to schemes of labor-management cooperation, and less likely to risk being fired, if their actions risked the loss of retirement benefits as well as of their present job. They would think twice about disaffiliating from a union that administered their pensions, and that administrative role proved particularly appealing to some union leaders who saw it as a model for co-management in other aspects of political and economic decision-making.

Within a year of the agreement between GM and the UAW, more than eight thousand new pension plans went into effect in the United States—four times as many as had been established in the previous one hundred years.[82] True to the principles of corporate liberalism, the pension fund strengthened the institutional power of the company and the union at the expense of individual workers. It made the gains of some employees dependent on the deprivations of others, and it attempted to connect workers to the interests of capital, preventing them from formulating a countervision of social organization. In short, it did everything necessary to undermine working-class strategies of independence. But it did not stop them completely.

James Boggs worked at a Chrysler plant in Detroit when that company adopted the five-year contract and pension plan initiated at General Motors. He saw the agreement as a landmark, but not in the way that it was intended. As he later wrote, "It was with this contract that the workers began to realize how nailed down they really were to the company and how they were being made into part of it. The contract evoked from the workers, particularly the younger ones who were unable to see any benefits for themselves in the pension schemes, the first serious opposition from the ranks."[83] For these workers, the material security afforded by the pension plan paled in significance next to the psychological threat it posed to their independence. Management wanted to make its investment in labor as secure as its investment in machinery, but the needs of human beings go beyond mere maintenance.

As the company managers impinged on every area of a worker's life, the wildcat strike became more important, not less. It asserted one's humanity and capacity to act in a power structure that demanded passivity. It undermined the bargain between unions and management by subverting labor peace, and it hit the companies where they could be hurt most—by interrupting production. The more energy business and labor expended on building stability, the more effective strategies of disruption became.

Workers in the auto industries staged constant wildcat strikes during the five-year life of the 1950 contract. They forced the UAW to renegotiate two years before the contract expired, and the union never again risked a five-year agreement. Centers of speedup and resistance to it among rank-and-file militants like Ford's River Rouge plant in Detroit, or the Linden, New Jersey, General Motors operation suffered repeatedly from strikes.[84] Yet the true importance of the wildcat strike went beyond its frequency. Often more effective as a threat than as an actuality, the existence of even a single wildcat strike raised the specter of similar strikes everywhere. A state of mind as well as an event, the possibility of a wildcat made each supervisor a little more cautious and each worker a little bolder. In an age of deteriorating working conditions, slow grievance procedures, and labor-management collusion, the wildcat strike served as a great equalizer.

Wildcat strikes also superseded many of the traditional functions of the trade union. As the processing of grievances moved farther away from the shop floor, and as union negotiating strategies increasingly asked workers to trade their working lives for monetary rewards, the shop floor became even more important as a crucible of working-class identity and conscious-ness. Primary work groups rearranged production on a day-to-day level, and the sanctioned strike became largely a symbolic demonstration of accumulated grievances. Nearly every union experienced a serious decline in attendance at meetings in the early fifties, but sanctioned strikes none-theless remained frequent. For years, workers had "soldiered" on the job, going through the motions of work while denying the bosses their full sup-port. Now workers began to "soldier" in the union hall as well, displaying a studied apathy for forums in which they had no real power. But they re-mained militant when circumstances and opportunities permitted.[85]

Despite the comprehensive co-optation of pension plans and the coer-cive control exercised by union leaders and business executives at the point of production, working-class resistance to speedups and automation still limited the ability of capitalists to solve the economy's problems. Unre-strained speedup provoked too much resistance, and mass unemployment remained politically untenable. Some mechanism had to be devised to sus-tain economic growth, full production, and full employment. Rank-and-file resistance forced corporate liberals to externalize the contradictions of the factory onto the society at large. Through spatial reorganization of cities and suburbs, subsidies for home ownership and increased consump-tion, and calls for new ideologies based on the moral authority of business, corporate liberals in the postwar era countered working-class strategies of independence with the construction of a new public sphere firmly grounded in business principles.

NOTES

1. The United Electrical Workers union in St. Louis and Evansville, Indiana, staged mass demonstrations against postwar housing shortages, while CIO coun-cils across the country demanded Keynesian measures to address collective ma-terial needs. See also David Brody's discussion of how Walter Reuther's ambitious postwar planning program for rapid transit and public housing emerged from "the mainstream of CIO progressivism," in *Workers in Industrial America: Essays on the Twentieth Century Struggle* (New York: Oxford University Press, 1980), 177.

2. Howell John Harris, *The Right to Manage: Industrial Relations Policies of American Business in the 1940s* (Madison: University of Wisconsin Press, 1982), 8.

3. Ibid., 180.

4. Ronald W. Schatz, *The Electrical Workers: A History of Labor at General Electric and Westinghouse, 1923–60* (Urbana: University of Illinois Press, 1987), 151.

5. Brody, *Workers in Industrial America*, 191.

6. Schatz, *The Electrical Workers*, 153, 152.

7. Brody, *Workers in Industrial America*, 187–88.

8. Harris, *The Right to Manage*, 150.

9. American Vocational Association Committee on Research, "Factors Affecting the Satisfaction of Home Economics Teachers," *American Vocational Association Journal*, 1948.

10. Eugene J. Benge, "Non-financial Incentives: A Management Motivation Analysis," *Advanced Management* 19, no. 6 (1954); Benjamin Selekman, "Resistance to Shop Changes," *Harvard Business Review* 24, no. 1 (Autumn 1945): 123.

11. Alvin Gouldner, *Wildcat Strike* (Yellow Springs, Ohio: Antioch University Press, 1954).

12. Ross Stagner, "Psychological Aspects of Industrial Conflict," *Personnel Psychology* 3, no. 1 (1950): 15.

13. Robert Guest, "Men and Machines," *Personnel* 31, no. 6 (May 1955): 496.

14. H. Meltzer, "Personal Values: Root of Wage Disputes," *American Journal of Orthopsychiatry* 15 (1945).

15. P. F. Hurst, "This Small Plant Made a Morale Survey," *Factory Management and Maintenance* (May 1948).

16. Glen Cleeton, "Human Factors in Industry," *Annual of the American Academy of Political and Social Science*, no. 274 (1951): 17–24.

17. Reinhard Bendix, *Work and Authority in Industry* (New York: Harper and Row, 1963), 338.

18. *New York Times*, Oct. 26, 1945, 1.

19. *Time*, Dec. 17, 1945, 79.

20. *Newsweek*, Dec. 15, 1947, 64.

21. Loren Baritz, *Servants of Power* (Middletown, Conn.: Wesleyan University Press, 1960), 142, details the relationship between social scientists and industry stimulated by World War II, especially in respect to job-attitude surveys.

22. Herbert Gutman, "Work, Culture, and Society in Industrializing America," *American Historical Review* (July 1973): 531–88.

23. Ibid.

24. Virginia McLaughlin, "South Italian Immigrants Confront New York Experience," *Journal of Social History* 7 (Summer 1974): 429–45.

25. Tamara Hareven, "Laborers of Manchester 1912–1922," *Labor History* (Spring 1975): 249–65.

26. David Montgomery, "The New Unions, 1909–1922," *Journal of Social History* 7 (Summer 1974): 509–29; Jeremy Brecher, *Strike* (San Francisco: Straight Arrow, 1972), 98.

27. Frederick W. Taylor, "Shop Management," *The Principles of Scientific Management* (New York: Harper, 1947), 33.

28. Martin Glaberman, *Wartime Strikes: The Struggle against the No-Strike Pledge in the UAW during World War II* (Detroit: Bewick, 1980).

29. Allison Davis, "The Motivation of the Underprivileged Worker," in W. F. Whyte, ed., *Industry and Society* (New York: McGraw-Hill, 1946), 86.

30. E. William Noland, "Worker Attitudes and Industrial Absenteeism: A Statistical Appraisal," *American Sociological Review* (June 1945).

31. H. G. Martin, "Locating the Troublemaker with the Guilford Martin Personnel Inventory," *Journal of Applied Psychology* 28 (1944).

32. Lester Coch and John French, "Overcoming Resistance to Change," *Human Relations* 1, no. 4 (1948); Paul Lawrence, "How to Deal with Resistance to Change," *Harvard Business Review* 32, no. 3 (1954); Selekman, "Resistance to Shop Changes."

33. James Francis Kelly and Thomas W. Harrell, "Job Satisfaction among Coal Miners," *Personnel Psychology* 2 (Summer 1949).

34. Frederick Herzberg, Bernard Mausner, Richard O. Peterson, and Dora Capwell, *Job Attitudes: Review of Research and Opinion* (Pittsburgh: University of Pittsburgh Press, 1957), 4.

35. Walter H. Eaton, "Hypotheses Relating to Worker Frustration," *Journal of Social Psychology* (1952): 35.

36. Herzberg, Mausner, Peterson, and Capwell, *Job Attitudes*, 21.

37. Richard Centers, "Motivational Aspects of Occupational Stratification," *Journal of Social Psychology* (1948): 28.

38. Robert Guest, "Work Careers and Aspirations of Automobile Workers," *American Sociological Review* 19, no. 2 (Apr. 1954).

39. Gladys Palmer, "Attitudes toward Work in an Industrial Community," *American Journal of Sociology* 63 (July 1957): 17.

40. Fred Blum, *Towards a Democratic Work Process* (New York: Harper, 1953).

41. Guest, "Work Careers," 319.

42. Nancy Morse and Robert Weiss, "Function and Meaning of Work," *American Sociological Review* 20 (Apr. 1955).

43. James Francis Kelly and Thomas W. Harrell, "Job Satisfaction among Coal Miners," *Personnel Psychology* 2 (Summer 1949).

44. John P. Troxell, "Elements in Job Satisfaction: A Study of Attitudes among Different Occupational Status Groups," *Personnel* 31, no. 3 (Nov. 1954).

45. Herzberg, Mausner, Peterson, and Capwell, *Job Attitudes*, 44.

46. Guest, "Work Careers."

47. W. Lloyd Warner, *Social Life of a Modern Community* (New Haven: Yale University Press, 1941), and *Status System of a Modern Community* (New Haven: Yale University Press, 1942).

48. Blum, *Towards a Democratic Work Process.*

49. F. J. Roethlisberger and W. J. Dickson, *Management and the Worker* (Cambridge: Harvard University Press, 1939), 459–92.

50. Raymond E. Bernberg, "Socio-psychological Factors in Industrial Morale," *Journal of Applied Psychology* 37 (1953): 249–50.

51. Centers, "Motivational Aspects."

52. Adam Curle, "Incentives to Work: An Anthropological Appraisal," *Human Relations* 2 (1949).

53. Coch and French, "Overcoming Resistance to Change."

54. Selekman, "Resistance to Shop Changes."

55. Charles Walker, *Steeltown* (New York: Harper, 1950), 69.

56. Palmer, "Attitudes toward Work."

57. Blum, *Towards a Democratic Work Process*, 124–25; Centers, "Motivational Aspects."

58. Lloyd G. Reynolds and Joseph Shister, *Job Horizons* (New York: Harper, 1949).

59. William Form, "Toward an Occupational Social Psychology," *Journal of Social Psychology* 24 (1946).

60. Morse and Weiss, "Function and Meaning of Work."

61. Centers, "Motivational Aspects"; Robert Blauner, "Work Satisfaction and Industrial Trends in Modern Society" in *Labor and Trade Unionism*, ed. Seymour Martin Lipset and Walter Galenson (New York: Wiley, 1960), 339–60; Lloyd Reynolds and Joseph Shister, *Job Horizons* (New York: Harper, 1949); Ely Chinoy, *Automobile Workers and the American Dream* (Garden City, N.Y.: Doubleday, 1955).

62. Selekman, "Resistance to Shop Changes."

63. Clifford E. Jurgensen, "Selected Factors Which Influence Job Preferences," *Journal of Applied Psychology* 31 (Dec. 1947).

64. Arthur Kornhauser, *Detroit as the People See It* (Detroit: Wayne State University Press, 1952).

65. Blum, *Towards a Democratic Work Process*; Eugene H. Jacobsen, *Foremen-Steward Participation Practices and Worker Attitudes in a Unionized Factory*, cited in Herzberg, Mausner, Peterson, and Capwell, *Job Attitudes*.

66. Harry Braverman, *Labor and Monopoly Capital* (New York: Monthly Review Press, 1974), 87.

67. Gabriel Kolko, *Main Currents in Modern American History* (New York: Harper and Row, 1976), 317.

68. *Monthly Labor Review* (Feb. 1950): 129; Kolko, *Main Currents in Modern American History*.

69. *Business Week*, Apr. 24, 1948, 100; *Detroit Times*, May 20, 1948, 1.

70. *Business Week*, Nov. 6, 1948, 107.

71. *Time*, Nov. 22, 1948, 24.

72. *Monthly Labor Review* (May 1950): 493.

73. Brody, *Workers in Industrial America*, 203.

74. *Detroit Times*, May 1, 1949, 1; *Time*, May 16, 1949, 25.

75. *Detroit Times*, May 24, 1950, 1.

76. *Time*, Oct. 10, 1949, 22, Jan. 30, 1950, 14.

77. Harris, *The Right to Manage*, 169.

78. *Vital Speeches* 17 (July 15, 1950): 605.

79. Gwendolyn Mink offers an excellent analysis of the ways in which both private welfare capitalism and state-sponsored social welfare in the United States have been guided by stratified categories of race and gender in "The Lady and the Tramp: Gender, Race, and the Origins of the American Welfare State," in Linda Gordon, ed., *Women, the State, and Welfare* (Madison: University of Wisconsin Press, 1990), 92–122.

80. See for example, Rick Fantasia, *Cultures of Solidarity: Consciousness, Action, and Contemporary American Workers* (Berkeley: University of California Press, 1988), 60.

81. Letter from General Motors to employees, Apr. 8, 1948, box 2, Louis Ciccone Collection, Labor History Archives, Wayne State University, Detroit, Mich.

82. Peter Drucker, *The Unseen Revolution* (New York: Harper and Row, 1976), 7.

83. James Boggs, *Monthly Review* (July 1963): 117.

84. Stanley Aronowitz, *False Promises* (New York: McGraw-Hill, 1973), 368.

85. James Green, "Fighting on Two Fronts," *Radical America* 9, nos. 3–4 (1975): 38. Almost every account of this period mentions rising apathy toward union meetings. See Matthew Ward (Charles Denby), *Indignant Heart* (New York: New Books, 1952), K. B. Gilden's wonderful novel *Between the Hills and the Sea* (Ithaca: ILR Press, 1989), Charles Walker, *Steeltown* (New York: Harper, 1950), and Elmer Matyi, "A Pleasure to Go to Work," 1976 oral history interview, Western Historical Manuscripts Collection, University of Missouri–St. Louis. St. Louis, Mo.

CHAPTER ELEVEN

Corporate Culture, Conformity, and Commodities

The Fight for Moral Authority

WORKING-CLASS militants during the forties faced powerful opponents. Journalists, business executives, politicians, and even labor leaders vilified rank-and-file struggles, denouncing the workers who staged them as immature, irresponsible, and incompetent, but somehow also as diabolical conspirators slavishly devoted to following the dictates and designs of corrupt, ambitious, and unacceptably radical local leaders. These judgments seriously misrepresented the dynamics of working-class grass-roots activism, but they contained more than a grain of truth in their assessment of the political and cultural radicalism behind the direct-action protests of the decade.

Of course, there was no conspiracy (diabolical or otherwise) propelling rank-and-file strategies of independence during the war and postwar eras. For all of their ingenuity and solidarity, militant workers lacked organizations capable of transforming their short-term local coalitions into a permanent political force. The institutions that did seem open to them—like the trade unions or the Communist party—generally served conservative ends, removing decision-making and implementation from the rank and file in the interest of their own institutional ambitions. But the political weaknesses of workers should not be used to obscure the political and cultural radicalism of their movement; on that score, their enemies correctly perceived a profound threat to the status quo.

Working-class activism in the forties embraced direct action and direct democracy. In the face of dominant ideologies riddled with individualism, privatism, and materialism, they mobilized collectively and publicly for material *and* moral rewards. In some cases, this radicalism manifested itself directly in the form of political demands—like the argument mounted by members of the United Auto Workers for conversion of wartime defense plants into postwar government-run institutions devoted to meeting consumer needs for housing and rapid transit, or the insistence during the 1945–46 strike that GM pay wage increases from profits rather than from price hikes.[1] But in most cases, the radicalism of the wartime and postwar strike wave expressed itself in more immediate and tangible ways—by stopping or reorganizing production against the wishes of management, by forging new communities among workers through collective action, and by transforming city streets from conduits for commerce into sites for the enactment of carnival-like demonstrations that created and celebrated a new working-class public sphere.

Public demonstrations played out the consequences of private and previously individual anger. As Leonard Sayles argued in *The Harvard Business Review*, "The average worker does not contemplate a walkout lightly, being aware that this is a serious breach of plant discipline and that a stiff penalty—perhaps discharge—may result. . . . Fellow workers may support the walkout of one small group because they recognize that to fail to do so may subject the few who do leave the plant to 'capital' punishment, while if they all go out together, management cannot easily discharge the entire department or plant."[2] Solidarity with other workers in these cases does not come so much from ideology or from innate militancy among workers, but rather from experience with the harsh discipline of the factory and from accumulated resentments against the humiliating deference institutionalized in working-class life by the power imbalance between workers and employers.[3]

To many workers, unionism became popular largely because of the dignity that the protection of a contract could bring to them as individuals and as a group. When asked about the difference that union representation made in the lives of workers, one United Electrical Workers union officer explained that "it made a big difference," because "if a foreman started riding a member, why, all a member had to do [was] to tell the steward and the steward would get after the foreman. It made a lot of difference. Where before, why you could stand there and hear a foreman bawl a guy out for something that didn't amount to anything. Make him look like a damn fool. And you couldn't do nothing about it, see? That's before unionism was in the shop."[4]

It should not be surprising then, that cultural and "quality of life" considerations loomed large in the grass-roots activism of the forties. To be sure, strikes sought concessions on wages and working conditions from management, but they also served in some ways as ends in themselves, as actions designed to call into being the working-class "public sphere" latent in the process of incipient class formation. Thus, it was no accident that shop-floor activism took playful forms in order to deny the hegemony of work over pleasure—that jitterbug dancing accompanied the Oakland general strike as well as the 1946 walkout at the Tennessee Coal and Iron Company in Alabama as a way of dramatizing how work stoppages transformed the daily routine, or that workers brought their disputes with management into the streets to demonstrate the support they could mobilize from their neighbors, friends, and sympathizers.

The militancy and solidarity that fueled the mass demonstrations and general strikes of the forties offered the possibility that workers might remake society along more egalitarian, collective, and democratic lines. In order to defeat this challenge from labor, business leaders had to respond with a cultural and political mobilization of their own. To win, they needed to defeat workers inside the factories, in union halls, and in legislative battles. But they also needed to reconstitute U. S. politics and culture along individualistic, private, and materialist lines by creating public spheres and private spaces dominated by the imperatives of capital accumulation.

For business, political and economic victories came more easily than cultural triumphs. The close collaboration in the fifties among labor leaders, government officials, and business executives in support of industrial peace at home and economic expansion abroad revealed few traces of the serious disagreements of the previous decade. The Taft-Hartley Act's ban on secondary boycotts and sympathy strikes effectively terminated the tactics that had proven so successful in the 1946 general strikes, while the law's provisions against wildcat strikes strengthened the hand of unions as agents of industrial peace. Closed-door meetings between representatives of management and labor took on increasing importance as sites where grievances could be resolved, while low-key lobbying within the Democratic party became the privileged site for politics among labor's leaders. On the local level, trade unions generally threw their support behind "pro-growth" coalitions dominated by business interests. The ensuing urban renewal, highway construction, and downtown redevelopment programs won jobs for workers, especially in the building trades. But they also demolished the urban ethnic working-class neighborhoods that had formed the focal point of working-class life and culture since the nineteenth century.[5] As had happened so many times before in U. S. history, working people once again found themselves unable to translate mass mobilization and social struggle into lasting institutional power or structural reform.

Perhaps one reason why historians have paid so little attention to the labor disputes of the forties is that working-class political and social quiescence in the fifties and sixties makes the turmoil of the forties look like some kind of mirage—a temporary "blowing off steam" caused by wartime anxieties and postwar adjustments. But such an analysis underestimates the important transformations brought to U. S. society by the social and political contestations of the World War II experience and its aftermath. The hegemony enjoyed by business interests in the fifties came about as a result of ferocious struggle and a calculated strategy to transform American society and culture. The problem for workers was not that things failed to change in the fifties, but that the revolutionary changes that took place reflected the interests and aspirations of capital, rather than those of labor.

Closer cooperation between companies and unions, the nationalist imperatives of the cold war, expulsions of leftists from labor and from other institutions in American society, and an expanding economy all accounted for some aspects of labor's defeat. But the transformation from the forties to the fifties in working-class life also entailed an ideological and cultural struggle that touched every individual, institution, and organization. Business leaders responded to working-class strategies of independence with strategies of their own, strategies involving concessions, containment, and control.

In the postwar period, business executives conceded higher wages and fringe benefits to organized labor, and they supported as well an increased social wage for unorganized workers in the form of government-sponsored housing, education, and welfare programs. But they also sought to contain working-class demands for a greater share of the nation's material abundance and for greater political power by confining concessions within programs designed to guarantee expanded opportunities for private profit. They favored highway construction over rapid transit, loans for the purchase of single-family detached housing in the suburbs rather than for public housing or renovation of inner-city neighborhoods, private pension plans and limited government loans for veterans rather than universal plans underwriting pensions, housing, and education like those adopted in nearly every other industrialized country.

Like earlier attempts at welfare capitalism, these measures aimed to give some workers a possessive stake in the expansion of capitalism. The underlying philosophy behind them sought to portray economic security as a private and personal matter—a reward for specific services rendered rather than a general right. They also sought to discourage highly paid trade unionists from allying with unorganized workers to demand collective state-sponsored social democratic solutions to public problems. Along with concessions and containment, corporate leaders also aggressively deployed their political power and economic influence to secure control over production inside of factories and over the cultural and social possibilities outside them.

State power proved to be the most important resource available to business executives in this fight. In the emerging corporate-liberal system of

the postwar era, government assumed a twin burden of assisting business in capital accumulation and ideological legitimation. Capital accumulation depended on defense expenditures for the cold war, enhanced
access to markets and raw materials overseas, laws limiting labor activism at home, and state-sponsored programs subsidizing private consumer
spending. Ideological legitimation came from the ways in which federally supported home-loan programs, highway-construction projects, aid to
education, and welfare payments all increased consumer confidence and
decreased the likelihood of broad-based alliances for radical social change.
In almost every instance, government policies and programs delivered crucial advantages to business interests and their policies of concessions, containment, and control.

Concessions made to workers in the wake of the postwar strike wave
established the basic contours of what we have come to call the "American
standard of living." For the first time, ordinary workers won two to four
weeks of paid vacations and holidays, wage increases guaranteed to keep
up with the cost of living, adequate medical plans, and supplementary unemployment benefits. During the fifties real wages increased by almost 20
percent; by 1966 half of all workers and three-fourths of those under the
age of forty had taken up residence in suburbs.[6]

Builders constructed 30 million new housing units in the twenty years
after World War II, and federal highway-building and home-loan programs
helped raise the percentage of home owners in the United States from
below 40 percent in 1940 to above 60 percent by 1960. Consumer spending
on private automobiles had averaged $7.5 billion per year in the thirties
and forties, but by 1950 it had reached $22 billion, and by 1955 the figure
approached $30 billion.[7]

Workers clearly made material gains in the postwar era, but not all
gained equally. Welfare capitalism channeled benefits to workers in large
industries that could not be secured by employees in smaller nonunion
shops. Federal Housing Agency loans backed by the federal treasury made
it possible for workers to acquire equity in homes and to spend more on
consumer goods because they did not have to save as much to make down
payments on houses. But racial discrimination written right into FHA appraisers' manuals meant that most of the benefits of the FHA went to
white workers.[8] Almost 80 percent of the male population over the age of
seventeen could avail themselves of aid to education and home ownership
through the GI Bill and Veterans Administration programs, but very few
women qualified for help under these plans.[9]

Corporate-liberal strategies of concessions, containment, and control
not only exacerbated divisions within the working class along lines of race
and gender but they also directly attacked the environments that gave rise

to the challenges of the forties. Through direct and conscious political attacks as well as through the indirect and sometimes unintended consequences of government support for the most profitable housing, transportation, and communication systems, postwar corporate-liberal policies undermined the importance of the factory floor, urban inner-city neighborhoods, labor unions, ethnic lodges, public meeting places, day care centers, and public transportation in U. S. society.

On the shop floor, contract provisions increasingly conceded to management an unchallenged right to organize work at the point of production, consequently undermining primary work groups and assisting management's ability to automate jobs in order to lessen the power of workers to stop production. Here too, government played a crucial role for corporations, funding research and development on new production methods, offering generous tax breaks for investments in new equipment, and even intervening directly to help companies replace workers with machines. Labor analyst (and former longshore worker) Stan Weir has found that automation of longshoring and shipping in the early seventies originated in an initiative in 1952 proposed by the Department of Defense and ship owners, conducted with the secret cooperation of the International Longshoreman's and Warehouseman's Union. They used the resources of the National Academy of Sciences and the National Research Council to devise and experiment with the "containerization" that eventually provided multinational corporations with the resources to move their manufacturing establishments outside the United States and to eliminate the jobs of hundreds of thousands of longshore and manufacturing workers.[10]

Government planners and business executives also collaborated in undermining the spatial bases for the working-class mobilizations of the forties. Federal decisions to locate defense plants in suburban areas during the war, expenditures on highway-building programs, and home-loan policies that overwhelmingly favored construction of new homes in the suburbs over renovation of older buildings or construction of new ones in central cities combined to pull workers out of ethnic working-class neighborhoods into new and diverse (although generally white) suburbs. The racially discriminatory dimensions of federal home-loan policies not only provided positive incentives for "white flight" from central cities, but for the most part they also penalized borrowers who wanted to invest in housing in older ethnic working-class neighborhoods by subjecting them to far less favorable loan conditions. In addition, urban renewal destroyed tax-paying properties, created new slums composed of escapees from the former renewal areas, and raised taxes on the remaining urban homeowners by granting tax abatements and other subsidies to downtown developers.

A vice-president of the American Trust Company told a postwar gathering of executives in San Francisco how labor militancy had influenced decisions by businesses in respect to the location of new plants, explaining, "In this period good employee relations have become a number one goal. Labor costs have expanded markedly. Conditions under which employees live, as well as work, vitally influence management-labor relations. Generally, large aggregations of labor in one big plant are more subject to outside disrupting influences, and have less happy relations with management than in smaller [suburban] plants."[11]

Suburbanization not only pulled workers away from sources of solidarity and support during strikes, but it also encouraged a less public life, especially in the area of amusements and popular culture. Although the dollar amount spent on commercialized leisure increased markedly in the postwar era, in terms of real disposable income the 1955 sum amounted to a 2 percent decline since 1947. Spectator amusements including motion pictures, professional sports, and concert attendance suffered declines, while spending on home-centered entertainments including television sets and high fidelity sound systems increased markedly.[12]

Many industrialists and advertisers viewed suburbs as ideal sites for consumption. They worked to cultivate that market by presenting new images of gender and family roles that promised fulfillment through commodities. Idealized portrayals of women as mothers played an important role in their appeals. The Seven-Up soft drink company placed advertisements in women's magazines extolling its product as conducive to "family harmony and contentment" because it was one drink the entire family could share. Ipana toothpaste displayed the dazzling smiles of models identified as mothers whose good looks were explained to be no threat to their proper role as mothers with small children. The Revere Camera Company used a picture of a baby in an apron to urge mothers to take pictures of their little girls before they grew up and became homemakers of their own.[13] At the same time, popular advice literature, psychoanalytic treatises, and sociological studies advanced a "breadwinner ethos" for men that "required men to grow up, marry and support their wives."[14]

Yet for all of these idealized portraits of motherhood, femininity, and commodities, tensions between men and women also appeared vividly in postwar consumer culture. In some respects, this stemmed from strategies by advertisers who could play on gender antagonisms as a way of creating a constant anxiety in people's lives that commodities might fill. But in other ways, it doubtless emerged from disillusionment with the over-inflated promises about the "happiness" connected with suburban consumer family life.

For example, family magazines often built the content of their stories around new definitions of gender. In one, a faculty member at Stephens

College in Columbia, Missouri, boasted that the school's "emphasis on marriage and appearance" had been successful in that "a high proportion of our graduates marry successfully." He went on to describe the key to that success: the institution's definition of femininity as "the opposite of direct-ness, aggressiveness, and forcefulness." [15] Yet, in the same issue, "humor-ous" features played on monstrous images of uncontained femininity. In one story, two men are humiliated because their wives kill more deer on a hunting trip than they do. In another, a wife in Los Angeles complains that her husband locked her in the house for two days and made her play chess with him until she cheated and he "chased her out into the street and conked her." The final "joke" concerns the explanation by a man in Cam-den, New Jersey, charged with punching a woman neighbor in the jaw—he said, "[I] thought it was my wife." [16]

Anxieties about relations between men and women appeared in a popu-lar radio format of the postwar era as well. It presented husbands and wives pretending to have breakfast in their homes while their listeners eaves-dropped. Pioneered by Dorothy Killgallen and Dick Kollmar as well as Tex McCrary and Jinx Falkenberg in New York, thirty-seven different shows of this type played to 80 million listeners in 1948. On the one hand these shows reinforced the cult of the home, but on the other hand, they evi-denced great anxiety about it. Most of the time, the husbands functioned as either slow-witted bumblers or as polite sounding boards for their wives' conversation. Ed Fitzgerald provided an exception to this, but the Fitz-geralds hardly seemed like a model of marital bliss either, what with Ed's hostile comments about Peegen's weight and dyed hair that always pro-moted bickering between the two of them. [17]

In the same vein, one of the most popular country-and-western records of 1952 expressed female outrage at men's double standards about extra-marital affairs. In an obvious answer to Hank Thompson's "Wild Side of Life," a lament by a husband whose wife has deserted him for the glamor of night life "where the wine and liquor flows," Kitty Wells's million-selling "It Wasn't God Who Made Honky Tonk Angels" identified male mistreat-ment of women as the main cause of infidelity in marriage.

In the late forties and early fifties, television became the most impor-tant form of home entertainment, with its own combination of idealized portrayals of motherhood and stoical acceptance of an unbridgeable gap between men and women. Whatever their merits as sociology, these por-trayals worked to attract audiences and sell products to them. Business leaders quickly recognized television as one of the best marketing devices ever. But here too, the federal government played an important role. [18]

Tax-sponsored research and development projects oriented the new me-dium toward home units financed by selling advertising, following the model used for radio rather than developing closed-circuit theatrical television, educational television, or publicly financed entertainment television. The Federal Communications Commission sanctioned the network system for television at the same time that federal antitrust actions broke up the motion picture industry's "network" of ties between studios and theaters. Early decisions by the FCC limited the number of stations on the air, while the 1948–52 freeze on new stations protected the competitive position of television's first investors. All of these decisions gave television important advantages over live spectator events. Combined with the ways that suburbanization and the decline of public transit made it more difficult for audiences to reach downtown arenas and theaters, they helped shift the focal point of popular culture away from public spaces and toward the privacy of single-family homes, where advertising messages mediated between the family and the larger society. Television eclipsed radio, but it also made gains at the expense of union and fraternal lodge halls, stadiums, theaters, night clubs, and city streets.

Federal policies also encouraged the expansion of private consumer debt and installment buying. During the period from 1946 to 1965, residential mortgage debt grew three times as fast as disposable income and the gross national product. In 1946 mortgage debt accounted for only about 18 percent of disposable income, but it accounted for almost 55 percent by 1965.[19] These policies gave workers more access to consumer goods of all kinds, but they also gave them substantial debts that made it more risky to go on strike while giving individual workers a profound stake in economic expansion so that tomorrow's growth might pay off today's debts.

Installment buying, television, and suburbanization functioned as powerful agents for the nationalization and homogenization of U.S. culture. They placed consumer purchases at the forefront of individual and collective consciousness and they quickly rendered obsolete old attachments to neighborhood, ethnicity, and class. In the context of the cold war, even religion took on a profoundly new identity.

Almost alone among the nations of the world, the United States experienced a great renewal of religious enthusiasm in the years immediately following World War II. Church membership had increased only slightly between 1910 and 1940, from 43 percent to 48 percent of the population. By 1950, more than 55 percent claimed to be church members, a figure that grew to 62 percent in 1956 and 69 percent by 1960. Between 1945 and 1960, the amount of money spent on building new churches increased every year, from a "low" of $26 million at the war's end to more than $1 billion just fifteen years later.[20]

Impressive in quantitative terms, the postwar religious revival also altered the quality of religion in the United States. Modern mass-media techniques won new constituencies for the traditional fundamentalist beliefs articulated by Dr. Billy Graham, for the Catholic anticommunism of Bishop Fulton J. Sheen, and for the liberal theology of Norman Vincent Peale, who translated the "good news" of the gospels into a self-help strategy for career success and professional advancement. Cardinal Mooney of Detroit's Catholic Archdiocese led seven thousand people onto that city's Washington Boulevard on May Day 1948 to pray for an end to communism and for the conversion of the entire Soviet people.[21]

During President Eisenhower's inaugural parade in 1953, wealthy contributors showed off their jewelry and mink coats while riding in limousines lined up behind "God's Float" at the head of the procession.[22] As religion increasingly became identified with U.S. foreign policy and U.S. capitalism, Congress inserted the words "under God" into the Pledge of Allegiance in 1954, and two years later "In God We Trust" became the official national motto.[23] The incorporation of popular religion into an increasingly important ideological justification for consumer capitalism and anticommunism represented another significant victory in the quest by capital and the state for moral authority in the fifties, particularly because of the close relationship between religion and rank-and-file struggles in the forties.

Especially on the local level, religious leaders often stood firmly behind the rank-and-file revolts of the forties. Priests joined picket lines in support of striking packinghouse workers in Chicago in 1946, and clergy from many faiths spoke out on behalf of the general strikes in Stamford, Lancaster, and Rochester. A letter supporting the Pittsburgh general strike in one of that city's daily newspapers asked, "Who made the Duquesne Electric Light Company but the poor working man? Now the poor working man must strike and fight for a living wage. No wonder the 19th chapter of St. Matthew in the Bible says 'Then said Jesus unto his disciples—verily I say unto you that a rich man shall hardly ever enter into the Kingdom of Heaven.' "[24]

Of course, clerical anticommunists also played an important role in opposing rank-and-file insurgencies during the New York longshore strike in 1945, the Pittsburgh General Strike, and in the Evansville and Fairmont City strikes in 1948. The Association of Catholic Trade Unionists played a particularly visible role within the labor movement, arguing that communist-influenced insurgencies undermined the opportunity for the substantive social justice that might be attained through Catholic corporatism.[25] At the peak of anticommunism in the labor movement, the ACTU received credit for very important changes in leadership in locals of the UE, IUMMSW, TWU, and other left-led unions.

Monsignor Charles Owen Rice of Pittsburgh advanced the ACTU agenda vigorously and effectively; for years he served as the organization's best-known spokesperson. CIO president Philip Murray secretly gave money to Rice to support the ACTU, and Rice received an automobile from executives of the Chevrolet corporation in recognition of his efforts on behalf of "sane industrial relations."[26] Looking back on his role years later, Rice admitted that his crusade never really caught on with the rank and file. "This anti-communism was hard work," Rice confessed. "For the most part, the rank-and-file was nonideological and was interested in bread and butter, which the leftist leadership provided as well as any and better than most."[27]

As Rice discovered many times, even devoutly religious workers had no compunction about opposing members of the clergy on issues of union politics and workers' control at the point of production. When Reverend Owen J. Kirby of Monessen, Pennsylvania, claimed that the forthcoming 1946 steel strike was unnecessary and inspired by Communists, union members in his parish sent him a sharp letter of reprimand. They condemned the "unchristian-like attitude which you have on numerous occasions voiced from the pulpit which is entirely devoid of the principles of the brotherhood of man." Denying communist inspiration for their decision to strike, they countered that they viewed Kirby's utterances as "company inspired and originating from an unreliable source."[28]

Catholic members of UE Local 813 in Evansville, Indiana, and IUMMSW in Fairmont City, Illinois, displayed similar loyalty to their unions in the face of anticommunist attacks by local priests. They won important victories, but workers elsewhere were not as successful. In New York City, 250 grave diggers at the Catholic Diocese's Calvary and Gate of Heaven cemeteries in 1948 remained loyal to the officers of their Food and Tobacco Workers of America union despite attacks by Francis Cardinal Spellman. Refusing to negotiate with a union whose officers refused to sign the noncommunist affidavits of the Taft-Hartley Act, the cardinal personally ordered the grave diggers to halt their work stoppage. They obediently kissed his ring—and then calmly resumed their strike as a backlog of one thousand corpses piled up. But eventually, they were persuaded by their attorney, a member of the ACTU, to join the AFL Building Service Employees Union, which allowed Spellman to settle the strike on his own terms.[29]

The cold war incorporated anticommunist religious leaders into the corporate-liberal consensus and effectively isolated radical workers from any significant support from the religious hierarchy. The religious metaphors that had proved so effective in dramatizing workers' struggles during the forties now became inverted as clerics began to embrace what Robert Bellah has called the American "civil religion." Because "Communists" stood for atheism, the U.S. government could be portrayed as an agent of God, while support for its foreign and domestic policy interests could be presented as part of a divine obligation beyond question or debate.

Cold war appeals to patriotism and nationalism also inverted radical metaphors from the forties. In the postwar demonstrations and general strikes, workers wore their army uniforms. They carried American flags, and they invoked "the spirit of the American way" in their appeals for fair treatment. Building on the "Americanism" celebrated in New Deal and Popular Front culture and politics in the thirties, they equated their egalitarian and anti-authoritarian aspirations with the goals of the nation at large. But the cold war enabled big business, the government, and anticommunist labor leaders to recapture the imagery of nationalism and patriotism away from the rank and file, to deploy their symbols in the service of labor peace, anticommunism, increased production, and support for economic expansion overseas. In doing so, they built upon a more conservative nationalist tradition—one that equated the nation's interests with the interests of private property and that found the national culture embodied best in the national market for standardized consumer goods.

In the postwar era, corporate liberals built political alliances that radically restructured the economy, politics, and culture of U. S. society. They countered the emerging working-class public sphere of the forties with a well-integrated capitalism in the fifties. Their policies succeeded in placing consumption and commodity exchange at the core of community and cultural life, transforming the family into a consuming unit defined by the needs of television advertisers and remaking the community into an entity held together by shared experiences with mortgage debt and commodity purchases. They elevated consumption over production, conformity over dissent, and bureaucratically administered social harmony over direct democracy. They succeeded in utilizing the state as an instrument of both capital accumulation and ideological legitimation, while at the same time colonizing for capital new areas of investment opportunity.

The postwar triumph of corporate liberalism represents a clear case of a successful struggle for hegemony. Corporate liberals secured control over key resources and institutions by unifying antagonistic elements into an effective coalition. They won widespread support for a worldview that made their view of society synonymous with the general interest. They recruited allies from among competitive-sector conservatives and trade-union liberals by making concessions to the material interests of both groups. Most important, by combining countersubversive rhetoric with policies geared toward economic expansion, they found a basis for uniting the interests and ideologies of groups capable of working together to control the key institutions of the economy and the state.

Yet hegemony is never a fixed fact, it is more of a floating equilibrium, a temporary solution that has to be remade each day. In modern societies, ideology and culture play crucial roles in maintaining hegemony; a police officer in people's heads is ultimately cheaper and more effective than a police officer on every corner. But ideological and cultural hegemony are innately unstable; no sooner are they established do they start to come apart, as excluded individuals and groups struggle to create new alliances capable of transforming inequitable power relations.

The working class won concessions from corporate liberals in the postwar era because direct-action protest proved that workers had to be acknowledged and their needs satisfied to some extent if there were to be labor peace and social harmony. These hard-won concessions may have helped co-opt the social movement, whose struggles made them possible in the first place, but they also gave public recognition and legitimacy to working-class desires for the good life, for happiness and abundance. As the main focus of U. S. ideology and culture shifted from the primacy of production to the primacy of consumption, workers transferred their struggles for control over the pace and purpose of production to battles for control over the reception, uses, and effects of new forms of commercialized leisure.

Just as demonstrations of popular power produced the necessity for concessions from corporate liberals in the postwar era, the solidarity and militancy of grass-roots direct action also brought containment and control. For example, public policies that undermined ethnic working-class neighborhoods and fraternal organizations stemmed in part from efforts to constitute a new public more receptive to the needs of capital accumulation. But these efforts would have been effective as repression only if workers depended solely on residual entities from the past as a basis for waging struggles in the present. In the forties upheavals, ethnic and neighborhood solidarity did play a strong role in providing supportive atmospheres for shop-floor militancy and general strikes. But in just as many cases, labor militancy called into existence a new sense of community and a new sense of class that transcended old ethnic divisions and barriers. Emergent possibilities from the present informed these strikes just as much, or more, as did residual elements of struggle from the past. As Nelson Lichtenstein notes, "The decline in the importance of ethnic divisions within the white working class meant that in the forties, American patriotism enjoyed a broader cultural base than at any time in the twentieth century. A homogeneous blue-collar Americanism was re-forged out of the more insular sense of self-identity that had long characterized so many immigrant and second-generation workers from southern and eastern Europe."[30] If capital's policies encouraged assimilation and incorporation from the top down, working-class experiences in the forties demonstrated the possibilities of assimilation and incorporation from the bottom up.

Even on the factory floor, the area where employers exercised the greatest amount of direct control, policies of control, concessions, and containment had their limits. Strikes, slowdowns, sabotage, and stealing continued, despite the sophisticated contracts negotiated and policed by unions and employers. Writing in 1961, industrial relations expert James Kuhn asked, "Why, after twenty years of experience with the best grievance procedures which able men could devise, do American workers regularly engage in grievance tactics which are disruptive to production and disruptive of harmonious shop relations?"[31]

Working-class strategies of independence persisted inside the plants, at least in part, because they flourished outside the factory gates. Corporate-liberal attempts to externalize the tensions of the factory onto the larger society, to obscure class conflicts by "naturalizing" them in hierarchies of race and gender, and to cultivate a consumer rather than a producer consciousness all served to broaden, rather than narrow, popular aspirations for control at work and for better life chances at home and in the community. Working-class dissent did not disappear in the fifties. On the contrary, aspirations denied expression through politics, suppressed on the shop floor, and contained in the community often found powerful expression with emergent forms of popular culture and commercialized leisure.

Just as general strikes and mass demonstrations transformed places designed for work or commerce into zones occupied for purposes of community and carnival, new forms of consumer culture in the fifties could become sites for symbolic inversion. For example, highway-construction programs, suburbanization, and urban renewal dispersed working-class populations over broader areas, necessitated more purchases of automobiles, and destroyed familiar gathering places and meeting sites. But subcultures of working-class "car customizers" claimed these new realities for their own forms of play. They used unfinished or largely untraveled highways as sites for drag racing. They used their skills as mechanics and artisans to turn standardized, mass-produced "family" cars into individualized, stylish, high-performance machines. They rummaged through junkyards and abandoned lots to salvage old cars and car parts and make something new, useful, and beautiful out of them.

When automobile manufacturers converted to military production during World War II, consumers lost access to new-model automobiles until the postwar period. But because of wartime scarcities, many people became accustomed to working on their own cars, repairing them, and sometimes changing their design. In the immediate postwar years, two groups emerged expressing a new creativity—car racers and car customizers. Both groups turned the standardized commodities produced in Detroit into highly personal creations, embodying completely different principles of aesthetics and engineering from the ones marketed by the auto industry. The racers modified their machines to improve their speed and acceleration, while the customizers centered their concerns on design. But both fashioned changes in the automobile that eventually forced even manufacturers to respond.

By 1950, hot rod magazines had 200,000 readers, and car clubs began to operate across the nation. In October 1946, car races in Oakland, California, attracted crowds of 6,000 people; by the following spring they were racing three nights a week. The Southern California Timing Association held its first exposition in January 1948, attracting 55,000 people. California led the way, but drag-racing clubs organized in Indiana, Pennsylvania, and New Mexico at the same time.[32] Young people who got their cars from junkyards—and who had to learn about them to make them run—joined with experienced mechanics in increasing the power and streamlining the bodies of Detroit's automobiles. They fashioned a new kind of "prestige from below" that focused unprecedented public attention on working-class skills and creativity.

Customizers lowered the body and took the chrome trim off of their cars, assembling parts from various models to create their own styles. They created individual statements out of mass-produced commodities, and at the same time sneered at the auto industry by demonstrating untapped possibilities in engineering and design. For mechanics and body-shop repairers, customizing allowed a playful outlet for creativity not permitted at work. In an age of automation and standardization, customizing provided a rare opportunity for anyone with an interest in doing mechanical work. For others, the car culture offered an intimate relationship with a supportive community forged in opposition to the consumer norms of American capitalism.

Some of the customizers stole their parts from auto supply stores and junkyards, terrorizing their communities with dangerous street racing. A member of a midwestern hot rod club recalls, "There are some things I'm not too proud of. We did steal from other people; we did make regular trips into South St. Louis because it was so easy to steal fender skirts, hubcaps, taillights, or whatever was big at the time. . . . A lot of us that was all we had. We weren't scholars, most of us weren't that attractive to the women otherwise. We didn't have money, wore the same pair of jeans to school most days. But we had our cars. And we would angle park at school and no one would leave till everybody got there and we'd all leave a strip of rubber as we took off. They knew who we were."[33]

Even individuals involved in the incredibly sophisticated craft work of painting and lowering the bodies of cars, as well as those who saw working on cars as an outlet for their mechanical prowess, often found themselves considered outcasts. An electrical engineer—who learned the basics of troubleshooting while working on racing cars in the early fifties—remembers, "I was always hit with this being a childish endeavor, and something that you should have grown out of at 16, nothing permanent, nothing substantial. It was really a normal cross section of people, but it was a grouping of young men, and if they weren't on a rugby team or polo team had

to be bad. You know, you don't want small dissident groups to huddle any-
place, it would be bad!"[34]

In the South, much of the grass-roots creativity about cars became
channeled into stock-car racing. Often local police would help out race
promoters by identifying the town bootleggers, whose driving skill came
from the peculiar requirements of their illegal activities. In the early days,
stock-car racing drew upon any rivalries of interest, including all-women
races, women against men, or blacks against whites. Wendell Scott, a
black driver from Virginia, earned great respect from his fellow drivers but
never secured the support from automobile manufacturers that would have
allowed him to race with equipment equal to that of other drivers.[35]

Women made particularly important contributions to the early development of the sport. Acting on the advice of local police officers exasperated
by her reckless driving and flamboyant customizing, Louise Smith of Green-
ville, South Carolina, entered and won numerous stock-car races in 1946.
Ethel Flock Smith, Sara Christian, and Mildred Williams all participated
in the early days of stock-car racing, and female drivers and customizers
appeared all over the country. Women wrote in to *Hot Rod* magazine to
inquire about car clubs in their areas, and racing journals frequently publicized the exploits of women racers who attained outstanding speeds.[36]

Rooted in the folklore of southern communities, stock-car racing so captured public attention after the war that it spawned a mass spectator sport,
with important impact on the automobile industry as a whole. Customizers and drag racers also affected the automobile industry. Stylistically,
Detroit followed the lead of customizers throughout the fifties. The industry introduced the V-8 engine and 12-volt electrical systems to appeal expressly to the drag racing and customizing audiences. These craftspeople
found that their art and engineering became co-opted into just another
mass-mediated commodity, but for the marginal subculture that spawned
it, car customizing retained its subversive social content.

Car customizing requires detailed and painstaking work. "Chopping and
channeling" a car, applying ten coats of enamel paint, and keeping an engine in racing shape all require precision, skill, and patience. But they also
enable workers to preserve in their "hobby" the control over the job and the
commitment to it that was invariably denied them at work. Management
techniques for organizing production try to leave workers with as little
leverage as possible. Automation aims to contain the creative aspects of
work inside machines, so that workers will have less power to influence the
nature, purpose, or pace of production. With customizing, the artisan can
work on the whole machine, not just a part. A personal vision guides design and ornamentation decisions, and the finished product shows off one's
own labors to the rest of society. In their appropriations of new spaces,

customizers also showed the traces of old ones, keeping alive memories of meaningful self-paced production in an age of automation and speedup.

The active labor of remaking cars created by Detroit drew the attention of two important sociologists in 1950, who saw customizing as an emblematic experience within the new practices of popular culture in the postwar era. David Riesman and Reuel Denny formulated a general theory about the uses and effects of popular culture based on their observations of customizers, claiming, "As the hot rodder visibly breaks down the car as Detroit made it, and builds it up again with his own tools and energies, so the allegedly passive recipient of movies or radio, less visibly but just as surely builds up his own amalgam of what he reads, sees, and hears; and in this, far from being manipulated, he is often the manipulator."[37]

In their insistence on the active nature of media reception, Riesman and Denny followed in the footsteps of Robert K. Merton. In his study of a 1943 war propaganda broadcast, Merton found that listeners heard different things from the same program. Merton asked listeners why they responded favorably to an eighteen-hour marathon designed to sell war bonds and to its host, Kate Smith. Surprisingly, the content of the program and the patriotic purpose of the event had little to do with people's reasons for liking it. Many women respondents volunteered that they liked Kate Smith because her large body did not conform to generally accepted Hollywood standards of beauty, and they surmised that she must be a good person with values much like their own. They projected onto Smith their personal discomfort with the oppressive standards of beauty and personal worth devised by the beauty and glamor industries, and consequently they discerned a message in Smith's broadcast more important to them than its ostensible purpose. Similarly, almost half of the respondents addressed class questions in their remarks about the broadcast, praising Kate Smith's humble background, asserting that her good character came from having to work for a living, and condemning rich people as selfish and lazy. None of these responses seemed stimulated by the content of the program; they came instead from the explosive confrontation between symbols in the mass media and real, lived experience.[38]

The meaning given to Smith's broadcast by the audience stemmed largely from its own consciousness, but creators of mass-mediated entertainment also tried to create sights and sounds that would win popularity with working-class audiences. In absorbing and exploiting traditional forms of working-class culture like ethnic humor, working-class music, and popular legends, the mass media also formed a new body of common folk knowledge susceptible to popular manipulation. Precisely because working-class culture in the United States could not be autonomous from capitalism or from the imagination of other classes, elements of it became available to the society at large, and working-class worldviews permeated all quarters of American life.

In order to attract and retain the allegiance of working-class customers, the culture industry had to present images that reflected the situated knowledge and experiences of working-class people. Capitalists can market culture, but they cannot create it. They must keep their eye in the organic artistry of everyday life in working-class communities to find the fads, fashions, images, and ideas that will strike a resonant chord with a mass audience. In the early years of commercial home television, one unusual popular spectacle emerged out of working-class life to grab the attention of a mass audience—the roller derby.

Just as car customizers and drag racers placed their mark on the automobiles and highways that had done so much to transform working-class life, roller derby audiences marked early local and network television broadcasts with a distinctly working-class character. In the years when attendance at motion pictures and other public spectator events began to decline, the number of television sets in use in the United States increased dramatically, going from 14,000 units in 1947 to 1 million by 1949, then increasing to 4 million in 1950, a one-year jump of 400 percent.[39] Television's biggest investors knew that they wanted to follow the example of radio and base their industry on private home units suited to selling mass audiences to advertisers. But they were less sure about what kinds of programming would make people actually purchase television sets. Hungry for something to put on the air, the industry experimented with a variety of programs that might attract viewers, including televised roller derby matches.

Part sport and part theater, half carnival and half truth, roller derby floundered as a touring exhibition for over a decade until television turned it into a commercial success. The "sport" originated in the creative and commercial mind of Leo Seltzer, a film distributor and theater owner who needed an entertainment attraction to fill empty arenas and theaters in the depression years of the thirties. Seltzer came across an article in *Literary Digest* that estimated that 93 percent of the American public roller-skated at one time or another. Coming from the same journal that predicted victory for Alf Landon in the 1936 presidential election, that figure may be taken with a grain of salt, but fortunately for Seltzer, the magazine's enthusiasm for roller skating proved profitable even if empirically groundless. Seltzer staged marathon races in the Chicago Coliseum in 1935, but few fans could maintain interest in watching skaters circle a small track again and again for hours on end. So Seltzer devised a set of rules and a format for team play based on the goal of having selected skaters try to pass (by a full lap) members of the other team. The attraction built up a small but faithful following that enabled it to survive until 1949, when television created new possibilities.[40]

Capitalizing on CBS's confusion as to what could be done with the new medium, Seltzer convinced the network to broadcast a sparsely attended game from New York. The next night crowds packed the arena, and roller derby became a staple of early television, featuring two local (in New York) and one network telecast per week. In the next several years, the game used extensive television exposure to spur live attendance, partially because the illusion of the medium made the game look more exciting and legitimate than it actually was. Camera angles made the track look smaller and the action more exciting. Skilled announcers like Ken Nydell helped by preserving the illusion of genuine competition. Fans came in person to see what they remembered from television; in this case, the copy (the television broadcast) was better than the original (live roller derby matches).

Roller Derby News had 50,000 subscribers by 1953. Paid admissions to roller derby exhibitions that year exceeded $5 million. Flushed with success, the official roller derby program boasted that "in the past decade two impacts have hit the American public—the atom bomb and the Roller Derby—and it appears the latter will have the most permanent effect."[41] Like televised wrestling, another staple of the early years of the medium, roller derby involved fans in a spectacle that spoke to the needs and fears of working-class life in postwar America. How else can one explain the appeal of a sport in which the results are predetermined, in which play depends more on dramatic embellishment than athletic skill, and in which staged violence caters to the wildest prejudices of the fans? Roller derby relied on drama because it was drama, offending only those who cherished the illusion that competition in sports or in life actually separates the deserving from the undeserving. Roller derby served as a kind of ritual, unifying its followers in a deeply emotional experience, rather than dividing them into antagonistic groups in the manner of competitive sport.

Roller derby villains demonstrated such uncompromising and unyielding evil that the fans enjoyed a continuing relationship with them because they were fun to hate. Flaunting their malevolence and never expressing remorse, roller derby villains gloated about how the established authorities and rules could not stop them. Every match proceeded with a long series of manipulations, tricks, and cheating by the villains, until at last, the home team heroes struck back. Their retribution proved particularly exciting because it invariably occurred outside the hated parameters of legality.

The rules constituted a living hypocrisy in roller derby, always susceptible to the whims of the powerful or the brazenly antisocial; small wonder that the sport would resonate mightily for working-class audiences. In roller derby, covert and illegitimate means became necessary to end long periods of suffering and defeat, much in the manner that Roland Barthes has identified as characteristic of professional wrestling in France.[42] Roller derby presented setbacks as a result of the unfair manipulation of rules by others, and it carefully constructed revenge fantasies of vigilante action, giving voice to deep feelings of resentment allowed few other forms of expression.

Rooted in a leisure-time activity open to all regardless of gender or income, roller derby provided credible heroes in familiar situations for working-class audiences, stressing its class, gender, and racial dynamics in its publicity. Josephine "Ma" Bogash, the wife of a railroad fire tender, explained that she wanted to be an entertainer of some kind and consequently took to skating as a way out of the kitchen and the old neighborhood. Buddy Atkinson, Sr.'s, father was a machinist, and Atkinson himself entered the games directly from a job as a garment worker. His brother Tommy billed himself as the "skating bartender," a salute to his former trade. Ken Monte's father drove taxi cabs, Midge "Toughie" Brashun's was a plumber, and the legendary Charlie O'Connell turned his back on a career as an auto mechanic to take up skating.[43]

The marketing and public relations personnel behind roller derby took pains to maintain the working-class identity of the stars with their fans. A 1953 article in *Popular Science* featured Mary Lou Palermo and boasted of her skill as a machinist: "Nobody touches her magic skates but Mary Lou herself. An artist with the abrasive wheel she grinds down a new set of wheels, then removes a couple of ball bearings and adjusts the axle-bearing keeper loosely. She thinks slight friction improves control."[44] In addition, gender loomed large in the roller derby universe. Voice-overs by announcer Ken Nydell told television audiences that "this is the only sport where men and women are placed on an equal basis, so that when the gals are skating, they've got control of the game."[45] Not surprisingly, roller derby had a particular appeal to working-class women, who made up from 50 to 65 percent of its audience.[46] Reflecting the increase in the number of women in the industrial work force, roller derby heroines provided strong and assertive models of female independence. In its equality between men and women, its teamwork, and its unifying rituals, roller derby provided a utopian vision of social relations present but not yet realized in everyday life.

As a spectacle lampooning the seriousness of competition, asserting ritualistic unity in the face of aggressive division, and emphasizing a preference for direct justice over legitimate channels, roller derby stemmed from the same passions as the mass demonstration and wildcat strike. Its working-class performers and spectators acted out in symbolic form what direct political action enabled them to do in real life. A stepchild of the gap between the logic of capitalist production and the fulfillment of human needs and aspirations, roller derby made fun of the present as it preserved utopian hopes for the future. Its success came from the happy combination of the needs of television and the political agenda shaped by postwar labor strife, but it also made such an impact because it spoke the language of working-class experience.

The exaggerated melodramatic posturing by roller derby performers proved perfectly well suited to the internal properties of the television medium. The media scholar Harold Innis has explained how electronic media tend to obliterate the past and future, stressing the emotional experience of the moment. Television has the capacity to turn each moment into an end in itself, unlike linear media such as books, which depend on chronology, sequence, and a firm sense of past and future. Unlike linear sports such as boxing and baseball—where each moment is part of a logical sequence leading to an inexorable conclusion—roller derby thrives on the spontaneous outburst that overturns the logic of previous events. The persecuted hero endures repeated and unbearable indignities before miraculously turning things upside down and exacting revenge.

Roller derby's emphasis on emotional catharsis, augmented by the immediacy of the electronic media, fulfilled possibilities long latent in working-class culture, particularly working-class speech. Sociolinguists differ as to the effect of class background on speech, but the work of Leonard Schatzman and Anselm Strauss in the fifties, and more recent studies by Basil Bernstein, suggest some fascinating connections between working-class ways of talking and the adaptability of working-class culture to the electronic media.[47]

Interviewing witnesses at a disaster, Schatzman and Strauss found that middle-class observers detached themselves from their experience. They described the event in neutral terms, making careful distinctions and qualifications. They took care to step back and summarize the meaning of the event. But working-class witnesses, on the other hand, related the same event in a decidedly personal way that made themselves a part of the experience. They took pains to express empathy for the victims and to underline the emotional content of the event, assuming an empathy between speaker and listener. Basil Bernstein's research on the speech patterns of British school children shows some of the same class-based dynamics at work. He observed that working-class speakers stressed immediate emotional reactions to lived experience. They relied on collective forms (especially the second person plural) to emphasize collective experience, and they did little to order events in a linear way. But Bernstein's investigations into the speech patterns among middle-class children found them making careful distinctions among people, stressing the unique perceptions of the speaker, and arranging information to stress analysis and evaluation rather than subjective emotions.

These studies provide a framework for understanding some of the covert class implications of popular culture practices in the forties. Calo, the colorful street slang employed by Mexican-American zoot-suiters in the Southwest, contained many of the tendencies toward exaggeration, rhyme, and melodrama found in English working-class speech. The pachuco argot violated rules of grammar in order to assert familiarity with others, and it relied on repetition of stock slang phrases to build unity among those who spoke it. Lalo Guerrero, who had worked in California aircraft factories during World War II, recorded a series of Spanish-language hit records in the postwar era including "El Pachuco," "Pachuco Boogie," and "Marijuana Boogie." These songs displayed a delightful and mischievous sense of wordplay and helped popularize calo among new audiences.[48]

Similarly, recorded music also helped articulate a new sense of prestige from below through "jive talk," the linguistic code of urban working-class blacks. Like working-class English or pachuco Spanish, "hip" or "bop" talk varied the meanings of words, employed internal rhymes, exaggeration, and ungrammatical familiarity, creating an in-group code that flaunted social norms.[49] To the "hip" talker (probably derived from the Wolof word "hipi cat," meaning one with open eyes) something good could be "crazy" —a violation of rational considerations—and to understand meant "to dig," as if to get beneath the surface.

Dizzy Gillespie—whose musical creativity and effusive personality focused public attention on "bop" music and speech—identifies the unity between music and speech emanating from their history in the experience of black people. In his autobiography, he asserts, "We didn't have to try; as black people we just naturally spoke that way. People who wished to communicate with us had to consider our manner of speech, and sometimes adopted it. As we played with musical notes, bending them into new and different meanings that constantly changed, we played with words."[50]

Like jive talk, bop music played with existing forms and made them come out different. Bop musicians played the melody of popular songs, but liberated it by changing its rhythms and tune, retaining only some of its chord progressions. Bop musicians interpolated bits of popular songs as humorous phrases into their songs, but they also changed keys and tempos frequently. The hidden melodies and complex rhythms of bop led some to condemn it as unlistenable. "You can't dance to it," they'd say—although bop aficionados like Amiri Baraka would reply, "*You* can't dance to it." It was something for black people, designed to be difficult to steal. "Something they can't play," Thelonius Monk called it. Of course they could play it, but only by accepting and trying to understand the worldview behind it.

Just as bebop rejected American musical and grammatical standards, it also involved a political critique of American society. Some bop artists expressed interest in Islam because it enabled them to break with Christianity and the white supremacists who preached it, while others made a direct political critique. "We refused to accept racism, poverty, or economic exploitation, nor would we live out uncreative humdrum lives merely for the sake of survival," Gillespie proclaimed.[51] Apparently his views had broad appeal, as bebop records began selling well to both blacks and whites between 1947 and 1949. *Life* magazine ran a cover story on Dizzy Gillespie, who found his concerts attended by young people eager to speak bop talk and emulate their heroes. As he remembers, "I looked around, and everybody was trying to look like me. Now, why in hell did they want to do that? They even pretended to laugh like me (the newspapers said) and it was not a racial phenomenon. These were black and white people alike, by the tens of thousands, willing to stand up and testify for bebop."[52]

The language of bop musicians quickly became conventional American slang. Their philosophies helped inspire an entire generation of social critics, whose bohemian culture itself reached a mass acceptance in the sixties. The bop musicians may have been too intellectual and too internalized to enjoy total acceptance, and of course, the music industry, law enforcement agencies, and others certainly worked hard to destroy bebop and its followers. Yet whatever the shortcomings of their movement, they established the ability of the electronic media to help spread culture and speech rooted in the emotional, collective, and empathetic world of the working class and its ethnic subcultures.

Richard Wright realized the importance of speech in his 1944 memoir, *American Memoir*. Relating his experiences at work in a restaurant, Wright emphasized the difference between his worldview as a black man and that of the white waitresses he encountered. "All my life," Wright observed, "I have done nothing but feel and cultivate my feelings; all their lives they had done nothing but strive for petty goals, the trivial material prizes of American life. We shared a common tongue, but my language was a different language from theirs."[53] Yet after the war, Wright's speech and the depth of feeling behind it became transmitted to millions of people through the language of jazz musicians.

Postwar popular culture revealed the disunity of the working class as well as its unity. The visibility of African-American artists revealed old antagonisms and provoked new ones. The same dynamics that drew women into stock-car racing and the roller derby also generated a seemingly endless series of images of women as domestic and dependent. But class did not disappear from view; in popular culture its contours and dimensions remained evident and accessible.

Working-class culture, with its emotionalism and collectivity, contained an affinity for the electronic media that print-oriented, middle-class culture could not match. Television turned to the language of roller derby in part because that spectacle's class origins gave it an immediacy and an exaggerated emotionalism perfectly suited to televised presentation. The speech of working-class people dramatically embodied in bebop became adopted as the national slang when records disseminated it to a mass audience.

Of course, jive talk, roller derby, and car customizing are no substitutes for state power. On the job, at home, and in popular culture, workers and others paid a terrible price for their inability to convert grass-roots militancy into a social movement capable of fighting to reform society along democratic and egalitarian lines. But the traces of working-class consciousness within popular culture in the postwar period also show the limits of corporate-liberal hegemony. They testify to profound popular dissatisfaction with the hierarchies and exploitations of the cold war era. They also demonstrate the emergent possibilities of the affinity between electronic mass media and working-class culture, an affinity most powerfully demonstrated by the class dimensions of popular film and popular music during the postwar years.

NOTES

1. In *Workers in Industrial America: Essays on the Twentieth Century Struggle* (New York: Oxford University Press, 1980), 177, David Brody presents the reconversion proposal as "acting within the mainstream of CIO progressivism."

2. Quoted in Rick Fantasia, *Cultures of Solidarity: Consciousness, Action, and Contemporary American Workers* (Berkeley: University of California Press, 1988), 113.

3. I am indebted to Stan Weir for alerting me to the importance of resentment against deference in working-class life as a source of rank-and-file activism.

4. Quote from interview with Art M. McCollough, June 4, 1976, Pennsylvania Historical and Museum Commission, in Ronald W. Schatz, *The Electrical Workers: A History of Labor at General Electric and Westinghouse, 1923–60* (Urbana: University of Illinois Press, 1987), 113.

5. See, for example, labor's support for Mayor Jerome Cavanaugh in Detroit, David Lawrence in Pittsburgh, Oscar Holcombe in Houston, or Raymond Tucker in St. Louis. For information about progrowth coalitions, see John Mollenkopf, *The Contested City* (Princeton: Princeton University Press, 1983).

6. Brody, *Workers in Industrial America*, 192.

7. Susan Hartmann, *The Home Front and Beyond* (Boston: Twayne, 1982), 165–68; Mollenkopf, *The Contested City*, 111.

8. Kenneth Jackson, *Crabgrass Frontier: The Suburbanization of the United States* (New York: Oxford, 1985).

9. Gwendolyn Mink, "The Lady and the Tramp: Gender, Race, and the Origins of the American Welfare State," in Linda Gordon, ed., *Women, the State, and Welfare* (Madison: University of Wisconsin Press, 1990), 113.

10. Stan Weir, "The Human Cost of Automation," *New Politics* 3, no. 4 (1992): 175.

11. John Mollenkopf, "The Postwar Politics of Urban Development," in William Tabb and Larry Sawers, eds., *Marxism and the Metropolis: New Perspectives in Urban Political Economy* (New York: Oxford University Press, 1978), 131.

12. Lynn Spigel, "Installing the Television Set: Popular Discourses on Television and Domestic Space, 1948–1955," *Camera Obscura* 16 (1988): 20. For Spigel's full (and fully convincing) argument, see her *Make Room for TV: Television and the Family Ideal in Postwar America* (Chicago: University of Chicago Press, 1992).

13. *American Magazine*, Jan. 1948, 10, Feb. 1948, 3, 8.

14. Barbara Ehrenreich, *The Hearts of Men: American Dreams and the Flight from Commitment* (New York: Anchor, 1983), 11; see also Wendy Kozol, *Life's America* (Philadelphia: Temple University Press, 1994).

15. *American Magazine*, Jan. 1948, 125.

16. Ibid., 11.

17. Ibid., Feb. 1948, 42.

18. George Lipsitz, *Time Passages: Collective Memory and American Popular Culture* (Minneapolis: University of Minnesota Press, 1990), 45–47; Spigel, *Make Room for TV*, 59–60.

19. Michael Stone, "Housing: The Economic Crisis," in Chester Hartman, ed., *America's Housing Crisis: What Is to Be Done?* (London: Routledge and Kegan Paul, 1983), 122.

20. Sydney Ahlstrom, *A Religious History of the American People* (New Haven: Yale University Press, 1972), 952–53.

21. *Detroit News*, May 1, 1948, 4C.

22. Merle Curti, *The Growth of American Thought* (New York: Harper and Row, 1964), 771.

23. Ahlstrom, *A Religious History of the American People*, 954.

24. *Pittsburgh Sun Telegraph*, Sept. 26, 1946, 14.

25. Neil Betten, *Catholic Activism and the Industrial Worker* (Gainesville: University of Florida Press, 1976); Michael Harrington, "Catholics and the Labor Movement," *Labor History* (Fall 1960): 231–63; Douglas P. Seaton, *Catholics and Radicals: The Association of Catholic Trade Unionists and the American Labor Movement* (Lewisburg: Bucknell University Press, 1981).

26. Steve Rosswurm, "The Catholic Church and the Left-Led Unions: Labor Priests, Labor Schools, and the ACTU," in Steve Rosswurm, ed., *The CIO's Left-Led Unions* (New Brunswick: Rutgers University Press, 1992), 130, 132.

27. Monsignor Charles Owen Rice, "The Tragic Purge of 1948: A Personal Recollection," in James C. Foster, ed., *American Labor in the Southwest* (Tucson: University of Arizona Press, 1982), 228.

28. Letter to Father Owen J. Kirby from Tony Ortolona, Recording Secretary of United Steelworkers of America Local 1229, Jan. 25, 1946, CIO Papers, Department of Archives and Manuscripts, Catholic University of America, Washington, D.C.

29. Harvey Levenstein, *Communism, Anticommunism, and the CIO* (Westport, Conn.: Greenwood Press, 1981), 276.

30. Nelson Lichtenstein, *Labor's War at Home* (Cambridge: Cambridge University Press, 1982), 237.

31. Quoted in Brody, *Workers in Industrial America*, 205.

32. Gene Balsley, "The Hod Rod Culture," *American Quarterly* 2, no. 2 (Winter 1950): 353; *Hot Rod*, Mar. 1948, 18, Aug. 1948, 41.

33. Quoted in George Lipsitz, "They Knew Who We Were," *Cultural Correspondence* 5 (Summer-Fall 1977).

34. Ibid.

35. Jerry Bledsoe, *The World's Number One, Flat-Out, All-Time Great, Stock Car Racing Book* (New York: Bantam, 1976), 212.

36. Ibid., 80; *Hot Rod Magazine*, Mar. 1949, May 1949.

37. Quoted in Balsley, "The Hot Rod Culture," 357.

38. Robert K. Merton, *Mass Persuasion: The Social Psychology of a War Bond Drive* (New York: Harper and Brothers, 1946).

39. Tino Balio, "Retrenchment, Reappraisal, and Reorganization," in Tino Balio, ed., *The American Film Industry* (Madison: University of Wisconsin Press, 1976), 315.

40. Frank Deford, *Five Strides on the Banked Track* (Boston: Little and Brown, 1971).

41. *America*, Mar. 1953. See also H. Cohn, "Rough in the Curves: Roller Derby," *Colliers*, Jan. 1953, 22–23; C. McLendon, "How to Watch Roller Derby," *Popular Science*, Mar. 1953, 172–77.

42. Roland Barthes, *Mythologies* (New York: Hill and Wang, 1970), 15–26.

43. Herb Michelson, *A Very Simple Game* (Oakland: Occasional Publications, 1971).

44. McLendon, "How to Watch Roller Derby," 173.

45. *Presenting Roller Derby*, kinescope recording, Television Archives, University of California, Los Angeles.

46. Michelson, *A Very Simple Game*.

47. Leonard Schatzman and Anselm Strauss, "Social Class and Modes of Communication," *American Journal of Sociology* (Jan. 1955); Basil Bernstein, *Class, Codes, and Control* (London: Schocken, 1972).

48. George Barker, *Pachuco: A Spanish-American Argot* (Tucson: University of Arizona Press, 1950).

49. Haskell Cohen, "Mello like a Cello," *Negro Digest* 1, no. 1 (Aug. 1943): 7.

50. Dizzy Gillespie, *To Be, or not . . . to Bop* (Garden City, N.Y.: Doubleday, 1979), 281.

51. Ibid., 287.

52. Ibid., 342.

53. Richard Wright, *American Hunger* (New York: Harper, 1944), 13.

CHAPTER TWELVE

Reel America

The Working Class and Hollywood

IN THE EARLY forties, Hollywood films about working-class life presented complex and contradictory images. They portrayed workers as unhappy, fatalistic, and self-destructive, but also as honest, creative, and mutually supportive. They depicted physical labor as dangerous, degrading, and alienating, but also as necessary, virtuous, and satisfying. Sympathetic to workers as individuals but not as a class, these films invariably depicted escape to small-business ownership as the only real solution to the indignities and alienations of waged work.[1]

After 1945, working-class life appeared less frequently and less favorably in feature films. The postwar strike wave so politicized labor issues that motion pictures dealing with working-class life automatically ran the risk of polarizing the audience. Militant trade-union activism within the film industry itself hardened antilabor attitudes among studio executives, and congressional investigations into alleged Communist influence in Hollywood sent a sharp warning to filmmakers and financiers to avoid scripts that portrayed capitalism in a negative light.

Yet in order to make money, filmmakers still needed to present a picture, however distorted, of some of the experiences and aspirations of the public. Work did not lend itself easily to cinematic representation, but labor played too central a role in U.S. society in the postwar era for Hollywood to ignore it altogether. Although only a few films of the postwar era tackled labor issues head-on, representations of working-class life often appeared indirectly within films ostensibly centered on other themes and concerns. Transformations in traditional genres like gangster films, family melodramas, and westerns vividly reflected the transformations taking place in working-class life outside the motion picture theaters. Two new genres, known to critics and scholars as "film noir" and "film gris," powerfully registered the unstable state of class relations in the postwar United States.

In addition, directors with strong personal ties or intense ideological commitments to working people sometimes inserted strong class messages in their cinematic productions.

Many mainstream films of the postwar period retrospectively rewrote the history of World War II as a battle fought to ensure the future of free enterprise. The freedom preserved in combat in these films has little to do with free elections, free expression, or freedom from racist oppression. Instead, in these articulations freedom comes to mean the freedom to own more commodities, to experience upward mobility, and to form nuclear families built upon male authority and female domesticity.

The film scholar Dana Polan notes that the great goal of George Bailey in Frank Capra's 1946 *It's a Wonderful Life* is to build suburban housing for workers. If he fails, workers will sink into amoral depravity; but if he succeeds the whole community will live decently and harmoniously.[2] In William Wyler's 1946 *The Best Years of Our Lives*, returning war veterans adjust to civilian life by assuming responsible family roles that make their experiences similar despite their very different class positions. Yet in Michael Curtiz's 1945 *Mildred Pierce*, a working-class housewife turned successful entrepreneur loses everything because she fails as a mother.[3]

While constructed around narratives that ultimately deny the importance of social class, these films also reveal great anxiety about class issues. The villainous capitalist in *It's a Wonderful Life* puts his own greed above the general interest. In *The Best Years of Our Lives*, war profiteers have enjoyed themselves on the home front while virtuous soldiers have suffered overseas. Mildred Pierce is disgusted by poverty, but her efforts to make her daughter's life economically secure depend too much on cold-blooded materialism. In the end, the daughter's social-climbing aspirations and greed prove monstrous.

Even socially conservative films like *It's a Wonderful Life*, *The Best Years of Our Lives*, and *Mildred Pierce* had to recognize the existence of class tensions and the danger they posed to the free-enterprise vision of the postwar world. As Fredric Jameson argues in his important essay "Reification and Utopia in Mass Culture," successful commercial films often open up wounds and air out social tensions in order to contain them. But they always run the risk that the problems exposed will have more meaning to audiences than the ways in which the film "resolves" them.[4] Polan points out that the range of subject positions presented in films allows viewers to experiment with many different points of view, that the preferred ideological resolutions inscribed in film texts must always make us aware that other choices are possible.[5] Consequently, class tensions still appeared in feature films during the late forties, even when the filmmakers intended to suppress or contain them.

One measure of the impact of the class struggles of the forties on the cinematic imagination can be found in the transformation of traditional genres
during the postwar era. In innovative and imaginative research, Jonathan
Munby has shown how gangster films in the early thirties generally attributed criminal behavior to the debilitating effects of economic deprivation
and ethnic exclusion. Mervyn LeRoy's 1930 *Little Caesar*, William Well-
man's 1931 *Public Enemy*, and Howard Hawks's 1932 *Scarface* viciously
libeled Italian-American and Irish-American culture, but their depictions
of the resentments that can grow from being poor in a rich country resonate with the egalitarian populism of the thirties. By the late forties, however, Munby argues that gangster films, including Raoul Walsh's 1949 *White
Heat*, Nicholas Ray's 1949 *They Live by Night*, and Joseph H. Lewis's 1949
Gun Crazy built dramatic tension largely from sexual frustration as well
as from oedipal conflicts between parents and children. Where the gangster film had once been a site for exploring tensions between social classes,
criminal behavior now became internalized and psychologized, more a
matter of individual repression and desire than a question of systematic
social injustice.[6]

Family melodramas underwent a similar transformation from a focus
on ethnicity and class to a focus on parent-child tensions and coming-of-
age stories. Andrea Walsh has shown how film versions of fiction centered
on ethnicity and class like Elia Kazan's 1945 *A Tree Grows in Brooklyn*
and George Stevens's 1948 *I Remember Mama* emphasize relationships between "traditional" mothers and independent daughters. Similarly, Robert
Warshow notes the ways in which Laslo Benedek's 1951 *Death of a Sales-
man* and Mark Robson's 1951 *I Want You* discursively transcode class tensions into psychological dramas about fathers and sons.[7]

Western films also changed amidst the ferment of the forties. In John
Ford's 1939 *Stagecoach*, John Wayne plays an escaped convict determined
to avenge a purely personal grievance. He winds up on a stagecoach with
six respectable citizens and two other outcasts—a prostitute and an alco-
holic physician. When crises confront the party, the people with the highest status (a banker, a southern gentleman, and an army officer's wife) all
display severe character flaws, while the outcasts acquit themselves nobly.
But in Ford's 1948 film *Fort Apache*, when a dogmatic and vain cavalry
commander endangers his own troops and all of society, John Wayne's character praises him as a hero—even though he knows that the commander
is undeserving of this praise. The imperatives of the organization man in
corporate society dominate *Fort Apache*. Wayne no longer plays a rebel;
instead he is a good soldier who carries out orders even when he knows
they are wrong and who praises his leaders even when their policies have
proven disastrous.

The genre of the social-problem film also changed direction in the forties. For all their romantic individualism and unrealistic resolutions, thirties explorations into social tensions like King Vidor's 1934 *Our Daily Bread*, Michael Curtiz's 1935 anti-union *Black Fury*, and John Ford's 1940 *Grapes of Wrath* took class seriously as a social category. But social-problem films of the forties shifted the terrain of social contestation away from class and onto issues of ethnicity and race. They addressed issues like anti-Semitism and racial segregation, especially in Elia Kazan's 1947 *Gentleman's Agreement*, Edward Dmytryk's 1947 *Crossfire*, and Mark Robson's 1949 *Home of the Brave*.

The social turmoil of the forties left its mark on traditional genres, but it also helped bring into being two new genres with important implications for mass-mediated discourse about the working class—film noir and film gris. Film noir began in the early forties, but produced its great classics mostly in the late forties, while film gris emerged as a politicized response to film noir primarily in the early fifties.

The federal government inadvertently helped expand the film noir genre in 1943 when the War Production Board imposed a budget of only $5,000 on set construction for wartime films. Less than a third of what producers spent for B movies before the war—and less than a tenth of what they would pay for sets on A films—this budget mandated indoor rather than on-location filming and it encouraged directors to make the most of limited resources, especially in respect to lighting and editing.[8]

Film noir stories typically involve an isolated male hero trapped by confusing and threatening circumstances. A stranger in town or a returning veteran, the hero belongs to no community and often finds himself unjustly accused of a crime by hostile or incompetent authorities. As he tries to clear himself, other men present threats of violence from the outside, while women symbolize the possibility of betrayal from within. In film noir, fate and circumstance dwarf human will, and socially provoked violence overwhelms people's better qualities.

Characterized as much by their moods as their plots, film noir pictures convey claustrophobia, paranoia, despair, and frustration. Most of their action takes place indoors and at night; relatively simple activities are frustrated by the intrusion of outside circumstances, and characters express regret and uneasiness over lost or misspent time. Their titles often encapsulate their dominant mood or theme—as in *Detour, Out of the Past, Deadline at Dawn, They Live by Night, Journey into Fear, In a Lonely Place,* and *Clash by Night*.

The film scholar Frank Krutnik observes that the film noir genre is characterized by a complicated confluence of specific stylistic devices, consistent plots and themes, and recurring narrative techniques.[9] Although they are not exclusive to film noir, a common body of film techniques gives these films their distinctive look. Flashbacks draw viewers back through time, emphasizing the irresistible pull of the past and the powerlessness of the present. Door frames, mirrors, and small rooms confine the faces and bodies of film noir characters to make them seem like captives of their surroundings. High-contrast lighting makes it difficult to distinguish objects from shadows or friends from foes, while it exposes the shadows and harsher features of people's faces. Off-center camera angles disorient the viewer and accentuate the difficulty of getting the film noir world into manageable perspective. These techniques of film noir brilliantly communicate its moods, and those moods underscore its themes.

Urban working-class life provides an important setting for film noir stories, although the sense of powerlessness they convey comes from a societal malaise that affects all classes. Fritz Lang opened his 1953 *Clash by Night*, set in a California fishing town, with a long documentary sequence showing the hard labor performed by workers in the fishing and cannery industries in order to establish an aura of confinement underscoring the alienation of the film's middle-class characters. Taxi cab drivers, nightclub entertainers, private detectives, and restless war veterans often serve as film noir protagonists because their isolation symbolizes the anxieties of others. Those who work (and live) by night see the dark side, and in film noir that means the true side of human behavior, replete with all its corruption, greed, and violence. "The logic is that there's no logic," opines a character in *Deadline at Dawn*, adding that "the horror and terror that you feel comes from being alive."

The film noir hero is vulnerable because he is alone, and he must remain alone because he is vulnerable. Longing for the understanding and sympathy of neighbors, relatives, or friends, he meets only strangers who show him hostility at worst and indifference at best. Estrangement from others becomes aggravated by a fear of disapproval, a presumption that society will blame and punish the hero for acts he never committed. In many cases, circumstantial evidence makes the hero look guilty. Often he would have had a good motive for committing the crime of which he is accused. Through malevolence or misunderstanding, legally constituted authorities offer no relief. In fact, their incompetence and corruption assure that they will persecute the hero unless he clears himself by his own efforts. That task must be accomplished in the face of overwhelming odds and cruel blows of fate that constantly undermine the accused. Film noir depicts the struggles of isolated, outcast, unlucky, and ostensibly guilty individuals to become free in a world that allows no freedom.

The popularity of the film noir scenario in postwar America represents more than a commercial trend or an artistic cliché. In its portrayal of a frustrated search for community, film noir addressed the central political issue in U.S. society in the wake of World War II. The war experience disrupted communities and families, compelled soldiers and civilians alike to accept unprecedented regulation of their lives, and forced people to face the ignoble realities of armed conflict. The transition to peace only compounded accumulated wartime resentments. People who learned to work purposefully with others in military, community, or industrial projects now faced the future alone. Submerged tensions between competing interests surfaced in the postwar era, replacing national unity with vigorous internal disputes. Those who sacrificed and killed in pursuit of a better world found their loftiest aspirations betrayed by a society that demanded continued sacrifice and preparation for the next war. Under those circumstances, film noir dramas about isolation, lost time, guilt, frustration, powerlessness, and betrayal arbitrated the core tensions in the social lives of their viewers.

Mysteries and nightmares given dramatic expression in film noir stemmed directly from the mysterious nightmare of life in postwar America, a life often as complex and confusing as the films that described it. Precisely because they captured the ambiguities of American society so well, the mood and worldview of film noir movies encompassed the inner logic of diametrically opposite social actions—the wildcat strike and the cold war. The genre's writers, directors, and producers had no conscious intention of commenting on either of those events—none of these films include the cold war or wildcat strikes in their plots or depictions. Yet in their sensitivity to the national mood, they reproduced the motivations behind each.

By emphasizing a desire for community, fear of isolation, the necessity to struggle for a decent life, and hostility to authority, film noir reproduced the motivations behind wildcat strikes and mass demonstrations. Even the genre's paranoid expectation of social disapproval echoed the recognition that personal goals were likely to be viewed as illegitimate by conventional standards. As Alvin Gouldner shows in *Wildcat Strike*, this sense of illegitimacy can be an everyday part of working-class life. Gouldner argues that workers understand that the logic and hierarchy of production does not allow them to control their own lives, so they engage in acts of covert resistance, like stealing materials from the workplace, using company tools for their own projects, defying supervisors, or violating contract provisions. They scrupulously pursue conventional trade-union strategies to win what can be rightfully secured within the scope of collective bargaining, but they also want things that the system refuses to grant them. Their actions bring censure from authorities and cannot be justified by ordinary rules. The wildcat strike and mass demonstration circumvent legitimate channels to assert, however temporarily, the powers and freedoms considered illegitimate within the rules of labor-management law and custom. In similar fashion, film noir heroes break the law and avoid authorities to advance their own interests. They expect and fear disapproval and they battle enormous guilt. But ultimately they choose to be true to themselves even at the risk of appearing "illegitimate" to others. In film noir, the wildcat strike's rebellion against legitimacy becomes generalized into a means of survival and a standard of behavior for all of society.[10]

Yet film noir also expresses fear of other people, rugged individualism, fatalism about the constraints on human action, and projection of one's own guilt onto other people. In its paranoid delusions of conspiracy, its persecution fantasies, and its arrogant faith that all evil comes from outside sources, film noir contains the psychological prerequisites for the cold war. Senseless assaults from the outside and cunning betrayal from within undermine the film noir hero and force him to respond. That sense of persecution closely corresponds to the official explanations for the cold war, which posited an innocent America forced into an active role in world politics by aggressive enemies abroad aided by subversives at home.[11] Placing the blame for domestic conflicts on foreigners and alleged traitors has long been a staple of conservative ideology in the United States, shoring up those in power by evading an honest exploration of the real injustices that produce social unrest.[12] Film noir encouraged that worldview in its self-pitying portrayal of Americans as the hapless victims of cruel and immutable outside forces. Anxieties about loss of freedom in the postwar world could be channeled against communism at home and abroad, while presumptions about the evil lurking within each individual could short-circuit hopes for community. The same sense of alienation that could lead to a grudging acceptance of the need to go outside legitimate channels in the mass demonstration and wildcat strike could also produce authoritarian obedience to an aggressive foreign policy and a deep cynicism about collective solutions to the nightmares of postwar America.

In its ability to encompass the psychic structures behind both the cold war and the wildcat strike, the film noir genre demonstrates how popular culture can serve as a site for the negotiation of social contradictions. The gender politics of this genre reveal a similar complexity.

On one hand, film noir stories depart sharply from the family-centered patriarchy of the postwar era. Their male heroes display psychic (and sometimes physical) scars from family abuse and failed relationships. They generally live alone, fear women, and petulantly refuse to take on responsible adult roles. On the other hand, noir films enthusiastically embrace the misogyny of the postwar era in their portrayals of women as menacing, sinister, and calculating. In their flight from work, authority, and the law, film noir heroes also run away from domestic entanglements, romance, and responsibility. Noir films offer many examples of assertive and capable women, but only to heighten the horror of threats to male freedom by locating them within the bodies of the opposite gender.

Negative depictions of independent women in film noir dramas resonate with the antifemale backlash of the late forties. During those years, employers, unions, and government officials discouraged women from seeking high-paying jobs, while psychologists, members of the clergy, and educators counseled women to devote their primary energies to child rearing. Philip Wylie's 1942 best-seller, *Generation of Vipers*, blamed overprotective mothers for undermining the nation's strength by raising insufficiently masculine sons lacking in patriotic resolve. Dr. Benjamin Spock's equally popular advice manuals also counseled mothers against being suffocatingly overprotective, but at the same time advised mothers to respond to their child's every need. Marynia Farnham and Ferdinand Lundberg's popular *The Modern Woman: The Lost Sex* insisted that women could find true happiness only through motherhood. In the context of these efforts to condemn and contain female subjectivity, the "rebellions" of film noir heroes take on a decidedly conservative cast.

The film critic and feminist theorist Tania Modleski astutely notes how the male heroes in film noir pictures struggle to remain at what Freudian psychologists call the "pre-oedipal" state.[13] Their needy narcissism reflects a "refusal to be oedipalized," a resistance to adult male sexual and social identities. This behavior displays rebellion against authority, hierarchy, and patriarchy, but in its pursuit of pleasure and immediate gratification it also manifests the psychic state necessary for commodity capitalism. As Barbara Ehrenreich argues about other ostensible male rebels of the postwar years—the readers of *Playboy* magazine and the poets of the "beat" generation—popular culture's depictions of masculine pleasure and freedom increasingly entailed a "flight from responsibility."[14] Like these later forms of popular culture, film noir translated justified resentments against a corporatist culture of conformity into atomized individualistic self-pity. The genre aestheticized alienation, redirecting desire for connections with other people into a craving for revenge and reparations for hurts too deep to be mended.

The failure of the film noir genre to rise above cynicism or to pose anything other than compensatory individualistic strategies for combating complex social problems meant that motion pictures in the postwar era provided viewers with very few serious criticisms of the emerging corporate culture of consumerism. But one genre of films did offer such a critique. Although few in number and for the most part ignored by film historians, the genre identified by the film historian Thom Andersen as film gris (grey film) offers instructive lessons about Hollywood's treatment of class contradictions and class conflict in the decade following World War II.

Andersen discovered film gris in the course of his research into the Hollywood blacklist that denied employment to people suspected of holding subversive views. In 1947, the House Un-American Activities Committee held widely publicized hearings investigating allegations of "communist" influence in the film industry. At first the film community mobilized against this intrusion into the private beliefs and associations of ordinary citizens. But when studio executives caved in to the committee and pledged their full cooperation with it, they touched off an epidemic of accusations (often false and unsubstantiated) that had a chilling effect on civil liberties in Hollywood and all across the country. Ten witnesses who refused to accept the legitimacy of HUAC's inquiry received jail terms for contempt of Congress, while other opponents of the committee found that they could no longer work in the industry.

Most of the auteurs involved in film gris opposed the House Un-American Activities Committee's inquiry. Some of them had been members of the Communist party; some worked with Popular Front organizations closely associated with the party, others simply held antifascist or radical political views. The committee found no credible evidence of any subversive or "un-American" propaganda in films, and consequently most scholars have concluded that while the inquiry clearly abridged the civil liberties of citizens, it had no real impact on the content of motion pictures. But Andersen found that many of the victims of the Hollywood purge were just coming into their own as filmmakers and that the few films that they did get to make up until about 1951 reveal extraordinarily radical criticisms of the emerging cold war culture.[15]

The motion pictures in the film gris genre explore the role of money and materialism in working-class life. Like film noir dramas, they express bitter cynicism about upward mobility, suburbanization, and commodity capitalism. Their protagonists struggle to get by in unglamorous urban settings. But the torment of film gris protagonists is more material than psychological, and instead of blaming their problems on one deceitful woman or a few conspiring criminals, they point an accusing finger at society at large.

Film gris expressed the disappointment and frustration of Hollywood radicals with the emerging culture of the postwar period. Joseph Losey spoke for this group when he told an interviewer, "The struggle and optimism of the Thirties made it hard to accept the brutalisation and the degradation of the late Forties. . . . [During the war] one kept a certain optimism particularly as the war turned into an anti-fascist war. But after Hiroshima, after the death of Roosevelt and after the investigations, only then did one begin to see the complete unreality of the American dream."[16] This "un-reality of the American dream" formed the core of Losey's last film in 1951 before the blacklist caught up with him, the film gris drama *The Prowler*.

In *The Prowler*, Van Heflin plays a working-class police officer consumed with resentments about the "lousy breaks" that have left him with such a low-status job. He seems to hate everybody—his father for being only a worker, his partner for having idealistic notions about police work, and the rich because they have the things that he wants. Driven by trivial goals, his ultimate wish is to be a small businessman, to own a motel in Las Vegas that will make money for him even while he sleeps.

Heflin's character has an affair with a married woman, and he plans the murder of her wealthy husband so that he can marry her and collect the inheritance. He lures the husband out of the house by pretending to be a prowler, then answers the call when the couple phone the police. The officer executes the husband and then wounds himself to make it look like he shot in self-defense. The wife is suspicious, but hides their affair from a coroner's jury and eventually marries Heflin's character after convincing herself of his innocence.

When her advanced pregnancy proves that they had been having an affair before her husband died (the husband was sterile), she runs off with Heflin's character to a deserted ghost town. He plans to deliver the baby himself, but when his wife's labor proves difficult he calls in a doctor. After the successful delivery, Heflin's character confesses to having murdered the husband, and the wife realizes that he plans to kill the doctor too. She calls the authorities and they trap him in a shoot-out. He grasps his way to the top of a mining slag heap, but the police shoot and kill him. As the film ends, he falls back into the pile of worthless junk.

Secretly scripted by the already blacklisted Hollywood Ten defendant Dalton Trumbo, *The Prowler* makes no effort to mute its criticisms of U.S. society.[17] It depicts a handsome police officer as a murderer and a thief, a wealthy and popular radio commentator as an untrustworthy demagogue and an inadequate husband, and a beautiful housewife as a liar and a cheat. The connection between the family and the economy forms an important subtext in *The Prowler*, as its working titles—"The Cost of Loving" and "The Cost of Living"—indicate. Van Heflin's Webb Garwood looks like the All-American boy; he starred in high school sports, drinks milk, and reads muscle magazines. But he is motivated only by self-pity and greed, as he ruthlessly kills people who pose obstacles to his modest and unimaginative goals. The one time he succumbs to sentiment by summoning the doctor proves fatal to him.

Losey had attended Ivy League schools and served as a theater director and critic in New York before arriving in Hollywood. Active in antifascist activities, he directed an English-language version of Clifford Odets's *Waiting for Lefty* in Moscow in 1935. Aware that he was about to be blacklisted, Losey left the United States for residence in England shortly after completing *The Prowler*. He offered what he believed might be his last U.S. film as a summary statement on the blacklist and on postwar culture in general: "false values demand their own price in the people who accept them."[18]

If *The Prowler* portrays the pursuit of the American Dream as a shallow and amoral quest, John Berry's 1946 film gris *From This Day Forward* shows the dreadful price people pay for failure. In it, a man loses his job and battles to maintain self-respect in the face of his failure to provide for his family. Before him lies the desperate example of his chronically employed brother-in-law who has to borrow money from his recalcitrant mother and who sends his son to beg the butcher for bones ostensibly for a dog but really so the family can cook them in water and call it soup. The film ends with modest hope, as one of the men buys a chicken farm and the other lines up a promising job interview. But because their unemployment stemmed from no personal fault of their own ("things happen sometimes that are bigger than a guy and his trade," one of the men observes) their future is anything but certain.[19]

Similarly, in Cy Endfield's *Try and Get Me*, which Andersen calls "the masterpiece of film gris and certainly the blackest, most uncompromising film of the early Fifties," unemployment threatens another man and his family. His failure to provide for them drives his wife and son to the ultimate postwar indignity, they must go to neighbors' houses to watch television! In his despair, he joins forces with a vain and materialistic criminal on a spree of robbery and murder. But Endfield's critique does not end there. A liberal newspaper reporter condemns their crimes in such passionate terms that he unintentionally provokes a mob to lynch the two in a grotesquely violent twelve-minute scene. Too late, the reporter realizes that he and the lynch mob and the criminals have all been shaped by the same vicious and competitive values.[20]

For all of their searing social criticisms, the auteurs of the film gris genre remained middle-class intellectuals, despairing about mass politics and culture but unconnected to any constituency capable of change. Their efforts in this respect stand in sharp contrast to those of four filmmakers who did to a greater or lesser degree connect their postwar ruminations on working-class life to active political constituencies—Edward Dmytryk, Herbert Biberman, Edgar Ulmer, and Nicholas Ray.

Edward Dmytryk directed one of the most important films of the postwar period when he made *Till the End of Time* in 1946. Unlike film noir or film gris, this motion picture presents individuals who are connected to networks of family, friends, and co-workers, whose problems are political and social as well as personal, and who know that they need other people.[21] Its narrative focuses on the experiences of a marine coming home after World War II to his middle-class home, but many of the challenges he faces concern how he responds to the ways in which the war changed the meaning of class, gender, and ethnicity.

The lengthy opening sequences in *Till the End of Time* depict the mustering out of the service of three marines. These scenes establish clearly the impersonal and bureaucratic aspects of military life, with its endless lines to follow and forms to fill out. But they also convey a sense that the military is virtuously egalitarian, that everyone is treated alike and no one is forgotten. Counselors give friendly advice about adjusting to civilian life, and they indicate that the Veterans Administration will be there to help them if they need it.[22]

The hero returns to his house but finds no one home, the first of many frustrations in his transition to civilian life. He visits the local candy store only to find it has been transformed into a tavern, a symbol of moral decay on the home front. The store's proprietor explains the switch by saying that he couldn't resist the money-making opportunities provided by the war. Everywhere he turns, the returning soldier feels himself estranged from a society that seems to value money more than anything else. His parents push him to return to college so that he can pursue a career in engineering. From his perspective, everyone on the home front seems to have already forgotten the war and its lessons. More than anything, he feels a loss of the camaraderie he had become used to during the war. He tells another veteran, "We were a team in the war; everybody was together. There was a guy next to you, you could depend on. Now we're civilians again, rugged individuals. We're on our own, all of us."

Only when he falls in love with a working-class widow does the veteran begin to solve his problems. Like him, she feels that the war robbed her of precious time. Yet, she has more of a sense of purpose about her life than he has, largely because her work in an electronics factory connects her to other people. With her help, he gets a factory job. After some rough moments, he learns a sense of community and connection from working-class life that reunites him with the best aspects of his war experience. At the film's end, he joins with his former army friends to battle against a fascist veterans' organization. Even in peacetime, a united front against fascism enables diverse individuals to work together in a spirit of unity and cooperation.

Till the End of Time shares many of the preoccupations of film noir, without its pessimistic conclusions. Corruption, isolation, loss of community, guilt, and betrayal manifest themselves, but in this film the positive values of working-class life offer an antidote.

Yet, it is only through the military or some paramilitary antifascist project that *Till the End of Time* can find a way for its characters to solve their problems. From its friendly view toward the marines as a benign bureaucracy at the beginning of the film to the fistfight at the end that unites the ex-GIs in one more battle of fascism, Dmytryk tends to find solutions only in actions coordinated through big institutions. One reason for that came from his role as a former member of and sympathizer with the Communist party. Like many other antifascists in Hollywood, Dmytryk viewed the Communists as resolute opponents of Nazism, and their belief in disciplined collective struggle seems consistent with his own inclinations. But in the postwar era, his beliefs and associations attracted the attention of congressional investigating communities.

Along with Dalton Trumbo, Herbert Biberman, and seven other writers and directors, Dmytryk went to jail rather than answer the committee's questions about his politics. But when the dimensions of the Hollywood blacklist became clear to him, he denounced the Communist party from prison and announced that he would appear before the Committee as a friendly witness. In April 1951, he testified before HUAC and charged more than two dozen of his former friends and associates with having been Communists. He sought the advice and assistance of Hollywood's most active anticommunists to rehabilitate himself. Like so many ex-Communists, he embraced the authoritarian bureaucrats of the Right after severing his ties with the authoritarian bureaucrats of the Left.

Dmytryk became an important symbol for the House Un-American Activities Committee, a repentant former "traitor," and the only one of the Hollywood Ten to renounce his beliefs under pressure. In 1952 he directed *The Sniper*, a film in which a psychiatrist convinces homicide detectives and civic leaders that they should lock up sex offenders and other deviates in mental hospitals. He argues that those who can be cured should be cured and that those who cannot be cured should not be free to attack innocent citizens.

Dmytryk moved from defending preventive detention in *The Sniper* to an even more authoritarian message with his 1954 *The Caine Mutiny*, based on the best-selling novel by Herman Wouk. An excellent film, *The Caine Mutiny* nonetheless carried the rather authoritarian message that even incompetent, paranoid, and vindictive leaders deserve more respect than their critics because they alone face the responsibility of command. A more pointed, or more totalitarian, moral for the cold war could hardly have been invented by even its most dogmatic defenders. The real villain in *The Caine Mutiny* turns out to be an intellectual whose irreverence toward the military poisons the minds of two young working-class lieutenants. When an eminently fair and scrupulous Navy court-martial board benignly acquits them of the charges of mutiny, they come to their senses and reject the subversive in their midsts.

Just as the blacklist drove Edward Dmytryk to make connections with countersubversive right-wing activists, blacklisting motivated Herbert Biberman to link up with working-class activists on the Left soon after he completed his term in a federal prison for contempt of Congress. Blacklisted by the film industry and harassed by the government, Biberman went outside traditional Hollywood channels to make *Salt of the Earth* in 1953, a film far superior to anything he had ever done before in Hollywood.

A member of Congress denounced *Salt of the Earth* on the floor of the House of Representatives while it was still in production. The motion picture industry threatened to blacklist actors or technicians who worked on any part of it, and the secretary of commerce pledged his determination to prevent the picture from being exhibited abroad. Herbert Biberman defied these pressures to create one of the best cinematic portrayals of working-class life in the history of motion pictures.[23]

Biberman formed an independent production company and secured financing from the International Union of Mine, Mill, and Smelter Workers to make a film about a 1951 strike by that union's Local 890 in Silver City, New Mexico. He recruited the services of blacklisted Academy Award–winning screenwriter Michael Wilson, enlisted members of the local union that conducted the actual strike to appear in the film, assembled technicians barred from employment in Hollywood for reasons of racial or political discrimination, and devised new techniques to adapt to the limits of his antiquated equipment. *Salt of the Earth* drew its performers and its drama from real life; in order to secure their cooperation with the film, Biberman had to grant the workers and their families considerable control over the script to ensure its accuracy and sensitivity to the miners' concerns.

The members of Local 890 vociferously challenged the Hollywood conventions in the original script. They objected to the story that portrayed the white union organizer as the hero saving workers from danger and insisted that the film portray how they had saved themselves. They acknowledged the realism of plans to portray an affair between the union president and the wife of another miner, but vetoed it as a subplot because they felt it would play into audience stereotypes and expectations about Chicano men. One stage direction had the heroine wiping up some spilled beer with her dress, but the community members objected to its inclusion in the film because they felt it reinforced stereotypes about the lack of cleanliness in their community. Biberman and his staff heeded these objections and worked cooperatively with the miners and their families to produce a film in which they could all take pride.[24]

Salt of the Earth presents the story of miners in "Zinc Town," New Mexico, by focusing on the experiences of Esperanza Quintero and her husband, Ramon. The mining company exploits its Chicano employees with low wages, allows poor safety conditions, and supplies inadequate housing and plumbing facilities. Ramon, a union militant (played by the local's president, Juan Chacon), attempts to organize his fellow workers against those conditions while Esperanza stays at home, caring for the children and chopping the wood needed to stoke the fire that heats the water in their home.

When their husbands go on strike in protest against an accident in the mine, the women of Zinc Town send a delegation to the strike meeting to request that adequate plumbing be made one of the strike issues. The men ignore their request and resist even discussing the possibility of a women's auxiliary to help win the strike. But when the company gets an injunction against union picketing, the strike appears doomed. One woman suggests that the women take over the picket line, since the injunction doesn't say anything about them. The men resist her offer, but when the women force a vote of everyone in the room, the community decides to send women to the picket line. Many of the men feel humiliated about having to "hide behind their women," and they contemptuously predict that they will have to take over the picket line themselves at the first sign of violence. But they allow the decision to stand.

Ramon tries to stop Esperanza from joining the picketing, but she goes anyway. With the other women, she holds the line against an attack by the sheriff and his deputies. Instead of being frightened by her experience, as Ramon hopes, Esperanza returns home even more committed to the struggle. He warns her that he will not play nursemaid to the children any more, but she informs him that she will simply bring them with her to the picket line. The male miners become demoralized and embarrassed by the heroic actions of the women, but with their wives in jail periodically, the men get a taste of housework. And they do not like it one bit. As he hangs laundry on a clothesline, Ramon informs his neighbor that the union should include plumbing as one of its demands, apparently forgetting that he scoffed at that when Esperanza proposed it. Gradually the men come to respect the women's role in the strike and at the same time come to the realization that they have been oppressing their wives in much the same way that their bosses have been exploiting them. The company urges the sheriff to evict the strikers, but the community mobilizes en masse against him and the workers win the strike. Ramon acknowledges that his own struggle for freedom cannot be separated from Esperanza's, and thanking her for her dignity, he vows to fight side by side with her to "push everyone up along with us."

Salt of the Earth received a favorable response in the few places where it was exhibited upon release, and its very existence demonstrates the difficulties of completely censoring working-class life out of contemporary cinema. Yet most theaters bowed to right-wing pressure and would not exhibit it. Herbert Biberman did not make another film until the blacklist of suspected Communists waned in 1969, and the repression of *Salt of the Earth* served to warn others against making films with "unacceptable" themes or participants. But by being forced to share his skills with ordinary workers, Biberman produced a work of art and politics far superior to anything he had done when he had virtually full control over production in Hollywood. His contact with the concrete struggles of a working-class community led him to see how class and gender functioned as mutually constitutive categories, and the dignified and complex feminism of *Salt of the Earth* stands in stark contrast to the masculinist militaristic message of *The Caine Mutiny*.

Biberman and Dmytryk both came out of the Communist party and its orbit of intellectuals friendly to its goals, but they moved in opposite directions. In the forties, independent radicals Edgar Ulmer and Nicholas Ray shared the general left-wing outlook of Biberman and Dmytryk but they followed very different paths in their efforts to identify a social constituency capable of fighting for radical change.

Edgar Ulmer is best known for his direction of *Detour*, a low-budget 1945 picture often considered to be the consummate film noir. Working people played an important role in Ulmer's cinematic and social imagination; he employed class as a crucial component of his work, and he conceived of film noir as a commentary on the dilemmas facing workers.

A silhouette cutter, set designer, and director in his native Austria, Ulmer came to the United States in 1923 to design sets, and he soon started directing westerns at Universal Studios. After achieving commercial and artistic success with *The Black Cat* in 1934, a film he intended as a commentary on the moral bankruptcy of war, Ulmer left Hollywood to make a series of motion pictures whose form and content challenged prevailing assumptions about the medium.

Throughout the thirties, Ulmer directed films that dramatized the cultures of ethnic minorities, that made the everyday lives of ordinary people the focus of his art, and that attempted to demystify the processes of filmmaking so that people without specialized training could participate in them. Financed by the New York City Union of Ukrainian Window Washers, *Natalka Poltavka* was directed by Ulmer in 1936 and was a musical celebrating the folk culture of that country. To compensate for his own ignorance of Ukrainian language and culture, Ulmer enlisted a committee of dancers, designers, and window washers to rewrite the script. His actors and actresses came directly from the community. Ukrainians in the Carpenters Union built the set and rebuilt it when a hurricane destroyed their initial effort.

Encouraged by his experiences with *Natalka Poltavka*, Ulmer drew upon the resources of the International Ladies Garment Workers Union and the Yiddish theater of New York to make a series of films about European Jews. Although he spoke no Yiddish, Ulmer again proved that community effort could overcome technical shortcomings and make successful motion pictures. In 1938, he secured money from the Department of the Interior to make a film about tuberculosis, *Let My People Live*; he then made one about the black community titled *Moon over Harlem*. Ulmer used black people off the street as actors and actresses, involved others in the technical aspects of production, and wound up as the only white person with any important role in the production at all.[25]

During World War II, Ulmer chose to make B movies at minor studios rather than endure the lack of artistic freedom imposed by the industry's giants. Always an innovator, Ulmer had pioneered the use of the tracking dolly for movable camera shots years before as an economy measure, and his talents proved uniquely suited for the exigencies of making low-budget films. In his work for Producer's Releasing Corporation, Ulmer shot as little as one and a half or two feet of film for every one foot that he eventually used, and he made several motion pictures in less than seven days. Without elaborate scripts or sophisticated equipment, Ulmer had to draw on the drama of everyday life, relying on his cinematic skills to compensate for the weaknesses in his stories. He had already developed those skills in his ethnic films of the thirties, and his direction of *Detour* in 1945 continued, and in many ways culminated, his earlier efforts.

Detour tells the story of a musician whose fiancee somewhat callously leaves him to advance her career in California. To be reunited with her, he hitchhikes west, enduring repeated hardships as a stranger without money or friends. A generous driver gives him a ride, pays for his meals, and promises to take him all the way west. Just when his problems seem to be over, the driver passes out and accidentally dies, hitting his head on a rock. The hero panics, afraid that the police will think he murdered the driver in order to get his car and money. Because he thinks that no one will believe the truth, he hides the body and takes the money and car to continue the journey.

The hero picks up a woman hitchhiker who knew the murdered man, and she immediately concludes that he did murder the owner of the car. Worse yet, she threatens to go to the police if he doesn't do as she says. Even after they reach California, he must yield to her schemes to pose as the murdered man to try to collect an inheritance. The two quarrel, and when the woman goes into another room to call the police and turn in the hero, he pulls on the phone cord through the door, unaware that she has draped it around her neck. Without realizing it, his actions strangle her. This time he not only appears guilty, he is guilty, even though he is simply a prisoner of circumstance. As the film ends, the hero wanders off bemoaning the power of fate and gloomily predicting that one day he will be apprehended for his misdeeds.

Detour contains all of the standard ingredients of film noir: betrayal, greed, isolation, bad luck, fear of authorities, and a view of fate as overpowering and overwhelming. Ulmer's techniques underscore the film's story: he uses flashbacks mercilessly, shoots scenes in dim lighting, and has the action take place in enclosed automobiles and small rooms. The circumstances in *Detour* fit together so preposterously that one may be tempted to view the film as a desperate cry for help, as an impassioned protest against the powerlessness of individuals. Whatever Ulmer's motivation may have been, the fact remains that the man who found dignity and drama in the vitality of working-class communities in the thirties saw only guilt, frustration, and hopelessness by 1945.

Yet in 1948, Ulmer joined forces with Hollywood Ten defendant Alvah Bessie to make *Ruthless*. Ulmer felt close to Berthold Brecht and others targeted by the House Un-American Activities Committee, and he saw in the committee's actions the emergence of an American fascism that he had long feared. His response was to make *Ruthless*, which hid a searing critique of capitalism beneath its somewhat predictable biography of a business tycoon. In this film, Ulmer hoped to draw upon antimonopoly traditions among members of all classes in order to encourage the creation of a renewed New Deal Popular Front against fascism.

With *Ruthless*, Ulmer moved from film noir to film gris. The tycoon rises to the top of the business world by betraying his friends and enemies alike, destroying everyone in his way. In this film, Ulmer presents capitalism as a zero sum game in which individuals make advances only at the expense of other people. At the end of the film, two millionaires wrestle on a pier and fall into the water. Their "competition" destroys both of them as they drown with their hands around each other's necks. In case the audience misses the moral in all this, the female protagonist of the film tells her companion that the businessman "hero" of the film "wasn't just a man, he was a way of life."[26]

Nicholas Ray contributed to the film gris genre in 1947 with his first film, *They Live by Night*. Ray had previously worked with left-wing theater groups in New York in the thirties where his productions played "every strike, every picket line, political campaigns, the backs of trucks."[27] He went to Hollywood in 1946 to serve as assistant director on Elia Kazan's adaptation of Betty Smith's working-class coming-of-age novel *A Tree Grows in Brooklyn*. Enraptured by popular culture and vernacular expressions, Ray brought comic strips to film editors and tried to convince them to make cuts the way cartoonists did.

Ray persuaded Dore Schary to let him direct a screen adaptation of Edward Anderson's novel *Thieves like Us*. The story concerned a young couple on a crime spree desperately trying to be "free." The film is filled with images of poverty and corruption; the overwhelming materialism of their society leaves the young heroes of the film with the recognition that their lives have no "value." Ray started filming in 1947 and immediately ran into trouble with the film industry's censors, the Production Code Administration. They ordered him to leave out dialogue that connected the plight of the young couple to social conditions. Ray's original script made references to war profiteers, but the censors made him delete those references. Yet *They Live by Night* still conveys a strong sense of social criticism, and Ray later remarked that he thought of it as his favorite film: "Man, look! *They Live by Night* was done in a period of post-war affluence. Nobody was making pictures about poor people. Nobody was saying that used car lot owners are thieves."[28]

Ray went on to make *Johnny Guitar*, an anti-McCarthy western critiquing the red scare in 1954. Somehow, he got Ward Bond, one of the industry's leading anticommunists, to play the leader of a lynch mob that coerces suspects into informing on each other. In 1955, he made *Rebel without a Cause* with James Dean, where he reworked traditional themes about working-class youth in a middle-class setting. Critics have long noted the gender conservatism of *Rebel without a Cause*, and for good reason. The young rebel craves paternal authority more than anything else, he despises his father for being henpecked, and the film reaches ideological and narrative closure only when a police officer gets the young man to accept adult responsibility. Yet, the film also offers a voluntary family made up of young Jim, his girlfriend, Judy, and their friend Plato as an alternative to the oppressive biological families that the three of them are running away from. At one point, Judy tells Jim he is the kind of man girls like because he doesn't try to prove he's tough all the time and because he's willing to defy the "crowd" by being Plato's friend.

As a thirties radical making a film about fifties teenagers, Ray found that the anger and rebellions once tied directly to class now cut across class lines, that working-class forms served as a model for other groups. To prepare his young cast for their roles, Ray went "cruising" with them to drive-in teen hangouts in Los Angeles, and he encouraged his actors to improvise to make the film relevant to contemporary circumstances. Many of the subcultural practices depicted in the film, including its customized cars and clothes, came from Chicano subcultural styles that Ray took from the streets of L.A. and put on screen in a largely middle-class Anglo environment. Alone among the politically conscious auteurs of the forties, Ray found in youth culture in the fifties a potential constituency to stand in for the working-class movement that had been so sharply curtailed by the cold war, anticommunism, and its own contradictions.

Given the existence of censorship, the centralization of power within the Hollywood studio system, and the political and cultural climate of the cold war, the persistence of working-class images in films, however attenuated, calls for analysis and comment. Commercial motion pictures have never really been a working-class form, but the image of the working class has long served important functions for middle-class filmmakers, while working-class audiences have long represented an important source of revenue for wealthy film producers. Yet few forms of popular culture have been as resistant to grass-roots creation and transformation as motion pictures have been.

Perhaps no communications medium contains as much potential for uni-vocality—for telling one story from one point of view—as film. Spectators concentrate on larger-than-life images flickering in a dark room. They see only what the director and cinematographer allow them to see, while editing techniques undermine their normal senses of time and space. These internal properties of the film form take on an even more sinister character when one considers the social context of the film industry in the United States.

The large capital investment necessary for making and distributing motion pictures severely limits access to the industry. The history of collusion among major studios and investors has worked to reduce risks for those who control Hollywood, but it has also severely limited the range of ideas and images available to a mass audience. In order to secure the confidence of investors and calculate costs by predicting the size of a given film's anticipated audience, the industrial and commercial imperatives of film-making in Hollywood discourage novelty and innovation, while encouraging the recycling of genres, themes, and images that have been successful in the past.

As commodities seeking maximum returns on investment for a wealthy oligarchy, Hollywood films make no direct claim to represent social or historical truth. Audiences know that films have scripts, that the people they see rarely look like the actors on screen, and that the happy endings that always happen in Hollywood too often elude them in everyday life. Yet there is something about the film form and the "realism" of its images that makes it seem like much more than a mere simulation. For images to succeed with audiences, they must in some way ring "true." They must contain a credibility that engages people and makes them want to invest their emotions in the film's outcome.

In order to attract mass audiences, Hollywood films function through historically learned codes. Genre conventions teach us to have different expectations about comedies than we have for war films, and the repetition of forms within commercial films unite audiences around a common frame of reference. As William Howze demonstrates, John Ford's westerns looked like the West because he composed scenes to look like Remington paintings and like the lithographs of the Old West that had circulated widely on calendars, in magazines, and in advertising during the nineteenth century. Similarly, racist imagery in films built upon visual codes well established by the nineteenth century minstrel shows and reinforced by images in children's toys, in advertising, and in racist caricatures. This overdetermination of images has embedded deeply within the nation's cultural imagination images of the genocide of Native Americans and the enslavement of African Americans in a way that has had an extraordinarily reactionary effect on politics and culture in the United States for centuries.

Yet, just as reactionary images succeed in part because of their antecedents, egalitarian images also persist within popular culture. The legacy of immigrant ethnic working-class humor has shaped generations of stage and screen comedians. The rich interaction between Euro-American and African-American forms in popular music has sometimes undermined the reach and scope of white supremacy. The history of the film industry's origins in nickelodeons patronized by working-class audiences persists in egalitarian and anti-elitist images pervading comedy, melodrama, action adventure, and social-problem films.

Thus, the "materials memory" that inscribes the working-class history of previous popular culture creations in contemporary artifacts accounts for one important source of the working-class presence on motion picture screens in the United States during the postwar period. The commercial imperative for the film industry to attract mass audiences and engage them in issues worth spending time and money on provided another reason for the persistence of working-class images. Finally, political and cultural identification with the working class by educated middle-class filmmakers often motivated them to select working-class settings and themes, even in the face of great risks.[29]

Filmmakers in the film noir and film gris genres most often utilized working-class settings to symbolize the failures of capitalism and to provide dramatic force for their own middle-class alienation. Edward Dmytryk's films of the postwar period demonstrate what can happen when that

alienation becomes connected to a right-wing political and cultural movement. Herbert Biberman's *Salt of the Earth*, on the other hand, indicates
what can happen when that alienation becomes connected to a left-wing
working-class political and cultural movement. The postwar films of Edgar
Ulmer and Nicholas Ray represent opposing strategies by filmmakers once
grounded in working-class cultural production to find potential allies to
substitute for or to extend the political and cultural critique that they once
believed could only come from the working class.

The monopoly structure of the film industry, direct censorship, inten-
sive government repression, and the rapid decline in the motion picture
audience in the postwar years all combined to limit their efforts to defensive, rear-guard actions. But in another realm of commercialized leisure—
popular music—a significant number of working-class artists and entrepreneurs had a very different experience. They brought their traditional
creations and concerns before new audiences in ways that had important
ramifications for the cultural politics of the postwar era. As the least centralized popular culture industry distributing the most widely accessible
popular art, music became one of the main vehicles for the transformation
of particular working-class perspectives into general mass cultural articulations offering leadership and guidance to all.

NOTES

1. George Lipsitz, "Rank and File Fantasy in Films of the Forties," *Jump Cut*,
nos. 12–13 (1976).
2. Dana Polan, *Power and Paranoia: History, Narrative, and the American
Cinema, 1940–1950* (New York: Columbia University Press, 1986), 254.
3. Leonard Quart and Albert Auster, *American Film and Society since 1945*
(New York: Praeger, 1991), 21–23; Andrea Walsh, *Women's Film and Female Experience, 1940–1950* (New York: Praeger, 1984), 123–31.
4. Fredric Jameson, "Reification and Utopia in Mass Culture," *Social Text* 1
(1979).
5. Polan, *Power and Paranoia*, 9–10.
6. I thank Munby for calling this very important dynamic to my attention and
look forward to the forthcoming completion of his dissertation, "Public Enemies/
Public Heroes: Hollywood's Gangster Film, 1930–1950," and its rewriting into a book
that will make this case at greater length.
7. Walsh, *Women's Film and Female Experience*, 103–12; Robert Warshow, *The
Immediate Experience* (New York: Atheneum, 1979), 173–88.
8. Frank Krutnik, *In a Lonely Street: Film Noir, Genre, Masculinity* (London:
Routledge, 1991), 21.
9. Ibid., 19.

10. Alvin Gouldner, *Wildcat Strike* (Yellow Springs, Ohio: Antioch University Press, 1954), especially chap. 3.

11. *Journey into Fear* directed by Norman Foster and Orson Welles in 1942 functions as a direct allegory for the cold war even though it was probably not intended to do so.

12. See Bernard Bailyn, *The Ideological Origins of the American Revolution* (Cambridge: Belknap Press of Harvard University Press, 1967); Martin Sklar, "Woodrow Wilson and the Political Economy of Modern United States Liberalism," in Ronald Radosh and Murray Rothbard, eds., *A New History of Leviathan* (New York: Dutton, 1972); and Michael P. Rogin, *Ronald Reagan, the Movie: And Other Episodes in Political Demonology* (Berkeley: University of California Press, 1987).

13. Tania Modleski, "Film Theory's Detour," *Screen* 23, no. 5 (Nov.–Dec. 1982): 74.

14. Barbara Ehrenreich, *The Hearts of Men: American Dreams and the Flight from Commitment* (New York: Anchor, 1983).

15. See Thom Andersen, "Red Hollywood," in Suzanne Ferguson and Barbara Groseclose, eds., *Literature and the Visual Arts in Contemporary Society* (Columbus: Ohio State University Press, 1985), 141–96, and also his "The Time of the Toad," *20th Film Festival Rotterdam Program*, 1990, 15–23. I am grateful to Andersen for calling my attention to these films and to their importance.

16. Andersen, "The Time of the Toad," 20.

17. Trumbo's friend Hugo Butler co-wrote the script and fronted for Trumbo by having his name appear alone in the screen credits. Trumbo also played the voice of the right-wing radio broadcaster and even appeared in a brief shot when the film showed the husband's face just before being murdered.

18. Quoted in Andersen, "The Time of the Toad," 19.

19. Ibid., 21.

20. Ibid.

21. Perhaps we should assign this film to a new genre, film blanc (white film), although that category seems to be too large to take a generic identity of its own.

22. Serafina Bathrick, "The True Woman and the Family Film: The Industrial Production of Memory" (Ph.D. diss., University of Wisconsin, 1981). Bathrick provides an excellent analysis of this film, which she first called to my attention in 1977. I am indebted to her writing for its important insights on this film in particular and on the role of film as a social force in general.

23. Herbert Biberman, *Salt of the Earth* (Boston: Beacon Press, 1965); Deborah Silverton Rosenfelt and Michael Wilson, *Salt of the Earth* (Old Westbury, N.Y.: Feminist Press, 1978); George Lipsitz, "Herbert Biberman and the Art of Subjectivity," *Telos*, no. 32 (Summer 1977).

24. Tom Miller, "Salt of the Earth Revisited," *Cineaste* 13, no. 3 (1984): 32.

25. Peter Bogdanovich, "Interview with Edgar Ulmer," *Film Culture*, nos. 58–60 (1970).

26. See interview with Shirley Castle Ulmer, *San Francisco Chronicle*, Nov. 21, 1982, 33; additional information from personal interview with Shirley Castle Ulmer, Mar. 10, 1983, Houston, Tex.

27. Michael Goodwin and Naomi Wise, "Nicholas Ray, Rebel!" *Take One* (Jan 1977): 9.

28. Nicholas Ray quote from ibid., 10; information about censorship from Andersen, "The Time of the Toad," 20.

29. I am indebted to Stan Weir for calling my attention to the costs incurred by left-wing middle-class intellectuals from not facing up to their own alienations and instead using the working class as a surrogate for their own frustrations.

CHAPTER THIRTEEN

"Ain't Nobody Here but Us Chickens"

The Class Origins of Rock and Roll

WHEN LABOR UNIONS conducted organizing drives in the steel mill and mining towns around Birmingham, Alabama, in the twenties and thirties, they could usually count on drawing large and enthusiastic crowds to their rallies. Some workers came to hear what the union had to say about their wages and working conditions, while others no doubt showed up primarily out of curiosity. But they could all count on hearing from one of the CIO's secret weapons—one of the pro-union jubilee gospel quartets whose singing fused together class solidarity, Christian fellowship, and hopes for material gain.[1]

As the folklore scholar Brenda McCallum relates in her excellent study, the founding period of black gospel quartet singing in Birmingham coincided with the region's industrialization and unionization. Singing on the job seemed to make work time pass more quickly, while singing associations in the community provided workers status and prestige rarely available to them at work. The emphasis on harmony in jubilee gospel singing provided a metaphorical enactment of the cooperation and collectivity that black workers needed on the factory floor and in their communities. Gospel groups functioned as fraternal orders, offering opportunities for individuals to think creatively, supervise their own work, plan public appearances, administer funds, and speak out on issues of importance to them.[2]

Jubilee gospel quartet singing enabled black workers to blend religious activities with union activism. When unionism became a force in their lives, they organized their own quartets rather than continue to participate in the welfare society choral groups and bands run by their employers. New songs including "This What the Union Done" and "Union Boys Are We" celebrated labor's victories, while old songs like "Satisfied" acquired new lyrics depicting the Last Supper as an occasion where Jesus told his disciples to "stay in union." Groups calling themselves the Sterling Jubilee

CIO Singers and the Bessemer CIO Singers flaunted their membership in the trade-union movement. They sang at organizing rallies and union meetings and in the forties became regular participants in a weekly Sunday morning radio broadcast sponsored by the CIO.[3]

During the postwar period all across the country, faction fights between competing unions, contracts that ceded more power to management, labor's disinterest in aggressive organizing campaigns, anticommunism, and the emergence of powerful new forms of commercial popular culture all contributed to the eclipse of working-class musical organizations like the Birmingham jubilee gospel quartets. Between 1946 and 1949, a group of intellectuals in and around the Communist party attempted to stem the tide of what they thought of as "corrupt, mindless popular culture" by building an alternative political popular culture based on traditional rural folk music.[4] Although many of the individuals involved in People's Songs went on to play an important role in the folk revival within popular music in the sixties, the sectarianism and isolation of the Communist party in the forties provided a poor environment for efforts to create popular culture. Most of the participants in People's Songs concluded from the success of anticommunism and cold war ideology in the United States that the times were simply against them, that the people were simply too conservative to respond to their appeals. But their greatest artist, Woody Guthrie, was closer to the mark when he observed, "The people are lots more ready than our songs and our songleaders are ready to admit. . . . We are not allowing our songs to be radical enough in the proper way."[5]

Commercial popular music in the forties and fifties evidenced some of the ways in which songs could be radical, or at least how they had the potential to function in radical ways. As was the case with television and film, industrial modes of production, commodity form, monopoly control, private censorship, and state regulation all narrowed the range of what could be done within popular music. For all of its shortcomings, commercial popular music in the postwar period emerged as one site where the blasted hopes and utopian aspirations of working-class life found expression.

Throughout the winter of 1946–47, radios, record players, and jukeboxes featured a song titled "Ain't Nobody Here but Us Chickens." Performed by Louis Jordan, a black singer and saxophonist from Brinkley, Arkansas, the song told a story about a farmer drawn to a disturbance in his henhouse. Arriving on the scene with gun in hand, he leaves reassured when a voice informs him that "there ain't nobody here but us chickens." The voice goes on to remind the farmer that laying eggs and pecking for worms requires full concentration and a good night's rest and appeals to his greed as a reason to leave the henhouse alone. The song's humor lies not so much in the thief's foolishness or the farmer's gullibility, but in a brazen triumph by the powerless over the powerful. At the record's end, a jubilant voice intones, "It's easy pickin's, ain't nobody here but us chickens," clearly establishing the culpable bandit as the song's hero.[6]

Louis Jordan probably had no intention of making a serious social statement with this song. But in the context of postwar labor strife, the song's popularity added a new phrase to popular speech and a new metaphor for resistance to authority. In an age of anticommunism and countersubversion, covert struggles could continue among people whose public posture insisted that "there ain't nobody here but us chickens." The success of this song—with its ethic of playful rebellion in an era of intense anticommunism and systematic countersubversion—demonstrates the diversity of possible subject positions available to individuals through the texts of commercial culture.

Appropriately enough, the lyrics of "Ain't Nobody Here but Us Chickens" had their origins in the culture of America's first and most oppressive system of labor exploitation—slavery. As George Rawick demonstrates in his important study of slave culture, African legends about "trickster-hero buffoons" provided instruction and encouragement in the arts of resistance. Slaves told stories in which animals or lesser gods outwitted stronger opponents, never fully overcoming their own weaknesses, but employing deception and guile to win small victories. Although often misused and misunderstood by whites, to the slaves these stories kept alive utopian hopes for the future and reasserted their own interests in the face of oppressive power. As they became absorbed into the nation's folklore, these stories served as guides to other groups and individuals interested in mounting opposition to centralized authority and power.[7]

One can easily understand why a black artist like Louis Jordan would turn to the traditions of slavery for a model of resistance to authority, but "Ain't Nobody Here but Us Chickens" was written by two white songwriters and had enormous appeal for both white and black audiences.[8] Of course, white writers like Joel Chandler Harris had long ago discovered ways of popularizing (and changing the meanings of) slave stories. White audiences may have been laughing at, rather than with, Louis Jordan. But another explanation is also possible. With the growth of bureaucratic regimentation in all aspects of social life, methods of carving away limited spheres of autonomy by outwitting those in power became increasingly relevant to more and more people. White Americans may have turned to black culture for guidance because black culture contains the most sophisticated strategies of signification and the richest grammars of opposition available to aggrieved populations.

Black music has traditionally provided the basis for American popular music, but it did so most often when pirated by whites and played in diluted form, or when distorted to conform to white expectations as to how blacks should sound.[9] Jordan won approval from white audiences, but he did it with distinctly black music. Just as the lyrics of "Ain't Nobody Here but Us Chickens" offered whites a worldview rooted in the slave experience, its musical content consisted of blues and jazz forms originating in that same history.

Excellent research by scholars including Melville Herskovits, George Rawick, Amiri Baraka, Ben Sidran, and Sterling Stuckey has located the origins of much of modern popular music in the experience of slavery.[10] Africans kidnapped into slavery carried their most important possession with them in their minds—their culture.[11] Like other preindustrial peoples, they made no rigid distinction between work and art, and they developed a music that served important social functions in everyday life. Work, courtship, worship, gossip, and collective popular memory became expressed musically—not as a commentary after the fact—but as an integral part of performing the activities themselves. Work songs stressed the collective nature of slave labor while making tasks seem less onerous. Spirituals utilized hidden metaphors to preserve memories of past freedom in Africa and hopes for future liberation in America. Dance tunes maintained a spirit of celebration and self-affirmation in the midst of oppression. Drums took on special meaning, both as a retention from a proud past and as a means of communication under circumstances that prohibited free verbal interaction.[12]

Slave music retained African forms as well as functions. The banjo originated as an African instrument, lyrics of slave songs contained the grammar and idioms of West African speech, and the distinctive integration of voice, instruments, and rhythm as interchangeable forms stemmed from the culture of the slaves' home continent. As one would expect from a society with a strong oral tradition, African speech provided the basis for many musical conventions. The conversational interplay between one voice and another appeared in slave music as antiphony, or call and response, in which a lead vocal or instrumental "voice" drew an answer from another. African speech explored a wide range of sounds, altered meanings by changing registers of tone, and relied on circumlocution rather than direct assertion. Musically, this meant use of tones spanning the entire range of instruments and voice, subtle alterations in meaning by changing pitch, and articulation of notes by attacking them indirectly and exploring their boundaries.

Survival of African musical forms in America helped remind slaves of an alternative to their servitude, but the forms themselves contained important social implications for the present as well. Emphasis on music as communication and the use of the human voice as the model for instrumental sounds produced an emotional art seeking to involve, rather than awe, the listener. The wide range of available sounds stimulated innovation and improvisation, leading to an active and original art constantly building on past conventions and not just repeating them. Most important, polyrhythms expressed a sense of time as a flexible human creation rather than an external objective force. Because they asserted a fundamental unity among artists, art, and the audience, slave musical forms maintained a preindustrial worldview that not only conflicted with the slave owners' view of culture but with their view of work as well. Slaves resisted a labor system that deprived them of a stake in their work, of pride in their labor, and of control over their time, and they preserved in their music the social forms denied them in work.

After emancipation, racism and labor exploitation continued to oppress black people, but music remained an important defense. New experiences led to new forms supplementing traditional songs for work, church, and dance, as blacks drew upon all available sources to make a distinctly African-American statement. Instruments ranged from boxes, sticks, animal skulls, and parts of tools to guitars brought to this hemisphere by Spaniards and to horns discarded by army bands after the Civil War. European melodies and harmonies interacted with African poetic and vocal styles to form a new synthesis. By the early twentieth century, African-American music became America's most important original art form, particularly through the styles known as blues and jazz.

A creative tension between European and African harmonies gave the blues its distinctive sound. When musicians accustomed to the African five-tone scale played or sang music designed for the European eight-tone scale, it sounded better to them when they flattened or bent certain sounds, thus creating "blue" notes. To those trained in European harmony, the resulting music seemed to involve flattening the third, fifth, or seventh steps of the eight-tone scale, but a more accurate description would recognize that blues musicians used their own system of harmony and chord progressions. The musicologist Rob Walser points out that the use of blue notes by African Americans displays an understanding of pitch as an expressive parameter in direct contrast to the rigid European system of fixed pitches.[13] Blues artists employed a three-line verse common to West African poetry, repeating the first line as the second, and then adding a new rhyme with the third. In its changing time signatures, playing off the beat, and use of more than one rhythm at a time, blues music often manifested the complexities of the African rhythmic tradition, while call and response, changes in register, and vocal improvisation incorporated into the blues still other musical forms of African origin.

African functions made their presence felt in the blues. Blind singers played a particularly important role in disseminating the blues, partially because their disability kept them close to the oral traditions of African music. Male blues musicians wandered all over the South, surviving by a combination of their wits and their music, duplicating the role played in some parts of Africa by wandering griots. Yet blues singers were not Africans, and their art did not develop in isolation. White racism ensured that blacks could not make a complete break with their African past; that past held them together and accounted for their present. However, labor exploitation in America played an important role in defining black identity, and blues music expressed class as well as racial perceptions.

"The blues were born behind a mule," Bukka White once observed, and they traveled to the cities when sharecroppers and farm laborers became industrial workers. The success of blues records by Bessie Smith helped establish the profitability of the recording industry in the twenties, and blues influences played an important role in shaping the music of African-American improvisational ensembles popularly known as "jazz" bands. The term "jazz" often was used imprecisely outside the black community to describe a wide variety of music. Because of its insulting connotations to some black musicians, the music described as jazz might more properly be called black music, or as Duke Ellington insisted, American music. Whatever its classification, the music popularly known as "jazz" formed the basis for almost all modern popular music and dance. African-American songs seldom spoke directly about work, but they nonetheless reflected the worldview of the working people who played and listened to them. In a society that extolled individual alienated labor, African-American music asserted a connection between people and their creations, it presumed the collectivity of labor, and it spoke the language and articulated the concerns of subjective everyday experience.

By the time Louis Jordan began making hit records in the forties, he had mastered the heritage of blues and African-American ensemble music. His first professional job—as a clarinetist and dancer with the Rabbit Foot Minstrels—exposed him to the blues singing of the legendary Ma Rainey. Once during World War II, when Jordan performed on a bill with Lionel Hampton, he stole the show by singing nothing but the blues for his entire set. In the thirties, Jordan played alto saxophone and sang with an orchestra directed by Chick Webb, the brilliant drummer whose innovative use of rhythms transformed American dancing. In "Ain't Nobody Here but Us Chickens" and other songs, Jordan transposed old forms into a new synthesis. In the best tradition of the blues, Louis Jordan's saxophone playing and singing complemented each other, and both displayed his facility for improvisation. "Ain't Nobody Here but Us Chickens" employed call and response, blue notes, and blues chord progressions, but it also displayed the rhythmic influences of Chick Webb and the big bands of the thirties. "With my little band, I did everything they did with a big band," he later recalled, adding that "I made the blues jump."[14]

Musical forms popularized in Jordan's music existed for many years before white racism abated sufficiently to allow their dissemination to a mass audience. Discrimination prevented whites and blacks from living and working together freely, and the sheet music, phonograph, and radio industries deliberately isolated white audiences from black music. Unlike its African-American counterparts, white popular music generally imitated European forms, stressing direct reproduction of a limited range of sounds and separating vocal and instrumental styles. The resulting art proved well suited to producing cultural commodities that turned listeners into passive consumers and that made art itself a special sphere removed from the concerns and language of everyday life. But the very sterility of this popular music often drove its creators to plunder the riches of black culture, albeit through insulting forms like the minstrel show where whites masqueraded as blacks, the "coon song," which presented white interpretations of black music under the guise of "humor," and through much of the recycled popular music of the twentieth century wherein white musicians bought or stole the arrangements of blacks and presented them to the white public in diluted form. White America almost always refused to acknowledge its debt to black music and tragically shunned some of its greatest artists because of their skin color.[15]

Louis Jordan succeeded where other blacks had failed, not because his music departed from previously unacceptable forms, but because three historical developments created conditions conducive to his success. Jordan profited from the evolution of white working-class music, from the ability of the mass media to create a common frame of reference for diverse groups, and from changes in social conditions stimulated by World War II. Immediately prior to the release of "Ain't Nobody Here but Us Chickens," Jordan enjoyed commercial success with a country-and-western song, "Choo Choo Ch'Boogie."[16] Although his version contained the twelve-bar phrases and unevenly accented 8/8 time pioneered in black music, the song's musical and lyrical structure, as well as Jordan's vocal style, originated in the music of rural working-class whites. White country music also preserved a preindustrial worldview parallel to the one articulated within the blues, and the historical interactions between those two kinds of music and between their creators helped lay the foundation for Louis Jordan's accomplishments in the forties.

White working-class music has been as diverse as the class itself, preserving remnants of dozens of cultures transformed by emigration to North

America and by adaptation to industrial labor. Music created by poor whites in the rural South proved particularly suited for synthesizing a wide variety of European forms, including polkas, marches, waltzes, and quadrilles into a common musical vocabulary. But the most important influences on white working-class music came from black culture. Although white racism prevented completely free and reciprocal interactions, many of the Euro-Americans who lived and worked closest to blacks learned from them and developed a music that shared with blacks a vision of a world in which people's creations remained connected to the totality of their lives.

Country music combined European harmonies, dance rhythms, and song styles with African-influenced three-line twelve-bar blues, call and response, blue notes, and changes in pitch. The resulting synthesis encouraged individual improvisation within traditional collective musical forms, creating a delicate balance between individual initiative and collective traditions. Because they drew on folk traditions that made no distinctions between life and art, white country musicians found that they understood much of the inner logic of black music. Even when they held racist views about black people, southern white musicians found that the immediacy and emotion of black music powerfully expressed their own feelings of alienation from a society that also worked them too hard and too long.

Like blues artists, country musicians often used collective memory about the past as a defense against the injustices of the present. Whether recalling the joys of happier times, recounting stories of past tribulations, or merely preserving traditional stories, speech, and dance forms, country songs allowed artists and audiences to root their present identity in a usable past.

Racial segregation restrained face-to-face contacts between whites and blacks, but interactions at work, at play, and even at home still allowed for exchanges of musical forms. The rise of commercial popular music accelerated these interactions by distributing elements of white and black southern culture to new audiences. The transformation of music into commodities like sheet music, vaudeville-variety house performances, phonograph records, and radio programs undermined some of the situatedness and use value of country music and blues by separating music from everyday life functions, by turning human communication between artists and audiences into a commercial transaction, and by imposing narrow marketing categories on innovative, improvisational, and infinitely plastic art. But that same commercialism preserved music that might otherwise have been lost. It enabled people from diverse backgrounds to discover how much they had in common and consequently accelerated the mixing of peoples and musical forms. Commercialism altered, but did not significantly subvert, the best traditions of country music and blues, just as waged labor assaulted but did not destroy the sense of pride and service traditionally associated with work before the industrial revolution.

From the start, connections between commerce and class identity influenced and affected blues and country music. Black musicians followed the migrations of black workers, learning from them which songs would bring the best response when passing the hat or playing for tips in bars. Field hands supplemented their incomes by playing for local dances and parties, seeking the approval of their community to ensure future money-making opportunities. Country musicians sought similar rewards and played a similar role in their communities.[17]

In some instances, commercialism led to ingenious fusions of folk arts with unfamiliar forms. In the nineteenth century, touring musical shows popularized classical European harmonies, and music publishers distributed song sheets that enabled country musicians to learn harmony via the shape-note system. Country musicians learned from the new without discarding the old, by adapting traditional solo singing to the new harmonies—creating the beautiful and haunting blending of voices evident in records by the Delmore Brothers and so many other country artists.[18]

The development of commercial radio and recording in the twenties might have led to the obliteration of folk music by the new forms' cultural commodities. But instead, radio station owners contributed to even greater circulation of folk culture once they found that programs featuring "old-time" music motivated people to purchase radio sets. Station WSB in Atlanta built its earliest audience around the music of Fiddlin' John Carson, a cotton mill worker who played traditional country songs. Similarly, WSM in Nashville drew large audiences by featuring performances by a former farmer and wagon driver, Uncle Dave Macon, and WBAP in Fort Worth experimented with a variety of programs before letters from listeners convinced the station to adopt a country-music format.[19]

Record companies attempted to capitalize on the popularity of southern country music radio stations by recording their star performers in an enthusiastic, if uncomprehending, way. Fiddlin' John Carson's earliest vocal efforts seemed so crude to record company executives that they refused to release them, reasoning that no one would really want to listen to them. But demand from audiences familiar with the nuances of country singing secured their release and led to a profitable relationship between the company and country singers.[20]

Radio stations routinely ignored blues music, but the spectacular sales of blues records by Bessie Smith, Ma Rainey, Mamie Smith, and others established the viability of commercial recording and encouraged record producers to scour the country seeking out musicians who could play and sing the blues. Racism pervaded this process. Record company executives frequently cheated the artists out of their royalties, taking advantage of the dearth of opportunities for black people in America. Producers censored lyrics that offended them and insisted that performers imitate previous commercial successes rather than giving free rein to their own creativity. Sometimes people in the music business justified their appropriation of the efforts of the artists by claiming they assumed that making blues music required no special talents. These abuses often plagued country music performers as well, but as in every other industry, racism in the music industry made exploitation even worse for blacks.

To make their marketing tasks easier, record company executives imposed artificial categories on music that had always grown through creative fusions between different forms. Gid Tanner and the Skillet Lickers (a country string band featuring the talents of Tanner, a former chicken farmer, and Clayton McMichen, a one-time automobile mechanic) played all sorts of popular music including Dixieland "jazz" numbers like Louis Armstrong's "Royal Garden Blues," but their record company confined them to traditional mountain music when they recorded. Blind Willie McTell, a black blues singer who attended a state school for the blind at the same time as the lead vocalist for the Skillet Lickers, Riley Puckett, incorporated country songs into his repertoire, but only on rare occasions would producers let him record the full range of his music.[21] Record companies divided their products into "race" (black) music and "hillbilly" or "country" (white) songs, which they recorded and marketed separately.

Despite these efforts by the music industry to maintain a separation between black and white working-class music, country and blues records revealed the enormous interaction that had already existed between the two forms. Jimmie Rodgers, a former railroad water boy and brake operator, became one of country music's most successful recording artists with his varied repertoire of mountain tunes, yodels popularized in vaudeville, Hawaiian steel guitar sounds, blues, work songs, and Dixieland instrumentals. Drawing on his own experiences with black work crews on the railroads and on the rich storehouse of recorded black music, Rodgers sang three-line, twelve-bar blues, played guitar in the chordal style of Mississippi blacks, and inserted talking phrases in between verses in the manner of contemporary blues singers. In a stunning example of the creative possibilities engendered by mixing African-American and country traditions, Rodgers recorded "Blue Yodel No. 9" in 1930 accompanied by trumpeter Louis Armstrong and (probably) pianist Earl "Fatha" Hines. One of the first recorded collaborations between black and white musicians, the record came about because of the mutual admiration between Armstrong and Rodgers, and it featured an enthusiastic demonstration of call and response between them.[22]

Rodgers incorporated aspects of black music into an already diverse style. It needs to be acknowledged that a prejudiced society rewarded him financially for that music while virtually ignoring black blues singers, but his own artistry also contributed to Rodgers's popularity. The combination of kinds of music present in Jimmie Rodgers's songs created a new storehouse of folk art, inspiring and influencing black and white musicians alike. Chester Burnett, a black field hand from Arkansas, patterned his own music after that of the "Singing Brakeman," but his attempts at yodeling fell short and instead produced a deep-throated but high-pitched howl. Because of that sound he became known as Howlin' Wolf, and he went on to become one of the best and one of the most influential urban blues singers of the postwar years. Another bluesman, Lowell Fulson, learned country music as a boy from Coot Mason, "a white boy who played with Jimmie Rodgers."[23]

A black musician named Leslie Riddles provided an important element in the success of the Carter Family, one of country music's most popular acts in the thirties. Sara, Maybelle, and A. P. Carter generally played traditional mountain songs of the Southeast, but part of their distinctive sound came from the guitar style that Maybelle Carter had learned from Riddles. More of a song collector than a songwriter, A. P. Carter added to his stock by swapping songs with local musicians on family excursions, and he relied on Riddles's near-total recall to preserve all the melodies they heard. Songs like "Cannonball Blues" and "Lonesome for You" came directly from Riddles, while others bore his musical imprint in more subtle ways. The friendship and musical collaboration between the Carter Family and Leslie Riddles contributed substantially to the quality of the family's music, and it seems plausible to surmise that a large part of the audience had experienced similar interactions in formulating their own musical preferences.[24]

During the depression, large record companies pared down their catalogs, and many smaller firms specializing in country music and blues went out of business. Mainstream popular music consisted largely of romantic ballads and watered-down African-American dance music, but the industry still generated great wealth abetted by interlocking financial interests among publishers, record companies, and radio stations. Country music and blues comprised only a minor part of the industry and remained relatively isolated from the public at large, although they continued to thrive among a limited audience. The music industry marketed "hillbilly" and "race" music on a regional and racial basis, while distributing symphonic and popular music to everybody else. But industrial mobilization for World War II created a set of opportunities and possibilities.

When rural whites and blacks moved to take jobs in industrial cities, they confronted new social realities and new cultural forms. From the oil fields of Texas and the steel mills of Chicago to the booming shipyards on both coasts, black and white workers with money to spend longed to hear the music they left behind them when they moved to the city. Musicians among them discovered lucrative opportunities to play and sing blues and country music in taverns that catered to the dry throats and full wallets of war-plant workers. But the new conditions demanded changes in the old music as well. When McKinley Morganfield arrived in Chicago from Mississippi in 1943, he took a job as a truck driver by day, but really hoped to make his living as a blues singer by night. Morganfield played country blues on acoustic guitar at rent parties, but found it necessary to use an amplified instrument to be heard above the noise in small lounges. Although he still preferred the acoustic sound, Morganfield adapted brilliantly to the electric guitar. He became the leading practitioner of the Chicago style of urban blues using the nickname Muddy Waters, a name he received as a young boy because of his fondness for the river. Switching to amplification enabled blues musicians to play louder, to explore rhythms more compatible with the hectic pace and corresponding tensions of mass-production work, and display skills on the guitar that would have been inaudible before amplification.[25]

Country musicians made similar adaptations when they played at boisterous "honky tonk" bars. The pedal steel guitar, a homemade instrument designed in basements and garages by musicians searching for a new sound, became a prominent part of country music bands—as much for its volume as for its expressiveness. William "Lefty" Frizzell, an oil driller from Corsicana, Texas, pioneered a melodramatic vocal style that could command attention in a noisy bar, but also proved perfectly suited to either up-tempo dance numbers or plaintive ballads.

Urban blues and honky-tonk country music did not sound alike, but they shared a similar mission. Commercial considerations led to the abandonment of some traditional forms, but also created a means of performing some traditional styles better. The technical possibilities of the electric and pedal steel guitars made it easier to duplicate the human voice, adding a new dimension to the interaction between voice and accompaniment common to both blues and country music. That propensity to imitate the sounds of the human voice on instruments was what initially attracted blues singer Ray Charles to country-and-western music. "They'd made them steel guitars cry and whine," he recalled, "and it really attracted me."[26] Amplified bass guitars encouraged dancing and maintained the important social functions of rural music in the urban environment. Personal innovation flowered with the new forms, but artists still had to give dancers the music they came to hear.

Adaptability to commercial demands also won attention from people with little or no previous exposure to country music and blues. The rhythmic energy of country music and blues records of the forties helped win them a place in the hearts of jukebox owners who needed attention-grabbing music to place on the more than 350,000 boxes in America's bars, cafes, and bus stations.[27] The nickels and dimes of transplanted southerners introduced their co-workers and neighbors to country and blues music, and many found it to their liking. In 1943, Detroit jukebox operators observed that their customers preferred country music to any other form, and one of the best-selling records of the year turned out to be a jukebox favorite inspired by life in the East Texas oil fields—Al Dexter's "Pistol-Packin' Mama."[28] The music industry responded to the unexpected popularity of country music and blues by having popular singers record the new music in a smoother and less interesting style. Bing Crosby, whose facility for imitating black singers had earned him popularity as a "jazz" singer as early as the twenties, "covered" country songs including Dexter's "Pistol-Packin' Mama" and Bob Wills's "New San Antonio Rose," as well as blues and dance numbers including Louis Jordan's "Is You Is Or Is You Ain't."[29] Of all the popular singers, Crosby best preserved the properties of the songs he expropriated, and his records did help to prepare a mass audience for the country and blues artists who would soon enjoy great success among the pop audience.

Interactions between country music and blues, working-class migrations during World War II, and the capacity of the music industry for creating shared musical experiences among diverse people all helped set the stage for Louis Jordan's success. Five of his records sold more than one million copies, and in 1946 alone eleven of his songs made the best-seller lists.[30] His artistic synthesis of blues and country-music traditions moved black and white working-class musicians even closer together, and his success both shaped and reflected the demand for a new kind of music. Aided by social and technological developments, working-class musicians in the new industrial centers followed Jordan's example. The blues became transformed into rhythm and blues, country music into rockabilly, and both eventually blended into a new form that revolutionized American music and culture—rock and roll.

Two technological developments aided the growth in popularity of working-class music in the forties. The invention of the 33⅓ record led to great improvements in sound quality, while the use of magnetic recording tape allowed producers to make records without needing the services of a major studio. When wartime shortages of shellac (combined with their own cultural biases) led producers for major recording companies to neglect blues and country artists, independent entrepreneurs saw an opportunity to make money by serving the markets ignored by the majors. Some four hundred new recording companies started operations during the forties, most of them specializing in making music for the working-class populations of industrial cities. Small business people turned into music impresarios as a means of preserving their own autonomy in an increasingly centralized economy, while working-class musicians pursued careers as entertainers in part to escape the pain and alienation of waged work.

A former record-pressing plant worker from Los Angeles demonstrated the opportunities awaiting entrepreneurs in the music industry in 1945. Cliff McDonald heard Army Private Cecil Gant singing at a war bond rally and subsequently persuaded him to make a record in a homemade studio in McDonald's garage. The session produced "I Wonder," which became one of the best-selling records of the year, launching both Gant and McDonald into successful careers in music. Jules Bihari, a jukebox operator whose territory covered black neighborhoods in Los Angeles, became so frustrated trying to obtain copies of "I Wonder" that he talked his brothers into starting a record company of their own. The Bihari brothers' label, Modern Records, soared to success in the late forties on the strength of hits by a former janitor at a Dodge Auto factory in Detroit, John Lee Hooker; by B. B. King, who had been a tractor driver and farm worker in Mississippi; and by an ex-shipyard worker from Northern California, Jimmy Witherspoon.[31]

In every city affected by wartime working-class migrations, new record companies tapped the talents of musicians to meet the demands of the new residents. In Oakland, California, record store owner Bob Geddins entered the recording business with songs by Lowell Fulson, a shipyard worker, and by Johnny Fuller, a mechanic. The Chess brothers had owned a night club in Chicago, but they achieved their first real success in music with the recording business that they started in 1946 with their first product, Andrew Tibbs's "Union Man Blues." Syd Nathan abandoned his department store business in Cincinnati to set up King Records in 1945. Herman Lubinsky, the founder of the Savoy label, boasted that he made records "for the man with the dinner pail and the lady over the washtub."[32]

Although the record industry still marketed black and white music in separate categories, the cultural interplay between them exemplified by Louis Jordan's songs continued to accelerate. In place of divisions by race and region, a new national culture was being forged. The resulting music market so puzzled the editors of *Billboard*, the industry's trade journal, that they groped for appropriate labels to describe working-class music throughout the forties, eventually discarding "race" in favor of "rhythm and blues," and replacing "hillbilly" and "folk" with "country and western." The new classifications proved more useful to many in the industry, but they still failed to realize the full significance of the embrace of black musical styles by large numbers of whites and the impending destruction of some of the major barriers that had divided blacks and whites in popular music.

When those barriers did fall, Bob Wills was ready. Country music's "king of western swing" had been a construction worker and barber in his hometown of Turkey, Texas. His band had been playing a mixture of country music, blues, and jazz for over twenty years, but they attained their greatest popularity during and immediately after World War II. Bob Wills and his Texas Playboys blended a seemingly inexhaustible inventory of fiddle tunes with ensemble styles from Dixieland, the harmonies of Mexican fiddles and horns in mariachi and ranchera music, the instrumentation of swing big bands, and most important, with blues forms.

As a young boy working in the cotton fields of East Texas, Wills lived and worked alongside black people, and he never lost his reverence for the music he heard from them. In the twenties, Wills rode more than thirty miles on horseback just to hear a performance by Bessie Smith, and he later recalled, "She was about the greatest thing I had ever heard. In fact there was no doubt about it. She was the greatest thing I ever heard."[33] Wills slurred notes on the fiddle to produce a blues feel, and he once proclaimed, "I have always been a blues singer."[34] When he started to assemble western swing groups in the thirties, he demanded that his musicians display mastery of black musical styles.

Wills insisted that his band never play a song the same way twice. He encouraged his musicians to learn how to improvise, and suggested blues singers and black dance bands as appropriate models. Lead singer Tommy Duncan got his job with the Texas Playboys when Wills heard him sing the Bessie Smith favorite "I Ain't Got Nobody." Drummer Smokey Dacus learned the band's distinctive 2/4 beat while playing in Dixieland ensembles. Fiddler Jesse Ashlock patterned his playing after the trumpet parts in big bands. Bob Wills and the Texas Playboys offered the public an eclectic music deeply rooted in the diverse traditions of the American working class, and audiences of the postwar era responded enthusiastically.[35]

Although he recorded numerous hit songs in the postwar years, Wills's greatest success came as a live performer for dances. The son and grandson of champion fiddlers as well as a connoisseur of "hot jazz," Wills took dancing seriously and never allowed the individual virtuosity of band members to interfere with the audience's desire to move their bodies. All across the country—but particularly in California where he moved in 1943—people wanted to dance to the music of the Texas Playboys. Reporting on a dance in Bakersfield, California, in 1946, *Time* magazine lauded Wills as a "backwoods Lombardo" for the manner in which he stimulated over 1,300 oil workers, farmers, and "fruit cannery girls" to "jive," "jump," and "jog" to his music.[36] Somewhere in the midst of all that jiving, jumping, and jogging lay the rough beast of rock and roll waiting to be born.

In songs like "Bob Wills Boogie" (1946) and "Ida Red Likes the Boogie" (1949), one can hear the beat and chord progressions later popularized in rock and roll.[37] As Wills told a newspaper reporter in 1958, "Rock and roll???

Why, man, that's the same kind of music we've been playing since 1928! . . . We didn't call it 'rock and roll' back when we introduced it as our style in 1928, and we don't call it rock and roll the way we play it now. But it's just basic rhythm and has gone by a lot of different names in my time. It's the same, whether you follow just a drum beat like in Africa or surround it with a lot of instruments. The rhythm's what's important."[38]

The Texas Playboys used the same "shuffle boogie" employed by Louis Jordan in "Choo Choo Ch'Boogie," a song later recorded by Leon McAuliffe (who played steel guitar in Wills's band), as well as by countless other black musicians. Yet Wills had an influence on blacks as well. Blues singer and guitarist Albert King once worked as a chauffeur in El Paso, where his job took him to a ranch party featuring the Texas Playboys. King recognized the 8/8 time and the uneven accents as a staple of black jitterbug music, but later contended that "the Bob Wills band could play that stuff better than anybody I've ever heard."[39] Chuck Berry's rock-and-roll classic "Maybelline," recorded for Chess Records in 1955, bears such a close resemblance to "Ida Red Likes the Boogie" that if Berry did not listen to Wills, he must have listened to Cowboy Copas or whomever Wills listened to.[40]

The line dividing black and white working-class music became even more indeterminate with the success of Hank Williams (see chapter 1). In his eleven million-selling records between 1949 and 1953, Williams employed emotional solo singing, fiddle and pedal steel guitar as accompaniment, and four-line, rhymed-couplet verses that made him an exemplary representative of country-music traditions. But it was his sophisticated exploration of black musical styles that set him apart from other country singers and made him a pivotal figure in the rise of rock and roll.[41] Hank Williams's vocals utilized changes in tone and falsetto singing, his performances displayed call and response, and his compositions utilized the circumlocution and preoccupation with creating a mood characteristic of many blues singers.

With little formal education, minimal competence on the guitar, and an interesting but unpolished voice, Hank Williams wrote lyrics, composed melodies, and sang in a way that touched listeners' hearts as profoundly as any musician before or since. His talent as a composer and interpreter of songs deserve most of the credit for his success, but Williams also shared with his listeners the contradictions and confusions of their time. Williams's affinity for black music made him a credible voice at a time of increased cultural interaction between blacks and whites. His yearning for connection to others addressed the loneliness of mass society, and his pessimism about romance signaled a sharp dissent from the hegemony of narratives about domestic happiness in postwar America. With his chaotic marriages and the drinking and drug use that made him unable to fulfill so many obligations, Williams displayed in music the same "refusal to be oedipalized" characteristic of male heroes in film noir. His lyrics elevated immediate pleasure over deferred gratification and they articulated a sense of betrayal and abandon as the explanation for a life of loneliness. Like film noir stories, his songs rebel against "respectable" patriarchal roles, but they offer only a self-pitying isolation as an alternative way of living. But it may have been precisely the relevance of his lyrics to new family and gender roles that enabled Hank Williams to cross over into popular music so successfully.

In addition to his own best-selling records, "cover" versions of Hank Williams's songs by pop singers distributed his work to a wide audience. His compositions "Cold, Cold Heart" and "Jambalaya" rapidly became classics in both popular and country music, and his up-tempo numbers influenced the structure of early rock-and-roll songs, particularly "Move It on Over" and "Mind Your Own Business," which bear a marked resemblance to "Rock around the Clock."[42]

Louis Jordan, Bob Wills, and Hank Williams attacked the artificial walls dividing white and black music, but it took spontaneous collective action by young urban dwellers to launch an all-out attack on those barriers. The small independent record labels inaugurated in the forties tapped the talents of rhythm-and-blues artists in the cities, while radio stations catering to the growing black communities in industrial areas made that music accessible to all within earshot. In a 1947 story about expanding opportunities for black disc jockeys, a writer for *Ebony* magazine observed that the "discovery that a voice has no color has opened new vistas to Negroes in radio, where disc jockeys have demonstrated once again that race is only skin deep."[43] But many listeners recognized these disc jockeys as black and listened to them for that reason.

White teenagers soon played an important role in transforming rhythm-and-blues records into a $15 million a year business.[44] In the early fifties radio stations aimed at white listeners began to allocate time for rhythm and blues in order to stem the flight of young audiences to black-oriented stations. In every major city, local radio boasted at least one disc jockey playing black music for a presumably white audience, and record sales reflected that trend. Los Angeles's Dolphin Record Store sold over 40 percent of its rhythm-and-blues records to whites in 1952, where previously its clientele had been almost exclusively black. That same year, New Orleans record dealers noticed numerous purchases of rhythm-and-blues music by white housewives, some of whom pretended to be running errands for their maid or housekeeper.[45]

When they listened to "rhythm and blues," whites became exposed to a wide range of black musical styles. Paul Williams's "The Hucklebuck," the big rhythm-and-blues hit of 1949, took its melody from a part of bop saxophonist Charlie Parker's "Now's the Time." Duke Ellington's "Happy Go Lucky Local" provided the melody for Jimmy Forrest's 1952 best-seller "Night Train." Art Rupe's Specialty label in Los Angeles recorded the Swan Silvertones, Soul Stirrers, Pilgrim Travelers, and other gospel groups at the same time as rhythm-and-blues artists with a "church" sound like Roy Milton, Lloyd Price, and Little Richard. Roy Milton, who placed twelve records on the rhythm-and-blues best-seller lists between 1949 and 1953, regularly listened to gospel songs immediately before recording. Popular vocal groups like the Ravens and Clovers also drew heavily on gospel influences. Blues singers Charles Brown and Joe Turner found new popularity with old forms, as Brown's "Trouble Blues" remained on the charts for twenty-seven weeks in 1949, and Turner's "Chains of Love" stayed on them for twenty-five weeks in 1951.[46]

Like previous genres of black popular music, rhythm and blues displayed an interaction with country music. Bull Moose Jackson's 1949 rhythm-and-blues hit "Why Don't You Haul Off and Love Me" copied the original version recorded three months earlier by country singer Wayne Raney. Jackson drew blacks and whites to his popular stage shows; in Knoxville, Tennessee, in 1949, seven hundred whites jammed the segregated balcony during his show for a black audience and demanded "the right to go onto the floor, mingle with the Negroes, and get a better look at 'the Moose.' "[47]

The recording by California western swing artist Hank Penny provided the model for Wynonie Harris's successful "cover" of "Bloodshot Eyes" in 1951.[48] The Orioles placed eight records on the rhythm-and-blues best-seller lists between 1948 and 1953, culminating in their biggest hit, "Crying in the Chapel," written by Artie Glenn, first released as a country song by his son Darrell, and delivered in a decidedly country vocal style by Orioles lead singer Sonny Til.[49] Although building on the traditional relationship between country music and blues, these records also reflected the blurring of racial and ethnic lines in everyday urban life. Anticommunist xenophobia made immigrants and their descendants more assimilationist, while accelerating consumer spending and an emerging national popular culture made the music industry more significant as a social force. As remnants of older immigrant cultures blended with the new forms emerging from rhythm and blues or country musicians, they created a fusion that mixed regions and races but that also revealed the enduring strengths of the Euro-American immigrant experience in the United States as well. Elements of French, Spanish, German, Polish, and other European music provided part of the mix for the emerging national popular music.

Antoine "Fats" Domino, who quit a job in a bedspring factory because he feared an industrial accident might hamper his piano playing, recorded nine best-selling rhythm-and-blues records between 1950 and 1953. His exotic pronunciation of words, his dance-oriented rhythms, and above all, his use of dense, swirling instrumental backgrounds reflected the historical interactions between French accordion music and black blues in Louisiana and East Texas. This music relied on the wheezing sounds of the squeezebox for both chords and rhythm, an effect later duplicated in many New Orleans rhythm-and-blues records (including those by Fats Domino) by horns and saxophones played with a loose embouchure.[50] Known as "zydeco"—a corruption of the pronunciation of the French word for snap beans employed in the title of one of the genre's most popular songs, "Les Haricots Sont Pas Sale"—the combination of blues and French music had an impact on country music as well. The same French influences appeared in pianist Moon Mullican's 1947 rendition of the Cajun song "Jole Blon," as well as in the 1952 Hank Williams composition "Jambalaya," based on another Cajun song, "Grand Texas." In 1956, Domino capitalized on that shared heritage by applying elements of blues and French music to an old big band song from the early forties previously recorded in country versions, "Blueberry Hill." Domino may have sounded bluesy or Cajun to pop audiences, but his black producer Dave Bartholomew remembers that "we all thought of him as a country and western singer."[51]

Spanish, Mexican, and Caribbean influences popped up in the music of Fats Domino and other rhythm-and-blues artists due to the inspiration of Henry Roeland (Roy) Byrd, the undisputed king of New Orleans piano players and the guiding light to a generation of musicians in the Crescent City. A one-time professional gambler, cook, and jitney driver, Byrd developed his extraordinary knowledge of rhythms as a tap dancer and later transferred that sophistication to the piano. Recording under a variety of names, including Professor Longhair, Byrd played calypso, mambo, and rhumba rhythms, often adding one melodic line with his right hand, another with his voice, and, on occasion, yet another by whistling. Latin time signatures had a long history in New Orleans dating back at least as far as the *habaniera* music of the nineteenth century, and calypso singers Cabana Joe and Jamaica Johnnie had popular records in the city in the forties. But Byrd's synthesis of styles added a new dimension. Although he had few hits of his own, subsequent rock-and-roll stars from New Orleans like Archibald, the Spiders, James Wayne, Huey Smith, and Robert Parker all owed a debt to the rhythms of Professor Longhair. Yet Spanish influence had already pervaded many forms of American music via other sources.[52]

Big bands such as Xavier Cugat's and Jimmy Dorsey's had enjoyed commercial success in the early forties with Spanish-sounding novelty numbers ("Perfidia," "Maria Elena") and the vogue continued after the war, reaching its nadir with Frank Sinatra's insulting "The Coffee Song." In a more serious vein, Dizzy Gillespie brought African-Cuban cult drummer Chano Pozo from Cuba to New York to add more authentic and sophisticated Latin rhythm to jazz. Operating somewhere between the frivolity of "The Coffee Song" and the artistry of Chano Pozo, Louis Jordan recorded a calypso number, "Run Joe," that became a best-seller in 1948. Country musicians drew on a long history of Latin influences in their music, but they also followed trends in jazz and popular music, as evidenced by Jim Reeves's 1953 hit "Mexican Joe," Hank Snow's "Rhumba Boogie" in 1951, and Snow's ode to cultural pluralism, "When Mexican Joe met Jole Blon," a hit in 1953.

German, Polish, and other European music also contributed to the new urban music of the postwar era. Berl Adams and Irving Green formed Mercury Records in 1947 with the intention of specializing in polka music and rhythm and blues. Frankie Laine became the label's first big star by copying the vocal style of blues singer Charles Brown on "That's My Desire," by imitating Gene Autry and other western singers on "Mule Train," and even by adopting polka music as his own with "Metro Polka." Laine could listen to blues and polka musicians in Mercury's studios, then use the same producers on his records, but the interactions between polka, blues, and country music had already been well established before then. Early New Orleans Dixieland music grew out of the application of African rhythms to European instruments and song forms. When black musicians played the marches, quadrilles, and polkas popularized by white bands, they syncopated the polka and they applied the off-beats of the polka to marches, creating a two-beat sound with the accent on the second.[53] The resulting 2/4 beat became a staple of African-American dance music that made it accessible to country musicians like Bob Wills, who grew up listening to polka music played by Czech and German musicians in Texas. Bill Boyd and his Cowboy Ramblers had a western swing hit record in 1936 with "Under the Double Eagle," a German marching song that Bob Wills later converted into a classic polka, "Texas Double Eagle." Bill Monroe, the founder of modern bluegrass music, learned the "Heel and Toe Polka" from his mother, although he later refined his concept of instrumental music listening to black dance ensembles while working as a barrel loader and washer in an oil refinery in East Chicago, Indiana, in the thirties. Willie Nelson, an admirer of Bob Wills, supplemented his income as a country musician in the postwar years by performing in polka bands in his native central Texas. The composer of "Pistol Packin' Mama," Al Dexter, made the best-seller lists in 1946 with "Guitar Polka No. 1." When country and blues musicians moved to the cities, their music contained elements of those interactions with the polka, and they quickly attracted the attention of Polish and German working-class people.[54]

After World War II, polka music became closer to commercial country music, in part because of the emergence of a more country sound from within. During the war, big band music heavily influenced polka styles due to numbers like Johnny Mercer's "Strip Polka." But as country music began to win the approval of northern audiences, Li'l Wally Jagiello from Chicago rose to prominence in polka circles with a country-oriented polka sound. Based on the folk music of rural Poland, Jagiello's "Chicago Style" emphasized a unity between instrument and voice featuring heartfelt, emotional interpretations of standard songs. In place of the sophisticated ensemble work of clarinet and saxophone players common to popular polka music of the war years, Jagiello accompanied his plaintive singing with a whining concertina and a bass drum, which he played with his foot. The "Chicago Style" seemed primitive, repetitive, and hopelessly sentimental to some listeners, particularly those from the East Coast, but its immediacy and emotion captured the affections of many more and it became the dominant force in polka music by the early fifties.[55]

Li'l Wally Jagiello's success paved the way for new interactions between country and polka musicians. Frankie Yankovic and his Yanks made a best-selling polka record in 1948 out of an old country song, "Just Because," and the same group enjoyed commercial success in 1949 with "The Blue Skirt Waltz," another polka-country hybrid. The ever-observant Louis Jordan responded to the conversation among different kinds of music with an urban cross-breed of his own in 1950, "Tamburitza Boogie," celebrating the popular Eastern European stringed instrument by placing it inside blues chord progressions and rhythms.

Workers drawn to the cities by the work force needs of American industry retained features of their traditional cultures, but they also combined them with others to form a polyglot urban working-class culture. The social meanings previously conveyed in isolation through blues, country, polka, zydeco, and tango music took on new dimensions as they blended together in an urban setting. Rock and roll music grew out of this crucible, accelerating and intensifying interactions among ethnic groups. The careers of Bill Haley, Chuck Berry, and Elvis Presley demonstrate the dramatically new interracial context made possible in the postwar era.

Bill Haley grew up in Detroit and led a series of western swing ensembles in the forties. While working as a record librarian in a radio station in Chester, Pennsylvania (a shipbuilding center), he became intrigued by Louis Jordan's music and by the idea of a country-and-western group that could perform rhythm and blues. After "covering" blues singer Jackie Brenston's "Rocket 88" for a local Philadelphia label, Haley and his group signed with Decca Records, where they worked with Milt Gabler, who had produced most of Louis Jordan's hits. Consciously copying the Tympany Five, but retaining more of a country sound, Bill Haley and His Comets found a musical formula that resulted in seventeen best-selling records between 1954 and 1956. The exaggerated beat of their records appealed to both black and white audiences, and the inclusion of "Rock around the Clock" in the 1955 film *Blackboard Jungle* made that song a symbol of teenage rebellion and desire. Music that had once expressed the worldview of primarily marginal groups now began to assume center stage.

A cosmetologist and a carpenter's son from St. Louis, Chuck Berry also developed new musical forms that spoke to changing social realities. Berry's music came from the same origins as Haley's: the blues, country, and Louis Jordan. "I identify myself with Louis Jordan more than any other artist," he told one interviewer. Berry's rhythms, vocal style, sense of humor, and versatility all bore the marks of Jordan's influence.[56] Berry could sing the blues so effectively that Muddy Waters personally recommended him for an audition at Chess Records, but he established himself as a commercial force by proving that he could sing country-and-western lyrics to a rhythm-and-blues background.

Berry eventually signed a contract to record for the Chess brothers in 1955, after having been rejected by both Mercury and Capitol Records because to the executives at those companies his demonstration song, "Ida Red," sounded too much like country music to be a hit for a black singer. Although Chess Records specialized in blues, they let Berry record "Ida Red," adding a stronger beat and changing its title to "Maybelline." The song became one of the best-selling records of the year, demonstrating the commercial viability of Berry's fusion between the blues and country music. Berry also recorded blues songs for Chess, and he had hits with many different styles. His songs became especially popular among country musicians, while Berry's fellow blues singers marveled at his mastery of both genres. As Jimmy Witherspoon declared, "Chuck Berry is a country singer. People put everybody in categories, black, white, this. Now if Chuck Berry was white, with the lyrics he writes, he would be the top country star in the world."[57]

Berry never received proper recognition for his important contributions to U.S. culture. Not until a white singer steeped in black musical forms crossed the same barriers did American popular music concede, however grudgingly, the worth of working-class musical forms. Possibilities submerged within the music of Jimmie Rodgers, Louis Jordan, Bob Wills, Hank Williams, Bill Haley, and Chuck Berry became realized in the commercial success of Elvis Presley.

Presley learned to sing at the Assembly of God church, at revival and camp meetings, and from the country and blues singers he heard on the radio as a youth in Tupelo, Mississippi. His family moved to Memphis in 1948, where his father secured employment packing paint cans into boxes for $.83 an hour. After graduating from high school in 1953, Elvis Presley went to work for the Crown Electric Company as a truck driver making a salary of $40 a week. But he looked to a career in music as a possible means of escape from a life of low-paying and unsatisfying jobs.[58]

Presley's deliveries sometimes took him past the Memphis Recording Service, a firm that invited the public to pay four dollars to make recordings for their personal use. A subsidiary of Sun Records, one of the small independent labels specializing in country music and blues that emerged after the war, the Memphis Recording Service beckoned to the truck driver with a passion for music. Sam Phillips, the founder of Sun Records, reputedly boasted that he would make a fortune if he could find a white singer who sounded black. Phillips's office manager heard Presley's recording and directed her boss's attention to the unusual qualities in the young man's voice. Sam Phillips arranged a recording session for Presley, but it was not until the session itself in August 1954 that the singer's true talents became evident. And then it happened by accident.

While the other musicians took a short break, Presley broke into an impromptu and half-joking rendition of "That's All Right," a 1946 hit by Arthur "Big Boy" Crudup, a black timber worker and field hand, whose music Presley heard on the radio as a boy. Bass player Bill Black and lead guitarist Scotty Moore joined in, and Sam Phillips liked what he heard so much that he decided to record the song just as they played it during the break. Presley's vocal copied the original, even mimicking Crudup's scat singing note for note at one point, but the rhythm came out of country music with its heavy accent on the first and third beats in the style of the Carter Family records of the thirties and forties. Phillips released "That's All Right" as a single record with "Blue Moon of Kentucky" on the other side, a selection that also came about because of some improvisation during a break. Bill Black did a deliberately exaggerated impersonation of bluegrass singer Bill Monroe, and the others joined in to do a rocking blues adaptation of the original. Thus, Presley's first record had a white interpretation of a black song on one side, and a black-influenced version of a white song on the other.[59] Presley's subsequent efforts for Sun Records followed the same pattern, culminating in the pairing of "Mystery Train," originally recorded by blues singer Junior Parker, and the country-oriented "I Forgot to Remember to Forget." Both sides of that record became hits, and their success led to the purchase of Presley's contract from Sun by RCA Records.

RCA producers never captured Presley's enormous talents in quite the same way that Sam Phillips had, but Presley's ability to rise above the deficient imagination of his producers coupled with the superior marketing power of RCA proved a potent combination. RCA purchased Presley's services for $35,000. For their investment he produced thirty-one of the company's thirty-nine million-selling records between 1956 and 1962, nine of their forty million-selling albums, and an estimated 25 percent of their total sales between 1956 and 1966.[60] Those accomplishments did a lot for RCA and a lot for Elvis Presley, but they also established the commercial viability of music previously considered "too black" to be taken seriously by a mass audience.

For black musicians, Elvis Presley's success presented a cruel paradox. With his extraordinary singing, hypnotic stage presence, and mastery of all forms of southern music, Presley deserved to succeed. But once again, black people found their culture serving as the basis for someone else's financial gain. The music-buying public rewarded Presley for his versions of "That's All Right," "Mystery Train," and "Hound Dog," while largely ignoring the black artists who made the original versions of those songs. The exciting and enticing gestures that provoked controversy and interest in Presley had long been part of the acts of several black entertainers who received no comparable attention paid to their art. Ray Charles, whose own definitive synthesis of black and white music has never attained its deserved acclaim, recalled the attention paid to Presley's stage movements as an insult to black entertainers, asserting, "Ain't no way they'd let anybody like us get on stage and do that but he could 'cause he's white."[61] In a similar vein, Louis Jordan refused to see rock and roll as anything other than a white expropriation of black music, bitterly remembering his own experiences: "I lived in New York for twelve years and I've had white musicians hang around me twenty-four hours if I would let 'em, hang around until they learned something from me. And then I couldn't go to hear them play!"[62]

The attention paid to Presley slighted the contributions of black musicians to his style, but his success did not work to the disadvantage of all black artists. Spurred by the rise of interest in rock and roll stimulated by the Presley phenomenon, record sales in 1955 reached $227 million (as opposed to $189 million in 1950), and they continued to increase in succeeding years, opening up opportunities for both black and white musicians—although, of course, not on an equal basis.[63] Presley's success assaulted some of the "standards" and conventions of popular music that served to exclude black styles. After Presley, all American popular music, in one way or another, acknowledged a debt to the rich musical heritage of black people, creating new possibilities for black artists. As the legendary blues musician Brownie McGhee expressed it, "See the blues was ostracized to the black man only once. But when rock 'n' roll came in, you understand, it opened up the valley of enjoyment for everyone! It wasn't the black people's music anymore. Was anybody's music! It became commercial when everybody started gettin' onto the train, see. Because when it was C.P. [colored people] and Race, that put you in your place."[64]

The transformation from black people's music into anybody's music also entailed a shift from working people's culture to anyone's culture. The ascendancy of rock and roll involved more than a change in popular taste; it represented the capacity of a working-class worldview to express the attitudes and interests of nearly all of society. The popularity of rock and roll was no accident; it came about because the working-class understanding of the world that was embodied in rock-and-roll's lyrics, functions, and forms gained credibility with large numbers of people.

Rock and roll originated in the traditional music of black and white working-class communities, and its leading artists came from working-class backgrounds. But its identity as working-class music went beyond that. As the heir to an oral tradition that stressed the primacy of human beings over the logic of production, rock-and-roll music expressed the same critique of work, hierarchy, and exploitation manifested in the strikes, demonstrations, and primary work groups of the postwar years. Rock and roll understood the world of work, but it expressed the hope of something better.

Originating in preindustrial societies, oral cultures carry an implicit critique of industrial organization. They stress group solidarity instead of the self-regulating individual, value immediate emotional experience more than deferred gratification, and assert the primacy of everyday experience over abstract ideas. Under industrial conditions, an oral tradition serves as a collective memory of better times, as well as a means of making the present more bearable. Country music and blues bequeathed the concerns of their respective oral traditions to rock and roll, and it carried their subversive message throughout society.

By the standards of a literate culture, rock-and-roll music may seem ill-suited to conveying any message, subversive or not. Its use of nonsense syllables and scat singing, reliance on stock musical and verbal phrases, immersion in the ordinary experiences of everyday life, and simplistic descriptions of reality hardly seem a challenge to the industrial system. Yet what fails by one standard may succeed by another. Whatever it lacked in analysis, description, and qualification, rock-and-roll music more than compensated for in emotion, empathy, and concreteness. Hank Williams once explained the art of country-music songwriting by warning, "You've got to know a lot about hard work."[65] Once you do, a music that expresses immediate personal feelings, that connects people with each other, and that finds meaning in the ordinary details of everyday life takes on increased importance. Rock-and-roll lyrics talked about loving, working, eating, sleeping, buying, and the connections between all those activities. If one views politics as only the public struggle for political power, then rock-and-roll songs were apolitical. But if one defines politics as the social struggle for a good life, then these songs represent politics of the highest order.

The politics of rock and roll expressed themselves in the process and experience of the music itself as well as in their inscribed message. They demanded a release of energy and emotion. Louis Jordan wanted his music to "make you forget what you'd had to do the day before and just have a good time, a great time," but he was never completely escapist. Tonight's good time always depended on the gap between "what you'd had to do the day before" and what you wanted to do, and it kept your mind on both.[66] Like the songs of Bob Wills and Hank Williams, Jordan's humor remained rooted in the experiences and language of everyday life, and it assumed particular dignity from persevering in the face of difficulties. That determination permeated the lyrics of rock-and-roll songs and crystallized their distinctive worldview.

Little Richard demonstrated one relationship between the world of work and the world of rock and roll in his first songwriting efforts. As he later recalled, "I was working in the Greyhound bus station in Macon, Georgia, oh my Lord, I was washing dishes. I couldn't talk back to my boss man. He would bring all those pots back for me to wash, and one day I said, 'I've got to do something to stop that man bringing back all those pots to me to wash,' and I said, 'Awap bop-a lop bop-a-wop bam boomm, take em out!' and that's how I came to write 'Tutti Frutti.' "[67]

Bill Haley's "Rock around the Clock," Elvis Presley's "Blue Suede Shoes," and Chuck Berry's "Roll Over Beethoven," became anthems of rock and roll because they proudly and defiantly asserted group solidarity and rejected respectability. In "Rip It Up," Little Richard boasts of his intention to have a wild evening rather than save his paycheck, an intention more consistent with the immediate emotional needs of working-class life than with the socially approved rational planning for the future encouraged by the middle class. Little Richard's glee comes as much from rebelling against those standards as it does from the anticipated good time. Chuck Berry glorifies the joys of rock and roll in "School Days" by depicting them as a response to the indignities of life in high school. The appeal of a Saturday night drinking spree in Fats Domino's "Blue Monday" comes in response to the pain of thinking about having to get up and go to work during the rest of the week. These songs do not plot social revolution, but they do keep alive hopes for a better life. Like the mass demonstration and wildcat strike, the good time in rock-and-roll songs elevates the world of play over the world of work, and it carves away a limited sphere of autonomy in an increasingly regimented world.

Rock and roll also served functions different from those provided by previous popular music. Artists and audiences remained close; in fact, they were sometimes interchangeable. Groups like Sonny Til and the Orioles or Frankie Lymon and the Teenagers had an amateurish quality about them, and they went right from singing on street corners to making records with no opportunity to polish their skills and gain a professional sound. What they lacked in technical virtuosity they more than made up for in emotion, sincerity, and audience identification. Even the stars with clearly superior musical talents had to reach their audiences in a personal or emotional way, a relation between performer and listener first developed on this continent in black music. As Max Roach, one of the leading African-American musicians of the postwar era, explained, "No matter how much technique you have got, if you don't create some kind of emotion or some kind of electricity between yourself and somebody else, it don't mean a damned thing—whether you are a writer, a painter, a musician, what have you. We have come from that school as black people that when somebody doesn't get something from you, then you don't have anything anyway."[68]

The Grand Old Opry comedienne Minnie Pearl expressed similar sentiments when defending Hank Williams against claims that other people could sing as well or better than he did. Acknowledging that she'd heard better voices, Pearl insisted that "they'd never get that cataclysmic reaction from the audience that Hank got."[69] The frenzied behavior of fans at concerts by Elvis Presley, Chuck Berry, or Little Richard sometimes seemed to outsiders to reflect uncontrolled hysteria; but in reality they demonstrated a collective understanding of the responsibility of artists to "give something" to their listeners.

As with past forms of working-class music, rock and roll enabled people to experience in their art what had been missing from their lives, but with a difference. Never before had working-class art and the worldview contained within it been as accessible to other groups, and never before had working-class resentments against hierarchy and exploitation expressed the feelings of so many people. Working-class music, with its active, original, collective, emotional, and self-affirming content, provided not only a different view of work and art, it prefigured an entirely different form of social organization. No artistic form by itself carries a liberating content, but rock and roll historically merged with resistance to capitalism in the past and a spirit of independence in the present to stimulate utopian hopes for the future.

The worldview and functions of rock-and-roll music came from traditional forms of country music and blues. Rock and roll stressed a unity between instruments and voice, evidenced call-and-response patterns and blues chord progressions, and explored the entire range of potential sounds by both voice and instruments. These forms appealed to the audience's collective memory of the past, but they also continued to contradict the values of alienated labor in the present.

As commodities produced and distributed by highly centralized monopolies, rock-and-roll records lost some of the spontaneity and variety of earlier working-class folk music. Record companies censored lyrics, narrowed the range of "acceptable" musical forms, cheated artists out of deserved royalties, standardized diverse musical styles in the pursuit of commercial success, and encouraged a division between artists and consumers. In addition, the masculine flight from responsibility and the needy narcissism in song lyrics often privileged men over women, individual pleasure over group obligations, and self-indulgent consumption over purposeful production.

Yet the people who sold culture could not create it. In order to attract the allegiance of a mass market, they had to make concessions to the tastes and musical histories of their customers, and they unwittingly preserved and extended the social criticisms contained in working-class music. The power of commercial distribution homogenized some aspects of working-class experience, but it also enabled people from diverse backgrounds to share a common experience, one that centered around a working-class critique of American society.

What the mass demonstration and wildcat strike provided in political life, rock-and-roll music realized in culture. Both originated in the working class, both expressed a resentment against hierarchy and a celebration of future possibilities, and both became symbols of liberation for people inside and outside the working class. Neither led to a revolution, but both imbedded themselves between the power of the system and popular resistance, where they remain to this day.

NOTES

1. Brenda McCallum, "Songs of Work and Songs of Worship: Sanctifying Black Unionism in the Southern City of Steel," *New York Folklore* 19, nos. 1–2 (1988): 20.

2. Ibid., 15, 17, 18, 19.

3. Ibid., 16, 22, 23, 27, 25.

4. Robbie Lieberman, *"My Song Is My Weapon": People's Songs, American Communism, and the Politics of Culture, 1930–50* (Urbana: University of Illinois Press, 1989), xix. The phrase "corrupt, mindless popular culture" is Lieberman's, but I use it here because I believe the phrase is an accurate, and telling, indication of the Communist party's view of popular culture, which differs sharply from my own.

5. Quoted in ibid., 135.

6. *Billboard*, Nov. 14, 1946; Louis Jordan, "Ain't Nobody Here but Us Chickens," Decca Records 23741.

7. George P. Rawick, *From Sundown to Sunup* (Westport, Conn.: Greenwood Press, 1972), 98.

8. Arnold Shaw, *Honkers and Shouters* (New York: Macmillan, 1978), 84. The story line of this song appeared in country music songs in the twenties, and varia-

tions of it have been found in a variety of ethnic folk tales. Yet even if this version of the story did not originate in Africa, it is clearly based on the form of African tales of the kind described by Rawick.

9. For example, Paul Whiteman became the "King of Jazz" in the twenties and Benny Goodman became the "King of Swing" in the thirties by playing watered-down versions of black music. To be fair, Goodman's appropriation was far more knowing than Whiteman's, and to his credit, Goodman desegregated white big bands by featuring Teddy Wilson and Billie Holiday in his quartet and orchestra. The Mills Brothers are an example of an African-American group that enjoyed commercial success by sounding "white."

10. Melville Herskovits, *The Myth of the Negro Past* (Boston: Beacon, 1958); Rawick, *From Sundown to Sunup*; Amiri Baraka (LeRoi Jones), *Blues People* (New York: William Morrow, 1963); Ben Sidran, *Black Talk* (New York: Holt, Rinehard, and Winston, 1971); Sterling Stuckey, *Slave Culture* (New York: Oxford, 1987).

11. Rawick, *From Sundown to Sunup*, 7.

12. Baraka, *Blues People*, 26; Rawick, *From Sundown to Sunup*, 45–46. Drums played such an important role in slave communications that slave owners often banned them or restricted their use.

13. Rob Walser to George Lipsitz, personal communication, Dec. 19, 1992.

14. Shaw, *Honkers and Shouters*, 87.

15. Nathan Irvin Huggins, *Harlem Renaissance* (New York: Oxford, 1971); David Roediger, *The Wages of Whiteness* (London: Verso, 1991).

16. Joel Whitburn, *Top Pop Records, 1940–1955* (Menomonee, Wisc.: Record Research, n.d.), 29; "Choo Choo Ch'Boogie," Decca 23610; Shaw, *Honkers and Shouters*, 70.

17. George Lipsitz and Daniel Czitrom, "We Don't Read Adorno in Muskogee," paper presented at the Mid-Atlantic Radical History Organization meeting, Apr. 17, 1977, New York, N.Y.

18. Bill C. Malone, *Country Music, U.S.A.* (Austin: University of Texas Press, 1968), 14–15.

19. Ibid., 36.

20. Robert Shelton and Burt Goldblatt, *The Country Music Story* (Secaucus, N.J.: Castle Books, 1966), 31–32.

21. *Old Time Music*, no. 2 (Autumn 1971): 15.

22. Chris Comber and Mike Paris, "Jimmie Rodgers," in Bill C. Malone and Judith McCulloh, eds., *Stars of Country Music: Uncle Dave Macon to Johnny Rodriguez* (Urbana: University of Illinois Press, 1975), 123–24; "Blue Yodel #9," on *My Rough and Rowdy Ways*, RCA Victor LPM 2112

23. Shaw, *Honkers and Shouters*, 302, 104.

24. John Atkins, "The Carter Family," in Malone and McCulloh, *Stars of Country Music*, 99.

25. Peter Guralnick, *Feel like Goin' Home* (New York: Harper and Row, 1971), 47; Shaw, *Honkers and Shouters*, 294–301.

26. Steve Chapple and Reebee Garofalo, *Rock'n'Roll Is Here to Pay* (Chicago: Nelson-Hall, 1977), 243.

27. Ibid., 6.

28. Ibid., 8; Malone, *Country Music, U.S.A.*, 200.

29. Whitburn, *Top Pop Records*, 16–17.

30. Shaw, *Honkers and Shouters*, 63.

31. Chapple and Garofalo, *Rock'n'Roll Is Here to Pay*, 29.

32. Shaw, *Honkers and Shouters*, 89–92, 275–314, 247–56; Tony Heilbut, *The Gospel Sound* (New York: Simon and Schuster, 1971), 297.

33. Charles R. Townsend, *San Antonio Rose: The Life and Music of Bob Wills* (Urbana: University of Illinois Press, 1986), 40. Rob Walser tells me that Wills follows an old tradition here; J.S. Bach walked two hundred miles to hear Buxtehude play the organ.

34. Ibid., 40.

35. Ibid., 60, 62, 74.

36. *Time*, Feb. 11, 1946.

37. Townsend, *San Antonio Rose*, 356, 348.

38. Ibid., 269.

39. Arnold Shaw, *The World of Soul* (New York: Cowles Book Company, 1970), 233.

40. Berry's original title for "Maybelline" was "Ida Red." See Chapple and Garofalo, *Rock'n'Roll Is Here To Pay*, 39.

41. Charlie Gillet, *The Sound of the City* (New York: E. P. Dutton, 1970), 16.

42. Roger M. Williams, "Hank Williams," in Malone and McCulloh, *Stars of Country Music*, 252.

43. "Disc Jockeys," *Ebony*, Dec. 1947, 44.

44. Chapple and Garofalo, *Rock'n'Roll Is Here to Pay*, 31, 34.

45. Ibid., 31, 57; Shaw, *Honkers and Shouters*, 188.

46. Joel Whitburn, *Top Rhythm and Blues Records, 1949–1971* (Menomonee, Wisc.: Record Research, n.d.), 103, 41, 96–97, 19; Shaw, *Honkers and Shouters*, 179–84.

47. "Bull Moose Jackson," *Ebony*, Jan. 1950, 27.

48. Shaw, *Honkers and Shouters*, 278. Jackson, Raney, Penny, and Harris all recorded for King Records, which used the cover system as a way to extend old publishing royalties into new markets. The executives at King felt that whites would not buy records by blacks and vice versa, but their own decisions may have helped change that.

49. Whitburn, *Top Rhythm and Blues Records*, 74. Rex Allen and Darrell Glenn had successful country versions of "Crying in the Chapel" and placed slightly higher on the pop charts with them than did the version by the Orioles.

50. See the liner notes to "Zydeco," Arhoolie Records, F1009.

51. Bill C. Malone, "A Shower of Stars," in Malone and McCulloh, *Stars of Country Music*, 403; John Broven, *Rhythm and Blues in New Orleans* (Gretna, La.: Pelican, 1974), 132.

52. John Storm Roberts, *The Latin Tinge* (New York: Oxford), 1979. See also the liner notes to Dr. John's album on Atco SD 7006 Gumbo and the article on Professor Longhair in *Living Blues*, Mar.–Apr. 1976, 16–29.

53. Andres Hodier, *Jazz: Its Evolution and Essence* (New York: Grove Press, 1956), 195, 211.

54. Ralph Rinzler, "Bill Monroe," in Malone and McCulloh, *Stars of Country Music*, 206; Malone, "A Shower of Stars," 438; Malone, *Country Music, U.S.A.*, 172–73; Townsend, *San Antonio Rose*, 367.

55. Angela and Charles Keil, "In Pursuit of Polka Happiness," *Cultural Correspondence*, no. 5 (Summer-Fall 1977): 9–10.

56. Shaw, *Honkers and Shouters*, 64.

57. Ibid., 215.

58. Jerry Hopkins, *Elvis* (New York: Simon and Schuster, 1971), 37.

59. Ibid., 62.

60. Chapple and Garofalo, *Rock'n'Roll Is Here to Pay*, 210.

61. Ibid., 246.

62. Shaw, *Honkers and Shouters*, 74.

63. Chapple and Garofalo, *Rock'n'Roll Is Here to Pay*, 69.

64. *Living Blues*, Summer 1973, 23.

65. *Nation's Business*, Feb. 1953, 51.

66. Shaw, *Honkers and Shouters*, 74.

67. Arnold Shaw, *The Rockin' 50s* (New York: Hawthorn Books, 1974), 162.

68. Max Roach, "What 'Jazz' Means to Me," *Black Scholar*, Summer 1972, 5.

69. Roger M. Williams, "Hank Williams," in Malone and McCulloh, *Stars of Country Music*, 245.

What Labor Lost, and Why

IT IS NEVER easy to make radical changes in society, to dislodge ideas and practices that have been around for centuries. In *The Eighteenth Brumaire of Louis Bonaparte*, Karl Marx explains that "the tradition of all the dead generations weighs like a nightmare on the brain of the living." Marx found it particularly galling that in potentially revolutionary situations, people sometimes subvert meaningful change because their old ideas and traditional categories hide from them the emerging possibilities of their moment in history.[1]

Through general strikes, mass demonstrations, shop-floor insurgencies, and cultural creativity, workers in the United States in the postwar years lifted some of the weight of "the tradition of all the dead generations" from their minds. They took advantage of new circumstances to struggle openly for power over their lives and to win space for private and public roles previously denied to them. They won important gains by relying on direct-action protest and mass mobilization.

Yet a massive counterattack by leaders of business, government, and even labor unions themselves prevented workers from finding the forms of struggle capable of realizing fully the new possibilities they saw all around them. In the end, the most powerful people and institutions in U. S. society succeeded in reinscribing what Marx called the old "names, battle cries and costumes" on the new realities, restoring the rule of the dead weight of tradition.

Understanding exactly how much labor won in those years helps us place in perspective how much they lost. At peak moments of the struggle, for instance when black workers won jobs in mass-production industries, secured apartments in government-sponsored housing projects, and gained prominent places within emerging forms of popular culture, they crippled a system of segregation that had seemed invincible before the war began. Women workers proved that they could perform production tasks efficiently, participate in union struggles, and pool their resources to make gains as individuals and as a group. In securing concessions on wages and benefits, workers from different backgrounds, job classifications, and industries united to challenge the prerogatives of management and the legitimacy of the state. They took direct action to secure greater participation in the decisions that affected their lives. Seemingly static categories of race, class, and gender shifted their meanings radically, while workers joined together to fashion a new public sphere and to advance an egalitarian agenda for new kinds of job and community relations.

Yet very rapidly, this "new scene of world history" became saturated with old battle cries and a borrowed language. Leaders of government, business, and labor worked together to remove women from high-paying production jobs, to relegate black and Latino workers to secondary segments of the labor market, and to repress direct democracy on the factory floor and in the community. In the wake of urban renewal and suburbanization, automation and job-control schemes on the factory floor, intense anticommunist assaults and the growth of a new corporate culture organized around patriarchy and consumption, rank-and-file workers never found the means to translate their strategies of independence into effective struggles for power.[2]

One legacy of labor's postwar struggles has been the increasing importance of gender and race in U.S. society, both as forms of domination and as focal points of resistance. In her studies of women workers in the auto and electronics industries during World War II, Ruth Milkman shows how employers and unions made it difficult for women to stay in high-paying production jobs. Companies feared political and shop-floor opposition to postwar male unemployment, but they reasoned correctly that working-class ideals of the male "family wage" would make unions and male workers unconcerned about female unemployment. In one of the few cases where a union did take a strong stand in favor of female workers (in the electrical industry), anticommunism so neutralized union power that management could easily ignore their demands.[3]

Women fought their employers and their unions in a valiant effort to maintain wartime gains. Even those relegated to gender-segregated jobs displayed tenacious militancy in the postwar period. For example, several hundred thousand women workers stunned the Bell Telephone System when they staged a militant nationwide strike in April 1947. In New Jersey, the governor invoked extremely harsh antistrike measures twelve minutes after the walkout began, but the women defied him and remained on strike.

The striking telephone workers complained about a wide variety of grievances, but statements by two of the workers demonstrate the role that working-class aspirations for independence played in the dispute. "We're telling the company we're not part of the switchboard any more," said one striker from Connecticut.[4] Another indicated a clear political direction when she said,

> I'm ready to admit our people could get a lot more done without really extending themselves. But why should they? They'll never do it as long as they believe the boss, not the worker, will get the benefit from their working harder. You can talk yourself blue in the face about how prosperity for everybody depends on high production. You'll never make it real to the worker in the shop unless he feels that he is a partner in the business. And when I say partner, I mean partner. That's not just something in an annual report or a Christmas message from the front office. Partnership is something that affects the whole running of the plant. You've got to give the workers a voice in how these things are done and how the profits are divided.[5]

Her sentiments reflected the social vision behind much of the postwar strike wave, a vision of democracy on the shop floor, production for human needs, and a society that respects people more than money.

Yet the trade unions and radical parties failed to mobilize a mass movement to advance the ideas expressed so cogently by that worker in the telephone industry and by millions like her. Leaders of these groups fought to maintain their own institutional positions and in the process collaborated with the sexism and racism that works so well to separate white male organized workers from women, racial "minorities," and the unorganized.

Of course, trade unions and radical parties had their own indigenous traditions of defining the class struggle in gendered terms. Their metaphors often posed labor activism as an essential part of the defense of working-class "manhood." Consequently, they never saw women as workers on equal terms with men.[6] The social democratic public and private welfare policies that emerged after the war also reflected traditional gender coding. Within them, men's welfare benefits stemmed from their wages, military service, or union membership while women's benefits came mainly in regard to their roles in child rearing. Like the New Deal and Progressive Era policies that preceded them, these policies defined men as workers and women as mothers and as a result countenanced lower pay and benefits for women while defining full employment only as full white male employment.[7]

In some cases during the postwar era, women attempted to use their social identities as women and mothers to make particular interventions in labor disputes. In at least four instances, women took over picket lines in postwar America when it appeared that male strikers were in difficulty. After particularly brutal arrests demoralized male strikers during the Rochester organizing campaign of 1946 (see chap. 5), women joined with the clergy to present police officers with a crowd that they might feel reticent about brutalizing.[8] In the Bucyrus-Erie strike in Evansville in 1948 (see chap. 9), a court injunction and 140 state police officers forced the opening of the factory, but a picket line composed of 7 women kept all but 420 of the firm's 1,100 workers from going to work.[9] Wives of striking workers took over a picket line at Bell Aircraft in New York in October 1949 and precipitated a full-fledged battle. Wearing helmets and swinging clubs, the women attacked three engineers crossing the union picket line. Deputy sheriffs tried to arrest some of the women, battling with them and their husbands until low-flying helicopters broke up the melee by dropping tear-gas bombs on the crowd.[10] A strike that appeared to be lost in Silver City, New Mexico (the one dramatized in the film *Salt of the Earth*, see chap. 12), turned around late in 1951 when the wives of members of the International Union of Mine, Mill, and Smelter Workers Local 890 assumed responsibility for the picket lines over their husband's objections. An injunction banned picketing by union members but said nothing about their wives, whose courage and dignity led the strikers to at least a partial victory.[11] But while these interventions proved effective tactically and politically, they also stand as poor substitutes for the struggles women workers were not able to wage on their own behalf.

Milkman points out that political mobilizations by black organizations in defense centers like Detroit enabled African-American workers to retain more of their wartime gains than did women. Her point about political mobilization is absolutely correct—it aided black workers in crucial ways, and more mobilization outside the factories would have helped all groups of workers. Yet, it is clear that the failure of trade unions to fight for full and nondiscriminatory employment also had a disastrous effect on the status of black workers in the economy. These failures hurt black women most of all; they lost more in the postwar period than any other group of workers.[12] Black male workers did secure more jobs in the late forties than they had access to previously, and they even temporarily closed the wage gap between themselves and white male workers. But they remained segmented in job classifications that excluded them from most of the benefits won by white male workers in the postwar era.

Black workers fought hard to retain the jobs in heavy industry that they won during the war. But their low seniority made them extremely vulnerable to layoffs in the postwar era. During the early reconversion period in 1945 and 1946, unemployment for blacks increased twice as fast as for whites. Black unemployment for 1947 stood at 5.4 percent at a time when only 3.3 percent of white workers were unemployed.[13]

In July 1949, the Westinghouse Refrigerator plant in Lima, Ohio, cut its entire work force by 50 percent, but the company laid off nearly 80 percent of the slightly more than 300 black workers employed there.[14] The business agent for United Electrical Workers Local 427 in Jersey City, New Jersey, told a statewide conference in 1950 that black workers bore the major burden of layoffs in the entire industry, noting that blacks made up 20 percent of the laid-off workers in New York, 50 percent of the laid-off workers in Toledo and Chicago, and 71 percent of all people on relief in Detroit.[15] By 1954, black unemployment levels were twice as high as the levels reported for whites.[16] Even more ominously, that ratio remained static for the next twenty years and was even more pronounced for educated black workers than it was for those with only a minimum amount of schooling.[17]

By redefining full employment as white male employment, trade unions and big corporations produced a racialized social democracy that relegated blacks to a separate segment of the economy. Black workers in the important twenty-five to forty-four age group faced unemployment levels three times greater than whites in the same age bracket. In addition, almost all of the job gains made by black workers came in semiskilled positions, which proved most vulnerable to automation and to seasonal layoffs. Underemployment also plagued black workers, as only 50 percent of blacks could expect year-round employment, while 67 percent of whites had regular full-time work. Government statistics indicated that blacks were overrepresented among the working poor, had lower median incomes, and were much more likely to be laid off or injured.[18]

Because of their segmentation in the labor market, black workers had far less access to union medical and pension plans than did white workers. Social democratic programs outside the factory also took on a racialized identity. Like other taxpayers, blacks helped support the FHA and other government-sponsored home-loan institutions, but they received few benefits from them. Discriminatory policies by private realtors and by FHA appraisers left black workers facing a chronic shortage of housing; they invariably wound up paying more for housing than other workers, but still received lower quality. Because they were less likely to be homeowners, black workers also lost out on the generous homeowners' tax deduction, and consequently they paid higher taxes on average on their incomes than white workers. Federal and state subsidies for locating new factories in suburban areas while cutting back on public transportation in central cities also further funneled the benefits of federal spending away from blacks and toward suburban whites.

The growing gap between black and white workers helped fuel the black civil rights movement of the postwar era. Returning black war veterans met in Atlanta in the winter of 1945–46 to pledge their efforts to pursue "a full share of democracy." A similar group marched on the courthouse in Birmingham, Alabama, to protest denial of voting rights to blacks. Yet with

the war emergency over, they faced declining support from the federal government and renewed racism from many civilians. South Carolina police
officers blinded a black veteran in uniform in February 1946, dragging him
off a bus and jabbing him in the eyes with their nightsticks. Five months
later, a mob of whites near Monroe, Georgia, pulled four blacks from their
car and fired sixty shots into their bodies.[19] Harry Truman's accession to
the presidency further blighted the picture for civil rights advocates, since
little in his career indicated sympathy or understanding of the status of
black people in America.

A. Philip Randolph, whose leadership of the March on Washington
Movement exploited the government's desire for consensus about World
War II to win major victories (see chap. 3), understood the relationship
between racism and America's militaristic drift in the postwar era. Recognizing that the ideological needs of the cold war mandated at least the
appearance of unanimity at home, and cognizant of the ways in which
racism made a mockery of rhetoric about democracy and freedom, Randolph saw the opportunity for more victories over race hatred.

When President Truman asked Congress for approval to implement
peacetime conscription, Randolph announced that he favored resistance to
the draft by blacks unless the armed forces ended segregation. Condemned
by many prominent blacks and urged to back down by former white allies,
Randolph stuck to his position. A poll conducted by the NAACP showed
that black newspaper publishers and other prominent people opposed him,
but 71 percent of black college students agreed with Randolph and intended
to follow his advice.

In a dramatic hearing before a United States Senate committee, longtime civil rights advocate Wayne Morse confronted Randolph about his
views and warned him that his position bordered on treason. When Randolph reiterated his stand, Morse tried to persuade him that blacks would
be the ones to suffer from such a strategy because it would provoke vigilante action against them by whites. Randolph replied, "I would anticipate
nationwide terrorism against Negroes who refused to participate in the
armed forces, but I believe that this is the price we have to pay for democracy that we want. In other words, if there are sacrifices and sufferings,
terrorism, concentration camps, whatever they may be, if that is the only
way by which Negroes can get their democratic rights, I unhesitatingly say
that we have to face it."[20]

A short time later, President Truman issued an executive order desegre-
gating the armed forces. Although the order was not fully implemented for
years, and although Truman's stance in favor of it came largely for political
reasons related to the 1948 election, once again, Randolph proved that the
system was vulnerable to the threat of mass protest. His tactic showed that

groups that had once been politically powerless and economically marginal could now take action to control their own destinies.

Subsequent events confirmed Randolph's vision. E. D. Nixon of Randolph's union, the Brotherhood of Sleeping Car Porters, planned the 1955–57 Montgomery bus boycott, and black workers made up an overwhelming majority of those withdrawing their business from the transportation company in that city. In a peculiar way, the centralization of corporate power after World War II and the marginalization of black people in economics and politics actually helped provoke the civil rights movement. Segregation and discrimination forced black communities to rely on their own resources, while the rhetoric of the cold war and the emergence of newly independent nations in Africa made American racism a liability in international affairs. The existence of concentrations of black people, alienated from the system and willing to engage in direct action, undermined corporate-liberal hopes for stability at home. Relying on civil disobedience and mass demonstrations, the civil rights movement of the fifties and sixties maneuvered the system into important concessions, providing a strategy for victory as well as a liberating process of direct action that spoke to the aspirations of all opponents of hierarchy and exploitation.

If in future years race and gender would loom larger as sources of oppositional social movements than would class, one reason stemmed from the ways in which the class conflict of the postwar era reached a distinctly racialized and genderized accommodation that met some of the needs of white male workers at the expense of women and aggrieved racial minorities.

Another source of labor's inability to keep up with changes by management has been the internationalization of the work force overseas and its changing demographic character in the United States. Leaders of the labor movement have been ill-prepared for organizing drives among the growing numbers of women, immigrants, and "people of color" in the working class, and they have had precious few strategies to challenge computer-generated automation or capital flight. Their organizations remain limited to national contexts at a time when capital has become international.

The inability and unwillingness of labor leaders to mobilize their own rank and file in direct action for social change has been even more devastating than their failures to unite workers across lines of race and gender or to organize the unorganized. For years, labor leaders assumed that their political influence in the Democratic party more than made up for their lack of militancy on shop-floor and community issues. Yet when capital unilaterally broke the postwar bargain with labor in the seventies, union leaders had no effective means of opposition. Distrustful of their own members and dependent upon favors from big business, they attempted to maintain their control over diminishing numbers of workers rather than participating in a broad-based social movement fighting for the preservation of good jobs and social-welfare institutions.

For organized workers in mass-production industries during the postwar period, the corporate-liberal solution to postwar conflict brought substantive short-range concessions in respect to wages, pensions, medical benefits, housing subsidies, and opportunities for early retirement. Concessions that had been forced out of management by labor in the postwar period proved to be good for business too, because high wages and high levels of employment created a broad-based consumer demand that stimulated economic growth. Real wages increased by almost 20 percent during the fifties; by 1966, 75 percent of industrial workers under the age of forty lived in the suburbs.[21] Yet installment buying, mortgage debt, automobile loans, and an inflationary spiral made workers dependent upon future wage increases to pay off present debts, a need which itself helped to fuel inflation. Most important, companies took back in working conditions nearly everything they conceded in wages; each increase in income meant a sacrifice on the job for the sake of productivity.

As grievances increasingly became settled behind closed doors by management and labor specialists, trade unions too often degenerated into glorified service organizations rather than institutions maintained by and for rank-and-file workers. Union officers received dues money directly from corporations by withholding it from workers' checks. This made union dues seem like just another tax on wages to the workers and made good relations with the company and uninterrupted production a prime goal of union leaders. Unions helped maintain peace on the shop floor to preserve their cooperative arrangements with business, and they helped maintain social peace in society in order to maintain their harmonious relationship with the Democratic party.[22]

Labor leaders staked their future on the arrangement that allowed them to win wage concessions from management in return for uninterrupted production. They felt that they did not need to organize the unorganized, generally finding organizing too risky and too unprofitable compared with the task of maintaining cordial relations with big employers who gave them millions of dollars in dues every time they signed a contract with automatic checkoff provisions. Under these arrangements, labor leaders did not have to educate their membership on political issues or to develop new shop-floor leaders. On the contrary, the principles of labor law and labor administration (NLRB rulings, court decisions, longer contracts covering broader geographic areas) increasingly made it more and more difficult for the rank and file to have any influence on union policies and procedures except at the most immediate local levels.

Outside the plants, labor leaders used their influence within the Democratic party to secure modest social democratic measures in respect to education, health care, minimum wage laws, and civil rights. But here their influence stemmed mostly from the fact that capital's heavy investment in plants and equipment in the United States made the corporations and their executives prisoners of their environment. They found it in their interests to make some short-term concessions on these issues to preserve the infrastructure of the society in which they had invested so much. But when companies adopted containerization in the shipping industry and computer automation in manufacturing (both with the enthusiastic support of unions), management became able to ship production overseas, undermining the terms for both of their agreements with labor. They no longer needed union help in controlling production, and no longer were they trapped where they had invested their money. The era of concessions and corporate liberalism was over. Union leaders had neither the will nor the power to challenge these decisions in the seventies and eighties, because their strategy all along had depended upon receiving gifts from the corporations rather than on political mobilization of their own rank and file.

For big business, the triumph of corporate liberalism provided a seemingly ideal solution to their postwar problems. They secured access to capital as a result of government spending, established virtually unchallenged control over production, and paid less in taxes for welfare benefits than almost any other nation's industrialists and financiers. With their new plants and equipment undamaged by war, with no real competitors in other nations, and with a permanent garrison state geared for war, it seemed as if they had attained complete security, stability, and predictability.

Yet they quickly squandered what had been given to them. Lavish defense spending removed incentives for developing better and cheaper consumer products. Military adventures drained capital from productive uses, while efforts to provide foreign countries with U.S. dollars helped create foreign competitors with superior technologies (and labor-management relations) to those in the United States. Failure to involve workers in meaningful decision-making lowered productivity and morale on the shop floor, while short-term tax savings dangerously undermined the health and education of the work force. U.S. corporations coasted on their oligopoly status, fixing prices rather than innovating and competing. Their arrogance proved extremely wasteful in the long run. In one emblematic example, when the attorney Ralph Nader began publicizing the safety hazards of one of General Motors's cars, they hired a detective to investigate Nader and provide the company with derogatory information so that they could discredit him. Had they instead simply followed Nader's advice to make smaller, safer, fuel-efficient cars, they probably would not have surrendered so much of their domestic market to foreign competitors. Business commitment to maintaining their own prerogatives and power proved stronger than their oft-proclaimed commitment to creating better products. All of us have paid a terrible price for their unwillingness to share decision-making and power.

The combination of years of corporate dominance and cold war anti-communism has meant that citizens have engaged in precious little debate about the future of their country. Whether the issue concerned civil rights, the war in Vietnam, or deindustrialization and economic restructuring, virtually the only meaningful dialogues open to most citizens have come from direct-action protests outside of the regular channels that have worked so effectively to silence them. Instead of solutions to our problems, the government and business give us spectacles to divert our attention. In the eighties and nineties, we have careened from one sensational media event to another—wars in Nicaragua, Grenada, Libya, Panama, and Iraq, national "moral panics" about missing children, drug use, allegedly obscene art, political correctness, family values, and a sinister countersubversive hysteria that conjures up the enemy of the day in the form of terrorists, gays and lesbians, single mothers, and, always, people of color. This contemporary version of rule by riot and manipulated moral panic vents anger and frustrations in order to divert our attention away from the most important questions we can ask—what has happened to the distribution of wealth, power, and life chances in the United States—who has held power over the past four decades and what have they done with their power?[23]

During wartime and reconversion in the forties, workers in the United States battled for another kind of politics. At their best, they fought against racism and sexism. They took direct action to influence the decisions that affected their lives and they formed new communities and alliances to look out for each other. Their decentralized struggles pointed toward a high-wage high-employment economy, toward a society where wage increases for one group of workers did not have to mean price hikes for everybody else, and where human needs had priority over private profit.

It may not be possible or even desirable to replicate the exact form of their insurgencies. Changes in the nature of work, in the composition of the working class, and in the relationship between multinational corporations and the nation state pose the risk of eliding the fundamentally new and potentially revolutionary possibilities of our own time if we try to stick too closely to the lessons of the past. But the differences between the postwar era and our own time do not obviate the enduring necessity for grass-roots mobilization, popular democracy, struggles against racism and sexism, comprehension of the ways in which popular culture inculcates corporate culture in us even as it exposes alternatives, and a willingness to embrace new identities and possibilities rather than retreating to the "borrowed language" and dead weight of traditions.

Just as Ernest Tubb's "A Rainbow at Midnight" captured the cautious optimism of the early postwar era in 1946, Hank Williams's song "I'll Never Get Out of This World Alive" expressed a good-natured pessimism appropriate for 1952. Williams often introduced the song by paraphrasing one of its key lines, telling the audience, "Don't worry, nothing's gonna turn out right no how." Workers who counted on the tranquility and prosperity promised within the "Rainbow at Midnight" had to be disappointed six years later. The cold war with the Soviet Union as well as the hot war in Korea signaled the start of seemingly permanent preparation for war. The bargain by union leaders to trade working conditions for wages led to speed-ups, industrial accidents, and ultimately to profit-based automation that eliminated jobs and lessened the value of workers' knowledge about their tasks. Failure to organize the unorganized left labor politically isolated and dependent upon business concessions for social reforms, consequently leaving the United States with a high-cost, low-coverage system of medical care, inadequate old-age pensions, and one of the most regressive tax structures in the industrialized world. When finance capital and management responded to the crises of the early seventies by unilaterally breaking their postwar bargain with labor and by moving investments and production overseas, labor could not or would not mobilize its own rank and file in protest, choosing instead disastrous strategies of "give-backs" and concessions that helped pay for the dismantling of the nation's economic and social infrastructure.

In their mass strikes and demonstrations in the postwar era, American workers employed the methods of direct democracy to retard the power of monopoly capital and secure greater control over their own lives. Yet their actions also inadvertently forced a closer relationship between big business and government, produced legislation that increased the power of unions at the expense of the rank and file, and made corporations more determined than ever to control the minute details of production.

Workers could not translate their momentary glimpses of new possibilities into a coherent program of action capable of implementing entirely new power relations. They remained divided by race, gender, and caste, and they often complied with management and union schemes to exacerbate those divisions. Despite the universal implications of their battle against hierarchy and exploitation, they often failed to transcend local and parochial interests.

Yet it would be foolish to dismiss working-class strategies of independence in the postwar era because they did not produce a revolution. Failures that leave a relevant legacy of struggle and resistance may lay the groundwork for important and necessary changes in the future. Working-class strategies of independence during the postwar period forced melioristic concessions in the factory and in society at large, they limited the initiatives of conservatives and corporate liberals, and they held open the potential for even more effective resistance in the future. The determination of workers to battle for full employment, and the resulting pressure placed on the economy because of it, led to some dramatic actions whose final consequences we have not seen to this day.

The legacies of postwar working-class strategies of independence have manifested themselves in the factory, in the civil rights, black power, student, antiwar, and women's movements of recent years, and in conscious countercommunities created around common interests and aspirations in many ways. Labor learned in the 1940s that trickle-down economics and trickle-down politics offer nothing of value to the majority of the population. Working people realized that they had a right to participate in making the decisions that affected their lives. They discovered that only mass mobilization could counter concentrated power. Nothing has happened since the forties to discredit mass mobilization and democratic contestation over resources and power as a necessary element in creating a livable world or an emancipatory future. To be sure, working-class resistance after the war did not quite generalize itself into human resistance, into a realizable vision of society without exploitation and hierarchy. But it remains a rainbow at midnight—a symbol of what could have been, and what might yet be.

NOTES

1. Karl Marx, *The Eighteenth Brumaire of Louis Bonaparte* (New York: International Publishers, 1981), 15.

2. My understanding of the importance of automation owes an enormous debt to many conversations with Stan Weir and to the tremendous knowledge and wisdom that he possesses on these issues.

3. Ruth Milkman, *Gender at Work: The Dynamics of Job Segregation by Sex during World War II* (Urbana: University of Illinois Press, 1987), 124–26, 151–52.

4. Labor School Notes, Diocesan Labor Institute, Hartford, Connecticut, part 2, Association of Catholic Trade Unionists File, Labor History Archives, Wayne State University, Detroit Mich.

5. Ibid.

6. Nick Salvatore, *Eugene V. Debs: Citizen and Socialist* (Urbana: University of Illinois Press, 1982); Paula Rabinowitz, *Labor and Desire* (Chapel Hill: University of North Carolina Press, 1991).

7. Gwendolyn Mink, "The Lady and the Tramp: Gender, Race, and the Origins of the American Welfare State," in Linda Gordon, ed., *Women, the State, and Welfare* (Madison: University of Wisconsin Press, 1990), 11–113.

8. David Lee Hardesty, "The Rochester General Strike of 1946" (Ph.D. diss., University of Rochester, 1983), 74–76.

9. *Evansville Press*, Aug. 31, 1948, 1.

10. *Time*, Oct. 10, 1949, 23.

11. Deborah Silverton Rosenfelt and Michael Wilson, *Salt of the Earth* (Old Westbury, N.Y.: Feminist Press, 1978), 117.

12. Karen Tucker Anderson, "Last Hired, First Fired: Black Women Workers during World War II," *Journal of American History* 69, no. 1 (June 1983): 95.

13. William H. Harris, *The Harder We Run: Black Workers since the Civil War* (New York: Oxford University Press, 1982), 125.

14. Ronald W. Schatz, *The Electrical Workers: A History of Labor at General Electric and Westinghouse, 1923–60* (Urbana: University of Illinois Press, 1983), 129.

15. Ibid., 129.

16. Harris, *The Harder We Run*, 125.

17. Ibid., 123.

18. Ibid., 128, 130, 131, 137, 133.

19. Richard M. Dalfiume, *Desegregation of the U.S. Armed Forces: Fighting on Two Fronts, 1939–1953* (Columbia: University of Missouri Press, 1969), 132–34.

20. *Congressional Record*, Apr. 12, 1948, 4312.

21. David Brody, *Workers in Industrial America: Essays on the Twentieth Century Struggle* (New York: Oxford University Press, 1980), 192.

22. I know that defenders of the AFL-CIO will point to their support for civil rights legislation as proof that they fought for social justice rather than for social peace. But when one looks closely at their role in the civil rights movement a different picture emerges. Walter Reuther paid for the sound system for the 1963 March on Washington, but then used his influence to censor John Lewis's speech. Social democrats like Joseph Rauh and Allard Lowenstein channeled civil rights workers within the Democratic party, urging acceptance of the decision to seat the segregationist Mississippi delegation at the 1964 convention instead of the integrated Mississippi Freedom Democratic party. In these instances and others, union leaders tried to do with the civil rights movement what they had done with the labor insurgencies of the thirties and forties—take power away from the rank and file and delegate power to leaders making deals with corporations and political parties. In both cases, in my judgment, the rank and file lost far more than it gained.

23. For accounts of capital in the seventies, eighties, and nineties that illumine the processes of deindustrialization and economic restructuring see Stanley Aronowitz, *Working Class Hero: A New Strategy for Labor* (New York: Pilgrim Press, 1983); Fred Block, *Postindustrial Possibilities: A Critique of Economic Discourse* (Berkeley: University of California Press, 1990); Mike Davis, *City of Quartz* (London: Verso, 1990); Barbara Ehrenreich, *Fear of Falling: The Inner Life of the Middle Class* (New York: Harper Perennial, 1990); Bennett Harrison and Barry Bluestone, *The Great U-Turn: Corporate Restructuring and the Polarizing of America* (New York: Basic Books, 1988); Thomas Ferguson and Joel Rogers, *Right Turn: The Decline of the Democrats and the Future of American Politics* (New York: Hill and Wang, 1986); and James O'Connor, *Accumulation Crisis* (London: Blackwell, 1984).

Index

GEORGE LIPSITZ is the author of *Class and Culture in Cold War America: A Rainbow at Midnight*, *A Life in the Struggle: Ivory Perry and the Culture of Opposition*, and *Time Passages: Collective Memory and American Popular Culture in the U.S.* He is currently a professor of ethnic studies at the University of California–San Diego.